28.95

Family Therapy Techniques
for Problem Behaviors
of Children and Teenagers

Charles E. Schaefer
James M. Briesmeister
Maureen E. Fitton

Family Therapy Techniques
for Problem Behaviors
of Children and Teenagers

Jossey-Bass Publishers
San Francisco • Washington • London • 1984

FAMILY THERAPY TECHNIQUES FOR PROBLEM BEHAVIORS
OF CHILDREN AND TEENAGERS
by Charles E. Schaefer, James M. Briesmeister,
and Maureen E. Fitton

Copyright © 1984 by: Jossey-Bass Inc., Publishers
433 California Street
San Francisco, California 94104
&
Jossey-Bass Limited
28 Banner Street
London EC1Y 8QE

Library of Congress Cataloging in Publication Data
Main entry under title:

Family therapy techniques for problem behaviors of
children and teenagers.

Includes bibliographies and index.
1. Family psychotherapy. 2. Child psychotherapy.
I. Schaefer, Charles E. II. Briesmeister, James M.
III. Fitton, Maureen E.
RC488.5.F348   1983   616.89'156'088055   83-48164
ISBN 0-87589-583-2

Manufactured in the United States of America

The paper in this book meets the guidelines for
permanence and durability of the Committee on
Production Guidelines for Book Longevity of the
Council on Library Resources.

JACKET DESIGN BY WILLI BAUM

FIRST EDITION

Code 8330

The Jossey-Bass
Social and Behavioral Science Series

GUIDEBOOKS FOR THERAPEUTIC PRACTICE
Charles E. Schaefer and Howard L. Millman
Consulting Editors

*Therapies for Children: A Handbook of Effective
Treatments for Problem Behaviors*
Charles E. Schaefer and Howard L. Millman
1977

Therapies for Psychosomatic Disorders in Children
Charles E. Schaefer, Howard L. Millman,
and Gary F. Levine
1979

Therapies for School Behavior Problems
Howard L. Millman, Charles E. Schaefer,
and Jeffrey J. Cohen
1980

*Therapies for Adolescents: Current Treatments
for Problem Behaviors*
Michael D. Stein and J. Kent Davis
1982

Group Therapies for Children and Youth
Charles E. Schaefer, Lynnette Johnson,
and Jeffrey N. Wherry
1982

Therapies for Adults
Howard L. Millman, Jack T. Huber,
and Dean R. Diggins
1982

*Family Therapy Techniques for Problem Behaviors
of Children and Teenagers*
Charles E. Schaefer, James M. Briesmeister,
and Maureen E. Fitton
1984

Preface

This book is intended to serve as a practical and comprehensive handbook of family therapies for therapists working with children and teenagers. Because family therapists need to learn about many kinds of approaches and techniques to change family dysfunction, all the major schools of family therapy are included in this volume, including structural, strategic, insight, and behavioral approaches.

Indeed, after reviewing the literature on family therapy, Gurman and Kniskern conclude that no beginning family therapist is justified in learning only one approach to family therapy.*

*A. S. Gurman and D. P. Kniskern, "Research on Marital and Family Therapy: Progress, Perspectives, and Prospects," in *Handbook of Psychotherapy and Behavior Change: An Empirical Analysis,* ed. S. L. Garfield and A. E. Bergin (New York: Wiley, 1978).

The effectiveness of highly diverse family interventions with the same and different disorders suggests the folly of a single-system approach to the field. While acquiring competency in a number of different family treatment methods may seem onerous, it is becoming increasingly clear that multiple technical skills are necessary to the broad practice of family therapy.

The prescriptive approach to therapy is reflected in this book; that is, given a specific behavior disorder of a child, what specific remedy or family therapy technique can best be applied? One sign of advancement in a field of therapy is practitioners' ability to recommend specific interventions for specific disorders, much as physicians do when they write individualized prescriptions for physical illnesses. Similarly, family therapists are now able to individualize treatment, to prescribe remedies or techniques particular to the needs of the child. The skillful application of this prescriptive approach requires the development of expertise in a variety of family therapy methods. As therapeutic methods are refined, therapists are better able to determine which method will be most effective given a certain child, therapist, and situational variables.

To present clinical information that is as practical and complete as possible, we provide detailed abstracts of the most relevant articles from the family therapy literature, with technical material clarified and simplified whenever possible. The abstracts focus on the practical, giving specific information about how to use the various techniques. Of course, readers should study the original articles to fully understand the theoretical and research base for the approaches and to avoid any tendency to mechanically apply the techniques. The exact reference for the article is listed at the end of each digest.

The digests in Part One describe family therapy approaches for a variety of behavioral and conduct disorders, including aggressiveness, delinquency, and drug abuse. Part Two is devoted to interventions for a wide range of other childhood problems, such as schizophrenia, phobias, and psychosomatic disorders. Part Three presents family therapy approaches to preventing psychological disturbances for high-risk children, such as children of divorce, victims of child abuse, and children whose families are in crisis.

This book is the seventh volume in the series Guidebooks for Therapeutic Practice.

August 1983   Charles E. Schaefer
Dobbs Ferry, New York

James M. Briesmeister
Purchase, New York

Maureen E. Fitton
Dobbs Ferry, New York

Contents

xiii

Contents

Contents xxi

Chapter 22: Psychotic Families   451

The Authors

Charles E. Schaefer is director of psychological services and research at The Children's Village, a residential treatment center in Dobbs Ferry, New York. He received the Ph.D. degree (1967) in clinical psychology from Fordham University and completed a clinical psychology internship at the Institute of Living in Hartford, Connecticut. He is a fellow in the American Orthopsychiatric Association and a member of the American Psychological Association. He is cofounder of the international Association for Play Therapy.

In addition to over fifty articles published in professional journals, Schaefer is the author or coauthor of many books on child therapy and childrearing, including *How to Influence Children* (2nd ed., 1983), *Handbook of Play Therapy* (1983),

Group Therapies for Children and Youth (1982), *How to Help Children with Common Problems* (1981), *Therapies for School Behavior Problems* (1980), *Therapies for Psychosomatic Disorders in Children* (1979), *Childhood Encopresis and Enuresis* (1979), and *Therapies for Children* (1977). He is the coeditor of the Guidebooks for Therapeutic Practice series published by Jossey-Bass.

Schaefer frequently conducts seminars on child therapy and effective parenting and has appeared on numerous radio and television shows across the country to discuss these topics. He maintains a private practice in Scarsdale, New York, for children and adolescents and their families.

James M. Briesmeister is a therapist at the Manhattanville College Counseling Center in Purchase, New York. He is a Ph.D. candidate in clinical psychology at the Graduate Faculty of The New School for Social Research in New York City. He received the M.A. degree in psychology (1970) and the M.A. degree in philosophy (1976), both from the University of Detroit. His previous professional experience includes counseling in a variety of clinical settings, including The Children's Village, where he completed an internship in clinical psychology, as well as drug abuse clinics, youth homes, and psychological testing services.

Briesmeister's articles on psychotherapy, mental retardation, and attentional deficit disorders have appeared in several professional publications, including those of the Association of Michigan School Counselors, the Association for Play Therapy, and the Detroit Archdiocesan Counselors Association. His current professional interests include the clinical management and treatment of depression and suicide, gender and sexual identity issues, and the interface between cognitive and dynamic therapies. He is a member of the American Psychological Association and the Association for Play Therapy.

Maureen E. Fitton is a school psychologist at The Children's Village. Fitton received the M.S. degree in school psychology (1971) and the Professional Diploma in School Psychology (1972), both from St. John's University. She has also studied at the Center for Family Learning in New Rochelle, New York.

Fitton organized and participated in workshops held at
New York University and Rutgers University on interviewing
emotionally disturbed children and the correlation between
psychological and educational diagnostic procedures. Her current areas of interest include increasing parental involvement in
educational programs for children in residential treatment; devising, organizing, and implementing curricula for The Children's Village human sexuality program (in progress for the
past seven years); and evaluating the relationship between improvement in children's academic skills and their self-images.
She is a member of the National Association of School Psychologists; the American Association of Sex Educators, Counselors,
and Therapists; and the Association for Play Therapy.

Family Therapy Techniques
for Problem Behaviors
of Children and Teenagers

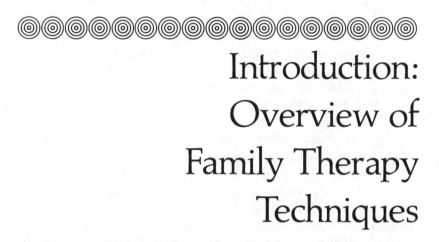

Introduction:
Overview of
Family Therapy
Techniques

During the past two decades, family therapy has emerged as a major innovative force in the field of psychotherapy. In this introductory essay, we offer a brief overview of the important concepts and issues in family therapy: definitions and descriptions of the major schools of family therapy, evaluative research findings, and indications and contraindications for its use in clinical practice.

In a broad sense, family therapy can be defined as any psychotherapeutic approach to the primary client that intentionally includes members of the client's family, seen either separately or jointly with the identified client. In this sense,

1

counseling parents about more effective parenting practices to resolve their child's particular problem is a form of family therapy. This broad definition of family therapy was used in selecting the articles abstracted in this book.

In a narrower sense, family therapy usually refers to conjoint family therapy in which two or more members of a family meet, either by themselves or with a group of other families, with one or more therapists. The term family therapy is also used to designate any form of therapy with one or more members of a family that is guided by a family systems conceptualization of psychotherapy. A cybernetic model of the family considers it a system in which the pattern of interrelationships is seen to affect the health and behavior of individual members. A change in one part of a family system is believed to be followed by compensatory changes in other parts of the system. Within this model, the goal of treatment is to change the family system of interaction. Individual change is believed to occur as a by-product of change in the dysfunctional system. Central to all forms of family therapy is the concept that family relationships are at least as important in influencing the behavior of individual members as are unconscious, intrapsychic events.

Schools of Family Therapy

Family therapy is not a treatment method but a clinical orientation that includes many different therapeutic approaches or schools. Each school has its own assumptions about family dysfunction, therapy goals, and the mechanisms of family change. The five main schools are: insight, structural, strategic, behavioral, and integrative. Let us briefly review the main tenets of each.

Insight Therapy. Insight-oriented therapists seek to lead the family to an understanding of its problems and enhance communication of thought and affect. Insight therapists generally follow a psychoanalytic orientation that incorporates many of the premises of Freudian psychology and strongly emphasizes the role of intrapsychic forces. The individual is seen as harboring nonrational and unconscious beliefs that need to be confronted and interpreted by the therapist, who uses such techniques as exploring feelings, gaining insight, and "working through" past events.

The clarification of verbal and nonverbal communications between family members is a common goal, with incongruous, or double-bind messages often the focus of clarification. Incongruous messages are those that are inconsistent in their aspects, levels, or elements; for example, there are inconsistencies between the verbal and nonverbal modalities, the literal and metaphorical levels, or the content and the context of the message. Family sculpting may be used as a nonverbal technique by which families communicate various aspects of family relationships, such as closeness or distance, and alignments or divisions among family members. Family sculpting involves asking all the family members to pose like statues to express a particular feeling or behavior.

A general belief of the psychodynamic or insight school of family therapy is that therapy must uncover historical or causal factors in order to achieve change, a principle based on Freud's theory of repression. The theory, in its simplest terms, is that if therapy uncovers a previously closed-off event and the family then relives it and abreacts it, the symptom attached to it will disappear. For example, if the family has not adequately worked through a death or loss, the therapist may initiate a family mourning process. Similarly, a family secret may have to be revealed to all family members in order to dissipate the anxiety and lack of closeness associated with keeping the secret.

Psychodynamic therapists are also concerned with the differentiation and autonomy of individual family members. Murray Bowen suggests that emotional disturbance has its origin in the difficulty that one's parents and older members had in separating from the core family. Bowenian family therapy is designed to identify the historical patterns that continue to exert present influences on the family members. One must differentiate oneself from one's family of origin, a therapeutic process that Bowen says can take many years. Interpretations are often used by Bowenian therapists to give insight into family factors impeding personal growth. A mature, autonomous self is the goal for every family member.

Another belief of psychodynamically oriented family

therapists is that individual family members' disturbances become family dysfunction through the mechanism of multiple interlocking pathologies. A major focus in therapy is to disentangle the identified patient from the web of distorted involvements among family members.

Structural Therapy. Salvador Minuchin describes structural family therapy as "a body of theory and techniques that approaches the individual in his social context. Therapy based on this framework is directed toward changing the organization of the family. When the structure of the family group is transformed, the positions of members in that group are altered accordingly. As a result, each individual's experiences change" (*Families and Family Therapy* [Cambridge, Mass.: Harvard University Press, 1974], p. 2). The basic assumption is that a symptom is a product of a dysfunctional family structure or organization, and that if the organization becomes more "normal" the symptom will disappear.

According to Minuchin's conceptual framework, a normal family has clearly marked boundaries. The parents' boundaries protect their privacy and marital relationship, and their children's boundaries are hierarchical with their tasks and privileges in accordance with age and sex. Structural therapy involves changing the family organization so that it more closely resembles normal family structure. For example, if a mother and son are acting like siblings, the mother is instructed to change their relationship by assuming charge of her son.

Moreover, the therapist seeks a "therapeutic alliance" with the family through the processes of joining and accommodation. *Joining* is the process whereby the therapist reaches out and empathizes with each individual member; *accommodation* refers to the changes the therapist must make in himself or herself in order to achieve joining. The therapist must accommodate to each family member's interactional style, affect, language, and cognitive development.

Strategic Therapy. Jay Haley first used the term *strategic* to describe any therapy in which the clinician actively designs interventions to solve the presenting problem (*Strategies of Psychotherapy* [New York: Grune & Stratton, 1963]). The strategic approach focuses on the problem—not on the family—as the unit of concern. According to the strategic school, the curative agent in family therapy is not insight or catharsis of affect, but the paradoxical manipulation of power. A systemic or circular etiology of psychopathology is postulated, and each member of the family system is seen as an active agent, even though one member may seem to be victimized by another.

Strategic therapists often see individuals or family subgroups separately, and they may seek change by secretly opposing one group against the other. Directives are deliberately planned and are the main therapeutic techniques. The therapist designs a strategy; if within a given time this strategy does not produce results, a new strategy is formulated. No interpretations are offered, and insight and understanding are not emphasized.

A hallmark technique of the strategic school is the paradoxical directive, *paradoxical* because the therapist instructs the family to continue to enact the very problem behavior they want to change. The therapist expresses agreement with the family members' inappropriate feelings, attitudes, or behaviors and then encourages them to exaggerate them. By prescribing the symptom, that is, apparently encouraging symptomatic or other undesirable behavior, the therapist seeks to lessen such behavior or bring it under control. For example, a child who exhibits temper tantrums may be told to make every effort to throw tantrums during the week. Acting on such a prescription usually decreases the symptom. Even if the symptom gets worse, the client has followed directions, a sign that he or she is capable of making directed change.

Another strategic technique is positive reframing, in which the therapist restates a situation so that it is perceived in a new, favorable way. Thus, a therapist may redefine a behavior that family members consider to be "hostile" as "concerned interest."

Behavioral Therapy. Behavioral approaches to the treatment of children and adolescents only haltingly adopt the notion of the family as a system, preferring to concentrate on dyadic and triadic models of parent-child interactions. Using techniques derived from learning principles, the behaviorist attempts to treat problems by changing specific behaviors in the family. Reinforcement contingencies are changed so that desired behaviors, rather than maladaptive acts, are attended to and rewarded. Typically the emphasis is placed on improving the parents' childrearing practices.

Integrative Therapy. In recent years the training of family therapists has tended to include instruction in more than one model of family theory and therapy, and articles in the family therapy literature that combine related approaches are becoming frequent. For example, a therapist might use behavioral techniques within a structural family therapy model. As P. H. Friedman explains, an integrative family therapist is one who does not assume that one particular family therapy approach is appropriate for every family ("Integrative Family Therapy," *Family Therapy,* 1981, *8,* 171-178). The integrative family therapist is flexible in orientation and interventions.

Evaluative Research

Until recently, few researchers performed evaluative studies of the effectiveness of family therapy. The difficulties inherent in evaluation are compounded by the complexity of the family therapy process, which is extremely difficult to define and equally difficult to measure. But in the last two decades empirical evidence relating the practice of family therapy has increased substantially.

A review of 200 research studies finds that improvement rates for nonbehavioral family therapy were greater than those reported for individual therapy (A. Gurman and D. P. Kniskern, "Research on Marital and Family Therapy—Progress, Perspective, and Prospects," in *Handbook of Psychotherapy and Behavior Change: An Empirical Analysis,* ed. S. L. Garfield and A. E. Bergin [New York: Wiley, 1978]). Largely positive results emerged on a wide variety of criteria and for family therapy conducted by clinicians of all major therapeutic disciplines. Among Gurman and Kniskern's conclusions are the following:

• Involvement of both parents in family therapy greatly enhances the probability of positive therapeutic outcome. Parents tend to terminate early if the father is not sufficiently involved.

• The effectiveness of family therapy is not correlated with the length of treatment. Therapists need not limit the number of sessions for a family, but they should be aware that the vast majority of families terminate within five months. Short-term family therapy is the rule, and family therapists are quite active and structuring in their style so as to effect change within this brief time span.

• At present, there is little substantive basis for the routine use of co-therapy teams in family therapy.

• The only treatment process that has received consistently positive empirical support as a curative factor in family therapy is the enhancement of communication skills for family members.

• As in all other methods of psychotherapy, the relationship skills of the therapist facilitates, and may even transcend the impact of specific therapeutic techniques.

A review of evaluations of delinquency prevention and treatment projects, focused on studies wherein matched or randomly assigned control groups were used and follow-up information on behavioral outcome was obtained, states that no studies reported success of individual therapy at preventing or reducing delinquent behavior (A. Romig, *Justice for Our Children: An Examination of Juvenile Delinquent Rehabilitation Programs* [Lexington, Mass.: Heath, 1978]). Family therapy showed mixed results: family treatment focused on improving the communication behavior toward a positive goal yielded significant decreases in delinquency, and crisis intervention counseling, especially when used to teach systematic problem solving, was successful. Another evaluative study indicates that family therapy results in more egalitarian participation by family members (T. M. Johnson and H. N. Malony, "Effects of Short-Term Family Therapy on Patterns of Verbal Interchange

in Disturbed Families," *Family Therapy,* 1977, *4,* 207-215).
This conclusion supports the common sense view that family
therapy should be much more influential than other therapeutic
modalities in establishing a balanced pattern in a family's patterns of verbal interchange.

Indications and Contraindications

The question of indications and contraindications of family therapy for children and adolescents is a controversial one.
There seems to be more agreement among various practitioners
about contraindications, including intrapsychic disorders that
seem more amenable to individual therapy (shyness, identity
confusion, severe depression, acute psychosis), habit disorders
(thumbsucking, tics, stuttering), and lack of family coping skills
(insufficient structure within the family to maintain regular
meetings; single-parent families with young children).
Indications for family therapy vary widely among clinicians. Generally, family therapy appears to be most appropriate
and effective if there is evidence of prominent interpersonal
problems within the family. Family therapy is warranted when
a child's problems seem directly correlated with family dysfunction or when family forces reinforce and sustain the child's disorder.
A growing variety of specific problems have been treated
successfully, including: school phobia, noncompliance, sibling
rivalry, adolescent acting-out behaviors (delinquency, promis-
cuity, drug abuse), adolescent separation problems, family crisis
(divorce, death of a family member), and anorexia nervosa.
These general guidelines should be regarded as tentative generalizations that need verification by additional research.
Changing a family system is the ultimate professional
challenge, perhaps the most difficult of all therapeutic tasks.
Thus we conclude this overview with a few brief words of caution to those engaged in the practice of family therapy. Because
family therapy is so exhausting, the therapist should be wary of
accepting a large caseload of families. In working with a family,
the therapist should avoid becoming caught up in the family

system; he or she must be careful not to do the talking for a family that does not want to become involved, or to respond in a hostile way to angry remarks by a family. Too, the overly active therapist can stir up a family but fail to build trust, while the overly passive therapist can miss the chance to change a family. The family therapist should not attempt to treat intrapsychic problems that are best treated in individual therapy. Finally, the drop-out rate in family therapy is quite high, in part because the sources of resistance in families as compared with individuals are greater. The beginning family therapist must learn to cope with the high early drop-out rate and "no-shows."

Clearly, family therapy is not an easy or simple form of intervention. It is, however, always exciting, challenging, and growth-producing for the therapist. It represents an emerging field that continues to increase in popularity and effectiveness. The studies described in this book should not be considered final answers but, rather, road maps or directions to be followed with a view toward improvement.

To maximize the useability of this handbook, we have included an author index and a subject index at the end of the book. The *Author Index* lists authors of the original articles as well as authors of all other references cited. In the *Subject Index* we have attempted to provide a comprehensive cross-referencing system to both problems and treatment modes.

Part One

Conduct
Disorders

Conduct disorders in children and adolescents refer to persistent patterns of impulsive, antisocial behavior that are not accompanied by neurotic anxiety or psychotic distortion of reality. Children with conduct disorders fail to conform to the norms set up by society and either break these rules or violate the basic rights of others. About 20 percent of the children in the overall population require attention and treatment for such emotional problems; of those seen at clinics, boys outnumber girls by two or three to one.

Many forms of unacceptable behavior fall under this classification, seven of which are addressed in this chapter. The behaviors covered in the digests vary in the severity of pathology and the negative effects they have on others. A family orienta-

11

tion is used in each case to modify the problem behavior, with techniques employed varying according to the child's symptoms and their consequences.

The literature abounds in studies on school behavior and learning problems, the topic of Chapter One. A child's home is his first school, from which he carries values and attitudes that affect his behavior in the school setting. In one of the digests it is noted that a child's identification with the parent of the same sex, as a learning person, occurs before the child enters school (Friedman, p. 61). Family therapy approaches for this disorder are very diverse and depend on the child's age.

Impulsive-aggressive behavior is the focus of Chapter Two. The wide spectrum of problems addressed ranges from name calling to violent assault. Active and direct involvement of the therapist is recommended.

Fire setting is covered in Chapter Three. Most often, the symptom of fire setting is characterized by a powerful urge that the child is unable to resist. The motivations to set fires include defiance of authority, expression of hostility and aggression, or an attempt to resolve sexual conflicts. Unique strategies for eliminating this dangerous behavior are offered.

Noncompliant behaviors, the subject of Chapter Four, include oppositional tactics that are sometimes very difficult to alter. If the child is enrolled in school and exhibits noncompliant behavior in that setting, the teacher may play a part in the treatment process. Consistency of limits is essential in order to change the noncompliant behavior.

Runaway behavior (Chapter Five) is described by Stierlin as a surface manifestation of complex psychosocial conditions and developments. It is hypothesized that various young people run away for different reasons: some to isolate themselves, while others run toward a person or group. Behavioral and crisis intervention techniques are frequently used in treating the families of runaways.

Delinquent behavior (Chapter Six) assumes many forms and frequently presents a challenge to therapists because, given that the child's behaviors are usually blatant, it is difficult to persuade the family not to focus only on the symptom. In many cases the family desires to eliminate the delinquent behavior but resists looking at the relationships among its members.

Drug abuse is the topic of the last chapter in this part. This behavior is seen primarily in adolescents and young adults, rather than young children. Among the conduct disorders discussed, it can be the most damaging to both physical and emotional development. Young drug abusers are sometimes the stabilizers in their families, and in most cases there is a dependent relationship between the drug abuser and at least one parent. Noone reports that the majority of drug abusers live with their families of origin. Therapy is geared toward change within the family system, so that a new drug-free equilibrium can be established.

1

School Behavior
and Learning Problems

The techniques reviewed in this chapter address school behavior and learning problems among a variety of age groups. Some family approaches use one modality, while others are multi-faceted. Modeling techniques in parent tutoring is one method used with young children. Behavioral techniques, some involving co-therapists, are recommended for children of different ages. The transition from elementary to junior high school is often a difficult one and multifamily group sessions may ease the adjustment. At times, paradoxical techniques are employed in short-term therapy with underachievers. Overall, a flexibility in the use of techniques is recommended for this group of childhood disorders. Close communication between the therapist, family, and school is strongly suggested.

Application of a Systems Model with Families and Schools

AUTHORS: Bennett I. Tittler and Valerie J. Cook

PRECIS: Clinic treatment of a child's learning and behavior problems through integrating the family and school systems.

INTRODUCTION: The Peabody Child Study Center was the setting used to integrate a child's family and school systems. This approach flowed from the working hypothesis at the clinic that both family and school were significant to children's lives. The authors acknowledge the influence of Hobbs and Bowen in formulating their systems approach. According to Hobbs, a community clinic should work toward supporting the child's family and school. An important aspect of Bowen's theory is to relate to each system in a clear and respectful way and to guard against becoming overly involved in the emotionality between the client systems.

CASE ILLUSTRATION: A ten-year-old boy, Bobby, was brought to the clinic by his parents at the recommendation of the Director of Special Education. The history revealed that Bobby had repeated kindergarten and was in his third year of special education in a learning disabled (LD) class. There was some question as to the appropriateness of Bobby's school placement and a "second opinion evaluation" was requested. A team approach was used at the clinic and included assessments by a family specialist, psychological assessor, educational assessor, and educational consultant. An emphasis was placed on the family by developing a support system for it and giving the family an important role to play in the assessment process.

Before meeting with the team at the clinic, the parents were asked to fill out a number of questionnaires that applied to each family member as well as the family unit. The first session was conducted by the family specialist. Independently of one another, Bobby and his parents were asked to explain why they had come to the clinic. A group discussion about their responses followed and then the parents were interviewed separately. They were asked to talk about themselves and how they related to one another and to their children. Throughout this interview, the parents were given a clear message that they would be very much a part of the emotional problem-solving process.

The family interview indicated that Bobby and his younger sister were the main focus of their parents. Although there was a great deal of emphasis placed on Bobby and his learning problems, he was prompted by his parents to participate in outside activities. Also, the father had experienced difficulties in school and yet had achieved career success as an adult. As the authors state, "The family assessment served as a guide for knowing where and how to intervene so that the child and the family would receive the help they needed."

Next, a knowledge of Bobby's school as a system was viewed as essential, since the way in which the school sees the child and the referring problem greatly influences the treatment process. Bobby's teacher completed a questionnaire that covered both academic and social functioning. The psychological assessor and educational consultant then met with his teacher, reviewed Bobby's curriculum and individual educational program and observed him in the classroom, noting in particular his relationships with others in the class. The school assessment thus gathered important information about the child and laid the groundwork for a continued relationship with school personnel to facilitate their acceptance of later educational recommendations and consultation.

A psychological assessment and educational assessment by respective professionals followed. Bobby was found to be of average intelligence with specific learning problems. Mild neurological impairment was seen as a contributing factor. The curriculum provided for Bobby was found to be appropriate, but the pacing of assignments left Bobby with free time on Thursdays and Fridays.

According to the authors, if the relationship between the family and school is flexible often an assessment is all that is necessary, although further work with the family and school in developing better communication may be indicated in other cases. Bobby's family fell into the latter category because over the years his parents so questioned the value of his special education placement and program that they gradually came to see themselves in an adversary relationship with the school. The clinic therefore assumed the role of helping to repair the communication between Bobby's family and the school. A family conference was held with all the team members to discuss the assessment and the recommendations to the parents and child. Although his parents wanted Bobby to be placed in a regular fifth-grade class, this was seen as unwise by the team and they presented a compromise plan. The next conference included people from the clinic, family, and school. Based on the reports of all involved, the following plan was drawn up: Bobby would go into a regular fourth-grade class the following year and would receive supplementary services and tutoring. The tutoring was to begin immediately and continue through the summer. Also, Bobby would participate in a cognitive training program during the summer, which if seen as beneficial to Bobby was to be continued during the regular school year. In order to bridge the gap between special-class placement and a regular program, Bobby was scheduled to attend a regular class for social studies or science.

COMMENTARY: The two most important systems in Bobby's life were identified as family and school, and the clinic served as a consultant to both these systems, enhancing communication between them to work toward solving the child's problems. Clinic personnel observed a high level of cooperation by the family members, which was attributed to requiring them to participate in the process and providing the support they needed; too, the level of participation by family members was viewed as related to the degree of their acceptance of the clinic's recommendations. By using the approach outlined in this paper, the clinic reported an increase from 25 to 50 percent in the number of families who would accept parent or family therapy.

SOURCE: Tittler, B. I., and Cook, V. J. "Relationships Among Family, School and Clinic: Toward a Systems Approach."

Journal of Clinical and Child Psychology, Fall 1981, 184–187.

===

The Treatment of a Child's Underachievement in School Using a Paradoxical Approach with the Family

AUTHOR: Peggy Papp

PRECIS: Paradoxical techniques are used with families to deal with resistance and to avoid a power struggle between therapist and family.

INTRODUCTION: Papp defines three concepts of family work: (1) the family as a self-regulatory system, (2) the symptom as a mechanism for self-regulation, and (3) the resulting resistance to change. Papp notes that the symptom serves to regulate a dysfunctional part of the system, and if the symptom is removed a part of the system is left unregulated.

Quite often the therapist working with a family with a symptomatic child is presented with a contradictory request: the family wants the symptom to change without changing the system. A paradoxical intervention is defined as "one that, if followed, will accomplish the opposite of what it is seemingly intended to accomplish." The decision to use this type of technique is made after the family has failed to respond to direct interventions. As stated by the author, "We reserve paradoxical interventions for those covert long-standing, repetitious patterns of interaction that do not respond to direct interventions such as logical explanations or rational suggestions." The degree of resistance to change determines the type of preferred intervention.

TREATMENT METHOD: The three most important techniques

used in paradoxical therapy are redefining, prescribing, and restraining. *Redefining* involves changing the family's perception of the problem by designating the symptom as an essential part of the system. For example, anger might be explained to the family as a sign of caring. In redefining the therapist supports the system rather than attempting to change it directly. Once the redefinition has taken place, the therapist prescribes the symptom-producing cycle as inevitable: "The secret rules of the game are made explicit and the family must take responsibility for its own actions." Papp cautions that before prescribing the therapist must have a clear understanding of the relationship between the symptom and the system as well as how they set each other off. After applying the first two techniques, the therapist would then need to restrain the family if any sign of change occurred. When the family insists on change, the therapist regulates the pace and points out the new problems as they emerge. Change is gradually permitted after much caution.

CASE EXAMPLE: The symptom of school failure in Billy, an eight-year-old boy, was presented. The therapist noted that the symptom kept Billy's mother from experiencing her disappointment in her husband's business failure. By focusing on Billy's underachievement, she circumvented the major issue. Her husband gave the family the message that he would fall apart if confronted directly with this problem, and she responded by protecting him. A typical scene: she was feeling angry at her husband's lack of motivation and would then pick on her son to do his homework or complete a household chore. A fight would ensue between mother and son, while the father distanced himself by watching TV. The couple denied any problem in their marital relationship.

In redefining the problem, the therapist instructed the wife to continue to show her disappointment in Billy rather than express any negative feelings toward her husband. It was explained that Billy could absorb the criticism and bounce back while her husband might become depressed. Billy was told to keep his mother's disappointment centered on him in order to protect his father, and the father was praised for his cooperation. In response to these instructions, the mother recoiled, asking, "Why should I damage my son to protect my husband?" But her husband agreed with the instructions and felt that his son was quite resilient. This difference of opinion between the couple provoked a fight, a conflict that centered on the couple's relationship, with Billy no longer in a middle position. The therapist's definition and prescription of the family system was both accurate and unacceptable—which is what made it untenable.

TREATMENT RESULTS: The outcome of paradoxical therapy depends to a great extent on the application of the techniques by the therapist. Papp outlines some common pitfalls. The most frequent error is to describe the symptom without relating it to the system. For example, if the therapist says, "Billy, you should keep failing in school and disappointing mother," he has failed to redefine the symptom as serving the system, while connoting both positively and prescribing both. Similarly ineffective is for the therapist to prescribe only the system; for instance, by saying, "Billy, you should continue to fail in school and disappoint mother. Mother, you should continue to fight with Billy, and father you should continue to withdraw." In contrast, the positive treatment result in the case described followed from the therapist making a clear connection between symptom and system.

COMMENTARY: Paradoxical therapy can yield dramatic positive results in a short period of time. However, it must be stressed that the therapist must connect the symptom to the family system. The manner in which the paradoxical message is delivered is also important. Therapists new to this method often lack the necessary conviction. But to be effective, the paradoxical message must be stated in a sincere way, no matter how absurd it sounds. As the author notes, someone in the family generally confirms its validity. (In the case presented, the father confirmed that it was better for his wife to fight with her son than with him.) In response to a question regarding the effect of this form of therapy on the child, the author notes that the child is already involved in destructive behavior in order to save his parents and that by making the covert overt, the child is released from the destructive position.

SOURCE: Papp, P. "The Greek Chorus and Other Techniques of Paradoxical Therapy." *Family Process,* 1980, *19,* 45–57.

A Family Therapy Approach
to Understanding and Accepting
a Learning Disabled Child

AUTHORS: Florence W. Kaslow and Bernard Cooper

PRECIS: Concurrent and conjoint family therapy for treating families in which a child has a learning disability.

INTRODUCTION: The basis for using family therapy as a treatment approach with families who have a learning disabled child is that no matter what the etiology of the disability, the child is strongly influenced by the family system. The authors adapt the definition of learning disability set forth by R. H. Barsch, "A child with learning disability is one with adequate mental ability, sensory processes, and emotional stability who has specific defects in perceptual, integrative or expressive processes which severely impair learning efficiency. This includes children who have central nervous system dysfunction which is expressed primarily in impaired learning efficiency" ("Neurological and Sensory Control Program," U.S. Department of Health, Education and Welfare, Publication no. 2015, 1969). The authors add that the child's external environment plays a part in the syndrome and that the family structure and the members' interrelations provides a context of living for the child.

Following a diagnosis of learning disability, most parents undergo a feeling of sadness and anger and sometimes a wish to reject the child. These feelings are often translated into their becoming overprotective and overindulgent of the child. Frequently, they see the disability as the totality, rather than as one aspect, of the child. At times, the problem permeates the entire family system and results in the whole family becoming immobilized. The siblings of the disabled child are sometimes not told about the diagnosis, which may provoke confusion and resentment. During family sessions, all these issues can be addressed.

TREATMENT METHOD: The authors present concurrent family therapy as the preferable choice in cases in which the conflict level in the family is high. When the parents and child have different therapists, the emphasis may be on educational methods for providing a predictable routine for the child and ways to cope with developmental tasks as well as environmental pressures. The child's therapist can support the child by accepting him as he is and helping him to see what he can accomplish. The concurrent family therapy model is seen as the method of choice when: (1) The parents are too angry or upset to be seen together with their child; (2) the family is characterized by an "undifferentiated ego mass"; (3) the parents need support in maintaining some independence from the child; (4) the child is so emotionally needy that sharing the therapist with the other family members is unfeasible; or, (5) the child requires protection from the criticism of the parents. Permission for the therapists to collaborate is essential.

Concurrent family therapy using the same therapist is recommended when the parents and child are individuated enough that they can share the same therapist. Two benefits of this form of approach include eliminating any rivalry that might develop between two therapists and precluding the members of the family from undoing therapeutic gains by playing one therapist against another. The authors view conjoint family therapy as the most advantageous method of treatment. This approach allows the whole family to be seen together, and all the hurts, frustrations, and misperceptions about the learning disabled child can be explored. Another benefit is that the

whole family can be mobilized to find ways to share the responsibility for the learning disabled child. At the same time, family
members can be shown how to promote the child's independence.

CASE STUDY:

> Many times, quite unconsciously, we cut off a
> child's feelings because they are so painful to us
> [S. H. Fraiberg, *The Magic Years*. New York: Scrib-
> ner's, 1959].

Twelve-year-old Mike was seen with his parents, with the
goal of the therapy to help his parents acknowledge their disappointment and thus move on to a more productive relationship with their son. Mike was functioning at a second-grade
level in reading, a first-grade level in writing, and a fourth-grade
level in math; his social friendships were minimal. During the
family sessions, Mike was urged to express his feelings verbally,
even though he had a language disability. Part of the therapy
involved teaching the parents how to facilitate communication
with Mike while encouraging them, at the same time, to be patient. To better understand Mike's perceptual difficulties, he
drew designs presented by the therapist and then his parents
drew the same designs. The family members noted the differences and discussed them, developing a closeness through these
shared experiences. A turning point in the therapy occurred
when Mike's father told him how disappointed he was that he
would never follow his career path. At the same time, he communicated to Mike how he loved him as he was and talked
about other career opportunities. These messages were also
communicated through tears and hugs, and this was seen as a
breakthrough by the therapist.

TREATMENT RESULTS: In Mike's case the results of family
therapy included his expanded ability to participate with his
peers in social activities and his improved academic achievement. On a global level, concurrent and conjoint family ther-

apy offers ways to reduce stress and confusion as well as calling upon the support family members can provide for one another.

COMMENTARY: Kaslow and Cooper clearly describe the important role that family therapy can play in aiding the family in accepting and understanding a child's learning disability. By specifying the dynamics of various families, they are able to recommend the use of concurrent or conjoint family approaches. Quite possibly, the helping approaches of remedial tutoring, individual psychotherapy, and special education are accelerated when family therapy is initiated; for the support and closeness family members can provide to a learning disabled child cannot easily be duplicated.

SOURCE: Kaslow, F. W., and Cooper, B. "Family Therapy with the Learning Disabled Child and His/Her Family." *Journal of Marriage and Family Counseling*, 1978, 4, 41–49.

The Treatment of a School Learning Problem Through Wholistic Family Therapy

AUTHOR: Dennis A. Bagarozzi

PRECIS: A family therapy approach that calls upon the theoretical frameworks and techniques of systems, psychoanalytic, and behavioral perspectives.

INTRODUCTION: Bagarozzi states the basis for a wholistic approach to family therapy by noting that "no one theory of human behavior and family process can adequately account for the complexities of family interaction, therefore, the procedure to be discussed is an attempt to utilize all three paradigms during the intervention process." When treating a family, the therapist first discovers the pattern of interaction in the family, then conceptualizes the dysfunctional pattern using three paradigms, and finally, formulates a treatment strategy.

CASE STUDY: The identified patient in the K family was the thirteen-year-old son, Fred, who was experiencing difficulty achieving in school. Over the years, Fred had been seen by many professionals and the diagnoses offered ranged from retardation to emotional disturbance. Fred was the adopted child of Mr. and Mrs. K, whose two older children were no longer living at home.

During the initial interview Mrs. K monopolized the conversation while Mr. K sat with his back to her. Fred positioned himself away from his parents with his head lowered. Her conversation indicated that she was very overprotective of her son and neglected her husband. Her overprotective behavior included doing Fred's homework, supervising his bike riding, forbidding him to mow the lawn, and cautioning him about becoming friendly with "bad girls."

The goals of treatment were identified as: (1) aiding Fred out of the triangle between him and his parents, (2) helping Fred through the developmental stages of adolescence, (3) reestablishing the parental bond and encouraging the parents to allow Fred to be separate from them, (4) changing the communication pattern between the parents, and (5) helping the parents to develop more positive and satisfying behaviors. During the first few sessions the therapist employed a behavioral approach to help Fred separate and cope with some developmental tasks of adolescence and to assist the parents in relating to each other more positively. The therapist used the behavioral technique of contingency contracting, and contracts were drawn up between Fred, his parents, and his teachers. By finishing academic assignments in class, Fred earned extra time to work with his vocational techniques teacher. To encourage the parents to communicate with each other about how to help their son and to experience their teamwork in a job well done, both were instructed to help Fred with his homework. Previously, Mrs. K had worked alone with Fred and when she became frustrated by his work habits she completed the assignments herself. Whenever Mr. K attempted to help his son, Mrs. K would interfere. The two rewards that Fred chose for completing his homework were riding his bike without his mother's supervision and being able to mow the lawn. As part of the strategy for treatment the therapist told the family that he was certain the family would have a very hard time carrying out the instructions and that they might give up after a brief period of time.

As Fred progressed in his academic standing, he contracted with his parents to ride his bike to school. His mother then discovered that he was riding his bike to school with a girl from his class. At first, she became depressed and then started to accuse her husband of being unable to prevent Fred from becoming involved with the "bad girl down the street." An understanding of how negative feedback was used by the K family system was formulated during this phase of treatment.

The parental dyad was the next focus of the treatment process. A family history was taken and the parents were given some communication exercises to break down the rigid and defensive ways they related to one another. After a more functional communication pattern was arrived at, the therapist began to deal with their unmet needs and expectations from childhood. Gradually, over several sessions, Mrs. K saw how her accusations of her husband were connected to feelings toward her incompetent mother as well as attacks on some denied aspects of herself. Mr. K discovered how he had chosen to marry Mrs. K to compensate for his own shortcomings. He also saw how his wife played the roles of his overprotective mother and critical father.

TREATMENT RESULTS: The outcome of the wholistic approach to family therapy with the K family was positive. By using techniques from behavioral systems and psychoanalytic perspectives, the therapist was able to assist the family in changing their communication pattern. The referral problem of underachievement was confronted by involving the parents in the process of working with their son. Fred's success in completing assignments was matched by opportunities for greater independence. In focusing on the communication pattern between the parents, the therapist laid the groundwork for long-lasting change within the family.

COMMENTARY: The wholistic approach to family therapy provides the therapist with a great deal of flexibility. Some families require a variety of techniques, while others respond well to one particular strategy. The well-equipped therapist must determine the techniques that will be most effective for a given family. The author cautions that the wholistic approach should not be construed as a "cookbook" method of family therapy. For each family taken for treatment the therapist needs to consider which interventions will be relevant. Bagarozzi suggests further research in using a wholistic approach with families and notes possible problems with devising a curriculum for wholistic family therapy and the practical application of training students in such a comprehensive way.

SOURCE: Bagarozzi, D. A. "Wholistic Family Therapy and Clinical Supervision: Systems, Behavioral & Psychoanalytic Perspectives." *Family Therapy*, 1980, *7*, 153–165.

The Use of Family Group Therapy to Solve School Behavior Problems with Adolescents

AUTHOR: Vivianne G. Durell

PRECIS: A short-term, multiple-family group approach to the solution of school behavior problems.

INTRODUCTION: The adjustment an adolescent faces going from elementary to junior high school is often a difficult one. Frequently, the student finds the new freedoms and responsibilities to be overwhelming. Results of these feelings may include withdrawn behavior, underachievement, and acting-out behavior. Early intervention in junior high school is seen as the best hope for treatment. Durell states that previous studies in clinical settings have shown good results by combining conjoint family therapy with group therapy. This approach allows family members to understand their own difficulties by sharing with others. She describes a short-term approach with a few specific goals, defining the purpose of the multiple-family group counseling as assisting the families in the development of a shared view of the students' difficulty and in the evaluation of a collaborative plan of action.

TREATMENT PROCESS: A group of four families with boys thirteen to fifteen years old was selected and the eleven sessions were one and one-half hours long. The boys were of average intelligence who had experienced academic difficulty and behavior problems. The group leader was a psychologist, and the chief counselor served as a liaison between the school and the group. The assistant to the supervisor of guidance observed the sessions and discussed the meetings with the leader. This assistant also served as a resource person during the group meetings, informing the group on school policy, administration, and education as needed.

Each family was telephoned by the chief counselor and asked to become a part of the group. The family was told that their son was having serious difficulty and that the school administration had become aware of the problems. It was emphasized that the group was being formed on a trial basis and that it was hoped that the student could be reached at this crucial time.

In addition to guiding the sessions, the group leader participated in peripheral meetings, which were twice as frequent as the sessions and often included the resource person. The meetings' participants included individual students, individual families, the group of four students, or the students' teachers. Most significant were the meetings with the school administrators and with the chief counselor. The chief counselor's role consisted of attending the first and last group meetings, meeting with the group leader and resource person before and after each session to share information, counseling the four students, and coordinating communication with the teachers.

A change in the role of the group leader occurred right before the third session. Originally, the families had been told that the group leader would not interfere with the school's administrative function. However, one of the students in the group was suspended the day before the third session. The leader told the group that she would request that the school administrators treat a potential suspension as a crisis in which the chief counselor should immediately contact her. This would allow for a discussion of the problem and a possible conference with the family and the school. The authority for suspension remained with the administrators, but the proposal provided for interim communication before the disciplinary action. This proposal was accepted. But the mother of the suspended student said she would not attend any further meetings. The chief counselor called her, explained the new policy of crisis meetings before disciplinary action, and, although some ambivalence was expressed during a family conference, the family recommitted itself to the counseling process.

As the group became more cohesive, less blame was expressed toward the school system. By the fifth session the focus was almost entirely on the relationships between family members and how they contributed to the students' difficulties. By sharing mutual concerns, the families created a setting in which school problems were more easily discussed. At times, a student required added support from family members and school staff, and this was more easily accomplished by the family group interaction.

TREATMENT RESULTS: By the fifth session a noticeable positive change in the boys' academic and behavioral functioning was observed by their teachers. Significant objective improvements were seen in each boy's school performance by the end of the sessions. Also, the boys seemed happier and were more cooperative. Some regression was observed after the sessions terminated, but all the boys did better than would have been expected without intervention. In the months following the group meetings the boys sometimes asked for meetings and benefited from the added sessions.

COMMENTARY: The short-term nature of the multiple-family group sessions had both positive and negative aspects. Unlike a clinic, where long-term therapy is an option, a school is often viewed as a setting in which problem solving is done "on the spot." Positive results were attained in a short amount of time, but when the support of the group was no longer available the students regressed. Some form of ongoing support might have been considered, for example, having an ongoing crisis team. However, the group family approach in a school system can have great value, especially when there is good communication with school administrators and staff who may have had negative experiences with the problem students.

SOURCE: Durell, V. G. "Adolescents in Multiple Family Group Therapy in a School Setting." *International Journal of Group Psychotherapy*, 1969, *19*, 44–52.

Teaching Parents to Modify Children's Behavior Through Family-Play Therapy

AUTHOR: Gary E. Stollak

PRECIS: Teaching parents to change their children's behavior by using supervised play encounters with follow-up discussions.

INTRODUCTION: Stollak cites literature over the last fifteen years in which play encounters between parents and children were used to modify behavior. Although most clinicians use the home as the setting, the clinic playroom is used by this author. The focus of treatment is to train family members to interact in ways that will be mutually satisfying.

TREATMENT METHOD: Through this treatment method, parents learn how to relate to their children in caring ways by using play techniques developed by Axline and Moustakas.* Children between the ages of three and ten are the target population. The weekly play sessions between parent and child are half-an-hour long, with the parents alternating sessions; each play session is videotaped. The number of sessions depends on the situation. Before the first session the clinician explains the procedure to the parents and child, and the parents are given a copy of instructions for the special play sessions. The instructions state that the parents are to let the child know at various intervals how much time is left in the session as well as the time limits of the session. The parent is advised to be within two to three feet of the child, at eye level, and to maintain eye contact as often as possible. The parent wears a device called "bug in the ear," a hearing aid, which enables him or her to hear the clinician during the session. The clinician can offer direction and encouragement to the parent or make suggestions for physical contact.

Following the playroom session the clinician and parent meet to discuss feelings and thoughts. These discussions often focus on the parent's experiences with his or her own parents and how these relate to the child. In addition, they discuss how the parent related with the child in the playroom and the parent's behavior in the marriage.

CASE STUDY: This method is typically used with boys between the ages of eight and ten years who are exhibiting both social and academic problems in school. The child may display aggression, disobedience, hostility, short attention span, and learning difficulties. Although the school is usually the referral source, an interview with the parents often uncovers problems with socialization at home.

In the early play sessions with the father, the boy generally engages in competitive activities like shooting darts, punching bags, or throwing a ball. Usually by the fifteenth session and

*V. Axline, *Play Therapy* (New York: Ballantine, 1969); C. Moustakas, *Children in Play Therapy* (New York: Aronson, 1973).

sometimes as early as the fifth session, the child changes his focus and seeks more physical contact from his father. At some point the boy may ask to sit on his father's lap. The father may be reluctant to comply with his son's request, feeling that such contact is babyish or feminine. The clinician may instruct the father to relax and say, "Billy, during our time here you may sit on my lap. I know that often at home I don't let you sit on my lap but in here, while we are here, you may sit on my lap if you wish to." After the child climbs onto his father's lap, the clinician asks the father to put his arms around his son if he has not done so and tell him how good it feels to have him on his lap. During the five or ten minutes the child is on his father's lap, the clinician encourages the father to give his son positive messages.

While issues of nurturance and physical demonstrations of affection are often the central focus of father-son play sessions, the issue of limit setting frequently dominates play sessions between mother and son. Difficulties with limit setting emerge in the play sessions when the mother has difficulty getting her son to leave the playroom. The child may ask to extend the session or begin running around the room. During the next session the clinician would give the mother practical instructions: fifteen seconds before the time is up, she could rest her hand on the child's shoulder, and then, just before leaving, she should grip him firmly and show him out of the room. If he resists, she may need to pick him up and carry him out. During this interaction the mother is instructed to say, "Billy, I know you have had a wonderful time here today. You've enjoyed yourself. You do not want to go, but it is time to go now." The message conveys enjoyment of the time spent together as well as the mother's control over the session ending.

TREATMENT RESULTS: The success of this family therapy method is based on the two-step process of supervised parent-child play sessions and follow-up discussions between clinician and parent. Through the play encounters, parents learn various ways to relate to their children in a caring, sensitive way. The discussions between clinician and parent serve to explore thoughts and feelings that emerge during the play session. Uncovering the connection between the parents' personal and marital conflicts and their behavior in the play sessions is important if long-term change is to take place within the family.

COMMENTARY: The approach appears to be a practical and unique way to intervene in school behavior problems because children feel comfortable and relaxed in a play setting. It also addresses the long-term results of the process by having clinician-parent discussions that bring other family issues to the surface to be handled. In a variation of this process, the family sits with the clinician and reviews the videotape of the session. In addition, at times the clinician may have a conjoint session with both parents and child. Siblings could also be included, which may provide a context for peer problems to emerge and be solved.

SOURCE: Stollak, G. E. "Variations and Extensions of Filial Therapy." *Family Process*, 1981, *20*, 305-309.

---

*Modifying School Behavior Problems
Through Short-Term Family Therapy
Using a Behavioral Approach*

AUTHOR: Barclay Martin

PRECIS: Teaching parents to use behavior modification techniques to improve school behavior.

INTRODUCTION: Martin makes a preliminary study of communication between mother, father, and preadolescent son in four families in which school behavior problems predominate. The author focuses on current behavior in these families, citing that very repetitive patterns of interaction are often set off especially in disturbed families. For example, a parent criticizes his son, which provokes the son's withdrawal or a counter-aggressive response, such as storming off or slamming doors, rather than the desired positive behavior.

TREATMENT METHOD: The mother, father, and son are asked to meet in the therapist's office so that their interaction pattern can be assessed. Family members sit facing each other around a circular table. Attached to the armrest of each chair is a movable panel that can be turned around to face the person. The two signs at the top of each panel say *Talk* and *Don't Talk*. The bottom of the panel is fitted with two switches, and above each switch is the name of the two other family members. When one member pushes a switch, the *Don't Talk* sign goes off and the *Talk* sign goes on. The family members are to push the correct switch when talking to guarantee that each person communicates to only one other person at a time. Also, a recording device in the panel measures the length of each message and to whom each message is expressed.

At the beginning of a session the members of the family are asked to talk among themselves and decide upon an upsetting incident. Then they are instructed to describe what happened and to relate their associated feelings. Generally, three of these incidents can be discussed during the allotted hour. Each unit of speech—defined as speech confined on either side by another person talking—is rated in five categories: indirect blaming, direct blaming, self-blaming, nonblaming description of the situation, and nonblaming description of each member's own feelings.

After the assessment phase has been completed the modification phase begins with procedures that are very similar. The goal is to break into the repetitive cue-response patterns of the family members and test out new responses. A three-step process is employed: the stereotyped communication is pointed out to the family as it occurs; a different form of communication is suggested; and listening to one another is emphasized. For instance, a father who indirectly expresses blame toward his son by asking him questions such as, "Why do you keep on doing such and such?" would be encouraged to express his feelings directly. The new ways of relating are reinforced by the therapist's verbal approval and, more importantly, by the satisfaction experienced by family members in being understood. The therapist points out that a change in the son's school behavior serves to reinforce any shift in the parents' behavior.

TREATMENT RESULTS: Four families participated in a pilot study. The results showed a trend toward decreasing blaming statements in the two families that received the modification procedures; conversely, blaming statements increased in the two families that did not receive intervention. The school behavior problems, as reported by teachers, of the treated children also decreased.

COMMENTARY: In this preliminary study Martin shows how school behavior problems can be decreased by changing the pattern of communication in families. The treatment method is short term (six sessions over two weeks), and in the four families studied, very positive changes were observed. This method is still in the developmental stage; some of the methods used during the assessment phase need to be objectified, and it may well be that more than six sessions are necessary to bring about long-term change.

SOURCE: Martin, B. "Family Interaction Associated with Child Disturbance: Assessment & Modification." *Psychotherapy: Theory, Research & Practice,* 1967, *4,* 30-35.

Increasing Accuracy in Classwork with High-Risk Children Using a Family Problem-Solving Method

AUTHORS: Elaine A. Blechman, Cynthia J. Taylor, and Sandra M. Schrader

PRECIS: Involving families in solving the problem of children's inconsistent, unsatisfactory schoolwork.

INTRODUCTION: Elementary school students were evaluated on math and reading classwork accuracy, and the inconsistent results suggested that they were at risk for the life problems that accompany underachievement. Several methods of treatment were conducted with these students; the one discussed here is family problem solving.

TREATMENT METHOD: Those conducting the study collected math classwork on a daily basis from October through May. This work was scored and returned to the teachers the following day. Each child's baseline mean (percentage of correct answers) was determined, and forty-five children were assigned to the family problem-solving group. The families chosen came individually to the clinic for a one-hour appointment during which they met with a project teacher, were instructed about intervention, and spent about fifteen minutes playing the "solutions" board game. A contingency contract was written and it was decided when, how often, and by whom a reward would be given. Communication of good work was made through a "good news note." The contract outlined math as the target subject, with the goal performance at or above the child's baseline mean.

The contracts were followed up weekly by the project teacher phoning the parents and children. The parents were instructed to provide the reward on a consistent basis when it was earned and to say nothing when the child did not bring home a note. The teachers scored the children's work each day and sent a note home if it was earned; for example, a typical "good news note" read: Good News! John's math work was at least 85 percent correct today. If there was no assignment on a particular day, a note stating that was sent home. Every time a child was given a note, the teacher explained it by referring to the work accomplished that day.

TREATMENT RESULTS: Positive results were observed for the children who participated in the family problem-solving project. Changes included both an increase in accuracy in the target classwork and a generalized improvement in nonreinforced areas. The assigned work became more difficult as the year progressed, yet the children maintained good results.

COMMENTARY: The goal of increasing classwork accuracy was achieved by the intervention of family problem solving that tapped the resource of parents' involvement in their child's performance. This factor may be the most significant contribution to the positive results. Yet despite the improvement achieved, the teachers' opinions of these children as underachievers did not change. In addition, the results of a timed math test did not show improvement. Thus it appears that the result of the family problem-solving method was specific to the target goal. Perhaps an expansion of the goal to include improved results on standardized tests might be considered for further studies.

SOURCE: Blechman, E. A., Taylor, C. J., and Schrader, S. M. "Family Problem Solving Versus Home Notes as Early Intervention with High-Risk Children." *Journal of Counseling and Clinical Psychology,* 1981, *6,* 919–926.

A Combination of Educational and Family Therapies to Treat School Problems

AUTHORS: Betty Haufrecht and Celia Mitchell

PRECIS: The integration of educational therapy into family treatment to improve a child's school performance.

INTRODUCTION: The authors' treatment approach was devised after therapists found that despite positive changes in the family and school, some children's learning problems persisted. The clinic personnel recognized that many forms of learning disabilities were not being treated effectively. A learning disability specialist was brought on staff at the family treatment clinic in 1970. Following a period of adjustment, the new staff member was accepted and became integrated into the clinic's overall treatment program. Treatment strategies were designed to address the reciprocal interaction between a child's educational and emotional difficulties.

TREATMENT APPROACH: During the initial assessment phase clinicians determine the place of the child's learning problem within the overall functioning of the family. As the authors state, "A most significant consideration in the timing of the introduction of learning therapy is the extent to which this problem is viewed by the family as the sole cause of family dysfunctioning." An initial conference is held by the two therapists to decide whether an educational assessment should be done immediately.

An example of the integration of educational therapy in the family treatment is illustrated by the G family. In this case, the decision to include educational therapy was made several months after treatment began, despite the fact that the presenting problem was ten-year-old Robert's behavioral and learning difficulties. Robert's problems included not completing assignments, giving up if faced with a difficult task, and blaming others for his difficulties. The family had set up two separate "camps." The younger son, Richard, was viewed positively by both parents, while Mrs. G saw Robert as cold and ungiving like his father. She described Richard as outgoing and achieving, like herself, and the behavior problems Richard experienced in school were minimized by his parents. In effect, Mr. G and Robert were designated the "failures," and Mrs. G and Richard were the "stars."

The therapy process consisted of Mr. and Mrs. G being seen in therapy together, and at times the whole family was seen. As the family looked at the conflict issues together, Robert was no longer the focal point. A dramatic improvement in Robert's behavior was reported, but his difficulties in school persisted, and an educational consultation was arranged. Following the evaluation, the educational consultant met with the family and conveyed the message that Robert was bright and did not have any specific learning disabilities. As Mr. G discussed his school experiences, he realized that he regretted the fact that his parents made career choices for him rather than allowing him to explore his own interests. Mr. G connected his own frustration and his treatment of Robert. Throughout the discussion, Robert listened with keen interest. A positive change took place as Robert started to accept responsibility for his failure. At a second meeting the focus was educational problems for father and son. At that meeting, a decision was reached that educational services were not indicated, a decision later reinforced by Robert's academic accomplishments. Another consequence of the two sessions was a new closeness between father and son.

A different intervention was called for in working with the B family. The authors point out that, "When the preoccupation with the learning disability is so anxiety-laden that no other issues can be profitably explored, it is advisable to intervene promptly." Mr. B had called the clinic to request help for his son, David; that the father, rather than the mother, initiated the contact was unusual. The first family session was held with Mr. and Mrs. B, David, age fifteen, and Benjy, age twelve. Due to the intense focus on David's learning problem, an educational consultation was initiated following the first session. It was evident that Mr. B strongly identified with David's learning difficulties. A description of his own early years and his relationship with his stepfather paralleled David's current difficulties. A definite sense of relief was expressed by Mr. B and David as the result of an educational consultation.

One session was held with Mr. and Mrs. B to assess their relationship and their role as parents, and David was interviewed alone to assess his needs without the intervention of his father. The educational consultation showed that David had a minor visual problem that caused some difficulty with reading. In another meeting, the school principal described David as bright, anxious, and perfectionistic. His methods of learning caused him to feel easily overwhelmed. In order to lessen the pressure on David, the principal allowed him to drop one course. During the session to discuss the educational evaluation, Mr. B reacted with some resistance, while Mrs. B, uncharacteristically, differed with her husband. Through receiving support from his mother and the educational therapist, David admitted that he had exaggerated his visual problem in order to reinforce his father's belief that he had a reading disability and as an excuse not to read the classics, which his father valued as an important part of his development. Once the issue of David's "disability" was cleared up and the family dynamics were explored, the rigid family patterns loosened. Other difficulties came to light, such as the younger son's very definite school problems. Some modifications were made in the family living schedule, so that the parents and children felt freer in their functioning. An educational therapy intern was provided for the two boys to assist them in developing better study skills.

COMMENTARY: The authors' model for working on a child's learning problems within a family context appears to have great applicability. There is no doubt that the learning process is greatly influenced by the family system and, as noted in the case studies presented, that children's functioning in school is related to their parents' own experiences. An important consideration is the timing in bringing an educational therapist into the treatment process, which is indicated by an assessment of family dynamics. The illustration of timing and techniques in this article has broad implications for those working with families, one of whose children has learning difficulties.

SOURCE: Haufrecht, B., and Mitchell, C. "Family Systems and Learning Problems: A Treatment Model." *Social Casework,* December 1978, 579–587.

===

Four Family-Oriented Approaches to School Behavior and Learning Problems

AUTHOR: Robert Friedman

PRECIS: Improving learning and school behavior through individual, parent-tutor, concurrent, or conjoint family therapy.

INTRODUCTION: In discussing family-oriented psychotherapy for school behavior and learning problems, the author states, "Emphasis on the family component of the school problems stems from a recognition that the family, both genetically and in an ongoing way, has a powerful effect on the behavior of the child in school." Friedman views parents as the child's first teachers and notes that a positive or negative identification with the parent of the same sex as a learning person is generally established by the time a child begins school. Structured family-oriented therapy assumes that the values, goals, and interpersonal relationships found in the home usually duplicate themselves in the school setting and therefore greatly influence the child's success or failure in school adjustment.

TREATMENT METHODS: Four treatment modalities are discussed:
Individual therapy. When using the individual approach, the therapist explores parental attitudes, values, and feelings about school, as well as any problems among family members

that may be having a negative influence on school adjustment. Frequently a family "educational history" discloses that one or both parents had school problems similar to the ones their child is now experiencing. The effect of the parents' school history on the child's adjustment in school can be significant. If parental attitudes and values are seen as hindering the child's development, the therapist will bring the issue into the open, while being sensitive to how difficult it may be for the parent to give up or modify the family value. If problems in family relationships are directly affecting school adjustment, the therapist introduces the conflict into the therapy in order to resolve the school problems.

Parent-tutor therapy. In the parent-tutor approach, the parent is seen as the primary agent of change. This approach was developed after a number of treatment failures with children whose problems resulted from identification with the inadequate, ineffective learning model of the parent of the same sex. In order to modify the inadequacy in the parent and child, the parent is brought into the therapy session as an observer or participant in the tutoring process. During the session, the therapist might model or define a constructive tutoring approach with the child and note the reaction of the child or parent. When the parent is asked to assume the tutor's role, the therapist would be somewhat passive, responding to the interaction between parent and child with silence, nonverbal cues, or verbal comments about the feelings or actual results of the tutoring.

There are many aspects of the therapist's role. The first is to ascertain what the child is capable of doing compared to what he is willing to do. During the assessment of the parent, the therapist observes the parent's readiness for the task, as well as his ability to follow through with the approach. Part of the assessment involves the ability of the parent and child to tolerate stress, as well as the parent's willingness to take interpretations and instructions from the therapist. Another aspect of the therapist's role is to "vote" the child competent to complete the task and encouraging the parent to join in the "vote." By modeling a realistic expectation to the parent, the therapist attempts to encourage the parent to model the same expectation for the child. Although the major role the therapist assumes with the parent is a supportive one, the therapist does reject any attempt by the parent to abdicate responsibility. As stated by the author, "The therapist gives only as much help to the parent as is truly needed, and expects the parent to follow suit with the child." At times, the therapist may leave the parent and child alone to work on a task and may recommend that the "tutoring" take place between therapy sessions as "homework."

Friedman presents the following as an example of the interactions between parent, child and therapist.

Father: Are you just sitting here, are you really trying to find the word?

Carl: Trying, but I can't.

Therapist: (Reflecting feelings.) If I tell my father I can't, maybe he'll believe me.

Therapist: (After a long pause.) If I wait long enough, maybe father will forget that I figured out where that word is and that I really can get it. His patience won't last, I think.

Concurrent therapy. Friedman views concurrent therapy as being particularly applicable when parents or family have an interest in maintaining the negative school behavior or learning problem. If more than one therapist is involved, they must communicate with one another on a regular basis to deal effectively with the interlocking family problems. Part of the process is to evaluate whether the parent will be able to gain and use insight into his need to have his child fail. In cases where this is not seen as possible, the goal is to help the parents change the most destructive aspects of their interaction with the child. As part of therapy with the child it is often helpful to explain to the child what causes his parent to behave in certain ways. If a parent has a strong resistance to his child making changes individual therapy will not be effective, and concurrent therapy might yield positive results.

Conjoint family therapy. The whole family was seen during most of the sessions in conjoint family therapy, with variations of this format (such as seeing individuals or family member combinations) kept to a minimum. The discussions focus on a school issue that emphasizes events and developments at school and the resulting effects in the home. The treatment goals include identifying situations that negatively affect school adjustment, establishing good communication within the family about the problem, and identifying and building on family strengths that could provide reinforcement for changing school behavior.

In a case example, Friedman outlines the relationship between the family process and the child's school behavior. Following this stage of treatment, an attempt was made to engender some understanding and acceptance of the feelings all family members experienced as a result of the school problem. Next, the therapist worked on establishing a cooperative effort between the parents on expectations and management. When the parents were seen together for one session, they expressed some mutual dissatisfaction and allowed the therapist to make some suggestions for compromise. The family was asked to call the therapist every evening for the first three days to talk about how the suggestions were working. As the home situation improved, the son was able to deal effectively with his school responsibilities.

COMMENTARY: The author emphasizes that careful evaluation of the family members as individuals, as well as the family as a unit, should be done before choosing a course of treatment. At times a change in the form of therapy or a combination of approaches may be necessary. Six important aspects of family-oriented therapy for school difficulties are outlined: (1) The therapist should find ways to include the father in treatment; if the father is not included in treatment with a boy, the prognosis is poor. (2) An important goal is for the parent to give the child permission to make positive changes. (3) A family's resistance to change requires close consideration; in rare cases a school problem may be necessary to maintain the equilibrium within a family. (4) It may be very difficult for a child to break away from his role as the family scapegoat for parental guilt or failure. (5) The school adjustment of siblings can contribute to the family's view of a child's school problems. (6) The overall communication pattern within a family may need to be altered before changes can take place in the child's school adjustment.

The family-oriented approaches outlined in this article are applicable in long- or short-term treatment, and they can be adapted by therapists with different psychological viewpoints.

SOURCE: Friedman, R. "Structured Family-Oriented Psychotherapy for School Behavior and Learning Disorders." In R. Friedman (Ed.), *Family Roots of School Learning and Behavior Disorders*. Springfield, Ill.: Thomas, 1973.

Identification of Social Roles in a Family to Determine Points for Intervention

AUTHORS: Charles R. Atherton, Sandra T. Mitchell, and Edna Biehl Schein

PRECIS: The therapist views the family in terms of the members' social roles and then finds points for intervention.

INTRODUCTION: Through the illustration of a four-generation family the authors show a therapy process using points for intervention. The stated purpose of this article is to answer two questions: How does the points-for-intervention approach work out in practice? If a point for intervention can be identified, what is the appropriate role of the therapist?

CASE ILLUSTRATION: Sixteen-year-old Mary, the identified client, was described as a high school dropout. The family consisted of four generations of women: Mary and her divorced mother lived in the home of her grandmother, and the great-grandmother also resided in the home for about eight months a year. Mary felt that she could no longer live at home and described her grandmother as always berating her. She asked the therapist to speak to her mother about allowing her "to live in a commune with her boyfriend." This request was denied but the therapist agreed to meet with her mother and talk about the current living situation.

According to the therapist, Mary experienced role confusion in that her grandmother functioned more as a mother than her own mother. Role confusion was noted in the mother, who had difficulty negotiating her own mothering role from her role as a daughter. The grandmother was in some interrole conflict between her expectations of being a mother and grandmother, while the great-grandmother was in a powerless, roleless position, her opinions ignored by the other family members.

A few days after the initial interview with Mary, the therapist was called by the mother who was very distressed. Mary had been picked up by the police in a raid on a house during a search for a runaway. In addition, Mary had complained about police brutality while she was detained at the station. In the conversation between the therapist and the mother, the mother decided that she could wait until the scheduled appointment a few days later to further discuss the problem. The joint session with Mary and her mother was focused on Mary's keeping late hours. Mary complained about her grandmother's demands and said that if she had privacy at home she would not stay out so much. The mother looked to the therapist to set limits for Mary and was told that this was not the therapist's role. Some suggestions for building trust between mother and daughter were offered. The mother stated that nothing had been accomplished in the session because there was no assurance that Mary would come home earlier. Before the session ended the therapist noted that the problems had not started in a week and could not be resolved immediately. The therapist noted how frustrating the situation must be to the mother.

The next session began on a more realistic note with both Mary and her mother seeing the therapy in a broader time frame. Both of them expressed the need for the grandmother to participate in further sessions, as she held the power within the family. As anticipated, the grandmother dominated the first session with the entire family. Most of the time was devoted to the grandmother's complaining about Mary's behavior, adding that she should go live with her father. This session took place in the family home, as did subsequent sessions, but the great-grandmother did not participate in the following meetings.

The goal of the sessions was to support the mother in her attempt to assume her role. Although a difficult task, she began to assert herself more often, and Mary's behavior improved. An important goal to the mother and grandmother was that Mary return to school. When this was presented to her, Mary said she would not be able to get the necessary courses, but a phone call to the school by the therapist clarified that the courses were open. Mary's reaction was ambivalent: she wanted to return to school but was fearful that the family's commitment to working on problems in the home would diminish. Her fear became a reality when the family told the therapist that services were no longer necessary.

A week later Mary called the therapist and said that her mother no longer protected her from her grandmother's demands. The following week the mother and school personnel called to say that Mary had left school. The therapist arranged a staff meeting with Mary's teachers and principal, and a subsequent parent conference. During the thirty-minute staff meeting the family was described in terms of its role network. The members were asked to support the mother in her mothering role and to encourage Mary to play her role. At the parent conference the mother and grandmother were introduced to the staff, who then related their experiences as Mary's teachers. Without exception, they viewed Mary positively, which shocked the grandmother and delighted the mother. A discussion of the needs of teenage girls followed, and the needs for privacy and independence were brought up. The mother suggested that Mary have her own room, and at first the grandmother agreed. But when it was suggested that Mary be allowed to lock her room and keep it her own way, the grandmother changed her opinion. However, with the support of the teachers, the mother insisted and the grandmother conceded. Many other issues between the grandmother and Mary were brought up by the mother. The following day Mary returned to school. The mother's effective playing of her role was praised by the therapist. In order to continue the process, the mother asked for weekly sessions.

TREATMENT RESULTS: The family was seen for six months, and during that time the roles shifted in the family. While the mother became more assertive, the grandmother exerted less control: "The grandmother also was better off because she no longer felt the need to continue to live in a state of interrole conflict now that her daughter was successfully functioning as a mother for Mary." Other results included improved communication between Mary and her grandmother as well as Mary's continued good progress in school and her keeping her curfew.

COMMENTARY: Through identifying the roles and role confusion in a family the therapist was able to plan a strategy for treatment to support the different members in assuming their appropriate roles. As a result, the symptoms of the identified patient were eliminated. The involvement of community resources such as school personnel enhanced the new role positions. While an active participant in the treatment process, the therapist clearly delineated her own role as facilitator and not authority figure. The six-month family treatment process was indeed effective.

SOURCE: Atherton, C. R., Mitchell, S. T., and Schein, E. B. "Using Points for Intervention." *Social Casework,* 1971, *52,* 223-233.

The Go-Between Process in Family Therapy

AUTHOR: Gerald H. Zuk

PRECIS: The structuring of the family treatment process by the therapist assuming the role of go-between.

INTRODUCTION: The technique of go-between—the transaction of a therapist with two or more individuals who have a long-term relationship—uses sources that are believed to be unique to family therapy. Family therapy, as presented in this paper, is defined as "the technique that explores and attempts to shift the balance of pathogenic relating among family members so that new forms of relating become possible." Further, the expression of conflict in family therapy fosters the energy necessary to change fixed patterns of relating among family members.

TREATMENT PROCESS: Three terms of the go-between process are described: (1) the definition of issues on which the family members are in serious conflict and the communication of that conflict; (2) the therapist's assumption of the role of go-between or "broker" in conflicts; (3) the therapist's siding with or against family members in conflicts.

During the first term, the therapist encourages the family members to express conflict. Therapists are instructed to look for two patterns of expression. First is the family who shows a lot of boisterous disagreement while deeper sources of conflict are left concealed, a process designated as "pseudohostility." Second is the family that denies disagreements, and when the therapist points out conflict issues the members become confused and perhaps hurt. The therapist invites the family to relate a recent conflict (its recentness increasing the likelihood that the facts presented are accurate). If a family member wants to relate a conflict with a family member who is not present, the therapist needs to evaluate the appropriateness of the disclosure. One guideline offered is that the therapist should allow the conflict to be expressed if it seems likely to "open up" sources of conflict among the members who are present.

The go-between process is initiated in the second term when the therapist selects certain conflicts as advantageous and rejects others. Also, the therapist must resist the anticipated attempts by the family to set up their own rules of priority. In another paper, Zuk states that "In family therapy the go-between may be very active, intrusive, and confronting, or inactive and passive. He may move into the role of go-between by the device of attacking two parties he hopes to make into principals; or he may move into the role by calmly pointing out a difference between two parties. On the other hand, he may become a go-between by refusing to take sides in a dispute that has erupted; or he may become one by presenting a new point of view in a dispute."* These different strategies illustrate how the therapist constantly structures and directs the treatment process.

An example of the second term of the go-between process involves a family whose presenting problem was the nine-year-old daughter's poor school performance, a symptom that appeared to have its origin in disturbed family living. For the first few sessions, much disagreement was expressed by family members; during the fourth session the opportunity arose for the therapist to assume the go-between role. The incident involved a used bike that the father had given his daughter; the bike broke down, and the brother ended up getting it because he was able to fix it. The go-between process started as the therapist asked each member to relate his or her version of the incident. Having the therapist as go-between afforded the family a new way to express conflicts. The therapist set the rules and made certain that everyone was dealt with fairly. One rule laid down by the therapist was that no one could interfere when another member was speaking. As stated by the author, "Temporarily freed by the therapist's action from a vicious repetitive pattern, the family may experience the good feeling of more positive and productive relating and explore the possibility of new means to relate in the future."

The third term of the go-between process is conducted by the therapist siding with one member against another in a conflict, or by siding with or against the whole family at times. The therapist has to decide whom to side with and when to take this action. The intervention of siding permits the therapist to shift the balance in favor of healthier relating. One pitfall is any effort by the family to get the therapist to side in a systematic way; preferably, the therapist keeps the family wondering

*G. H. Zuk, "The Go-Between Process in Family Therapy." *Family Process*. In press.

whether he will use siding and what form of siding he will use. During the fourth session with the family described above, the therapist used siding in several different ways. First, he set the rule of no interference while other members were talking. Also, he often sided against the father and with other family members in order to implement his rules for procedure.

Throughout the go-between process, the family may attempt to resist the therapist's efforts in a variety of ways. Three frequent defensive tactics are: the family's denying the allegations of conflict made by the therapist; the phenomenon of one member becoming a spokesman for the entire family unit, which sets up a role conflict as the family member competes with the therapist for the position of go-between; family members giving the therapist the message that he was a particular type of go-between or that he was repeatedly siding with one member against others.

Finally, the author notes that the go-between process may have dramatic results when the therapist states that treatment should be terminated because there has been no significant progress. Such an announcement is a case of siding against the whole family as a way of shaking up the system.

TREATMENT RESULTS: According to the author, the family described made significant positive changes by the tenth session. The changes allowed all family members to assume more appropriate, satisfying roles within the family structure.

COMMENTARY: Zuk describes in detail the intervention of the go-between and how it can be successfully used to shift the pathogenic ways of relating among family members. The go-between process has many complexities, and Zuk outlines various pitfalls. Positive change in the ways family members related to one another were noticed in a short period of time, which made for cost-effective family therapy.

SOURCE: Zuk, G. H. "Family Therapy: Formulation of a Technique and Its Theory." *International Journal of Group Psychotherapy*, 1968, *18*, 42-57.

Effective Family Intervention with an Adolescent's Serious Behavior Problems

AUTHORS: Lillian C. Scheiner and Andrew P. Musetto

PRECIS: Redefining an adolescent's symptomatic behavior as a consequence of problems in family relationships.

INTRODUCTION: The authors propose that the way a presenting problem is understood directs the course of treatment. For example, if the question is simply "What's wrong with Steve?" the therapy is conducted accordingly; but the question "What is going on in the family, parental, and marital relationships that maintain and is maintained by Steve's symptoms?" sets up a very different therapeutic framework.

CASE ILLUSTRATION: Fourteen-year-old Steve refused to attend school and prior to a new term had attempted suicide by ingesting iodine. An initial assessment revealed that he felt awkward socially and was quite isolated. He spent a good deal of his time at home with his mother, and he often criticized her and exploded when she requested him to do chores. Steve's parents viewed him as the cause of family problems, and the covert message he received from them was to hold the marriage together and through his behavior bring his father more actively into the family circle.

Family sessions were conducted by a male-female co-therapy team. The majority of the sessions involved only the parents, as Steve often refused to come and claimed that the problems belonged to his parents. However, he did participate in a number of sessions at both the beginning and end of treatment.

As part of the therapy, the school personnel were contacted, and a behavioral approach to reinvolve Steve in school was devised. This approach was unsuccessful at first, but after a year Steve started night classes.

Another intervention entailed helping the parents to see that Steve's problems were connected to family issues. A deli-

cate balance was maintained between pointing out their involvement and not placing blame on anyone. The family, however,
strongly resisted redefining the process. The therapists asked
questions about how the symptoms helped the family and how
they maintained a homeostasis in the family. A redefinition of
Steve's symptoms from being "bad" to being the only means he
had to help his parents was offered.

The next part of therapy concentrated on the parents'
relationship, and in looking at it the parents were faced with the
choice of making a commitment to a more productive relationship or separating. The therapists encouraged each of them to
develop individual interests and to take more risks. As Mrs. O
began to go out on her own more often, she found that she
could cope with problems on her own, a crucial realization that
reduced the demands she placed on her husband. Mr. O was encouraged to use the resources he displayed in business in his personal life. The therapists also suggested that they do more
things as a couple. As the bonds between his parents became
stronger, the relationship between Steve and his parents became
more differentiated. This left Steve free to develop a more active social life with his peers. During therapy the parents were
taught to set consistent limits for Steve and to assume mutually agreeable positions for handling any provocative behavior.

TREATMENT RESULTS: The therapy lasted two years. During
that time, several regressions into former patterns were made by
family members. At times they wanted to terminate treatment,
and the therapists often felt frustrated. However, by the end of
treatment, a good deal had been accomplished. The parents expressed greater satisfaction in their relationship, and as their
communication improved they became more effective parents.
Steve acted more appropriately and attended high school. Overall the family came to recognize that they had the ability to
deal with life issues as they emerged.

COMMENTARY: The seriousness of the problems that brought
the family for treatment were recognized and the redefinition
of the problem helped to relieve the symptoms. The course of

therapy was two years, which might be viewed as longer than other therapy processes. However, that the son did not have to be hospitalized following his suicide attempt and that the marital relationship stayed intact and improved are remarkable. The co-therapist model added to the success of therapy because the therapists were able to support one another during the regressions and move on. The family approach led to differentiation among family members and better communication.

SOURCE: Scheiner, L. C., and Musetto, A. P. "Redefining the Problem: Family Therapy with a Severely Symptomatic Adolescent." *Family Therapy*, 1979, 6, 195-203.

Concurrent Individual and Family Therapy for the Treatment of School Problems

AUTHOR: Israel W. Charney

PRECIS: Both individual and family sessions are used as parts of the total treatment process.

INTRODUCTION: According to Charney, the use of concurrent individual and family interviews taps the complementary roles of the client as individual and family member. Each case is evaluated separately; there is no set number of individual or family sessions nor is there a set ratio of one type of interview to another. This form of therapy is recommended when there are signs that neither approach in itself will be sufficient.

CASE EXAMPLES: The Wolf family came for treatment with the presenting problem the underachievement of one of the children. A look at the family background revealed that Mr. Wolf, a successful executive, had been raised by a psychotic mother and had learned to placate everyone around him. The other family members had followed his lead and were seen as deeply repressed. It was felt that the father was the key to the family's difficulties. A treatment process was devised: the mother was to be seen weekly for no more than a few months, the identified patient was directed to a brief casework experience as well as to an optometrist to help with perceptual problems, and the father was asked to come to weekly individual sessions. After a period of time it became apparent that the individual approach was not successful with the father and family sessions were initiated. Movement occurred as Mrs. Wolf and the children gradually lessened their appeasement of the father and let him know how angry and demanding of them he frequently was, although he believed himself to be so good. Mr. Wolf's anxiety level increased to a point at which meaningful therapy could take place.

The second family focused on the problem of the school difficulties of the preadolescent son who showed signs of nervousness, negativism, and poor peer relationships. During the intake interviews the family members requested individual sessions for the child and concurrent casework for the parents. However, the child did not respond to the individual method, as he would get to a certain point and then blank out emotionally. He was aware of this problem and said to the therapist, "I do want to come and yell and scream more . . . I guess it is me who is the dangerous person that I am afraid of here, and not you." Simultaneously, the mother was having extreme difficulty engaging in treatment with the caseworker. She threatened to leave treatment and was told that no other part of the program would be made available to the family if she left. The situation reached the explosive point, and family sessions with the parents and child were started. After an adjustment period, the prescribed treatment program combined family therapy with individual therapy for the child, in addition to periodic individual sessions for the parents. A dramatic change in the child's participation was noted. Whereas he had been almost mute in many individual sessions, he became quite talkative in family sessions. Concurrent family and individual sessions allowed the child to express his feelings in a mutually productive way. Through the family meetings, he was able to see that he was not alone and did have support, while in individual sessions he was able to experience his deep angry feelings toward his parents, which were expressed in his wish to kill them. As the author notes, "Supported by individual therapy, he could come back to family sessions to bring home to his father and then particularly to his mother his anger at them."

TREATMENT OUTCOMES: The use of concurrent individual and family interviews is indicated when neither approach appears sufficient. Charney suggests that the integration of experiences as an individual and as a member of a family creates a flow of mutual confrontation of defenses and supports of self-acceptance. This reciprocal pattern, offered by combining approaches into one process, brought about successful results.

COMMENTARY: In the beginning stage of integrated individual and family therapy, the therapist fairly well controls the situation by the selection of whom he invites to the sessions. The therapist gives the family a message by asking various members to return for further interviews. As the treatment progresses and the family senses the flow, the family members decide who should be present at the next session. The flexibility inherent in this approach moves the responsibility for continued growth from the therapist to the family.

Some questions are raised by the author. One involves the potential for an individual to run away from a significant experience by crisscrossing from one mode of therapy to another. A second essential issue is how the classical transference in individual therapy is affected by the relationship with the therapist in family sessions. Specific studies addressed to these issues might be considered.

SOURCE: Charney, I. W. "Integrated Individual and Family Psychotherapy." *Family Process,* 1966, *5,* 179–198.

Additional Readings

Burdon, A. P., Neely, J. H., and Thorpe, A. L. "Emotionally Disturbed Boys Failing in School: Treatment in an Outpatient Clinic School." *Journal of the Southern Medical Association,* 1964, *57,* 829–835.

    The operation of a clinic school for boys with learning and emotional difficulties is the topic of this paper. The creation of the school was prompted by families who had exhausted all the specialized agencies of the school and the community. Procedures for acceptance to the school were established, with the length of a child's stay at the clinic school set between four and five months. During this time, the parents are required to show a sincere desire to cooperate by attending group and individual psychotherapy; separate groups are held for mothers and fathers. The boys attend their regular school in the morning and the clinic school in the afternoon. Each child is assessed, and the clinic focuses on the most outstanding educational deficits. The program also includes daily individual tutorial sessions and weekly organized play therapy. A small percentage of the boys require medication, but that is the only psychiatric attention found to be necessary.

    Boys involved in this study were evaluated by psychiatrists, school personnel, and psychologists. A majority of the boys were able to adapt to regular placement and made significant gains while at the clinic school. The authors indicate that the selection of cases must be done carefully and the selection committee must understand the limitations of the program. The study shows that a major shift in a pathological emotional constellation involving the whole family can be responsible for freeing the child from a block to learning.

Esterson, H., Feldman, C., Krigsman, N., and Warshaw, S. "Time Limited Counseling with Parents of Pre-adolescent Underachievers: A Pilot Program." Paper presented at the 78th annual meeting of the American Psychological Association, Montreal, August 1973.

    The purpose of this time-limited group counseling program is to provide a group service to parents whose children have been identified as underachievers by their teachers. The hypothesis is that for a child with average or better intelligence, underachievement represents a symptom suggestive of some familial conflicts and disturbance. Three schools of different socioeconomic backgrounds were involved in the study. Underachieving students were selected from grades three through six. Teachers were given classroom-behavior forms to fill out and return to the psychologist. Parents of the selected students were notified and asked to respond to a questionnaire. The three groups met for twenty sessions. Results of the study showed that ten of eleven children improved. The authors conclude that time-limited group counseling seems a useful procedure for parents of preadolescent, underachieving children.

Gilmore, J. V. "The Effectiveness of Parental Counseling with Other Modalities in the Treatment of Children with Learning Disabilities." *Journal of Education,* 1971, *154,* 74–82.

This paper describes a study with children who have perceptual difficulties. Findings showed that the conditions were psychosomatic in nature, dependent on parent-child relationships, and best treated through a combination of group instruction, parent counseling, and play therapy.

Klein, R. S., Altman, S. D., Dreizen, K., Friedman, R., and Powers, L. "Restructuring Dysfunctional Parental Attitudes Toward Children's Learning and Behavior in School: Family-Oriented Psychoeducational Therapy." *The Professional Press,* 1981, *14* (issues 1 and 2).

The authors describe parental attitudes that interfere with a child's learning and behavior in school, presenting two case histories. In the first case, the parent's dysfunctional attitude was manifested in dissatisfaction with the educational system and its authority. The second case illustrated a dysfunctional parental attitude toward the responsibility of learning. The findings show that school learning and behavior disorders that result primarily from dysfunctional parental attitudes might be treated by using behavioral and psychodynamic interventions. Also discussed is the value of a psychoeducational therapist as a diagnostician and as an integral member of the

treatment team who decides on the advisability of psychoeducational treatment in the individual cases and participates in
some family sessions.

In the second part, two more case histories are cited. In
the first the child was the target for displaced negative feelings
between parents. The child acted out their unresolved conflicts
about authority, while they remained mildly involved in his
chronic underachievement. Therapeutic progress in this case
was slow, as the parents' participation was minimal. Some
changes occurred in the boy's behavior and these changes were
primarily the result of his identification with the therapist's
standards, rather than his parents. The second case illustrates
dysfunctional parental attitudes whereby parents furnish a cultural model not adaptable to the educational system. The therapist pursued an optimal course of action for the parents, but
they were able to accept only a portion of what was offered.
The family finally terminated the treatment with the parents
expressing satisfaction with their son's changes, while the therapist felt that the treatment was incomplete.

Midlarsky, E. "Family Therapy: A Very Proper Failure." Paper
    presented in the symposium "When Therapy Failed: Case
    Studies of Unsuccessful Therapy," at the 84th annual meet-
    ing of the American Psychological Association, New York,
    September 1979.

In both family therapy case studies presented, the patient
was a latency-aged boy with behavior problems. The first family
attended all the sessions, solved many of the problems and felt
they benefited from nearly perfect cooperating therapy sessions. The object of the therapy, the child, showed some improvement but then regressed such that his situation in the family and at school was worse than ever. Even after the therapist
discussed the obvious failure of the treatment, the family was
still reluctant to abandon the sessions. In the second case, the
therapy sessions were unproductive from the outset. The mother dominated the sessions and the father always became bellig-
erent. The father eventually stopped attending, while the mother
and two sons continued the sessions. The one son (the identified patient) improved vastly. All three reported that they were

enjoying life to a much greater degree. The mother and two boys accomplished their individual goals, and the therapy was considered a success and was discontinued. The author explains that proper technique and "model sessions" are least important in successful therapy. The author proposes that the best results are yielded by a flexible, caring, practical, goal-oriented program that is always open to the patient's perspective and that can be immediately adapted to the changing situation.

Moos, R. H., and Fuhr, R. "The Clinical Use of Social-Ecological Concepts: The Case of an Adolescent Girl." *American Journal of Orthopsychiatry*, 1982, *52*, 111–122.

The authors outline a system that identifies and describes the components of the family's environment. This environmental assessment encourages an explicit practical focus in relation to the family's present environment. The case study involves the family of a fifteen-year-old girl who had dropped out of school. The therapist's goals were to discover what caused her to drop out, what changes she wanted to have occur at school, how she spent her time outside the classroom, and the like. To gather this information, the therapist conducted two-hour sessions with the family, employing established assessment questionnaires (the "Real Form" of the classroom, family, and work scales, among others). The results of these assessment procedures were used to help organize the family's difficulties into small manageable units, and the therapist established a treatment program that addressed each individual problem. Among the advantages of this approach: the therapist uncovered a full picture of the family's problems and could separate and individualize the situation; the family did not become overwhelmed by the size of the problems and did not ramble from topic to topic; most importantly, the clinician was spared from the error of underestimating the relative importance of environmental, as compared to dispositional, determinants of behavior.

Westman, J. C., Miller, D. R., and Arthur, B. "Psychiatric Symptoms and Family Dynamics as Illustrated by the Retarded Reader." *Psychiatric Research Report* no. 20, American Psychiatric Association, February 1966, pp. 115–120.

This study describes a working model that identifies

symptoms that display a person's private subidentity (his subjective view of himself) and his public subidentity (an objective,
observable view of his personality). The retarded reader and his
particular subidentities are the focus of this study, and the
"pseudo-stupid" subidentity within the teacher-learner relationship is discussed. Other characteristic subidentities in the child's
family and school relationships are delineated, and this model
enables the therapist to synthesize a clear picture of the child's
total identity.

2

Impulsive-Aggressive
Behaviors

Children who act out in impulsive-aggressive behavior require firm, quick, and direct intervention. If the aggressive behavior is of a serious nature, the therapist may advise the parents to call the police should the situation become dangerous. In treating violent episodes, the therapist may also consider conferring with a colleague to help objectify and neutralize any fear of the young person's behavior. Among the family treatment methods included in this chapter are a home-based treatment procedure using behavioral techniques and a paradoxical approach using letter writing.

63

Paradoxical Letters to Treat Defeating
Patterns in Family Therapy

AUTHORS: Luciano L'Abate and Lynette Farr

PRECIS: A variety of letters written to counteract defeating patterns in families are outlined.

INTRODUCTION: The authors seek to garner valuable lessons from therapeutic failures, specifically in dealing with defeating patterns that result in the defeat of family members as well as the therapist. A novel method of altering these patterns is offered in the form of paradoxical letters to be presented to family members with instructions for use.

TREATMENT TECHNIQUES: Six patterns of coping with defeat are outlined:

1. Admitting defeat and helplessness. The intent of the therapist in acknowledging defeat is to create the opposite reaction in the family. Therapists are reminded that underlying the family's request for help is a hidden agenda that pulls for defeat, and the therapist should recognize the possibility of defeat in each family. An example of admission of defeat is presented: "I am aware that, because of the power of this family, I am feeling a real sense of defeat and helplessness. I do know I have power that you cannot speak to, but yours is also special. You are a special family that I cannot fight with. I don't know where I could have found a better family than you to defeat me."

2. Congratulating the family. The therapist repeatedly praises the family for their defeating pattern.

3. Positive reframing. The therapist presents the defeating pattern as linked to success, closeness, and other positive values. After positively reframing the pattern, the therapist can move on to the next step.

4. Prescribing the defeat. Given the fact that the pattern is positive, the family is told to continue and even escalate whatever they are doing to defeat one another. For example, a family that continued the same patterns despite all the interven-

tions was instructed to read the following letter in the following way:

>   To be read by son to other members of the family.
>   Please read on Mondays, Wednesdays, and Fridays after dinner.
>   Mother is to remind son to read and if she forgets, stepfather and daughter are to remind her.
>   Do not discuss contents outside of counseling.

> "I am impressed with the way in which you show how much you care about this family and especially your mother. I feel you need to be congratulated for having violent temper tantrums, because these tantrums serve as a safety valve for what your father and mother cannot do. I admire you for the way in which you show your loyalty to your mother.
> "If this is the way you want to protect your parents from each other and continue keeping them apart, you should continue to blow up, but do this on Monday, Wednesday, and Friday of each week. Be sure to break some inexpensive item in your home and continue these outbursts, because if you stop, they might get back together."

5. Balancing the family upset. Following the first letter, which changes the role of the identified patient from victim to rescuer, the children are given instructions to praise their parents. In a second letter, the children thank their parents for giving up part of themselves to bring up their children.

6. Dealing with disqualifications. In working with a family whose defeating pattern is disqualification, the therapist sends one letter admitting his helpless position and follows it up with another letter reframing the family's pattern as "high standards" of performance.

COMMENTARY: The authors acknowledge that the biggest drawback of their method is the effect this technique had on the families. From a subjective standpoint, it was seen as improbable that the families would have stayed in therapy without the last-resort intervention. The authors emphasize the value of homework assignments and propose that a selective use of these letters could shorten the therapy process and lessen the chance of defeat in therapy. The letters can be individualized to the needs of the particular family and therapist. Therapists are encouraged to report their experiences with this technique to the authors.

SOURCE: L'Abate, L., and Farr, L. "Coping with Defeating Patterns in Family Therapy." *Family Therapy,* 1981, *8,* 91–103.

Controlling Violent Behavior in Youth

AUTHOR: Henry T. Harbin

PRECIS: Treating adolescent dyscontrol episodes through family therapy.

INTRODUCTION: This paper describes treatment techniques for patients and families for whom the main symptom is periodic violent episodes. Violent episodes are defined as aggression directed at inanimate objects (windows or furniture), aggression toward other people (sometimes with intent to kill), dangerous misuse of automobiles, and repetitive violence during drinking bouts. Self-destructive acts sometimes accompany the aggressive outbursts, and contributing factors can include an organic problem that intensifies the patient's vulnerability to everyday pressures. This family therapy approach focuses on the communicational meaning of the aggressive outbursts and endeavors to alter the interactional patterns that sustain the dysfunctional symptom. Once the cycle of violence is set in motion, the episodes sometimes assume an adaptive function for the family.

TREATMENT METHOD: Harbin outlines a profile of family dynamics for families in which one of the children has episodes of violent behavior. The young person frequently has an overly close relationship with one parent, while the other parent is generally only superficially involved. In a majority of cases, marital discord of a covert and overt nature is evident. The author correlates the adolescent's struggle between the needs for separation and dependency and the parent's struggle with middle-age life crises.

According to Harbin, the therapist must be active and directive in attempts to change the violent episodes. A first step is to meet with the family and outline what to do if another episode should occur. This procedure serves to diminish fear and anxiety by giving family members a plan of action, and the instructions increase contact between the parents and the adolescent and encourage greater communication. The procedure also helps the parents become more specific and consistent in their limit setting with the adolescent and decreases the adolescent's fear of losing control as he sees that other people can help to manage his behavior.

The therapist serves as an authority model for the parents and aids them in assuming their own position of authority. Due to the serious nature of the problem, the parents need to be told that they should call the police and take the adolescent to an emergency facility if necessary. Support persons in the extended family are identified to help out in an emergency. If a dyscontrol episode should take place during treatment, the way that the family deals with it should be carefully observed and any inconsistency should be corrected. Once the behavioral limits have been established, the therapist can turn to underlying problems in the family. The author cautions, however, that whenever a sensitive issue is addressed, the possibility for the adolescent's loss of control increases.

A more complicated treatment process is necessary if the adolescent has been diagnosed as having a seizure disorder that requires medication. Although the family may tend to assume the adolescent innocent of blame for postseizure behavior, the therapist can help by noting that the seizures are set off by emotional conflicts. The family members can be told that their coping with this stress will diminish the chance of a violent episode. The adolescent must understand that he is responsible for any physical damage he inflicts during one of these episodes.

CASE STUDY: The author describes a six-month therapeutic process with A, a seventeen-year-old young man and his family. The referral problem was several episodes of violent behavior. It was observed that the mother was overinvolved with her son, while the father was distant. The first violent episode took place while A was with his girlfriend and became concerned about how much money he owed his mother and his inability to pay his debts. His anxiety took the form of breaking furniture, threatening to hit his girlfriend, and breaking a window with his hands. A had to be hospitalized; it was then discovered that he had an abnormal EEG. A appeared to be torn between his loyalties to his mother and girlfriend and seemed driven to destroy himself or someone else.

After A was released from the hospital, he had more episodes. During one of these, his parents called the police and had him taken to the emergency room. When the father reported that he had cleaned up after the episode and repaired the broken furniture, the therapist asked him not to do this in the future. The therapist also instructed the parents to clarify with their son his responsibility for his behavior. When A became angry and offered his medical problem as an excuse, the therapist acknowledged the problem but said that no one else was responsible for his behavior. Another violent episode occurred the following week and this time he had to repair the damages. This marked the end of the episodes; the other outcomes of therapy included greater independence and a reinvolvement of A's father in the family.

COMMENTARY: Research shows an increase in juvenile violence on a yearly basis in the United States. This finding points to the need for further study of family dynamics that may contribute to violent episodes in adolescents. The author reports that employing a family therapy approach provided greater leverage than individual therapy, as the people who are most significant to the adolescent are part of the process. An important consideration is the therapist's emotional reaction to the violent individuals. If he reacts with a fear similar to that of the family members, he may exacerbate the conflict. Harbin suggests that a position of neutrality and objectivity can more easily be sustained by meeting with colleagues to discuss the treatment process.

SOURCE: Harbin, H. T. "Episodic Dyscontrol and Family Dynamics." *American Journal of Psychiatry,* 1977, *134,* 1113–1116.

A Structural Analytic Model in Treating Aggressive Behavior

AUTHOR: Lorna Smith Benjamin

PRECIS: Presentation of a structural analytic model to measure and understand the changes within a family during psychotherapy.

INTRODUCTION: In an effort to objectify the relationship between therapist and patient, Benjamin uses a structural analytic model. The stated goal of using such a model is to more precisely understand effective therapist-patient relationships that can eventually yield more effective interventions. The model is based on two axes—affiliation and interdependence—and appears in three planes—parentlike, childlike, and introjected behaviors. Psychotherapy with one family over a three-year period illustrates the use of the model.

CASE HISTORY: The family presented came for treatment with the referring problem of the extremely abusive, defiant behavior of the first-born five-year-old son. On a regular basis, this child was reported to kick, swear, and threaten to kill his mother when he was older. His mother viewed his behavior as that of a monster. A previous attempt at treatment using behavior therapy was unsuccessful.

At the start of treatment the husband and wife each filled out a detailed questionnaire that focused on their parents as they remembered them from childhood and their problem son. The mother's ratings of her son's behavior depicted him as displaying very hostile, parentlike behavior toward her. The author states, "when the son was focusing on the mother (parentlike), he was attacking; and when he was focusing on himself (childlike), his position was one of hostile autonomy." The mother's ratings of her own father indicated that he was hostile and powerful. When the mother was filling out the questionnaire she observed a similarity in behaviors, and when she was shown the analysis of her answers she acknowledged that she felt the same about both her father and her son. Furthermore, she felt that she could find no way to please either her father or her son or to be rewarded for her efforts.

In contrast, her husband felt optimistic and comfortable with himself. The questionnaire revealed that his upbringing had been positive and nurturing. In his family of origin there was no fighting, and difficulties were avoided by withdrawal or compliance. The couple's relationship was marked by the husband assuming a childlike role. Soon after their marriage, the husband developed a stomach problem and he was subsequently nurtured and nursed by his wife. This in turn did not satisfy the wife's need to be cared for.

A change in focus was suggested by the therapist. Rather than continuing to try to get the son to "be good," the focus was to increase friendly autonomy. In other words, the mother would be helped to substitute friendly emancipation for her own hostile power. At the same time, the son would be assisted in developing a sense of himself as separate from his mother.

During treatment there were occasional references to the model. At times chosen by the therapist, the rating questionnaires were completed again, but after the discussion of the initial ratings there was no further review of results with the family until therapy ended. In the beginning phase of treatment, it was suggested that the mother and son engage in pleasant activities: playing baseball, making scrapbooks, and going on outings. The result of this recommendation was a critical change in the relationship between mother and son, the beginning of a mutual affection.

After seeing the results of the questionnaire, the father recognized how he had behaved in a childlike way with his mother and was now acting in a similar way with his wife. He reacted to this connection with a few angry outbursts but was able to become more assertive in constructive ways. This was the second crucial change noted in the therapy process: the father moved into a more powerful parentlike role with his son. He started to help his wife with household chores and became more involved in disciplining their son.

Approximately a year after therapy started, the mother seemed to feel worse despite positive changes in her relationship with her husband and son. She became quite passive around the house, and her husband assumed the principal responsibility for household duties. However, she remained enraged at him, viewing his help as weakness; at the same time her ratings about herself showed strong hostile feelings. Therapy then focused on the husband and wife discussing their needs and views of one another. The husband was able to see his wife's need to be treated in a parentlike way. They discovered that he had not understood the concept of being strong and parentlike and at the same time being a giver. Through the discussion the wife was able to allow herself to be more parental and nurtured. This new position gave her room to pursue her own interests, such as working toward acceptance by a professional school. Concurrently, the son began to respond positively to a behavior therapy program intended to reduce verbal abuse and increase self-care behaviors.

A regression in the treatment process occurred when the husband had to go away for a month. His wife saw his leaving as abandonment and reacted with anger and resentment. A visit from her parents enabled her to see some of the paradoxes in her family of origin. Following this insight, she was able to give up her parental identification with her own father and moved toward establishing a separate identity. She started professional school supported by her husband and children, who took on responsibilities around the house. She also was able to shift her focus from her older son to his brother, who required firmer limits.

TREATMENT RESULTS: Six months after the mother started school, the ratings showed that her hostile power had significantly decreased and the primary goals of decreasing her hostile control and increasing the son's friendly autonomy had been met. A follow-up with the family a year after termination of treatment showed that their feelings about the therapy process, as well as their feelings toward one another, remained positive. Also, the family was sent a copy of the case description and they verified its accuracy.

COMMENTARY: In the concluding remarks, Benjamin states that, "After using therapeutic techniques that lead to insights that are uncomfortable, it is important to actively assist in developing positive alternatives." The data that the family provided in the questionnaires enabled the therapist to outline new directions, and the structural analytic model provided a context for change. During therapy, the quantitative ratings showed the progress made and gave impetus to continue the sometimes difficult process of treatment.

SOURCE: Benjamin, L. S. "Structural Analysis of a Family in Therapy." *Journal of Consulting and Clinical Psychology,* 1977, *45,* 391–406.

A Home-Based Behavioral Approach to Improve Parent-Child Relations

AUTHORS: Robert P. Hawkins, Robert F. Peterson, Edda Schweid, and Sidney W. Bijou

PRECIS: Training parents at home in behavioral techniques to alter a child's disruptive behavior.

INTRODUCTION: The important role that parents play in the development of their children's personality is widely recognized. When problems occur, most treatment methods are employed in locations outside the home, such as clinics or hospitals. This paper presents a method for dealing with problem behavior in the home setting. The mother was instructed in behavioral techniques, and the interaction between the mother and child was observed and recorded.

TREATMENT METHOD: The authors present some background information about the family in the study. Four-year-old Peter was the identified patient, and his position in the family was third of four children. Specific problem behaviors were identified as kicking objects or people, removing or destroying his clothes, name calling, bothering his younger sister, hitting himself, and in general becoming easily frustrated. The relationship Peter had with his mother was described as uncooperative.

The procedure was initiated by the experimenters' observing the mother and child in the home. They discovered that many of Peter's problem behaviors were reinforced by his mother's responses: she would reason with him or attempt to distract him. If she took away one of his favorite possessions after an infraction, he was usually able to get her to quickly return it.

Before beginning the treatment, the mother met with the experimenters to review Peter's behavior. She was told that the study was experimental in nature, would involve her active participation, and might take several months. She agreed to these terms.

The treatment plan included two to three one-hour sessions a week. While Peter and his younger sister interacted, their mother went about her normal schedule. The experimenters observed Peter as he moved freely throughout the main living area of the house. They did not respond to Peter or his sister and if the children asked questions, their mother said, "Leave them alone, they are doing their work."

During these observation sessions, nine objectionable behaviors were recorded. Together they were labeled "objectionable behavior" and their frequency was noted. A ten-second interval was used to record behavior. This time frame was also used to note the frequency of verbalizations between Peter and his mother. For every session each observer collected total frequency scores for the objectionable behaviors, the child's verbalizations, and the mother's verbalizations.

The treatment consisted of five phases. During the *first baseline period* (sixteen sessions) the experimenters recorded the objectionable behavior to determine the pretreatment rate of objectionable behavior. During the *first experimental period* nine objectionable behaviors were selected for treatment. The mother was shown three signals that the experimenters would use to indicate how she was to respond to Peter. Signal A meant she was to tell Peter to stop whatever behavior he was displaying; signal B told her to immediately place Peter in his room and lock the door; and signal C meant that she should give Peter positive reinforcement in the form of praise and warm physical contact. Following signal B Peter had to spend a minimum of five minutes in his room (these time periods were not included in the experimental hour). Whenever restricted to his room he had to remain quiet for a short period of time before gaining permission to come out. All play things had previously been removed from his room and his mother and sister were not to talk to him during these times. The first time an objectionable behavior was observed, the mother was instructed to tell her son to stop but if this behavior was repeated during the same session, signal B was given. The mother was to use these techniques only during the sessions and to act in her usual way the rest of the time.

During the *second baseline period,* which followed six experimental sessions with a stable number of objectionable behaviors, the mother was asked to interact with Peter as she had before the study began. This period lasted fourteen sessions. For the next six sessions, the *second experimental period,* the experimental program was continued but without the use of signal C (praise, attention). In the final follow-up phase, the mother was told that she could use any of the behavioral techniques and was given no specific guidelines. There was no contact between the experimenters and the family for twenty-four days. This was followed by a three-session posttreatment check to observe any changes. During the follow-up sessions, the mother was asked to behave in her usual way.

TREATMENT RESULTS: Careful recording indicated a decrease in the frequency of objectionable behaviors between the first and second baseline periods. Observers noted differences in the way the mother handled Peter's behavior. She gave Peter firm commands and appeared to be much more confident. After the twenty-four–day interval, the follow-up showed that the frequency of Peter's objectionable behavior remained low.

COMMENTARY: The unique aspect of this study is using the home as the setting for treatment. Important to the success of such a program is the cooperation of the parent. The specific instructions over a period of time give the child a consistent message about how his parent will respond to his behavior. These clear limits, delivered directly by the parent in the environment in which the problems occur, made for a dramatic reduction in the objectionable behavior. The results may encourage therapists to duplicate these methods in home settings.

SOURCE: Hawkins, R. P., Peterson, R. F., Schweid, E., and Bijou, S. W. "Behavior Therapy in the Home: Amelioration of Problem Parent-Child Relations with the Parent in a Therapeutic Role." *Journal of Experimental Child Psychology,* 1966, *4,* 99–107.

Additional Readings

Arnold, J. E., Levine, A. G., and Patterson, G. R. "Changes in Sibling Behavior Following Family Intervention." *Journal of Consulting and Clinical Psychology,* 1975, *43,* 683–688.

    A comprehensive program for the treatment of predelinquents is described. Parents of the identified predelinquents were •trained in social learning techniques of child management. An analysis of the home-observation data showed significantly reduced rates of deviant behaviors for the children studied, and these were maintained over a twelve-month follow-up. This paper focuses on the changes in behavior of the fifty-five siblings of the twenty-seven treated predelinquents. Baseline data showed no significant differences between siblings and the identified predelinquents. Significant reductions in rates of deviant behavior for the siblings were noted and were maintained over a six-month period, confirmed by a follow-up study. The results suggest that the parents learned a set of skills that they were able to apply to all their children. These findings support the theory that families function as an interactive system.

McCord, J., McCord, W., and Howard, A. "Family Interaction as Antecedent to the Direction of Male Aggressiveness." *Journal of Abnormal and Social Psychology,* 1963, *66,* 239–242.

    This paper reports on findings of a longitudinal study of antisocial aggressiveness in males. The general level of aggressiveness was rated by using reports of direct observation of behavior in childhood and early adolescence. Criminal records were used to ascertain antisocial behavior during adolescence and adulthood. In order to distinguish between factors that contributed to socialized aggressiveness and those that directed aggression into antisocial channels, the family backgrounds of men who were equally aggressive in childhood were compared. The sample consisted of 255 boys between the ages of ten and fifteen. Results of the study suggest that extreme neglect and punitiveness in combination with a deviant-aggressive paternal model produce antisocial aggressiveness. The features that seemed to produce social aggressiveness include moderate neglect, moderate punitiveness, and ineffective controls.

Patterson, G. R. "Retraining of Aggressive Boys by Their Parents: Review of Recent Literature and Follow-up Evaluation." *Canadian Psychiatric Association Journal*, 1974, *19*, 142-161.

In the social learning approach to treating disturbed children, an emphasis is placed on the importance of changing the social environment in which the child lives. Parents are taught skills to decrease the rates of deviant child behavior and increase rates of more adaptive forms of interaction. Generally, the parent is also supervised as he or she works with the child. Two hypotheses of this approach are that it could be very efficient in requiring only a small amount of professional time and that having the parent as treatment agent would increase the persistence of the changes in child behavior.

This study involved twenty-seven families, with at least one boy in each family identified as aggressive. Some of the common problem behaviors were difficulties in getting along with siblings and peers, temper tantrums, lying, and stealing. Five staff members, each working two or more years on the project, were involved in the treatment. Observation procedures were used throughout the study, and generally the clinician and family decided together when it was appropriate to terminate. At the time of termination there was, on the average, a 60 percent reduction in observed targeted behaviors. Many of the families needed some minimal support or retraining, and these procedures were thought to be necessary for long-term maintenance.

Sargent, D. "Children Who Kill—A Family Conspiracy?" *Social Work*, 1962, *7*, 35-42.

Sargent's thesis is that a homicidal child may be acting as the unwitting agent of an adult in the family with whom he may have a special emotional bond, that this adult, usually a parent, unconsciously prompted the child to kill so that he or she could vicariously enjoy the benefits of the act. Five case studies show the relationship between a child's homicide and the adult's unconscious wish for the act to be carried out. Although the material presented is highly speculative, according to the author, two suggestions for treatment are offered. If the events that led to the child's act of homicide give strong evidence that he was acting upon the provocation of an adult whom he was unable to resist, this concept should be communicated to the child to relieve him of an excessive load of guilt. In addition, this evidence may be used in the child's behalf in court. Consideration should be given as to the extent that guilt serves to protect the child from further impulsive actions. The potential danger of homicide could possibly be identified if the therapist notices a parent's strong hostile feelings toward some member of the family accompanied by the child's tendency to act out one or both parents' unconscious impulses. Therapeutic intervention for both child and parents should be strongly considered. In some cases, removal of the child from the home may be necessary. In conclusion, the author remarks that no psychiatric evaluation of a child is complete without a simultaneous evaluation of his parents.

Patterson, G. R., Ray, R. S., and Shaw, D. A. "Direct Intervention in Families of Deviant Children." *Oregon Research Institute Resources Bulletin,* 1968, *8,* no. 9.

A series of pilot studies that outline some preliminary procedures for reprogramming are reported in this paper. Families, teachers, and peers were trained to manipulate some behaviors that could be observed in the classroom and the home. The sample consisted of six boys who displayed multiple problems of the type usually referred for outpatient treatment. Observations were made during baseline intervention and follow-up. The results demonstrate that parents of deviant children, and to some extent their teachers and peers, can be trained to produce consistent changes in the behavior of the problem child. Part of the success of the outcome is related to the professional's ability to train the family in the use of general intervention strategies for coping with new problems as they arise. More comprehensive training could include an increased number of training sessions for the parent, telephone supervision, tape training procedures, and the training of groups of parents.

3

Fire Setting

The psychodynamics of a child who sets fires varies from case to case. A family systems approach views the development of fire-setting behavior within the context of the family and notes that it may serve one or more purposes within the family. Fire setting may be initiated and maintained to keep the focus off marital problems and keep the parents together. Research on this childhood disturbance is limited. The two articles reviewed in this chapter concern a family systems approach that includes the unique technique of constructing an ordeal and a treatment procedure to be used when fire setting is one of several family problems.

79

A Family Systems Orientation
to the Problem of Fire Setting

AUTHORS: John M. Madonna and Robert Ciottone

PRECIS: Eliminating fire setting by utilizing a prescriptive (non-interpretive) strategy in combination with the institution of an ordeal.

INTRODUCTION: The treatment of fire-setting behavior in a five-year-old boy is the focus of this article. William was brought to the clinic by his mother and stepfather after four fire-setting incidents over a two-week period. These incidents became increasingly more serious; also, the first two times William set a fire with a friend, while on the last two occasions he was alone. The behavior assumed self-destructive features, as the fourth incident involved William lighting matches while in bed. The parents had talked to William about the dangers of playing with matches, had spanked him and confined him to his room, and had brought him to the fire station to talk to the chief. Each time William promised to stop playing with matches.

TREATMENT METHOD: The treatment consisted of three one-hour sessions. During the first session with William's parents, a family history was taken. Significant was that William's stepfather had served as a volunteer firefighter for many years, but when he relocated to marry William's mother he was told he was too old to serve in that capacity. The stepfather expressed disappointment about this and he appeared to be depressed.

The second session was devoted to formulating the problem and introducing a treatment strategy. A hypothesis was made that William was subconsciously trying to move his stepfather out of depression and into some activity with the fire department. During this second meeting, William was present with his parents. The therapist acknowledged the parents' efforts at curbing their son's fire-setting behavior and said that their further participation could yield positive results; they agreed to work with the therapist. A metal waste basket was brought into the room, and the therapist pointed out that while fires could be quite interesting, they were dangerous if they were lit improperly and in inappropriate places. He emphasizes that knowing how, when, and where to light matches was crucial. Next, the therapist lit a piece of paper, held it for an instant, and dropped it into the metal basket. The stepfather was instructed to do this three times while explaining to William each step of the process. The same actions were then repeated by William's mother. William watched his parents closely and appeared surprised when the therapist handed him the matches and told him it was his turn. His parents were asked to help him if he had any trouble completing the task. William's stepfather intervened after his son impulsively lit the paper and threw it into the basket, and his mother showed him how to hold the match so he would not burn his fingers. After William achieved the proper method for lighting the paper and demonstrated it several times, he was congratulated.

For homework the parents were asked to take turns carrying out the procedure in precisely the same way for the next seven evenings. The second week the parents were to do nothing, and at the end of that time they were to call the therapist. Following the two-week period, the mother called and reported that William had set no fires. The therapist responded by saying the results looked promising but guarded against too much optimism. The parents were asked to come in alone and were told that the next phase of treatment would be more critical and more difficult.

The third and final session lasted half an hour. After acknowledging the parents' efforts with William, the therapist told them that if they could carry out the next task there would be no need for long-term treatment at the clinic for them or William. The parents agreed to try and were directed to perform the same match-lighting procedure with William for five consecutive days at midnight. This was to be followed by a week without the match lighting, and at the end of that time they were to report to the therapist.

TREATMENT RESULTS: William was reported to be symptom-free during the two-week period and treatment was ended. When contacted three months later, William's mother said there had been no further incidents of fire setting. In fact, William had started to bring his mother matches that he found around the house.

COMMENTARY: According to the authors, the effective treatment of this case of fire setting is attributable to a family systems approach that includes: the maintenance of focus on the problem behavior, the confident prescription of the symptom, and the construction of an ordeal. The ordeal phase used work by Cloé Madanes,* who describes interventions that require individuals to display metaphorical versions of their symptomology at inconvenient times, such as during the middle of the night.

     It should be emphasized that in the case presented both parents fully cooperated, which is essential, particularly during the ordeal phase. Considerable skill on the part of the therapist is required to deliver the instructions in a confident way. It would be interesting and valuable to duplicate these techniques with children of different ages to determine whether such an approach has broad-based application.

SOURCE: Madonna, J. M., and Ciottone, R. "A Treatment of Firesetting: The Merger of Paradox and Ordeal." Unpublished manuscript, 1982.

---

     *C. Madanes, *Strategic Family Therapy* (San Francisco: Jossey-Bass, 1981).

Eliminating Fire-Setting Behavior Through
an Ecological Approach with the Family

AUTHORS: George W. Roix and John M. Madonna

PRECIS: Treating fire setting in young children through an ecological approach with the family.

INTRODUCTION: In a case illustration, the fire-setting behavior of seven- and eight-year-old boys was treated along with the broader problem of family violence. The boys' father had sought treatment after six months of rage reactions toward his wife. Conjoint sessions with the couple revealed that the husband's abusive behavior toward his wife had been frequent and that he had also behaved abusively toward his sons. An overall picture of loss of control and acting-out behavior was presented.

CASE ILLUSTRATION: The family consisted of Jim, Sally, and their three children: two sons, eight and seven years old, and a four-year-old daughter. In addition to the referral problem of the husband's abusive behavior toward his wife, both boys had been involved in fire setting. The younger son had destroyed a neighbor's house by setting it on fire, and after that incident he and his brother had set fire to a field.

Treatment was conducted by a male co-therapy team. Six sessions were held with the children alone and six with the family unit. The seven treatment interventions were: (1) stating the consequences to the father of his loss of control, such as "you will drive your wife away"; (2) assisting the children in expressing their feelings of fear and sadness to their father about family violence; (3) supporting a temporary separation between the parents; (4) asking for police support when violence was threatened during the therapy process; (5) reestablishing contact with the father's family of origin to support the treatment; (6) encouraging the father's use of self-dialogue to aid him in controlling anger, for example, by asking "What am I doing?"; and (7) encouraging the father to use the Veterans Administration hotline.

During the sessions with the parents alone, the motivation for their behavior was reframed in positive terms; for example, the husband's frequent demands for sex were reframed as an expression of his need for connection and nurturance. Similarly, the wife's resistance to her husband's sexual demands was reframed as her need for rest and respect. Other interventions included giving the father written assignments that required him to develop more positive involvement with his children and to reach out to support systems such as the veterans' hotline or police when needed. Jim was instructed to place his written assignments in the bathroom and to read them whenever he used that facility.

TREATMENT RESULTS: The interventions proved to be successful in eliminating family violence as well as the fire-setting behavior of the sons. It was reported at monthly follow-up sessions that in place of acting-out behavior, the family had established an atmosphere of mutual respect.

COMMENTARY: The authors cite several contributing factors as components of the successful outcome of this therapy approach. Above all, Jim was very motivated to change his violence. In order to defuse his aggressive impulses, he was encouraged to make contact with various support systems in his environment, such as the police and his family of origin. The authors note that impulsive individuals can gain control by relating to authority figures who demonstrate control and have the ability to exercise penalties for breakdowns in control. Too, the treatment process greatly encouraged expressions of love and appreciation among family members. This was accomplished by acknowledging acts of mutual appreciation between family members and at the same time encouraging displays of affection between the father and his children.

The use of an individual's environment to lend support to the therapeutic process is an important aspect of this approach. Whenever dangerous or even life-threatening situations are part of the referring problem a decisive form of intervention, sometimes using controls outside the family (e.g., police) is often necessary. Also, the practice of monthly follow-up contacts with the family to monitor their functioning is an important safeguard against recurrence of the symptom.

SOURCE: Roix, G. W., and Madonna, J. M. "An Ecological Treatment of Family Violence." *40th Annual Conference, American Association for Marriage and Family Therapy,* 1982, pp. 1-11.

4

Noncompliance

In family treatment involving a child who displays noncompliant behavior, the therapist asks the parent to be specific in describing the behavior. During this detailed description, the therapist looks for inconsistencies in how the child has been handled. It is essential that the parent set consistent limits and formulate effective methods of disciplining the child. If the child acts in a noncompliant way in school, as well as at home, the teacher should be involved in the process. This chapter describes behavioral techniques for use with parents and teachers. One approach focuses on the therapist assigning tasks to family members to improve interactions. Another approach includes conjoint family sessions interspersed with individual sessions with the child. In all approaches, the therapist provides active and firm assistance. The timing for the introduction of techniques is viewed as crucial for success.

Task Setting in the Family Treatment
of a Noncompliant Youngster

AUTHOR: Michael White

PRECIS: Introduction and use of direct and paradoxical tasks in family therapy.

INTRODUCTION: The tasks described in this article are called systemic as they focus on the whole family system. White explains an underlying premise of systemic task setting: "symptomatic or problem behavior is contextually based and such behavior should be evaluated in terms of its significance within the family system. Through the use of tasks, the therapist is aided in assuming the position of the most influential member within the therapeutic process."

TREATMENT PROCEDURES: In working with families, the therapist gathers information about the system by assigning tasks. Initial tasks are based on the early formulation of the family's structure and how the symptom is supported by the structure. The way in which the family members respond to the task provides the therapist with valuable information. Either new tasks are assigned or paradoxical tasks are introduced. The avoidance of tasks gives the therapist as much important knowledge about how the family organizes itself as the family's completion of the tasks. By engaging in a task, the family members are diverted from trying to get the therapist to help them prove points to other members. The focus is shifted from cause-effect reasoning to relational and contextual patterns. An increase in the intensity of the relationship between the family and the therapist can occur through task assignment whether the task is completed or not. Because there is a lot of work for the family to do between sessions, sessions are generally at least two weeks apart, sometimes as much as three months apart.

The author distinguishes direct and paradoxical tasks as follows: "Those systemic tasks which attempt to provoke change in family structure by directly harnessing a system's capacity for transformation are called 'direct'; those that attempt to provoke change in a family structure by taking into account the system's capacity for remaining the same are called 'paradoxical.' " The ground rules for the construction of direct tasks include: The therapist should prescribe the task in an assertive manner, for example by saying, "This is what I want you to do" or "Your task for next week is _____." When delivering the task, the therapist should command the attention of family members, speak with authority, and repeat the instructions, if indicated. He should give a rationale (either implicit or explicit) for the task to promote motivation. All family members should be included in the task, which serves to ensure the successful completion of the task, but the hierarchy of the family system must be respected and children should not be involved in tasks of the parents. Finally, the careful matching of the task to the family system should take into consideration such factors as the family's traditions, myths, rules, time, and available energy.

Following prescription of the task, the therapist devotes the next session to review. During task review, a paradoxical task may seem appropriate. The therapist tells the family that both the problem and the pattern of relationships in which the problem is embedded should continue unchanged. Generally, a rationale for continuing the pattern is given and if the family attempts any changes, they are restrained from doing so. The task review should not be hurried, and the details of the task should be reviewed first, followed by the family's responses.

CASE ILLUSTRATION: Fifteen-year-old Eric, the youngest of four children in the family, had been experiencing episodes of melancholy, had dropped out of school, and was found to be oppositional in his behavior. During the initial interview with the family, the therapist observed conflict in the relationship between Eric and his father, while the relationship between mother and son was overly close. The mother and father were critical of one another and offered each other no support.

A direct task was given by the therapist instructing the father to watch his son's behavior and stop his overinvolvement with Mrs. R. Eric was to be told that he was not the husband to Mrs. R and if necessary, a screen was to be placed between Eric and his mother if he insisted on being with her while she was working. Mrs. R was instructed to support her husband in these efforts and remind him if he failed to note the behavior. Eric's siblings were requested to discuss with him the experiences they had when they were his age.

At the next session it was clear that the family had completely failed to carry out the task, which opened the way for the introduction of paradox. The family was told that the task had been inappropriate and they were wise not to attempt it. The therapist added that the way they had arranged their lives seemed to be comfortable to them. Mrs. R was asked to persevere in challenging her husband in Eric's presence, and if Eric was not there to go get him. Mr. R was instructed to continue to retreat from his wife's challenges. Eric was told to annoy his father, and his father was to urge him to do this. Then Mr. R was directed to attack Eric and Mrs. R was prompted to take Eric's side in the conflict.

In response, Eric said he would not purposely annoy his father. The therapist said this was good because that would probably annoy his father even more, as Eric would not be doing what was requested. Mrs. R stated that the experiment was worth trying and was told that it was not an experiment. Mr. R found the whole thing ridiculous and felt it would be better for he and his wife to fight. The therapist advised Mr. R to restrain himself.

The review of the prescribed paradoxical task yielded the same results. The parents had met with each other twice for two hours each time and had struggled with some recurring problems and had found solutions to them. Most significantly, they had come to an understanding of how they could handle Eric's behavior.

COMMENTARY: Systemic family tasks can be an excellent vehicle for change within a family. The process of attempting a direct task and testing the response of the family promptly supplies a picture of how the family system functions. A switch to a paradoxical task can be accomplished by the third or fourth session. In the case presented, the noncompliant behavior of the son was changed by the prescription of a paradoxical task following the clear failure of a direct one. Considerable skill and experience on the part of the therapist are necessary in the prescription of the paradoxical task.

SOURCE: White, M. "Systematic Task Setting in Family Therapy." *Australian Journal of Family Therapy,* 1980, *1,* 171–182.

Implementing a Behavioral Technique in the Family Therapy of a Disruptive Child

AUTHOR: Stuart L. Kaplan

PRECIS: Family therapy utilizing behavior modification as a family task.

INTRODUCTION: The approach is for the therapist to give the family a task to use behavior modification to change the behavior of a disruptive child. When discussing the use of a family task in therapy, Kaplan states that the task provides information about the way in which the family system operates. In addition, a well-chosen family task considers the psychodynamics of individual family members, as well as their functioning as a family system. The described treatment of the family illustrates how behavior modification can be used as a family task. The treatment was set in an office in the youngster's school.

CASE STUDY: For the last five years, ten-year-old Y had been beyond his parents' control. Although in a special school for learning disabled and emotionally disturbed children, Y did not respond positively to special education and had been referred to as a "hopeless case." The disruptive behaviors that Y displayed at home and in school included somersaulting across rooms, loud belching, and defiance of any limit setting by parents or teachers. Socially, Y was seen as an isolated youngster. In addition to special education, Y had been seen in individul psychotherapy and had been given psychotropic medication. None of these interventions altered his disruptive behavior.

An initial family interview was held with Y and his parents. Y appeared an intelligent, verbal child, who expressed an interest in military history and seemed preoccupied with thoughts about violence and attack. The therapist confronted Y with his misbehavior and was met with rationalizations. The parents had differing reactions to their son's behavior. For the most part, his father saw Y as a victim of his environment, blaming his son's problems on incompetent teachers and undesirable classmates. The most prominent emotion displayed by the mother in response to her son's problems was despair. At the end of the interview the parents agreed to come for treatment, which included looking into the relationship between them and their son and carrying out a behavior modification program. It was agreed that they would come for about ten sessions.

Prior to the first treatment session, Y's teachers kept a detailed log of his misbehaviors. These logs served as a baseline to determine the effects of the behavior modification program and to show the family the extent of Y's problems. The parents met with the therapist during the early part of the first session. The therapist told them that Y's behavior had been deplorable. At a predetermined point Y and two of his teachers entered the room. The teachers read from the log 145 disruptive behaviors from the previous week. During the monotone reading of the behavior chart, Y smiled in a mischievous way, while his mother started to cry.

The therapist then explained the behavior modification program. Y would bring home a daily behavioral report card, and based on the report he would either be confined to his bedroom or have routine privileges or be provided with one or two points toward a special treat, in addition to his daily privileges.

In discussing the plan, both the parents and teachers concurred that Y had not previously responded to rewards. As an alternative, various degrees of punishment were discussed. The therapist suggested that Y should immediately go to his room if he received a poor report in school. He would be allowed to have dinner with his family but would have to forego dessert. After dinner, he would return to his room. The parents were reminded that Y had smiled in delight when his teachers had read the list of misbehaviors, which reinforced their doubts about enforcing the program.

Toward the end of the first session, the mother became visibly upset and stated that Y had previously responded to her setting limits by destroying the furniture in his room and hitting himself in the face. The therapist asked the father to comfort his wife, but he refused. The therapist told the parents that they were not ready to begin the program and that his task was to prepare them, which he would continue to do at the following session.

Again the parents were seen alone at the opening of the second session. The mother started by saying of Y, "I can't stand it when I have to make him behave." Then the mother discussed her relationship with her own parents—her father had abused her, while her mother passively stood by. She noted that her relationship with her father made it very difficult for her to handle Y's misbehavior. Y was asked to join the session, and the therapist reviewed the behavior log, which documented sixty-eight disruptive behaviors the previous week. In a very authoritarian voice, the therapist explained to Y and his parents that the misbehavior was unnecessary and could be controlled by Y. The following program was presented by the therapist: If on a given day Y displayed more than three of the behaviors listed, he would receive a "poor" report and be sent to his room right after school with no TV or dessert; if there were between one and three misbehaviors, he would receive an "OK" and his usual privileges; for one misbehavior or none, he would earn a "good" report, which meant he would receive a point toward a special treat in addition to his usual privileges. The teachers were designated as the arbitrators of whether Y received a point. As a safeguard to Y losing the report card, it was agreed that he would get a "poor" report if he failed to bring the report home. The day after the session Y had a poor day in school, and both parents confined him to his room. This was a turning point—Y averaged only two misbehaviors per school week for the next sixteen weeks.

Despite the dramatic improvement in Y's behavior, his father ridiculed the therapy process. He noted that his wife was too hard on the children and he would bring dessert to Y's room when he was being restricted. The discussion during the third session revealed that it was the father, and not the mother, who had the most difficulty setting limits for the children. One of the rules in the family was to avoid open conflict, thus the therapist took the role of disagreeing with the father about consistency in disciplining the children. The therapist was able to support the father on other issues and keep a balance in the therapeutic process.

The success of the therapist's siding with the mother on disciplining the children became apparent at the next session. At the fourth session, the mother announced that she had made a number of decisions about the children without consulting her husband. Marital issues were addressed in subsequent sessions. The operant program continued to be successful, with Y's school behavior close to perfect. Y was brought into the last third of the family sessions, and his good behavior was acknowledged and any difficulties in his relationship with peers was talked over. When Y's behavior showed a stabilized pattern over eight weeks, the operant program included Y's behavior at home. In a week's time, Y's negative behavior toward his peers in little league and cub scouts was eliminated.

TREATMENT RESULTS: Y's behavior dramatically improved both in school and at home. This was accomplished in eighteen sessions, with the abatement of negative school behaviors occurring after two sessions. Positive results were also seen in Y's social relationships: before treatment, Y had no relationships with any children in his class, but at the end of the program, he was inviting classmates home after school. Y's class status improved considerably after the fifteenth session when he was moved to a class where students were viewed as capable of returning to a public school.

COMMENTARY: In the case presented, the introduction of a behavior modification program in a family in which a child had resisted many other approaches was very successful, a success most likely due to the specific nature of the behavior modification program. Both the parents and teachers were instructed how to set limits for the child, while at the same time the underlying marital conflicts were addressed. The combination of the two treatment processes made for enduring change.

SOURCE: Kaplan, S. L. "Behavior Modification as a Limit-Setting Task in the Family Psychotherapy of a Disruptive Boy." *Journal of the American Academy of Child Psychiatry,* 1979, *18,* 492–504.

Short-Term Family Therapy to Treat Children's Behavior Problems

AUTHOR: Daniel J. Safer

PRECIS: Goal-directed family therapy over a short period of time to alleviate symptoms of disturbed behavior in children.

INTRODUCTION: Safer, noting that directive approaches in family therapy have become a trend, states that in order to set the structure of treatment the family therapist needs to give firm support and put forth a definite example.

    This study took place over a two-year period. Twenty-nine children with behavior disorders were given a diagnostic evaluation, and short-term family therapy was attempted. The children included ranged from four to sixteen years in age; all but two were from lower socioeconomic situations; seventeen lived with both parents, seven with one parent, and five with a natural parent and a step- or adoptive parent. In general, the children presented aggressive behavior.

TREATMENT METHOD: As stated by Safer, "With behavior problems, the primary, most pressing and most workable issue was felt to be behavior itself." Since behavior in the home usually preceded behavior elsewhere, the focus was on behavioral interaction in the home. Safer discovered that in practically every case of serious, long-lasting conflict between parents and child, the boundaries between their realms had been infringed upon; for example, the child had entered the parental domain by sleeping in the parents' bed, or the parents had entered the child's realm by selecting his friends. These infringements generally exacerbated the interpersonal conflicts.

To specify issues of family interaction, the therapist asks questions such as, Does the child have chores? What happens if he dawdles or refuses? The responses to these questions give the therapist clues as to parent-child conflicts, family alliances, and altered family boundaries.

After some diagnostic work, the therapist sets some general goals and the parents decide on specific goals. Sessions with one or both parents and the problem child are used to design the specific goals. The proposal arrived at is looked upon as a trial. The trial is intended to discover if intrafamily anxiety can be alleviated by parental modification of domain and control patterns. The therapist provides active and firm assistance, directing his attention to that which can be changed and ignoring or cutting off discussion when he feels no change is foreseeable. Behavioral change is seen as probable if an effort is made. As an "agent of change" the therapist often becomes included as a family member during the structuring process. To aid the plan the support of the referring agency may be elicited.

To reduce the probability of future resistance in family sessions, the therapist may mention this expectation, which seems to lessen the actual resistance. In addition, the therapist serves as an educator, showing the family how to discipline the child and how to define boundaries. For instance, the parents are held responsible for setting and carrying out the rules of the home, and the child for his actions outside the home. Ideas for effective discipline include having the child sit on a chair for five minutes when he disobeys. It is emphasized that both parents need to give the same message. Also, the therapist can point out that physical punishment does not lessen the fear of a frightened child and that direct pressure does not decrease negativism.

During the first sessions, the therapist looks for any movement on the part of the family. If no modifying move is seen, therapy soon ends. When even a small change is seen, a transition in the family equilibrium and communication pattern is noted. Patterns of resistance are also discovered during the beginning sessions. Often the most critical parent is the one who presents the first resistance. Because he or she is very involved with the child, this type of parent responds to a helpful approach by the therapist. The therapist might say, "You've taken the burden on yourself and it has been too nerve-racking, so let's structure things right here in order that your burden will be lessened." In the beginning, the child with the presenting problem is often the most resistful, and he should be curbed during the first few sessions so that his parents become involved in the therapeutic process.

The establishment of firm home authority leaves the child without the previous reinforcement for his actions, and at this point both parents and child seem more open to introspection. Therapy may shift to other directions, such as marital counseling, more positive interaction between child and parent of the same sex, and confronting the child with consequences of his behavior. The particular direction determines which family members are seen in later sessions. In the majority of cases discussed, the child was seen individually after the family focus decreased. Conjoint sessions were interspersed with the individual sessions. Sometimes the parent of the same sex was brought into treatment to reinforce identification. The objective during the later phase of treatment was to help the child become more independent.

TREATMENT RESULTS: In this study success was defined as a modification in the home atmosphere that decreased conflict in the parent-child relationship and that left the child without symptoms or having made significant improvement. In the follow-up evaluation, four to sixteen months after treatment, 40 percent of the cases were termed successful. Several other cases showed signs of some improvement.

COMMENTARY: The cases selected for this treatment approach had been classified as unmotivated or unacceptable for individual treatment. Using a direct method in conjoint sessions, the therapist was able to alter behavior patterns within the family, with the result that 40 percent of the cases had positive outcomes, a result that needs to be seen in light of the fact that the children had been labeled unmotivated. Safer carefully defines his direct and active methods such that in future cases they could be readily duplicated.

SOURCE: Safer, D. J. "Family Therapy for Children with Behavior Disorders." *Family Process,* 1966, *5,* 243-255.

Altering a Child's Behavior Through
Consistent Discipline by the Mother

AUTHOR: Maurice J. Rosenthal

PRECIS: The treatment method aims at reducing a mother's guilt over her handling of the child's problems.

INTRODUCTION: Among the many facets of maternal inconsistency, Rosenthal chose to study inconsistency with regard to discipline. He outlines four features of the inconsistent mother: (1) her chief spontaneous complaint is her child's disobedience; (2) she expresses ambivalence in her attitude toward her child; (3) she sometimes threatens to impose restrictions but does not carry them out, or she restricts the child but then apologizes, or she only selectively restricts her child for a particular behavior; (4) she offers such rationalizations as "I tried to reason with him" or "I've tried everything. Nothing works."

According to Rosenthal, the inconsistent mother regards her disciplinary efforts as proof of her hostility toward her child. A disciplinary effort is usually followed by a guilt reaction. Rosenthal reports that the hostile acts were more retaliatory than disciplinary, and as a result of her guilt the mother was unable to successfully discipline her child.

TREATMENT METHOD: The position taken by Rosenthal is that "the success of this therapy depends upon alleviating the guilt of the mothers in regard to placing and enforcing reasonable restrictions on their children." Six aspects of the therapy are outlined: (1) The therapy is seen as applicable only if the main issue is the mother's inability to get the child to obey her; the therapist must focus on this issue and not get caught up in other topics. (2) The therapist should elicit specific details of the misbehavior from the mother; a persistent approach may be necessary to uncover that part of the incident when the mother did not carry out effective discipline. (3) Next, the therapist gives the mother a clear message that despite her child's opposition he has a need for consistent limits; in addition, the therapist explains that the child's observable behavior may be an effort to prompt his mother to impose such limits. (4) Together, the therapist and mother formulate an effective method of disciplining the child. Rosenthal finds it prudent to allow the mother to take the initiative in this process. If she seems to be at a loss, the therapist can suggest a procedure. If the situation appears totally out of bounds, the mother should call the police to help. A consistent disciplinary measure also needs to be enforced if the child's misbehavior occurs when she is not present. (5) During later sessions, the therapist watches for any lapses in the mother's carrying out the disciplinary measures. If the child responds positively to the limits, the mother may express concern that her child is too submissive. The therapist should stand firm and not succumb to the mother's new manifestation of guilt. As Rosenthal states, "To agree with the mother imposes the risk of increasing her guilt and losing the gains made." (6) This approach frequently improves the seriously disturbed relationship without addressing the origin of the mother's attitudes toward the child.

CASE ILLUSTRATION: The family consisted of a recently divorced mother, her twelve-year-old daughter, nine-year-old Brad, who was the identified patient, and a three-year-old son. Problems had arisen between the parents due to the father's drinking and consequent abusive behavior. The mother called the therapist in a desperate predicament. Brad had been acting out since his father had left, and following a disagreement with his mother had threatened to kill her with his father's rifle. During the first interview, with the mother alone, the therapist reviewed the current situation with her and asked what she had done about Brad's behavior and what had happened after Brad's rampage. The approach was to elicit explicit details about her child's behavior and her reaction to it. This interview revealed the inconsistency in her handling of the situation. During an interview with Brad, the therapist found him to relate quite well and to display some insight into his problems. In the third interview, with the mother, the therapist explained in nontechnical language how Brad identified with his father's aggression. However, the more important motivation was pointed out as Brad's need to have his mother control his behavior. The therapist reviewed the inconsistency of the mother's approach and stated the need for firmness and consistency. A direct result of this interview was Brad's improved behavior. The mother was able to maintain her firm approach with Brad.

TREATMENT RESULTS: Rosenthal notes that following ten interviews over four and a half months Brad was doing well. He speculates that without this active, direct therapeutic approach Brad would most likely have been institutionalized.

COMMENTARY: Rosenthal considers this approach to treatment as fairly conventional. The deciding factor is the vigor with which the therapist pursues treatment. One of the pitfalls for the therapist is agreeing with the mother about her harsh treatment of the child and maintaining a passive role—a position that could contribute to the mother's guilt feelings rather than alleviate them. Rosenthal cautions that this method is not recommended for children under the age of four or for older adolescents. Although this form of treatment yielded positive short-term results, there is a need for long-term follow-up of the cases.

SOURCE: Rosenthal, M. J. "The Syndrome of the Inconsistent Mother." *The American Journal of Orthopsychiatry*, 1962, *22*, 637–644.

Additional Readings

Augenbraun, B., Reid, H. L., and Friedman, D. B. "Brief Intervention as a Preventive Force in Disorders of Early Childhood." *American Journal of Orthopsychiatry*, 1967, *37*, 697–702.

Techniques of brief intervention with families of symptomatic children include: (1) The therapist makes a quick identification of the aspects of family communication that contribute to the child's symptoms; (2) these factors are brought to the family's attention by the therapist confronting actual behavior as seen in the interview; (3) a rational framework of the origins and consequences of their behaviors is presented to the family; (4) once the members understand their family dynamics, the therapist demonstrates more appropriate behavior that could be modeled by the family members. The authors' case studies show how brief intervention strategies could be applied with noncompliant children. The authors suggest that these techniques could be applied in nursery school and well-baby clinics to identify problems at an early stage.

Bhatti, R. S., Jana Kiramaiah, N., and Channabasavanna, S. M.
   "Group Interaction as a Method of Family Therapy." *International Journal of Group Psychotherapy*, 1982, *32*, 103–114.

   Multiple-family group sessions are discussed, with non-compliant behavior in an adolescent girl as one of the case studies selected to demonstrate the method of treatment. Some of the advantages of this method are that in a group setting patients who are hesitant to discuss anything other than their symptoms are prompted to talk about interpersonal problems and certain conflictual themes that could not be effectively resolved in individual or conjoint family sessions. The authors report that the multiple-family group sessions had a positive influence on other forms of therapy (individual, conjoint) that were carried out concurrently.

Byng-Hall, J. "Family Myths Used as a Defense in Conjoint Family Therapy." *British Journal of Medical Psychology*, 1973, *46*, 239–250.

   The author's approach highlights mutual protection of family members, as illustrated by a case involving the rebellious behavior of a daughter. It was discovered that the mother covertly provoked the daughter into rebellious activity, which placed the burden of limit setting on the father. The capacities lost by the family members were listed by the therapist: the father gave up his tender, warm, loving potential; mother gave up her assertive abilities and the respect of her daughter; and the daughter removed herself from warm exchanges with her parents, which she actually desired. A more productive, healthier mode of family interaction was provided by implication.

Christensen, A., Johnson, S. M., Phillips, S., and Glasgow, R. E.
   "Cost Effectiveness in Behavioral Family Therapy." *Behavior Therapy*, 1980, *11*, 208–226.

   Three therapy conditions were studied as to cost effectiveness in behavioral family therapy. Thirty-six families were included, each with a child between the ages of four and twelve who had displayed problem behavior. These families were randomly assigned to individual treatment, group treatment, or minimal contact bibliotherapy. All families were given similar information about behavioral management of children, although the form of therapy and amount of contact with the therapist differed among the three groups. Parent attitude measures, data on defined problems from the parents, and audio recordings made in the homes of the families were collected. The results of the group- and individual-treatment conditions were judged superior to minimal-contact bibliotherapy, but the group condition required less than half the amount of professional time. The problem child in each family was reported by the parents to have significantly improved, with no differences between conditions.

Firestone, E., and Moschetta, P. "Behavioral Contracting in Family Therapy." *Journal of Family Counseling,* 1975, *3,* 27–31.

The family therapist's use of behavioral contracting is demonstrated through a case example involving a fifteen-year-old girl's rebellious behavior toward her parents. In two family sessions a contract was negotiated, and in two subsequent sessions some minor problems of implementation were discussed. The duration of the contract was three weeks and it was fulfilled. There were no major arguments during the weeks immediately following contract implementation. The contract became a jumping-off point for further family discussion of feelings. The authors emphasize that timing is very important and that using a contract approach during the beginning phase of treatment is an effective way to engage resistive families.

Friedman, R., Dreizen, K., Harris, L., Schoen, P., and Shulman, P. "Parent Power: A Holding Technique in the Treatment of Omnipotent Children." *International Journal of Family Counseling,* 1978, *6,* 66–73.

When a child opposes a parent's reasonable requests or directions, a holding technique can be quite effective. Prior to introducing the technique, the therapist explains it to the parents and obtains their written, informed consent. The holding technique consists of the parent holding the child firmly on the lap until the child stops struggling and verbally acknowledges that the parent is the boss. The authors report a 75 percent success rate with twenty-five children in a follow-up study.

Hare-Mustin, R. "Paradoxical Tasks in Family Therapy: Who Can Resist?" *Psychotherapy: Theory, Research and Practice*, 1976, *13*, 384–388.

The author finds that tasks in family therapy are especially appropriate in treating the parents' complaints about a child. By focusing on the problem and requiring it to be demonstrated, the family becomes open to a redefinition of the problem in terms that respond to treatment. Especially valuable are tasks that involve every family member. One case example concerns an eight-year-old boy brought for treatment because of bad behavior. The therapist assigned the boy the task of being bad all day for a specific day. If he tried to be good in any way, his parents were to remind him to be bad and his siblings were instructed not to interfere. The following week the parents reported that their son had not been bad. The child stated, "There was nothing to be bad about." The outcome of the task jolted the family and increased their desire for change.

Napier, A. Y. "Beginning Struggles with Families." *Journal of Marriage and Family Counseling*, 1976, *2*, 3–11.

Napier proposes that beginning with the telephone contact, the therapist should focus intently on the initial interviews and attempt to respond to the family's anxiety by showing firmness, insight, and sensitivity. Clearly, the most formidable problem is getting the family to shift the focus from the identified patient to the family as a whole. It is suggested that the therapist identify the members of the family who feel most threatened and attempt to reach them first. Areas in the family that are highly emotionally charged, such as the marriage, should be approached later using both strength and sensitivity. Specific techniques for accomplishing these goals are outlined.

5

Running Away

Reports indicate that the numbers of young people who run away from home is increasing. Runaway behavior in children is defined as situational and the family's participation in the treatment process is essential. This behavior may be just one in a series of social problems, as the young runaway becomes vulnerable to an antisocial segment of the population. A frequent precipitating cause of runaway behavior is the inadequate fulfillment of a child's social needs. The offering of alternative means for a child to develop social competence that will bring him or her reinforcement can prevent or reduce runaway behavior. A number of therapists report that behavioral approaches, some using contracts, are effective interventions.

A Comprehensive Behavioral Program
to Treat Families with Runaway Children

AUTHORS: John S. Wodarski and Paul W. Ammons

PRECIS: A behavioral approach to the problem of runaway children that uses child management, family enrichment, and interpersonal enrichment.

INTRODUCTION: The complexity of the runaway problem requires that the treatment approach to families provide a number of different services. The authors outline a treatment program whose major goals are to train the parents in child management methods that aid the child's social and psychological development; to work toward family enrichment through problem solving, conflict resolution, and positive interactions; and to establish for children social enrichment programs that emphasize the acquisition of social skills.

TREATMENT METHOD: The authors hypothesize that the lack of a comprehensive approach is the reason treatment programs have not achieved meaningful results for runaways. Their approach has three components. A *child management program* presents the family with an explanation of how certain stimuli and consequences can control behavior, procedures for identifying and defining a behavior to be modified, and methods for applying appropriate consequences to either increase or decrease a behavior. The family is then taught how to change the frequency of the child's objectionable behavior through stimulus control techniques, and how to use graphs and tables to record behavior changes.

Second, a *family enrichment program* is initiated to improve family communication. The procedures include: noting the problem and determining treatment procedures, formalizing the treatment process, and preliminary training in communication skills, problem solving, and conflict resolution strategies. This training also includes modeling of appropriate behavior, verbal and nonverbal instruction, behavioral demonstrations, instructional practice, giving feedback and reinforcement to make a response specific, and verbal descriptions of possible consequences for both appropriate and inappropriate behavior. The program also focuses on identifying relationships between family members, establishing exchange contracts, and substituting natural reinforcers for concrete reinforcers on a gradual basis to guarantee behavioral change. A follow-up evaluation concludes this program.

Third, a *social enrichment program* emphasizes the improvement of the child's interpersonal skills. Skills include learning how to: present and introduce oneself, start and develop a conversation, give and receive compliments, improve appearance, make and refuse requests, show feelings spontaneously, and express feelings appropriately by nonverbal means (posture, gestures, eye contact, touching, smiling, etc.).

Adolescents who were identified as high risk also received training in problem solving. They learned skills needed to generate information and solutions to problems, including ways of dealing with situations, selecting and implementing strategies, and confirming the results of a chosen course of action. Specific procedures included an introduction to using stimuli and consequences to control problem-solving behavior by identifying and defining a behavior to be modified, changing the rate of problem-solving behavior by using stimulus control techniques, and applying appropriate consequences to increase or decrease a behavior.

The training model presented was also used to train juvenile justice workers. The performance of these workers was evaluated, and a follow-up process was implemented to determine if the training procedures were relevant to practical situations and whether runaway behavior decreased.

COMMENTARY: The creation of an effective educational program for juvenile justice workers to use with families of runaways is a significant achievement, especially since the training program requires little additional effort on the part of the workers because training manuals, materials, and criterion-referenced evaluation procedures are provided. The program also uses predictive self-inventories and behavioral observation to determine which children are most likely to run away.

SOURCE: Wodarski, J. S., and Ammons, P. W. "Comprehensive Treatment of Runaway Children and Their Parents." *Family Therapy*, 1981, *8*, 229–240.

Dealing with Runaway Behavior Through Behavioral Contracts

AUTHOR: Robert Bruce Rutherford

PRECIS: Rules for behavioral contracting and case studies illustrating their application with different forms of delinquent behaviors.

INTRODUCTION: Rutherford points out that adolescents who display delinquent behavior may be skillful at developing alternate strategies for gaining reinforcers and avoiding mediator-imposed interventions. These adolescents need to be allowed to negotiate some aspects of the tasks and reinforcers in the intervention strategy. Behavioral contracting is one technique that invites the adolescent's involvement. The behavioral analysis that precedes the contract includes the determination of the antecedents that will cue the contract behavior, the contract behavior to be developed, and the consequences that will maintain the contract behavior. Consequences stated in a positive form are assumed to result in an increase in the frequency of the anticipated behavior.

TREATMENT PROCEDURES: The author cites ten rules for setting up behavioral contracts:
     1. The analysis of the behavior to be contracted must consider the antecedents, actual behavior, and consequences.

2. A precise and systematic format is necessary. Items such as dates, times, criterion behavior, amounts or range of consequences, names of contractor and contractee and all others involved in the contract should be listed.

3. Both parties should participate in the negotiation of the contract so that the terms will be balanced.

4. Positive wording in the contract is essential. The contractee is more likely to comply with the terms if positive reinforcement for appropriate behavior is built into the contract.

5. If the desired behavior is not part of the contractor's repertoire, the contract should include methods for the contractee to gain initial success. Behaviors already observed in the contractor must be built into the contract.

6. If both the contractor and contractee must change behaviors, the use of an arbitrator is beneficial.

7. The behavioral contract should be signed by both parties to emphasize their commitment to the contract.

8. The consequences that follow both the completion and the noncompletion of the contracted behavior must be outlined.

9. Upon completion of the contracted behavior, the reinforcing consequences should be immediately provided. Contracts may allow for small but continuous reinforcements for daily behaviors and a large reinforcement upon completion of the entire contract.

10. A progression from contractor-initiated to contractee-initiated behaviors should take place as quickly as possible: "Behavioral contracting will have more generalized results when the contractee (adolescent) proposes the privileges and responsibilities to be included in the contract."

CASE EXAMPLE: The following community contract illustrates the method's application to runaway behavior. Fourteen-year-old Pamela had been running away for periods of up to one year. She had her first sexual experience at age nine and she generally left home to be with older men. She had a four-month-old baby, who had been fathered by a twenty-one-year-old man. Two problems were identified by Pamela's mother:

her running away from home and the use of the $96.00 Pamela received from the county every two weeks for her baby. According to Pamela, she usually ran away because she felt her mother expected her to do more chores than her three sisters, and the county check was made out to her mother, while Pamela felt she should have control over the money.

The activities that Pamela said she enjoyed included going to parties with her friends, listening to music, and watching TV. Also, Pamela expressed a desire to go to Disneyland and to be taken out for a nice dinner. Other activities Pamela enjoyed were the ones organized by the county probation department.

Contract

Date: _____

1A. Pamela receives $96.00 every two weeks. Of that $96.00, she will pay her mother every two weeks:

Food	$30.00
Board	20.83
Utilities	3.00
Total	$53.83

2A. For following the chore chart each week (which divides the household chores evenly between Pamela and her sisters), Pamela will be able to attend any and all group activities provided by the probation department that week.

2B. For not following the chore chart each week, Pamela will not be able to attend group activities provided by the probation department that week.

3A. For each Friday or Saturday night that Pamela goes out and is home by 1:00 A.M., her mother will provide free baby-sitting for the baby that evening.

3B. For each Friday and Saturday night that Pamela is not home by 1:00 A.M., she will pay her mother fifty cents an hour for the time that she is gone past 1:00 A.M.

4A. Pamela will receive free baby-sitting from 9:00 A.M. to 1:00 P.M. from her mother on weekdays when Pamela is attending summer school.

4B. Pamela will pay fifty cents an hour to her mother for baby-sitting if she does not attend summer school.

As negotiator and overseer of this contract, Mr. Glen Hamilton, county probation officer, will see that all sections of this contract are followed and that said consequences will be paid. Mr. Hamilton will see that both Pamela and her mother are treated fairly by the contract.

Ms. Pamela Brooke, Student	Mr. Glen Hamilton Probation Officer

Ms. Sue Brooke, Mother

COMMENTARY: Rutherford summarizes the elements that appear to contribute to the effectiveness of behavioral contracting for delinquent adolescents. The contract supplies the adolescent with maximum negotiation power, directly observable contractor responsibilities, and a method for predicting the behavior of the contractor. At the same time, the contractor is supplied with the authority to negotiate change in the adolescent's behavior, observable contractee behaviors and contingencies, and a method for predicting contractee behavior.

In the turbulent emotional world of adolescence, the specific nature of behavioral contracting appears to provide a needed structure. Emphasis on the positive is important, while at the same time the recognition of consequences for failure to carry out the contract is essential.

SOURCE: Rutherford, R. B. "Establishing Behavioral Contracts with Delinquent Adolescents." *Federal Probation,* 1975.

Guidelines for Family Treatment
of Adolescent Runaways

AUTHOR: Helm Stierlin

PRECIS: Treatment of adolescent runaways based on an understanding of the dynamics between family members.

INTRODUCTION: Stierlin proposes that running away is a surface manifestation of complex psychosocial conditions and developments. Four forms of runaway behavior are presented. *Abortive runaways* are characterized by the ambivalence of the runaway attempts, which point to the adolescents' strong psychological ties to their families. *Lonely schizoid runaways* may behave so bizarrely or self-destructively that they are quickly institutionalized; they do not run toward people but remain isolated from others. *Casual runaways* experience no difficulty in leaving their families, moving easily from the parental orbit into the peer orbit. *Crisis runaways* act in ways that reflect a crisis in their own or their parents' lives. Frequently, they stay involved with their families and at some point return to the family orbit.

TREATMENT METHOD: Stierlin describes three major modes of runaway behavior as it relates to family dynamics. Adolescents who run away under the *binding mode* only run away abortively. Most of these adolescents tend to avoid peers, often lacking the necessary social skills to interact with peers. If the binding operates primarily on the archaic-loyalty level, the adolescents usually abort their runaway efforts with noticeable self-destructive acts. A majority of the lonely schizoid runaways belong to this group. The *expelling mode,* at the opposite end of the spectrum, is characterized by early and casual runaway behavior. Quite often, these adolescents are able to adapt to the tougher aspects of the runaway culture. Consistent neglect on the part of the parents is a hallmark of this group, although the parents often camouflage this neglect by observable protests of concern and claims to give their children everything. The *delegating mode* characterizes adolescents who are able to adapt to the runaway culture but eventually return home. Their running away is guided by the expectation of their fulfilling a mission for one or both parents; for example, an adolescent seeks to fulfill the ego mission of experimenting with lifestyles that his parents had not tested out for themselves.

Prior to treating the runaway adolescent, the therapist should look at the family context and consider the parents' middle-age crisis, their marital relationship, and their relations with their own parents. The author presents three guidelines for the treatment of runaways. (1) The primary therapeutic task with severely bound adolescents who run away abortively is to unbind them from their families. An exploration of the psychological ties that keep the family members bound together is necessary in order to find a way to loosen them. In this situation, an adolescent's successful running away could be a sign of progress, indicating the ability of family members to live apart from one another. (2) Adolescents who run away in the expelling mode require a very different therapeutic approach. Bonds of loyalty between the adolescent and his or her parents need to be developed. Helping the parents to set limits and express care and concern for their children is the therapeutic task. (3) Runaways who are delegated the intricate system of missions and loyalties require close investigation. Reconciliation of conflicts, both intrapsychic and interpersonal, as well as obligations within the family are the main goals of treatment. Generally, many runaways from this group and their families can make changes with brief therapeutic interventions.

COMMENTARY: According to Stierlin, an understanding of the family dynamics of the runaway adolescent is essential to the treatment process. His explanation of the various types of runaways provides guidelines for intervening with the families. These guidelines enable therapists working with runaways to better understand the family dynamics and devise effective strategies.

SOURCE: Stierlin, H. "A Family Perspective on Adolescent Runaways." *Archives of General Psychiatry*, 1973, 29, 46–62.

Curbing Runaway Behavior Through
Family Crisis Intervention

AUTHOR: Roy Grando

PRECIS: Mobilizing families to deal with crises by recognizing their strengths, setting goals, and implementing interventions.

INTRODUCTION: Family crisis intervention is an action-oriented approach in which problems are looked at within the framework of the family and both long- and short-term goals are formulated and implemented. Central to the effectiveness of this approach are participation by family members and constant evaluation. Each person is encouraged to express himself, particularly in any decision making about individual or family situations. Also, each person is viewed as being capable of selecting alternatives, making decisions, and accepting the consequences. The evaluation includes establishing definitions, selecting appropriate interventions, implementing the interventions, and assessing the outcomes.

TREATMENT INTERVENTIONS: The process of crisis assessment and intervention has four stages.

1. *Defining the problem.* The therapist is instructed to begin by asking the family members to state the presenting problem. While this is taking place, he must be fully aware of the emotional status of the individuals. Background information should be gathered as a basis for formulating intervention strategies. The way in which the therapist obtains the information and relates to the family members in itself constitutes an intervention. During the interview the therapist should attempt to establish the nature of the crisis in terms of event, resources, and meaning.

2. *Selecting interventions.* Making decisions about the course of treatment is the focus of this stage. If possible, these decisions should be made with the family, with the consequences of any intervention always given consideration. In cases of dangerous behavior, such as suicide or homicide, these issues are ad-

dressed immediately by involving the person or persons in taking alternative actions. When a family or person does not make a decision about a priority issue, the therapist should demand a decision and explain that authorities such as the police will have to be called upon if they do not come to a decision. If the situation does not require immediate resolution, the therapist should ask the family about the desired outcomes and attempt to work out an arrangement to achieve those goals.

3. *Implementing interventions.* A contract between the family and therapist is always made, whether implicitly or explicitly. If the family does not or cannot decide what to do, that is an agreement to continue as is. Implementing the contract with the family follows.

4. *Evaluation.* Seven questions are asked during this final phase: Was the contract fulfilled? What happened in the interview or intervention? What were the goals of the interview and intervention, and were they reached? Has the family performed changes or said that they had changed? What else could have been done, and what might have been the outcome? What has been learned about the family that could facilitate attempts to help them? What are the next steps toward the immediate and long-range goals?

CASE ILLUSTRATION: The crisis in the Tulley family was fifteen-year-old Alice's running away. When she returned home, she demanded that her boyfriend live with the family or she would leave forever. Alice expressed hurt feelings that her parents cared more about what the neighbors and community thought than about her.

During the initial interview, which included the parents, Alice, and her boyfriend, the therapist gathered information and watched the interaction between the family members. It was observed that Alice constantly threatened her parents and they in turn tried to control her. Although reluctant to set limits, Alice's parents would not allow her boyfriend to move in as they felt that would be morally wrong.

As the interview progressed, the therapist investigated Alice's reasons for running away. Alice explained that she had decided she could not get the emotional responses she wanted from her parents, felt too restricted by them, and wanted to be on her own. Tom, Alice's boyfriend, was willing to take her away from her family. Tom was twenty-two years old, divorced, not supporting his child, and unemployed. Alice and Tom had run out of money, and Alice's brother convinced her to come home. At this point, the therapist asked Alice why she had made such poor plans. She responded that she did not care about herself and based this feeling on her parent's lack of caring for her.

The therapist asked the parents if they cared, and they replied that they loved her. Alice did not believe them because she felt they always judged her by community standards. The therapist gave direct examples of the parents' caring feelings and their comparing behavior, and they recognized how they had disregarded Alice's feelings. The therapist offered a few recommendations, including that the parents express their love for Alice more directly and set appropriate limits for her while allowing her choice in other areas.

In discussing Alice's ultimatum with the family, the therapist tried to help the parents to distinguish between social approval and relationship. Rather than looking at Tom's living with the family in relation to the neighbors' viewpoint, they were asked to look at Tom's intentions. The therapist suggested that Tom could be in a lot of trouble with the law if they decided to press charges. An interchange between Alice and the therapist revealed that she was using Tom to embarrass her parents. The therapist told the parents that Tom had taken advantage of them and their daughter and that Alice needed their protection. Although the therapist felt that the parents might be uncomfortable with the situation, they should not be stopped by Alice's ultimatum and should take care of her. If Alice ran away, the parents were told that she would be brought back by the police; but if they accepted Alice's ultimatum, it would be just about impossible to show her that they cared.

At the next session, a few days later, the parents reported that they had put Tom out of the house and had pressed charges against him. Alice responded by feeling that her parents cared for her more than she thought.

COMMENTARY: In the case presented, the interventions focused on expanding resources and changing meanings. The parents were encouraged to define their priorities and set appropriate limits, which resulted in specific guidelines and protection for their daughter. Through active, direct discussion the parents became aware of the discrepancy between their love for their daughter and their desire for social approval.

This method of crisis intervention places the focus on the family members' strengths and ability to participate in the process. An active, direct role by the therapist and interventions that were clearly defined and implemented mobilized the family to positive action. This approach can be applied to a variety of crisis situations.

SOURCE: Grando, R. "An Approach to Family Crisis Intervention." *Family Therapy*, 1975, 2, 201-214.

Additional Readings

Chase, A. M., Crowley, C. D., and Weintraub, M. K. "Treating the Throwaway Child: A Model for Adolescent Service." *Social Casework: The Journal of Contemporary Social Work*, 1979, 538-546.

Treatment techniques with acting-out adolescents and their families are outlined. The setting was an adolescent unit of a family counseling agency. All of the young people were referred through the courts and their problems ranged from running away to felonies. Significant factors contributing to the success of the program include a focus on improving communication within the family, maintaining a flexible treatment approach, eliciting the support of the community resources, and conveying a sense of optimism in the relationship between therapist and family. A limited evaluation of the program shows that four of five of the adolescents were making positive adjustments within the community; the avoidance of institutionalization made the program cost effective.

Counts, R. M. "Family Crises and the Impulsive Adolescent."
    Archives of General Psychiatry, 1967, *17,* 64–71.

Running away, among other acting-out behaviors, is
viewed by Counts as a reaction to a family crisis. In the framework presented, the adolescent is seen as being in a precarious
state of equilibrium due to his phase of development. Frequently, the adolescent is designated the family scapegoat and, as
such, acts out the family crisis. The author recognizes the participation of the adolescent in the ensuing process and suggests
that family therapy is the treatment of choice, as the acting out
could be managed in the context of family functioning.

Gordon, J. "Working with Runaways and Their Families: How
    the SAJA Community Does It." *Family Process,* 1975, *14,*
    235–262.

This article addresses the delivery of services to runaways
and their families at a runaway house. The facility annually
serves 600 to 900 young people (ages ten to eighteen). The objective of the program is to provide concrete support for these
young people at the time of crisis. Family seminars are conducted, and the counselors attempt to work with the families in
whatever ways are mutually agreeable. Part of the overall philosophy of runaway house is to accept the young people and their
families on their own terms and to relate what happens in counseling to the family's involvement in the broader community.

Roberts, A. R. "Stress and Coping Patterns Among Adolescent
    Runaways." *Journal of Social Service Research,* 1982, *5,* 15–
    27.

This study of thirty suburban runaways and thirty non-
runaways investigates the extent to which specific stressful
events and deficient coping patterns contribute to the runaway
behavior. An interviewer asked each runaway, "What do you
feel was the 'last straw' that triggered your leaving home?" In
all cases, the runaways described a stressful situation within
their family as the trigger. Therapists working with families of
runaway youth can offer help by either direct treatment interventions or through referral to professionals for specific treatment, such as alcoholism counseling. However, when the latter is

the recommended approach, coordination of the overall treatment plan is essential.

Robey, A., Rosenwald, R. J., Snell, J. E., and Lee, R. E. "The Runaway Girl: A Reaction to Family Stress." *American Journal of Orthopsychiatry,* 1964, *34,* 760–768.

The authors study running away among adolescent girls from middle-class families. The thesis suggested by their work is that family interaction centers around a threatened unconscious incestuous relationship between father and daughter, which is motivated by the mother. From evaluations of forty-two runaway girls, a pattern of family interaction emerged: a troubled marital relationship, parents' lack of control over their own or their daughter's impulses, and subtle pressure by the mother for the daughter to take on her role while depriving the daughter of maternal love. Treatment is based on the crucial involvement of the mother in the process, with the main goal the improvement of the mother-daughter relationship. This can often be accomplished by an extremely direct interpretation of the girl's underlying dynamics to the mother. The daughter needs to be assured that she does not need to be seductive to be cared for. When this concept is conveyed, a dramatic improvement is often noted. However, maintaining the improvement depends on a continuation of treatment with mother and daughter. In the cases evaluated, the father's participation was not seen as essential to a successful outcome.

Stierlin, H. "Family Therapy with Adolescents and the Process of Intergenerational Reconciliation." Revised version of a paper presented at the symposium "Community and Family Psychiatry: Experiences, Assessment, and Problems of Evaluation," at the Institute of Community and Family Psychiatry, Montreal, Canada, 1969, pp. 194–204.

Through a case study of a family with an adolescent girl who had run away following a series of social problems, the author illustrates a unique therapy approach. The process of an adolescent's separation from his family entails three tasks: integrative reconciliation, adaptive reconciliation, and reparative reconciliation. In the case presented the therapists acted as facilitators of family communication. The bitter intergenerational and marital conflicts were deradicalized so that each family member was able to form a new perspective about the other members.

Stratton, J. G. "Effects of Crisis Intervention Counseling on Predelinquent and Misdemeanor Juvenile Offenders." *Juvenile Justice,* November 1975, pp. 7–18.

The effectiveness of family crisis intervention compared to traditional methods of dealing with runaways and other delinquent offenders is the focus of this study of 602 juvenile offenders. Compared to traditional methods, the crisis intervention counseling of these young people, who were accused of committing first or second misdemeanors, yielded a significant effect, measured by the number of rearrests, number of minors receiving probation services, and total number of days detained in juvenile hall. In addition, the crisis intervention counseling was by far the more economical approach.

Zastrow, C., and Navarre, R. "Help for Runaways and Their Parents." *Social Casework,* February 1975, pp. 74–78.

This follow-up study evaluates the effectiveness of counseling services that were provided, mainly by supervised volunteers, at a center for runaway youths. Thirty-one youths and their parents were studied. Results demonstrate that both the youths and their parents were generally satisfied with the services they received. Recommendations include that the agency's youth advocate role be conceptualized in ways that minimize problems in counseling the parents of runaways, that more extensive training for the volunteers be developed, that more objective screening be devised for accepting volunteers, and that experienced counselors handle contacts with parents.

6

Delinquency

Young people are classified as delinquent when they violate society's social norms. Depending on the young person's characteristic way of functioning, the infractions may be violent or nonaggressive; life-threatening behavior must receive immediate action. Some common goals of the family therapy approach with delinquents include involving the family in an understanding of the behavior, improving communication, and increasing parental responsibility and control of the young person. Another important objective is to keep the delinquent out of the criminal justice system. Behavioral techniques are employed in many of the approaches used with the family. Because many families of delinquents are resistant to engaging in the treatment process, paradoxical strategies are sometimes used to

121

break through their resistance so that therapy can begin. The momentum of the crisis may be used to encourage participation of all the members. In general, the therapist assumes an active, direct role in treating families of delinquents.

Family Therapy as an Alternative
to Legal Action with Juvenile Offenders

AUTHORS: Don Beal and Paul Duckro

PRECIS: Using a family systems approach as an intervention with juvenile offenders.

INTRODUCTION: A juvenile status offender (JSO) is defined as a youth whose offenses are of such a nature that they would not be considered criminal if committed by an adult. Acts of violence against person or property are not included in the definition of a JSO. The offenses frequently committed include running away, truancy, staying out late, and incorrigibility. Families who seek court action have to deal with several negative consequences: the self-fulfilling effects of the label, the removal of the youth from his family by placement in a correction center—where further negative influences are common—and the difficulty in placing the juvenile following detention.

TREATMENT INTERVENTIONS: A unique intervention program (Juvenile Status Offenders Unit) was developed to emphasize psychological perspectives in understanding the problem and rehabilitative procedures to effect the intervention. Counselors were trained in family and group counseling techniques, and supervision was provided on a regular basis. The goal of the intervention strategy was to resolve the family crisis without resorting to court action.

Most families in crisis with a juvenile offender approach the legal system expressing feelings of anger. At this critical time, families were offered the alternative of going to see a JSOU counselor for a series of prehearing meetings. The families were told that the procedure would be short term (six to eight sessions) and that the meetings would focus on finding a solution to the immediate problems without court action. Participation in the program was voluntary and was accepted by a majority of the families.

Crisis intervention techniques were used at the beginning

of the counseling process to work through the angry feelings and establish a broader base. The families met with the counselor once or twice a week, at which time a family therapy approach was used to modify communication patterns; group techniques were also used. The focus was on the family seeing the problems as an outgrowth of the family's functioning rather than as a problem within the juvenile offender.

Throughout treatment the disturbed communication pattern was gently and repeatedly illustrated as it occurred to bring it to the family's attention, and the underlying motivations were explained until they were understood. More adaptive transactional patterns emerged, and former nonproductive patterns disappeared as they became unnecessary. The counselor modeled communication skills for the family, and the family was instructed to check out messages and become aware of messages that were incongruent.

Following the treatment phase, families that were operating at a satisfactory level were allowed to terminate treatment. Families who required further help were able to request referral to another mental health agency. A few families selected the alternative of going before the court. Although this choice was in conflict with the oiginal goal, in a few cases this action was required. Some families continued in treatment during a probationary period and thereby continued to seek change in the family system.

TREATMENT RESULTS: A dramatic 83 percent of the families who participated in the prehearing program were terminated or referred without court action.

COMMENTARY: The prehearing program yielded many positive results for the juvenile offenders and their families, perhaps the most significant of which was the avoidance of court action. The authors propose that psychological, rather than legal, intervention benefits the total community in that legal action poses an economic hardship for the community. Another long-term result was the contribution the rehabilitated juvenile offenders could make to their communities.

SOURCE: Beal, D., and Duckro, P. "Family Counseling as an Alternative to Legal Action for the Juvenile Status Offender." *Journal of Marriage and Family Counseling*, January 1977, pp. 77-81.

Identification of System Precursors in the Treatment of Juvenile Delinquents

AUTHORS: William Gray and Lucille R. Gray

PRECIS: Determining the dysfunctional system precursor, blocking its momentum, and attempting to change it.

INTRODUCTION: The authors identify the first step in the treatment of juvenile delinquents as putting a "cap" on acting-out tendencies. They hypothesize that offenses result when inappropriate system precursors are activated and that there are specific system precursors for various delinquent acts. They state, "If system formation does not occur, then there should be no crime, and if our ability to system block is effective enough, hopefully there will be no recidivism in the near future, thus giving us opportunity and time to work out longer-range problems and needs."

TREATMENT METHODS: From their work with juvenile delinquents, the authors identify certain system precursors. The first precursor is difficulty in family relations, and the first step in all cases is to help parents relate to their children. The therapist can model behavior with the child for the parents and in other ways train them to relate differently to their child.

The second system precursor is a lack of adequate "answering time" in the family relationships. Associated with this is small allowance for "thinking time": although family members pause in their monologues, their pauses are not long enough to permit thinking about any complicated ideas. In many families difficulty in resolving problems reflects a lack of "give and take," and specific training in this skill, beginning with simple examples, was found useful. Any encounters that would have to be forced are avoided. Another behavior often seen in these families is that one member does most of the talking. Simple training exercises that activate "operon switches" for turn off and turn on can be useful.

The authors identify specific system precursors for young people who have committed particular offenses. For example, by working with many runaways, the authors found that the system precursor is the pressure of a mother who is too independent. This attitude of being able to handle everything on her own was modeled for the daughter. The runaway girls thus failed to see any danger in running away. A discussion with the mother and daughter about this behavior and a change in the mother's tendency toward independence often successfully blocks the daughter's inappropriate behavior. Once the running away stops other issues can be dealt with under less dangerous conditions.

COMMENTARY: Acts of juvenile delinquency are dangerous and can sometimes be life threatening. The seriousness of the behaviors command immediate action. The authors describe methods used with families of delinquents when "capping" the acting-out behavior is seen as a priority. Once this has been accomplished, more intensive work with the family can be started. The identification of specific system precursors for certain offenses helps professionals working with young offenders to intervene quickly and establish a treatment plan.

SOURCE: Gray, W., and Gray, L. R. "System Specifics in Offender Therapy." *International Journal of Offender Therapy and Comparative Criminology*, 1977, *21*, 56-67.

Problems, Participants, and Pledges:
A Family Therapy Approach
to Juvenile Delinquency

AUTHOR: Harry J. Aponte

PRECIS: Structural family therapy to treat juvenile delinquents.

INTRODUCTION: Individuals concurrently belong to several systems; for example, a person who is part of a couple system is simultaneously a member of a larger system such as a community. When a problem is presented to a therapist who uses a structural approach, he sets out to find the structural bases of family systems that have produced the problem.

TREATMENT METHOD: The therapist begins treatment by asking each family member to specify the problem he or she wishes to solve. By identifying the problems, the therapist can determine those issues that the members see themselves wanting to change. The author notes that the more specific the definition of the problem, the more specific the definition of its structural base.

During the initial phase of treatment, the therapist engages the family members in a discussion of their problems, which enables the therapist to determine the family structure and observe how the relationships between members contributes to the stated problems. The therapist also strives to know each participant to find out who can contribute to resolving the problem. This investigation may include looking into such subsystems as extended family and community organizations: "A whole set of overlapping systems can contribute to the development of a problem, as well as to its solution."

Depending on the nature of the problem and its structure, the therapist elicits commitments from certain family members. These commitments include pledges from the individuals for change in treatment. Both the changes and the means to enact the changes are agreed upon and the pledge may include family tasks.

CASE ILLUSTRATIONS: The presenting problem in the R family was the delinquent behavior of the twelve-year-old son. The family members, including the son, agreed on the problem. However, the readiness with which the family labeled the boy as delinquent gave the therapist a clue that there were other difficulties. The family requested that the therapist stop the boy's delinquent behavior, and he responded by addressing the family's other problem areas. In the first part of the initial session, the therapist offered concern about the problems of the other family members. By doing this, the therapist discovered that the mother felt inadequate, that the fourteen-year-old son was being kept at home to help his mother, and that the ten-year-old daughter was creating feelings of jealousy through being a mother's pet. As the therapist gave greater importance to these other family problems, the family responded by beginning to talk as though they had come for help with these other problems. The therapist and family established an unexpressed contract to work on these problems. According to the author, "the reidentification of the problem was in itself the cornerstone of the cure of the twelve-year old's misbehavior. It meant the spreading of stress in this family system throughout the structure and away from one of the participants in the problem." During the last phase of treatment, the boy was seen individually to secure his new position within the family.

To illustrate the way in which the treatment process was approached, the author offers the following outline:

Problem: a twelve-year-old "delinquent."
Participants: the boy, his family, and his school.
Pledges: the boy and his family will work on other family problems with the therapist (a pledge between the school and the family would have been useful, but the school did not cooperate).

Problem: an overburdened mother.
Participants: the mother and children.
Pledges: mother and children will work with therapist to redistribute more of the household responsibilities among the children, and to establish a more appropriate distance between the generations.

Problem: a fourteen-year-old homebound boy.
Participants: the boy, his mother, and his siblings.
Pledges: mother and boy will work with the therapist on the boy's assuming the responsibility and independence of the oldest in the sibling group, and he will join the twelve-year old in more peer activities.

Problem: a favored and pampered ten-year-old girl.
Participants: the girl, her mother, and her siblings.
Pledges: girl and mother will work with therapist to achieve more distance between mother and girl and to have the girl become more a part of her sibling subgroup.

COMMENTARY: The structural family therapy approach outlined by Aponte is direct in its focus. The author recommends that after the family has been interviewed, the therapist should appraise the overall situation and decide on the degree of urgency of the designated problems. Also, the issue of autonomy or dependence of problem structures should be considered to decide which problems should be handled first. When considering participants, the therapist should involve the current participants and not former ones. In addition, the participants in maintaining the problem should be differentiated from those who pledge participation in the solution; for example, the therapist is always a participant in the pledge though not a participant in the problem. Regarding pledges, the author states, "The burden is on the sensitivity of the therapist to determine when he does have a contract to work. In fact, the family may sometimes enunciate an explicit pledge to which they are not really committed. The pledge then has not been made." Throughout the entire process, the therapist plays a very active role and fully participates in the process of change with the family.

SOURCE: Aponte, H. J. "Organizing Treatment Around the Family's Problems and Their Structural Bases." *Psychiatric Quarterly*, 1974, *48*, 209–222.

An Interactional Approach to Treating
an Adolescent's Acting-Out Behavior

AUTHORS: Gerald Schneiderman and Harvey Evans

PRECIS: Curbing an adolescent's delinquent behavior through an interactional approach to the family system.

INTRODUCTION: A major impediment in dealing with families whose presenting problem is delinquency is keeping them in treatment. The authors indicate that families often come to the first few sessions and then terminate. In their work with families of delinquents, Schneiderman and Evans find that the acting out of the adolescent frequently expresses the parents' feelings of deprivation. The process of seeing the connection between their feelings of deprivation and the acting out of the adolescent may cause the family to become depressed and then to stop coming for treatment. The treatment technique described in this paper is proposed to counteract this breakdown in the treatment process.

CASE STUDY: The C family consisted of the parents and four children. Fifteen-year-old Paul was the oldest child and the identified patient. He had been caught stealing several times and was doing poorly in school.

The authors outline a typical interaction in the C family: "Mrs. C attacks Paul for stealing and not behaving as he should. Mr. C smiles in approbation. Mrs. C then metes out a punishment which 'does not fit the crime.' Mr. C then attacks his wife for being overwhelming in the punishment. Mrs. C then attacks Mr. C. Mr. C feels castrated and complains that Mrs. C does not help him feel like the 'one man in the family.' Mrs. C then attacks Mr. C for his past demeanors—that is, failure to pay his debts. Mr. C withdraws, and agrees with his wife that Paul should be punished."

The family history revealed that both Mr. and Mrs. C had experienced deprivation by not having a warm relationship with their respective fathers. It was felt that by stealing, Paul was ex-

pressing not only his parents' deprivations but his own deprivation, the lack of a warm relationship with his mother and father.
It was hypothesized that Paul's stealing represented frustration
at being deprived, an angry attempt to compensate for what he
was not receiving and a way of drawing attention to feelings he
was unable to express verbally.

During the beginning phase of therapy, the focus was on
Paul's aggressive feelings as expressed in stealing. Interpretations
were made about Paul's feeling angry at being deprived of a
strong father and an accepting, loving mother. Although these
interpretations seemed accurate, the family responded by talking about termination. The therapist felt that the family was
feeling guilty and depressed. When a change in focus from feelings of anger to feelings of deprivation was made, the family re-
sumed involvement in the treatment.

The family was shown how Paul's stealing was a vehicle
for bringing them together. Paul's desire to be loved by his parents was emphasized. The therapist shifted the focus to the expression of loving feelings between the parents and encouraged
them to state their needs and wishes to one another. Other family members then felt freer to talk about their own problems
with the expression of loving feelings.

Having established a foundation of positive feelings within the family, the members were able to deal more openly with
their angry feelings. At the same time, a change occurred in
Paul's behavior—he was doing better in school and had stopped
stealing. Other outcomes of the treatment process were Mr.
C's becoming increasingly assertive and more actively involved
with his family and Mrs. C's permitting herself to be more receptive.

COMMENTARY: By shifting the emphasis in the family from
dealing with their angry feelings to acknowledge their loving
feelings, the therapist was later able to focus the family on the
expression of angry feelings, which resulted in a decrease in the
adolescent's need to act out. This sequence in the treatment
process was successful with families whose members had warm
feelings toward each other. The authors caution that certain

families do not have enough positive experiences to elicit warm feelings. In these cases, another form of treatment is necessary.

SOURCE: Schneiderman, G., and Evans, H. "An Approach to Families of Acting-Out Adolescents—A Case Study." *Adolescence*, 1975, *10*, 495–498.

Changing Communication Patterns in Delinquent Families Using Behavioral and Family Therapy Techniques

AUTHORS: Bruce V. Parsons, Jr. and James F. Alexander

PRECIS: Short-term family therapy using behavior modification strategies with families having a delinquent member.

INTRODUCTION: Throughout the literature are reports that certain factors in family communication differ between abnormal and normal, or adjusted, families. These factors include activity level, equality of communication, frequency and duration of positive interruptions, and clarification. Parsons and Alexander's study delineates three main goals: to develop a clearly defined, behaviorally specific (short-term) family intervention program; to relate this program to a series of specific goals that are evaluated by both formal and content measures of family interaction; and to systematically extinguish maladaptive interaction patterns. They designed interventions intended to develop reciprocity and periods of positive reinforcement, to develop equality of verbal and nonverbal responsiveness, and to increase solution-oriented communication patterns.

TREATMENT METHOD: Forty male and female teenagers who had been designated delinquent and had been arrested or detained at juvenile court were selected for the study. The problems exhibited by the teenagers included running away, being declared ungovernable, or having been habitually truant. There were two experimental groups and two control groups, and the families were randomly assigned to a group.

Four specific features of the program are outlined. First, *rules* are defined as behavioral limits designed to regulate and control the conduct of the family, and *requests* are defined as asking with neither a yes or no response producing negative repercussions. The goal of this treatment strategy is to make rules explicit. Second, a token economy system was set up whereby each family member could name exactly which response he would like to see more often from the other family members. Each member identified three responses and the way in which he wanted to be rewarded. Third, family members were trained in solution-oriented communication patterns, including interruption for clarification, interruption to increase information about the topic or about oneself in relation to the topic, and interruption to offer positive feedback to other family members. During the training period the therapist explicitly stated the meaning and purposes of interruptions and the way in which he would reinforce these behaviors; he also engaged in active modeling, and prompted and dispensed social reinforcement (e.g., verbal and nonverbal praise). Fourth, families received a behavior modification manual, which familiarized them with the concepts and language of the treatment method and helped them develop the techniques.

After a three-week training period the therapists, who were graduate students in clinical psychology, started to see the families. During the initial interview, the family was told that both parents and child were expected to be involved. A prearranged seating order of father, child, and mother was followed, and the family was given a set of three tasks. In the first, the behavior specificity phase, each family member was given a pencil and clipboard with two mimeographed sheets attached. Each member was asked to list the three behaviors each would like to see changed in the other members. Also, each was requested to write down three behaviors that each other member might want to see changed. In the next phase, the vignette phase, each member was asked to list his responses to each of three situations that called for parental action in response to a child's behavior. Each member described the type of action he or she would expect each of the other members to take. The interaction phase followed completion of these tasks; during this part of the program, the family was asked to have a twenty-minute discussion about their responses during the previous two phases. They were told that it was not necessary to reach an agreement on the task. The family was also told that their discussion would be observed and recorded on an audio tape, and then the therapist left the room. When the time was up, the therapist gave the family members the manual and told them to read the manual at home and to check each page after reading it. It was explained to the family that it was important to read the manual because those families who read the manual did better in therapy. Therapy was conducted over a four-week period.

TREATMENT RESULTS: The communication patterns in the families treated improved significantly. The specific goals set forth in the beginning of the study were met. According to the authors, the results at least suggest that the family approach is valuable.

COMMENTARY: Parsons and Alexander emphasize that the intervention must be specific and focus on the communication processes that permit family systems to adjust to stress. In the study described, a sample of normal family behaviors—for example, communication variables—was defined and the therapist attempted to shape deviant families to that sample.

SOURCE: Parsons, B. V., Jr., and Alexander, J. F. "Short-Term Family Intervention: A Therapy Outcome Study." *Journal of Consulting and Clinical Psychology*, 1973, *41*, 195-201.

Techniques for Involving Families
of Delinquent Offspring
in the Treatment Process

AUTHOR: Thomas F. Johnson

PRECIS: Ways to deal with problems of motivation and resistance in families whose presenting symptom is delinquency.

INTRODUCTION: A common obstacle to engaging families of delinquents in treatment is their notable unwillingness to look at any problem that does not appear to be directly connected to the symptom. Families of delinquents tend to see their problem offspring as having a unique disability separate from the family system. Families often turn to the courts to deal with the delinquent member and sometimes have him removed. Although family members may recognize other difficulties, they are minimized or ignored. Treatment suggestions for dealing with these problems is the focus of this paper.

TREATMENT METHOD: After a young person is taken to court for an offense, in general family members resist the recommendation that they all participate in the treatment process. Johnson finds that part of the resistance reflects the fact that the court, and not the family, asks for the treatment. Also, any problems within the family are commonly projected onto the delinquent member.

The majority of families studied agreed to a contract for three meetings. At the first session, the family members usually wanted to relate numerous details of the delinquent member's activities. Sometimes the family was so determined to do this that the therapist could not redirect the focus. However, one effective technique with many families was to ask the members to talk about how the delinquencies had affected them, in this way placing the emphasis on their own feelings. This form of discussion frequently resulted in discrepancies among the family members and sometimes uncovered feelings previously unexpressed. In some cases, a consensus was reached and sometimes the family's defensive manner was altered. During the second session, the family was asked to think about what their lives would be like had the delinquency not occurred. This technique enabled the family to refocus their attention on the realities of daily life and often resulted in a clearer picture of connections within the family and differences of opinion.

During this process resistances that had lessened somewhat again became evident. Such resistance included a breach of the contract between the family and therapist by the absence of certain family members. When this happened, the therapist kept the focus on the reasons for the breach of contract with the understanding that it would be necessary for all members to attend the sessions, and a new appointment was scheduled. If the family did not agree, the therapist discontinued treatment but offered an option to start again should the family change its position. Johnson finds it crucial that the therapist set the conditions for treatment and recommends that a gentle approach, rather than an emphatic one, produces positive results.

A second form of resistance consisted of the delinquent member taking the stance of being "the family problem" and obstructing any of the therapist's efforts to involve other family members. Putting the delinquent member in charge of the session usually resulted in his becoming uncomfortable and allowing other members to be involved. A related form of resistance concerned the refusal of the delinquent member to participate. When this happened, the therapist instructed the young person to remain silent and sometimes requested that another family member help him to stay silent. Usually the resistant member responded by starting to participate.

When the resistances lessened during these early sessions, the parents often initiated discussion about some difficulty in their relationship. Johnson asserts that "willingness to shift from the initial concern with a child to consider this most important relationship is a favorable sign for treatment progress." The emergence of the parents' desire to address marital problems was considered such a positive sign that no contract for further work was attempted until this occurred; if the topic of the marriage was not addressed by the fourth or fifth session, treatment was discontinued with the offer to resume if the family's position changed. If the family discontinued treatment, the therapist reviewed for them what had been learned about the family up to that point and offered some recommendations. The summary statement was intended to give the nonresistant family members the chance to free themselves. As a result of this procedure some delinquents were able to free themselves from the family system and stop the delinquent acts and some families resolved to keep the entire family out of trouble to prove the therapist wrong.

COMMENTARY: Starting with the court referral, the author gives specific guidelines for engaging families of delinquents in treatment. Many of the strategies are paradoxical in nature and are aimed at breaking down the family's resistances to involvement in the treatment process. Although the families sometimes discontinued their participation in treatment, follow-up work found that the delinquent behavior had ceased.

SOURCE: Johnson, T. F. "Family Therapy with Families Having Delinquent Offspring." *Journal of Family Counseling,* 1975, *3,* 32–38.

The Treatment of Families Whose Double-Bind Messages Contribute to Delinquent Behavior

AUTHOR: Antonio J. Ferreira

PRECIS: Direct family therapy to change the communication in families whose presenting problem is delinquency.

INTRODUCTION: Ferreira asserts that a particular type of double-bind plays an important role in the origin of delinquent behavior. This situation, the "split-double-bind," occurs when the victim gets a bipolar message, for example, one message from the mother and one from the father; more precisely, a split-double-bind is "a somewhat formalized way of visualizing and describing at the communicational level, a pattern of inter-actions seemingly characteristic of families where delinquent be-havior occurs."

CASE STUDY: The parents of a fifteen-year-old boy who was being held in juvenile hall, came for help. A series of interviews were held to evaluate the problems, and the parents and son were seen both individually and together. Weekly family ther-apy was recommended and thirty sessions were held. During the second session the parents talked exclusively to the therapist, never to each other, and they expressed differing viewpoints. The father appeared very upset by his son's behavior, while the mother seemed aloof to the difficulties. For example, the father said that during a long talk his son had told him that he didn't like him; the father's response was to cry. During another early session, the therapist stressed several times that the problem was a family one and not exclusively a problem with the son. The father did not come to one meeting, at which the mother and son then talked to the therapist but not to each other. When the mother was not present, the father and son battled with each other.

At the ninth session, the father and son came and stated that the mother was not attending because she felt the problem was exclusively between the father and son. The therapist re-sponded by saying, "Perhaps this is the crux of your problem . . . perhaps when you (father and son) argue with each other, you are arguing about or for mother . . . in my opinion this is her problem as much as yours!" At the following meeting the family members seemed closer, more like a unit, and they were more verbally expressive. However, the parents still persisted in talking exclusively either about their son or to their son. The therapist commented on this and announced, "Next hour let's try not to talk about the boy." There were many spaces in the conversation during the next session, as the parents found it very difficult to talk about other things. The mother asked whether it was natural to be angry and, with the therapist's support, she expressed her complaints about her son and husband. At the twelfth session, the parents requested a session alone to talk about a topic they did not want to discuss in front of their son. This topic turned out to be the maternal grandmother's suicide, which had been a family secret. The therapist told them that their son might react to their request for a private meeting by imagining all sorts of things, such as the fantasy that he was not their son. He also indicated to the parents that they got angry with each other through their son.

In a later session, the son talked about his desire for his father to buy a new car. The father replied that they would not be getting a car for a long time, adding that the son wanted a new car so he could take it to school. While the father was objecting to his son's request, the mother was saying "there are exceptions . . . we wouldn't mind you taking that new car on Fridays for a date." The therapist pointed out that the father had just passed a law and the mother was simultaneously commenting on its "exceptions." During the twentieth session the parents were on the verge of discussing a serious topic when the son turned the conversation to a discussion of his hobby. The therapist interrupted and said, "It seems that when a serious subject comes up, someone interrupts it or jumps it to a lighter and more superficial topic."

TREATMENT RESULTS: The last eight appointments were kept by the couple and their son. Both positive and negative feelings were expressed more freely, and they reported things to be going quite well, both at home and in school. Also, the son was no longer getting into trouble with authority figures. Another change was that the father passed fewer "laws" and the mother interfered less with those "laws."

COMMENTARY: A distinction of the split-double-bind is that the young person gets conflicting messages from two equally important persons. In the middle, the child is unable to comply with the wishes of both parents. Because the parents are not consciously aware that they are giving different messages, the therapeutic approach uses an active participation by the therapist who confronts the family members in order to change the nonproductive communication patterns.

SOURCE: Ferreira, A. J. "The 'Double-Bind' and Delinquent Behavior." *Archives of General Psychiatry*, 1960, *3*, 359–367.

Additional Readings

Alexander, J. F. "Defensive and Supportive Communications in Normal and Deviant Families." *Journal of Consulting and Clinical Psychology*, 1973, *40*, 223–231.

The author's hypothesis is that abnormal families express high rates of system disintegrating by means of defensive communications, while normal families express more system integrating, or supportive communications. Performance of discussion and resolution-of-differences tasks were videotaped with twenty-two normal and twenty delinquent families to gather information about the processes through which some families adapt to stress and others disintegrate.

Alexander, J. F., Barton, C., Schiaro, R. S., and Parsons, B. V. "Systems-Behavioral Intervention with Families of Delinquents: Therapist Characteristics, Family Behavior, and Outcome." *Journal of Consulting and Clinical Psychology*, 1976, *44*(4), 656–664.

A short-term systems-behavioral model of family intervention was used to evaluate therapist characteristics, therapist process, and family process. Twenty-one families with delinquents participated in the program. Therapists were trained to modify family communication patterns and interaction sequences by modeling, prompting, and reinforcing clear communication of substance as well as feelings. Alternative solutions were clearly defined. Good and poor outcomes of therapy were defined as the family's staying in therapy or leaving. The therapist's relationship skills were found to have a significant effect on the outcome when they were displayed within a well-structured therapeutic agenda and operational framework.

Alexander, J. F., and Parsons, B. V. "Short-Term Behavioral Intervention with Delinquent Families: Impact on Family Process and Recidivism." *Journal of Abnormal Psychology,* 1973, *81,* 219-225.

The authors' program for delinquent adolescents consists of a specific short-term behaviorally oriented family approach. The goals of the program include an increase in family reciprocity, clarity of communication, and contingency contracting. Their results show a reduction in recidivism that is statistically and economically significant. Specific therapist interventions were noted to change family interaction patterns, while nonspecific interventions did not. Families that showed no changes in interaction also demonstrated no reduction in recidivism.

Austin, K. M., and Speidel, F. R. "Thunder: An Alternative to Juvenile Court Appearance." *California Youth Authority Quarterly,* 1972, *24,* 13-16.

An alternative to the probation department's standard procedure for juvenile court processing is proposed in this paper. The authors note that many of the juveniles brought before the court are not criminally oriented, but come from families that had lost control and were unable to deal with their children. They also point out that going to court entails a delay and these young people need immediate support and guidance. The specific objectives of Project Thunder were to: initiate crisis treatment, enhance communication and interaction between child and parents, support family strengths and reinforce the parents' roles as parents, reduce court calendars, and reduce probation officer workload. This intensive treatment program utilized short-term family group counseling. The outcome of the pilot study suggests that for delinquents group treatment techniques can be as effective as the traditional individual casework approach.

Barton, C., and Alexander, J. F. "The Effects of Competitive and Cooperative Set on Normal and Delinquent Families." Paper presented at the annual meeting of the American Psychological Association, New York, September 1979.

Thirty-two families participated in the study, half of whom had a delinquent adolescent. Parent-adolescent triads took part in an interaction-producing game under both conditions of a competitive and cooperative set instruction. The findings confirm the results of past studies showing that delinquent families interact less adaptively than normal families, and that interacting social units communicate more effectively in cooperative tasks. In addition, the study shows that delinquent families can significantly improve the qualities of their communication through use of cooperative set manipulation.

Foster, R. M. "A Basic Strategy for Family Therapy with Children." *American Journal of Psychotherapy*, 1973, *17*, 437–445.

The author outlines four steps in formulating a strategy for family therapy when a child is the identified patient. (1) Elicit and explore the parents' goals. (2) Explore in great detail parental views about what has led to the problem behavior. (3) Explore what the parents have done to encourage their child to change his behavior. The author notes, "Their corrective measures usually betray their ideas about the origin of the behavior; for example, if parents respond that they have tried to spend more time with him, further inquiry will reveal their view that his behavior resulted from some deprivation of contacts with them." (4) Arrange a confrontation during which the therapist notes that although the parents have done several things to encourage their child to change, these have not included *telling* the child to change. The therapist should then discuss the specific problem behavior and specific techniques and identify himself as available to help the parents to get their child to change his behavior. The unannounced goal is to demonstrate to the parents that they can and do direct their child's behavior. When the parents' conception of their child changes, their communication to the child changes.

Gruher, M. "Family Counseling and the Status Offender." *Juvenile and Family Court Journal,* February 1979, pp. 23–29.

The sample in this study consisted of an experimental group of fifty-four status offenders who received family counseling and a control group of seventy status offenders who received other dispositions. The results do not confirm the hypothesis that family counseling for status offenders results in fewer subsequent referrals; although there was a trend in the direction predicted, it was not statistically significant. The author suggests that family counseling is more effective for the younger male status offender who lives in an urban area, is referred for an offense other than runaway, and is not referred by a law enforcement agency.

Hampshire, P. A. J. "Family Therapy with Lower Socioeconomic Juvenile Offenders: Engagement and Outcome." *Dissertation Abstracts International,* 1981, *41* (7).

The author evaluates an engagement effort whose purpose was to increase attendance at family therapy sessions by forty-one lower-class juvenile delinquents and their families who were considered to be at high-risk for early termination. Over a two-month period, home visits, phone contact, appointment flexibility, agency interfacing, and individual meetings were used. The resulting increase in attendance at family sessions was attributed to changes in the family's perceptions of its own environment.

Johnson, T. F. "A Contextual Approach to Treatment of Juvenile Offenders." *Offender Rehabilitation,* 1978, *3,* 171–179.

The author asserts that a primary obstacle to helping juvenile delinquents is that they continue to be involved with their dysfunctional families. If the young person is physically separated from his or her family, the situation is modified but not eliminated. Thus the author recommends a therapy that takes into consideration the involuntary nature of the participation. The therapist is advised to accept the family definition of the problem and to design approaches concerned with the problems presented. For example, if the family presents a juvenile as disobedient, the task is to find ways to get the juvenile to obey. The therapy should include those family members who live together and should focus on getting family members to work on tasks to improve family functioning. Direct intervention in changing the behavior starts in therapy sessions. If the juvenile is rude during the session, the parents are instructed to handle the situation at that moment. Families should also be shown ways of conducting more appropriate interactions.

Johnson, T. F. "The Results of Family Therapy with Juvenile Offenders." *Juvenile Justice*, 1977, *28*, 29-33.

The study involves a comparison of juvenile delinquents who participated in family therapy and those who participated in casework-oriented probation with a range of auxiliary and allied services. Family therapy was found to have a strong effect on the continuation of delinquent behavior. During the first year of treatment there were no significant differences between the two groups; however, in the second year, the probation group showed increased delinquent activity, while the family therapy group did not. Thus long-term benefits were gained from family therapy as an intervention to modify delinquent behavior.

Kempler, W. "Experiential Family Therapy." *The International Journal of Group Psychotherapy*, 1965, *15*, 133-145.

Experiential family therapy is viewed as particularly applicable to individuals who are captive to family, either due to age (children) or inclination (adults who identify their problems as interpersonal). This approach has also been used successfully with individuals, couples, and groups whose needs have not been so apparent. The experiential family approach includes exploration, experimentation, and spontaneity. The underlying assumption is that within an accepted setting, the family members and the therapist have needs that will emerge. Such needs may be expressed in changes of posture, gestures, or even fantasies that are not conveyed to the group. Three principles govern the discussion: no interrupting, no questions, no gossip. The author's case example concerns the family of an adolescent female who showed signs of becoming a juvenile delinquent. All family members were asked to attend the first session. At the beginning of this session, the mother kept prodding her daughter to tell the doctor what had happened, but the daughter refused. After several attempts, the therapist remarked that the mother was trying to get the daughter to talk when she was apparently unwilling to reveal herself, that her repeated questioning precluded her direct involvement. Through the process of focusing on the "here and now," the family was able to develop new patterns of communication and was therefore better able to resolve difficulties.

7

Drug Abuse

Current work with drug abusers often focuses on the role of the family in the creation of the symptom, as well as in its maintenance. Many authors note a relationship between the symptom of drug abuse and the homeostasis of the family. It is hypothesized that when the family system is off balance a symptom such as drug abuse in a member is likely to emerge. If the person's abuse of drugs is assimilated into the family equilibrium, other members may sabotage treatment; thus treatment involving the entire family is often recommended. Structural, systems, and multifamily therapy approaches are among those advocated to eliminate the drug abusing behavior. Among the topics reviewed in this chapter are the influence of sibling roles in the treatment procedure, the identification and development of family loyalties, and the advantages of behavioral contracting between parents and their children. The nature of drug abuse requires that the therapist be available to families to lend support if crises arise.

Drug Abuse: Observations
of Family Functioning

AUTHOR: Robert J. Noone

PRECIS: Behavior patterns in drug-abusing individuals and their families.

INTRODUCTION: The author's description of drug abusers' behavior patterns is based on seven years' work with families of drug abusers. There are more similarities than differences in the behavior of these families compared to other families.

OBSERVATIONS: Noone offers seven principal observations.

"The abuse of drugs by an individual is directly related to the emotional process of that individual's family." A review of the literature reveals a consistent finding that the family is central to the development and maintenance of a drug-abuse problem.

"Changes in drug-abuse behavior are generally indicative of changes in the family emotional process." As a system, the family strives to maintain homeostasis. When the balance in a family is thrown off, a symptom such as drug abuse is likely to emerge. The author refers to Murray Bowen's* observation that the intensity and duration of anxiety and the degree of differentiation of family members are two of the main determinants of how the symptoms show themselves. For example, a family whose members have a relatively low level of differentiation but who have ongoing relationships with extended family members possesses a greater capacity to adapt to an increase in anxiety and is less inclined to develop symptoms than a family more differentiated but less involved in an extended family. Noone also discusses the relationship between nodal events (deaths, marriages, divorces, births) in the family and drug-abuse behavior. In the study of 500 families, drug-abuse behavior and changes in

*M. Bowen, "Theory in the Practice of Psychotherapy," in P. Guerin (Ed.), *Family Therapy: Theory and Practice* (New York: Gardner Press, 1976).

the family's homeostasis were consistently correlated for both acute and chronic drug cases.

"Drug abuse serves as an adaption mechanism for the individual and the family." Although a serious drug-abuse incident may greatly upset family members, it also seems to serve as a stabilizing force for the family. In times of acute upset, the abuse of drugs can serve as a concrete cause for the increase in anxiety felt within the family. By focusing on the drug-abusing member, the family relieves anxiety in other relationships within the family system.

"The presenting problem of drug abuse is generally indicative of the family projection process." At the clinic where the author worked, the average age of drug abusers seen was twenty-five. The majority of these individuals, even those who were married, lived with their parents. Noone notes that "the great difficulty drug abusers seem to have in separating from the parental home is evidence, I think, of how important the adaptive mechanism of the family projection process is for the ongoing functioning of the nuclear family."

"Drug abuse generally serves as a distancing mechanism in response to the anxiety generated by increased fusion." Family members constantly seek a balance between closeness and distance. Too much togetherness causes family members to become stuck; too much distance produces a sense of isolation between family members. In general, families of drug abusers are characterized by too much closeness. In fact, the abuse of drugs seems to emerge and intensify during those times when pressures for autonomy are at their strongest in a family. Once drug use becomes incorporated into the family's ongoing equilibrium, the cessation of drug use can severely disrupt the family balance.

"Drug abuse generally is seen in highly cohesive families which have traditionally utilized intrapsychic distancing mechanisms." The distancing mechanisms in drug abusing families are usually intrapsychic. Frequently the drug abuser is from a very cohesive family, but his or her parents had little contact with their families of origin, usually due to immigration.

"A decrease in chronic drug-abuse behavior by an individual will be disruptive to a family's equilibrium and result in an increase in anxiety." When the chronic drug abuser serves as a stabilizing force within the family, the decision to stop using drugs raises the anxiety level of the family. In some cases, the drug abuser reacts by returning to drugs; although family members may object to this, the anxiety level decreases. If the individual does not return to drug use, reactions within the family may include another sibling showing dysfunction, increasing conflict between parents or between a parent and grandparent, or one of the parents showing dysfunction. The pattern observed most often was that the overinvolved parent became depressed. The author finds it useful to predict such a reaction to a family and to suggest that it may indicate movement in the right direction.

COMMENTARY: Noone's observations about families of drug abusers provide other therapists reference points in their treatment of such cases. An understanding of these patterns can help the therapist formulate treatment interventions and analyze the family process.

SOURCE: Noone, R. J. "Observations on Drug Abuse and the Family." *The Family,* 1981, *9,* 46–52.

Treatment Based on the Link Between Family Loyalties and Drug Abuse

AUTHORS: Robert J. Noone and Robert L. Reddig

PRECIS: Treating drug abusers by acknowledging family loyalties and assisting family members in the positive expression of these loyalties.

INTRODUCTION: The authors' working premise is that drug

abuse reflects problems in the family system rather than an individual aberration. One important finding is that drug abusers generally maintain close ties with their families; thus all family members should be encouraged to participate in treatment from the beginning and it is critical to bring the family into treatment when the anxiety created by the drug abuse is high. Another finding is that the frequently destructive behavior of the drug abuser brings family loyalties to the fore. In treating these clients, the authors discovered that the families were experiencing difficulty moving beyond the phase of the life cycle when the children become independent of their parents. Among the implications of this difficulty is that the family views the drugs —and not the anxiety of impending independence—as the problem.

CASE STUDY: In the case illustrated, drug abuse was a mechanism for keeping the R family from dealing with more threatening problems. Fifteen-year-old Paul had been using and selling drugs, which resulted in his suspension from school. In response to his mother's request for intervention, the therapist requested the entire family to come in for an interview. The family constellation included Paul's parents and his three older sisters, two of whom were living away from home. During the initial stage of treatment, it was discovered that Mrs. R had been suffering from cancer for several years, but the topic had not been openly discussed within the family. The mother's illness resulted in the other family members feeling threatened for different reasons. Paul's needs for care and protection were in jeopardy, as his mother was the primary person who fulfilled these needs. During the interviews an intricate pattern of family loyalties emerged. Mrs. R was able to get her mind off her illness by focusing on Paul's problems, and this focus was reinforced by Paul, who gained more of his mother's attention through negative behaviors. Mr. R blamed his son for the upset in the family, rather than looking at his wife's illness and his own physical problems. At the same time, Paul's sisters focused on his problems instead of making decisions about their own lives. The authors assert, "Effective treatment for Paul's drug problem began when the therapist uncovered this complex pattern of loyalties within the R family and viewed Paul's behavior as a significant, though partial, expression of family bonds."

Treatment was approached by placing Paul's drug-abuse problem in the context of the impending losses of all the family members. As each member learned to grieve together, Paul's problems lessened. The therapeutic process aided the family in communicating feelings of pain and warmth, and resulted in the family regaining some stability.

COMMENTARY: This approach to drug abuse requires that the therapist affirm family loyalties and encourage the positive expression of these loyalties. Typical problems that need to be expressed are the resolution of grief that has built up over many generations or the resolution of separation anxiety. To uncover the pattern of loyalties within the family, the therapist needs a working knowledge of how the family system operates to maintain homeostasis. In addition, the therapist should involve all the family members in the process, as each member participates in maintaining the family equilibrium.

SOURCE: Noone, R. J., and Reddig, R. L. "Case Studies in the Family Treatment of Drug Abuse." *Family Process,* 1976, *15,* 325–332.

The Influence of the Sibling Subsystem in Adolescent Drug Abuse

AUTHOR: Martha Cleveland

PRECIS: Intervention with families of drug-abusing adolescents emphasizing structural analysis of sibling roles.

INTRODUCTION: Cleveland asserts that despite voluminous research into the relationship between parents and drug-abusing children, there has been little investigation into the role played by the siblings. She defines three general sibling roles and relates these roles to the family structure in drug-abusing families. A *parental child* is usually an older child who assumes a position of decision maker in regard to his drug-abusing sibling. A *good child* is the member of the family who exemplifies the overtly stated values of the family. One child may assume both the "parental" and "good" rules, but generally there is only one "good child" in a family. This role serves to make the family look successful to the outside world. The *symptomatic child* displays uncontrollable behavior that is characterized as either "sick" or "bad." Often a major marital conflict is detoured through this child.

TREATMENT STRATEGIES: If the family does not have a parental child, the treatment focuses on the difficulties in dominance-submission and closeness-distance between the parents and their symptomatic adolescent. Once changes start to occur in the behavior of the symptomatic child, the focus of treatment shifts to difficulties of dominance-submission and closeness-distance in the marital relationship. This shift in focus should not be made too quickly; premature timing may lead the family to terminate therapy. Concurrent sessions with the parents only are used to strengthen generational boundaries and provide an opportunity for discussing the couple's personal issues. As conflict between the couple usually increases during the beginning stages of marital treatment, the children, especially the symptomatic child, may fall into old behavior patterns. By seeing the couple and the family unit concurrently, the therapist can help the family separate the parent-child conflicts from those between husband and wife. The therapist helps the overinvolved parent to step back and encourages the less-involved parent to become more involved. They are helped to support each other in deciding on rules and carrying them out. Overall, the dominance-submission issues between parent (especially the less-involved one) and child are more difficult to resolve than the closeness-distance issues, in part because the former has implications about equality which dominating parents are uneasy in allotting to their adolescent sons and daughters.

Greater skill and more complex intervention are required in therapy with a family that has a parental child. The structure of such a family is a matched pair of strong coalitions, and members object to unbalancing this structure. The therapist seeks to remove the parental child from his or her position and then works with the husband-wife and parental child-symptomatic child relationships. Separate meetings with the parental child and symptomatic sibling may be very helpful, providing an opportunity to deal with the difficult issues of sibling rivalry without the parents being present and, at the same time, enabling the siblings to establish a more positive relationship.

COMMENTARY: Identifying sibling roles and relating them to the family structure conceptually broadens the treatment process of drug-abusing adolescents. Cleveland hypothesizes that treatment will be more effective if sibling roles are taken into consideration when planning treatment strategies. Her techniques require the therapist to be aware of appropriate timing, especially in shifting the focus from the symptomatic child's behavior to the marital relationship. The author recommends further investigation into her hypothesis as the data reported concern a small sample during a one-year period.

SOURCE: Cleveland, M. "Families and Adolescent Drug Abuse: Structural Analysis of Children's Roles." *Family Process,* 1981, *20,* 295–303.

Drug Abuse as an Outcome of a Family
Curse: Implications for Treatment

AUTHOR: James B. Raybin

PRECIS: Viewing the curse in relation to family communication and considering a family treatment approach.

INTRODUCTION: According to Raybin, a family curse is an expression of a wish that some harm will come to a member. The effect of myths and curses in a family can be understood by observing the amount of time and energy exerted by every family member in continuing the myth. Often the curses or prophecies span several generations and are passed down in quite complicated ways. Therapists should be aware that any challenge to a family's myth could unbalance the family equilibrium.

TREATMENT METHOD: Many authors observe that often only one member of a disturbed family group may seek help at a clinic or other facility. This person may have become the scapegoat or "sacrificial lamb" for the whole family. During interviews, family members might state that the one member had been identified for years as the "crazy one." Through these statements, the therapist is able to uncover complicated irrational beliefs and myths.

One of the case studies reported by Raybin involved Alice A, a twenty-year-old young woman who had been abusing drugs and behaving promiscuously. She was described as brilliant and well-liked until her senior year in high school, when these social problems developed. According to Alice's parents, her change in behavior came as a complete surprise to relatives, friends, and teachers. Two other daughters, ages eighteen and twelve, were described as wonderful, responsible children.

Many months of therapy with Alice and her family revealed some significant background events. For the past eight years, Alice had been identified by her mother as the "bad seed" in the family. This curse, or prophecy, was quite complicated and seemed to have been stimulated by Alice's emerging puberty. Mrs. A frequently told Alice that she was a bad child who would soon start to smoke and drink, and then become promiscuous, a drug addict, a criminal, and finally either commit suicide or become a chronic psychiatric patient.

Although Mrs. A discussed the curse from the time Alice was twelve, not until she turned eighteen did she start to display the predicted behaviors. Over a two-year period, Alice had accomplished all the "bad things" in the curse with the exception of committing suicide or becoming hospitalized. The aim of the psychotherapy was to help Alice to break away from her family and to show her that she had a choice in fulfilling the curse or not.

An analysis of the origin of the curse indicated that Alice's maternal grandmother had repeatedly given Mrs. A the message that she would someday get in trouble with a man. This was fulfilled by Mrs. A's becoming pregnant with Alice prior to marriage. Even before Alice was born, her grandmother predicted her gender and stated that she would turn out to be "rotten" like her mother. During the course of treatment, the participation of the other family members in the myth was identified. No one was either willing or able to challenge the curse. Alice's sisters felt the situation was awful and the father remained passive. Both the mother and grandmother assumed an "I told you so" attitude. Alice at first had not believed her mother's predictions, but as time went on she felt that her mother was right. Alice expressed the belief that she was bad and dirty and had no control over her own destiny. During the therapeutic process, her attitude toward herself changed.

COMMENTARY: The author comments that had Alice not been identified as the "bad seed" her mother's emotional status and the well-being of her siblings might have been at risk. The family therapy approach enabled the other members to relinquish the faith they had in the myth. In its place, a rational and adaptive adjustment was established.

Some guidelines for therapists are offered. If a family or individual seeks help when the resolution of the mythology seems impossible, the goal in treatment is to separate family members. If family mythology becomes apparent during therapy, the therapist should at an appropriate time begin to explore the complicated dynamics of the curse or myth.

Raybin stresses that the resistance within a family to giving up a myth can be tremendous, that the curse, as a specific type of family mythology, is very difficult to change. More extensive work with families having an operant myth may bring to light other effective strategies.

SOURCE: Raybin, J. B. "The Curse: A Study in Family Communication." *American Journal of Psychiatry,* 1970, *127* (5), 617–625.

A Behavioral Approach with Families of Drug-Abusing Adolescents

AUTHOR: John R. Cassady

PRECIS: Contracts between parents and adolescents are the basis for treatment of drug abuse.

INTRODUCTION: Cassady presents the results of a pilot study with drug-abusing adolescents in which their natural environment was used in the treatment process. A review of families with this problem revealed that parents tend to rely on social and physical punishment of their children rather than positive reinforcement, and the adolescent then seeks to escape this pattern through drug abuse. The pilot study had three objectives: parents and their children were to negotiate contracts that provide for positive reinforcers for appropriate behaviors; parents were to be trained in behavioral techniques to control their children's behavior, thus enabling them to serve as therapists to their children; all socially unacceptable behaviors (drug use, truancy, crimes) were to be eliminated.

TREATMENT METHOD: The hypothesis of the pilot study was that "if one could extinguish deviant behavior and at the same time shape in desirable behaviors incompatible with drug and alcohol use, then the use of mood-altering substances would decrease or even extinguish." The study included eight adolescents from the juvenile division of the Orange County Circuit Court, who participated in the project as part of their probation. Each adolescent had a history of extensive drug use, but was not physically addicted to the drug. Also, each had more than one arrest and conviction, and a somewhat intact family.

Right after their appearance in court, the adolescent and his or her parents were interviewed for a complete social history. The following day the family was seen at an out-patient clinic, and the adolescent was given the Thorp and Wetzel "M-R Incomplete Blank." From the responses, a hierarchy of reinforcers was determined and information on which punishments elicited rebellious behavior was gathered. At the same session, the parents were asked about the punishments they were using and their effectiveness, and the positive reinforcers they were using and their effectiveness. The parents were also asked about available positive reinforcers and the behaviors they would like their child to extinguish and those they would like him to acquire.

The goal of the next day's session was the negotiation of a contract between parents and adolescent with the counselor as mediator. The information gathered the previous day provided the basis for target behaviors to be extinguished or acquired by both parties. The reinforcing contingencies were established based on the "M-R Incomplete Blank," and the hierarchy of behaviors to be acquired from the parent interview. For instance, if a parent thought that a curfew was of the highest priority, then a contingency for being at home on time might gain points toward a motorcycle. In similar fashion, each behavior was matched with a contingency. This method was also used for extinguishing behaviors. Every time a parent gave a reinforcer, he or she was instructed to back it up with social reinforcement. A behavioral checklist was devised, and each time a contracted behavior occurred the parent was to check it off. If an adolescent received, for instance, 45 out of 50 checkmarks (90 percent) during a one-month period and had no negative legal contracts, a letter acknowledging his cooperation and progress was sent to his probation officer. In some cases, the contract included changes in the parents' behavior and the adolescent kept a checklist on his parents' progress.

Contracts followed a legal format and were signed by all parties. The family and the counselor met weekly to review the checklist and note any progress. The parents were given a copy of *Living with Children** and met once a week in a group to discuss relevant issues. During the week the counselor phoned the family to check on their progress, and family members were praised when positive changes occurred.

TREATMENT RESULTS: The average duration of treatment was eight and a half months. Five of the eight participants successfully completed treatment. Follow-ups made at three, six, and nine months revealed continued progress. Each of the five adolescents was living at home and was attending school or was employed. None had been arrested, and verbal reports stated that none was abusing drugs.

COMMENTARY: The author's evaluation of the successes and failures of this behavioral program notes that some young people do not respond to socially acceptable reinforcers and thus require other forms of treatment. Younger adolescents responded more positively to the program, while many older adolescents did not respond to conventional reinforcers or had learned to get reinforcers by illegal means. These findings give impetus to therapists, and the community in general, to intervene with families of drug-abusing adolescents at the earliest possible time and to give family members clear guidelines. That these young people responded positively without further legal action made for a cost-effective program.

SOURCE: Cassady, J. R. "The Use of Parents and Contract

*G. R. Patterson and M. E. Gullion, *Living with Children: New Methods for Parents and Teachers* (Champaign, Ill.: Research Press, 1971).

Therapy in Rehabilitating Delinquent Adolescents Involved in Drug and Alcohol Abuse." Paper presented at the 26th annual meeting of the Alcohol and Drug Problems Association of North America, Orlando, Florida, 1975.

Additional Readings

Alexander, B. K., and Dibb, G. S. "Interpersonal Perception in Addict Families." *Family Process,* 1977, *16,* 17–28.

This study used an "interperception matrix" technique to compare interpersonal perceptions in eight families in which the addicted young adults maintained close ties with their parents, and eight matched control families. The study focuses on the relationship between the addict and his or her parents, and the authors report that the parents overindulged the addict and did not help the addict to acquire the skills necessary for independence. Five families were seen individually and thirteen in groups of families. The majority of families participated in five to eight sessions of one to three hours. Some families were involved in as many as thirty sessions. In concluding, the authors note that prior to addiction, the addict appeared to serve as a stabilizing force in the addict family, and addiction seemed to perpetuate this function. Family therapists need to develop methods that are powerful and subtle enough to change families in which resistance is high, in which the connection between the symptom and family process is easily denied and there is a great need for intervention.

Bartlett, D. "The Use of Multiple-Family Therapy Groups with Adolescent Drug Addicts." In M. Sugar (Ed.), *The Adolescent in Group and Family Therapy.* New York: Brunner/ Mazel, 1975.

Multiple-family therapy was established for large groups of schizophrenics in a state hospital, and positive results were noted within a short period of time. Family conflicts were noted to be reproduced with less anxiety in the presence of other families than in individual family sessions. The author proposes that this method of treatment is appropriate in rehabilitating drug addicts as it could be used with large numbers, meet goals within a short period of time, and require a small staff of therapists. This form of therapy was used with a detoxification group, a parent couples group, and an addicted couples group. Limited time hampered the results in the detoxification group. The major stumbling block in the parent couples group was the adolescent's independence and separation from the family while in residential treatment. This feeling of independence combined with the parents' negation of that independence made a smooth reentry into the family extremely difficult. In the addicted couples group indignation of the spouses' families and the couples' sexual difficulties were the main adversities.

Bratter, T. E. "Helping Affluent Families Help Their Acting-Out Alienated Drug-Abusing Adolescent." *Journal of Family Counseling*, 1974, 2, 22–31.

The author cites background research on affluent families and drug abuse, examines methods for treating the affluent acting-out drug abuser through his family, and outlines the implications, traps, and pitfalls the therapist may encounter. Problems in enlisting the family's participation are explained in depth, as well as the common reactions of the parents and adolescents. A rationale and method to counter many of the negative situations that might arise are discussed. Upon establishing a relationship with the family, the therapist uses approaches to strengthen family ties. The many pitfalls of this process are explained; for instance, the affluent family may attempt to prolong the symbiotic relationship beyond the appropriate time. The author emphasizes that through the therapist's relationship with the acting-out, drug-abusing adolescent, goals can be formulated that reflect what is best for that individual.

Bratter, T. E. "Wealthy Families and Their Drug-Abusing Adolescents." *Journal of Family Counseling*, 1975, 3, 62–76.

This article is a clinical sequel to the preceding theoretically oriented paper. Four affluent families are described. These case studies illustrate a family member's ability to manipulate the therapist and the therapeutic process. In the first case, the therapist asked an adolescent drug-abuser to relinquish his driver's license. The boy agreed, but the father became extremely upset, arguing that he paid the insurance premiums and his son had a right to drive. This family was noted as rewarding self-destructive and dangerous behavior. The second family consisted of a father who spent all his time attending to his business, a mother who was totally engrossed in her social activities, and a barbiturate-addicted daughter. The parents showed little concern for their daughter or her problems; the therapist vainly attempted to bring the parents closer to their daughter, but after absolutely no progress she left home. Here the author emphasizes the merits of the therapy even when the initial goal is not accomplished. For the daughter proceeded to lead her own life, pursue a college degree, and marry; the therapist had helped her gain the strength to leave her pathological family instead of remaining in a no-win situation. The third case was characterized by the parents' inability to set limits for their addicted son. The therapist outlined a definitive treatment plan, but the parents were unable to comply. Finally, the son became drug-free by following the limits set by the therapist. In the fourth case study, an adolescent male was making progress in fighting his drug problem when his mother attempted to stop the therapy sessions. She attacked the therapist's competence and credentials, but then inquired about therapy for herself. The therapist said it was possible to treat only the adolescent. Through the therapist's taking a stand with the mother and consistently counseling the son, the adolescent became drug-free and acting out with his parents ceased. In all these cases, the therapist focused on his relationship with and responsibility to the adolescent. But Bratter points out that this method can be difficult to implement given the tendency of affluent parents to upset the relationship and negatively manipulate the therapeutic process.

Coleman, S. B., and Stanton, M. D. "The Role of Death in the Addict Family." *Journal of Marriage and Family Counseling,* 1978, *4,* 79-91.

In contrast to the traditional view of death as the cessation of life, the authors define the contemporary view that the death of a family member is not an isolated occurrence and that the dead family member has a distinct continuing role in the future of the family. This study focuses on how an addict's death affects the family. The authors note that addicts' families are of particular interest because drug abuse is a life-threatening behavior and the addicted family member is a premature slow-death victim. Also, families who experience a death caused by addiction have a greater propensity for future non–drug-related premature deaths. This article discusses family dynamics, some strategies for treatment, and a case example that unites theory and technique.

Everett, C. A. "Family Assessment and Intervention for Early Adolescent Problems." *Journal of Marriage and Family Counseling,* 1976, *2,* 155–165.

The author presents a clinical assessment model for initiating treatment with early adolescents and their parents. The approach consists of conjoint treatment using two therapists, one of whom works with the adolescent and the other with the parents. The first and second sessions require separation of the adolescent and the parents with the individual therapists. The third, fourth, and follow-up sessions involve the parents, adolescent, and both therapists. After these conjoint meetings, the therapists collaborate to direct future sessions. The author's case study involves a fourteen-year-old female drug abuser and her parents. The daughter totally dominated the first conjoint session. During the first collaborative meeting, the therapist discussed this and decided that the second conjoint session should focus on the issue of parental control and the daughter's reentry into the new family structure. As anticipated, the daughter dominated the second session. Toward the end of the second session, the parents' therapist identified this situation and asked the daughter to leave the session with her therapist. The parents met with their therapist for about four months, learning to implement firmer controls and planning for the daughter's reentry into the family. At the same time, the daughter met with her therapist. She became drug-free and responded to her parents' firmer guidelines and clearer expectations. The effectiveness of this treatment model was evaluated in fifty cases over a two-year period.

Haley, J. "The Process of Therapy: A Heroin Problem." In J. Haley, *Leaving Home: The Therapy of Disturbed Young People*. New York: McGraw-Hill, 1980.

The author describes a case in which intervention placed the father in charge of his addicted son at the first stage of therapy, the goal being to disengage the mother from her son. The son had been a heroin addict for five years and had recently been involved in a methadone program. By the end of the first interview, the therapeutic plan was in operation: the father was to deal directly with the son and the mother to deal with the father about the son's problems. The therapist had to be ready to handle the predictable increase in marital tension and the son's relapse to save the parents. The second stage of therapy was brought about by the therapist shifting the focus to the parents' marriage. He persuaded the parents that they would eventually have to accept their son's independence and face the problems in their marriage. Subsequent interviews focused on the young man's job, school, and disengagement from his parents. Therapy lasted a few months, at the end of which the son moved out. The therapist kept contact with the family over the next few years and after a few living adjustments by the three family members, the son remained drug-free, had a responsible job, and had moved to another state. Haley concludes that in working with drug addicts, once one discovers that heroin addicts are enmeshed in their families, it becomes apparent that the therapeutic approach should involve those families.

Harbin, H. T., and Maziar, H. M. "The Families of Drug Abusers: A Literature Review." *Family Process*, 1975, *14*, 411–431.

This review explores all available literature on the background of drug abusers. The authors note that treatment of drug abusers through family therapy has been slow to develop and research is even slower. This critical review of the literature is intended to enable future researchers and financial backers of research to determine more effectively the merits of proposed studies on families of drug abusers.

Kaufman, P. "Family Therapy with Adolescent Substance Abusers." In E. Kaufman (Ed.), *Family Therapy of Drug and Alcohol Abuse*. New York: Gardner Press, 1979.

    A special therapy program for adolescent substance abusers, which involved the entire family in the therapy, is discussed and illustrated by a case history. Kaufman suggests that the Step One of the Phoenix Programs might be a good model for the successful education of troubled adolescents from large urban environments. Some features of the program include small institutions; twenty students to a class in a school that is open from 9:00 A.M. to 6:00 P.M., with the nonschool hours filled with group activities; a comprehensive recreation program, and evening sessions in which parents and children participate in family therapy and family educational sessions.

Part Two

Emotional
Disorders

The problems of children and adolescents pose a dual task for the therapist: therapeutic intervention must attend to the immediate problems and symptomatic complaints, and treatment must also take into account the youngsters' developmental stages and abilities. "Psychopathology in children differs from adult psychopathology because of the overwhelming significance of the developmental process for all aspects of child behavior, normal or pathological" (T. M. Achenbach, *Developmental Psychopathology* [New York: Wiley, 1974], p. 3). The developmental process demands that treatment for children differ from treatment for adults. The family therapist, treating both children and adults, must be aware of these differences and the implications of the children's developmental stages.

167

Furthermore, pressures and problems within the home environment compound the developmental tasks and demands.

This part opens with a chapter on psychosomatic disorders. Our understanding of the relationship between psychological and physiological aspects of individuals' functioning has steadily improved during the last forty years. One way of conceptualizing a child's psychosomatic illness is as a circular process wherein family members respond to the symptomatic child in a characteristic way that reinforces and maintains the pattern. The forms of psychosomatic illness discussed in Chapter Eight include asthma, abdominal pain, ulcerative colitis, migraine, and failure-to-thrive; the treatment methods are addressed to the needs of infants, young children, and young adults. The family therapy approaches recommended include structural family therapy, behavior modification, systems family therapy, and a strategic approach. In some cases, depending on the disorder and particular family situation, combinations of these approaches may be the recommended course of treatment.

Chapters Nine through Fifteen concern seven categories of common disorders of childhood. Diverse in regard to symptom expression, all these disorders have adverse effects on a child's growth and development. While these disorders are not new, public awareness of their prevalence and severity has recently become more widespread, in part because, tragically, childhood suicide is more prevalent today.

A specific form of psychosomatic illness, anorexia nervosa, is the topic of Chapter Nine. Identification of the syndrome was noted as early as the seventeenth century, and in recent years it has been the subject of numerous studies. Anorexia nervosa can be defined as a process of self-starvation. This often life-threatening illness may occur in children as young as nine or ten, or in adults in their twenties, thirties, or forties. Because anorexia nervosa can prove fatal, the treatment plan must be carefully devised and quickly implemented. Forms of treatment discussed in this chapter include structural family therapy and family systems therapy, which is sometimes supplemented with operant reinforcement and combinations of insight, structural, and strategic approaches.

Chapter Ten addresses school phobia, which is quite often accompanied by psychosomatic symptoms. The symptom of school phobia is viewed as a sign of breakdown in the equilibrium of the family. A fear of separation from a significant person, rather than a fear of school, is a common feature of this disorder. Historically, school phobia was first thought to be a problem exclusively within the child, then a symptom of problems in the mother-child relationship, and more recently as a problem involving the entire family. Therapeutic approaches include a group-analytic approach to conjoint family therapy, multifamily therapy, and the restructuring of role functions within families; paradoxical techniques are also sometimes used with the families of school phobics.

Suicide (Chapter Eleven) is always a tragic phenomenon, but when it involves children and adolescents it is even more traumatic and poignant. The destruction of the unfulfilled potential and promise of youth carries a magnified burden of guilt and pain for the survivors, and the implications are far-reaching and frightening. Suicidal behavior is multidimensional and multidetermined. Family therapy may be an effective method for dealing with the multitude of factors involved in a child's suicide or attempted suicide. Family intervention is an approach in which the therapist enters into the suicidogenic family and attempts to alter the dysfunctional and debilitating family structure that fosters suicidal behaviors, thereby reducing the risk of further suicide attempts. When a child has committed suicide the therapist must help the family members resolve their individual and collective guilt. The grieving process must be allowed open expression, and family therapy should facilitate the communication of sadness and loss. Oftentimes, the therapist must intervene to halt the destructive perpetuation of guilt, blame (including self-blame), and anger that plagues the family members.

Schizophrenic disorder reactions (Chapter Twelve) result in severe, bizarre, and disabling symptoms. There are many theories about the etiology of this mysterious syndrome. Theories of single causation have now given way to the notion of multi-determination and the concept of a spectrum disorder. The extensive literature includes discussion of the schizophrenogenic family, the close and binding mother, the absent or distant father, the double-bind situation, severely disturbed styles of communication, and the implications of metacommunications. Similarly diverse, treatment approaches include individual, family, group, conjoint, and multiple-family programs that are dynamic, behavioral, cognitive, gestalt, or linguistically oriented, some of which involve community and helping services. Therapeutic intervention techniques for childhood schizophrenia are often multiple, sometimes at variance with each other, at other times collaborative and eclectic.

Chapter Thirteen is devoted to elective mutism, a relatively infrequent disorder in which the child is unable or refuses to communicate verbally with individuals outside the immediate family (parents and siblings) despite the fact that no organic, speech, or language deficits are in evidence. Usually these children will not even speak to grandparents or close members of the extended family. Elective mutism is accompanied by a complex of stresses and burdens upon the family, especially when the mute child reaches school age and the developmental phase during which he or she should be relating to persons beyond the immediate family, to teachers and peers and the like.

The subject of Chapter Fourteen is incontinence, a not infrequent disorder. Perhaps 20 percent of normal five- and six-year-olds exhibit enuresis (urinary incontinence during sleep) at some point, and about 3 percent of the children with this problem continue wetting their beds into their early twenties. Fortunately, the rate of spontaneous cure is relatively high. Encopresis (voluntary or involuntary defecation that results in soiled clothes) is far less common, with an overall incidence in the general population of about 1.5 percent. The problem of incontinence is usually related to a dysfunctional family system, and family-oriented intervention approaches that change family structural patterns reduce (or stop) the incidents.

Obsessive-compulsive disorders (Chapter Fifteen) refer to the persistent repetition of and preoccupation with irrational thoughts and actions. The child may use repeated actions or rituals to control or bind the anxiety related to the obsessive thoughts. These behaviors range from the mildly annoying to the seriously debilitating. They can interfere with the child's ability to function in school, relate to peers and family members, and cope with the stresses and demands of development. Often the child's obsessive-compulsive behavior serves some function within the family system. Family therapy is, then, the method of choice for revealing this functional element to family members and ameliorating the obsessive-compulsive behavior.

8

Psychosomatic
Disorders

Psychosomatic disorders include physical illnesses that can be
initiated, exacerbated, or prolonged by psychosocial factors.
Various forms of this disorder can afflict children beginning in
infancy. Interventions are conducted on many levels, namely,
intrapsychic, nuclear family, and extended multigeneration family. Some therapists advocate a combination of behavioral techniques and family therapy. A goal of behavioral techniques is to
aid the child in gaining mastery over the symptom. In school-
age children, an important aspect of treatment is the coordination of the medical, school, and family systems. During adolescence, when separation and individuation are developmental
objectives, the young person may be seen in individual as well as
family sessions. Particularly useful with families exhibiting

173

strong resistance is strategic family therapy, in which the therapeutic efforts are designed to produce change in families with symptomatic children by means of direct or paradoxical interventions.

A Family Orientation to the Treatment
of Childhood Psychosomatic Illness

AUTHORS: Salvador Minuchin and H. Charles Fishman

PRECIS: Alleviation of the psychosomatic symptom by working with the family to change patterns of interaction.

INTRODUCTION: One of the approaches described by the authors to treat psychosomatic illness is family-oriented therapy. The therapist examines the family system and specifies those interactions that established the behavior of family members in dysfunctional patterns and resulted in the child's psychosomatic symptoms. These psychosomatic symptoms are seen as the product of a circular system whereby the child responds to significant people with the symptoms and they react to him in a characteristic way that reinforces the symptoms. The authors note that, "it is the inherent circularity of this process of mutual affecting and reinforcing which maintains the fixed behavioral pattern in people who are viewed in this approach as imminently changeable."

TREATMENT METHOD: The authors present a case history to illustrate the family-oriented approach to a child's psychosomatic symptom. Members of the K family were the parents, their nine-year-old son Billy, and a five-year-old son. Billy, the identified patient, had breathing problems since the age of three and a half, but at age nine the asthmatic condition became severe. The symptoms required frequent treatment in emergency rooms and his daily living was difficult. Several changes had occurred within the family around the time that Billy's paternal grandfather died. Each member of the family, except the younger son, developed a psychosomatic or neurotic symptom. Of these, Billy's asthma was by far the most serious and required the greatest amount of intervention.

The focus of treatment with the K family was strengthening the boundaries around subsystems, namely the parental unit, the paternal grandmother with her contemporaries, and

Billy with his sibling and peers. Within the therapy sessions the parents were encouraged to resolve conflicts without involving a third party. The therapist suggested that they spend more time together pursuing common interests. At the same time, Billy was helped to assume more responsibility for his asthma. Through this process, he was able to depend more on himself and less on his parents, which in turn allowed them more time to relate to one another. A separate issue was pursued by the therapist with Mr. K. Following the death of his father, his mother became depressed and very dependent on him. The therapist encouraged Mr. K and the other family members to involve the grandmother in community groups so that she could build a wider social circle. Billy and his brother were instructed to support one another in staying out of parental conflicts and participating more with their peers.

TREATMENT RESULTS: Billy's asthmatic symptoms were alleviated within one month. He no longer needed emergency medical treatment and appeared to enjoy himself more as he did more things with his peers and brother.

At a follow-up contact with the family two and a half years later, it was reported that Billy no longer experienced true wheezing, although he did have infrequent episodes of shortness of breath. In his social life, Billy continued to be more independent, and his parents noted that they even had to punish him occasionally, which had not occurred before. Social and academic progress were both good. The parents noted an improvement in their relationship and the grandmother had made a better adjustment to widowhood.

COMMENTARY: Through placing the focus on the way in which the family members related to one another, rather than on the child and his symptom, the therapist achieved a successful outcome. After six months of weekly sessions, the family members were able to function in a much more satisfying way without the need of a psychosomatic symptom. The treatment described was cost effective, and the follow-up revealed its long-term positive results.

SOURCE: Minuchin, S., and Fishman, H. C. "The Psychosomatic Family in Child Psychiatry." *Journal of Child Psychiatry*, 1979, *18*, 76-90.

A Family Systems Approach to Treating Atypical Migraine

AUTHORS: Harvey A. Rosenstock and C. Glenn Cambor

PRECIS: The use of a family systems approach to alleviate the symptoms of incapacitating migraines.

INTRODUCTION: In a family system perspective the identified patient is seen as having a separate identity and simultaneously as an interacting member of a family. Over time, the family as a system has developed a model for communication. When the traditional method of interaction is threatened by an outside force or internal changes in its members, the family system either moves to preserve its homeostasis or to change.

CASE STUDY: Nine-year-old Corky had suffered for two years from migraine headaches and dizziness. During a period of hospitalization he had been given extensive tests and medical treatments, including a special diet, but none of these interventions produced positive results. Corky missed school for a whole month after going home and had to be rehospitalized.

Following a psychological evaluation, Corky was seen for several individual sessions. Corky then came to realize "that headaches would come on when teachers wouldn't slack off." When the family—parents, thirteen-year-old son, and Corky—was seen together a contract of six treatment goals was drawn up: to investigate the triggers for the headaches and determine if these could be reduced; to explore whether therapy would help Corky stay in school; to examine possible changes in the family's rules of interaction and transaction; to allow for more fun in the family; to allow for ventilation without retribution; and both to clarify the mother's role as a significant contributor to the family's interactions and to shift the focus from the father as the sole generator of family tension.

The therapist gave the family the assignment of determining rules about the expression of feelings, particularly anger. They answered that expressing anger meant breaking the family rules. A meeting with Corky and his father was set up, but prior to the session the therapist received a call that Corky was starting to get one of his headaches. Despite the emergence of the symptom, the therapist instructed the father and son to come together. The session began with Corky announcing that he had a very bad headache. He went on to talk about his father as being controlling, easily angered, noncompromising. According to the father, that role was one that had gone on for three generations in his own family. The father conjectured that he might be "locked in" to responding in an antagonistic way to his family. Following that admission Corky said he no longer had a headache.

At later sessions the mother was asked to look at ways she might be "locked in" to responding to her family. It was discovered that she saw Corky as violating a family tradition by expressing pain, and she was able to trace the origin of her response back to her own nuclear family.

The identification of interfamilial tensions was the focus of the family sessions during the next four months. During that phase of therapy some significant changes were noted in the family. Corky was more vocal about being asked to do more than his share around the house, while his mother became more involved in carrying her own load. The interaction between his parents changed and his mother would often say, "after years of marriage, I am speaking my own piece and I like it."

TREATMENT RESULTS: During the ten-month school year Corky did not have any migraines. His academic performance was satisfactory and he was not absent for somatic complaints. Peer relationships were reported to be good, and he became quite involved in sports.

The Sentence Completion Test, which had been administered before treatment, was readministered and the results were quite different. Corky's view of his parents was more positive, and he showed fewer hostile and aggressive responses toward his family.

Both parents continued in therapy for another ten months. The expression of negative feelings became much more accepted inside and outside the home. A follow-up, five years after treatment ended, revealed no recurrence of the migraine symptom.

COMMENTARY: The family systems treatment employed by the therapist addressed three areas: intrapsychic dynamics, the nuclear family, and the extended family over several generations. According to the authors, "The goals of therapy were also redefined for the family group: What had been regarded as the individual problems of one boy became a problem involving the entire family." The six goals that were defined and agreed upon were realized within the first ten months of treatment. An additional ten months of therapy for the parents helped to secure the changes that had taken place during the first phase of treatment. The long-lasting nature of the changes in the family was demonstrated by the five-year follow-up, which found the patient to be symptom-free.

SOURCE: Rosenstock, H. A., and Cambor, C. G. "Family Therapy Approach to Incapacitating Migraine." *International Journal of Family Therapy*, 1979, *1*, 46–55.

A Family Therapy Process for Treatment of Psychogenic Abdominal Pain

AUTHORS: Ronald Liebman, Paul Honig, and Henry Berger

PRECIS: The symptom of recurrent abdominal pain in children is alleviated using behavior modification techniques in conjunction with structural family therapy.

INTRODUCTION: The authors note that the combining of behavioral techniques and family therapy has been effective in treating such psychogenic illnesses as anorexia nervosa and asthma in children. The development and implementation of a successful program for recurrent abdominal pain is the focus of this paper.

TREATMENT METHOD: The ten families studied over a three-year period each had a child between the ages of six and fourteen who had recurrent abdominal pain for three to six months prior to treatment. Medical evaluations had shown negative results. While some of the children complained of pain before going to school, they all experienced pain at other times, indicating that the pain was not a form of school phobia.

The family therapist began the treatment process by interviewing the entire family and their pediatrician. The therapist and pediatrician worked as a team and instructed the parents to support each other in helping the child to gain control over the symptom. This emphasis on the parents' working together frequently served to uncover the couple's dysfunctional patterns. The family therapist and pediatrician met with school personnel to outline the treatment plan and explain that abdominal pain was not caused by organic disease. Throughout the treatment process the therapist was available to the parents and child in case a crisis developed.

Behavioral techniques were employed to increase the child's control over the symptoms. A daily record was kept by the child noting when he got the pain and how long it lasted. Every evening after dinner the child called the therapist to review the record. If the mother and child were overinvolved and the father underinvolved, the therapist appointed the father to go over the record with the child. After this review, the parents were to meet privately and discuss any problems between themselves or with their children. This set aside a time for the parents to be together and communicate with each other. Further, the mother was instructed to support her husband in his new role and not to usurp his new responsibilities.

Also, the father was to see that the child attended school each day. If the child wakened with the abdominal pain, he was told that the pain would lessen by eating breakfast. It was agreed that the child would be sent to school unless he had a fever or was obviously sick. If the pain continued after breakfast, the child was told that it would decrease during the morning and be gone by lunchtime. An arrangement was made with the school nurse whereby the child could go to the office to rest for fifteen minutes if he had pain. Such coordination of the treatment by the therapist, pediatrician, family, and school is essential.

Use of this treatment method resulted in the symptoms' gradually decreasing within two to three weeks. During this time the therapist also directed some attention to concrete problems presented by the siblings. One problem was handled at a time, and in this way the identified patient was no longer the sole focus. As the child became symptom-free he had more time and energy to be with peers and move out of a dependent role. The therapist cautioned the parents about giving the child preferential treatment as this would keep him from being part of the child subsystem.

Addressing the marital conflicts that emerged once the symptoms decreased was the last phase of the treatment process. Resolving the difficulties between the parents helped prevent the recycling of the child's symptoms.

TREATMENT RESULTS: The ten families in this study attended weekly family sessions for five to eleven months. Some of the children had individual sessions in addition to the family sessions. None of the children had to be hospitalized for abdominal pain in the follow-up period from eight to twenty-five months. In addition, there were no symptom substitutions or any incidents of another family member's developing symptoms. The children also developed more age-appropriate lifestyles, as measured by increased school attendance and greater social involvement with peers.

COMMENTARY: By viewing the symptom of the child's abdominal pain within a family system framework, the therapist placed the focus on changing the family structure. Behavior modification techniques aided the child and parents in gaining control over the symptom. Coordination between family and school provided a broad-based support system. A follow-up with the families, eight to twenty-five months after treatment, pointed to the substantial success of this treatment method.

SOURCE: Liebman, R., Honig, P., and Berger, H. "An Integrated Treatment Program for Psychogenic Pain." *Family Process,* 1976, *15,* 397–405.

Treating Psychosomatic Illness Within the Context of the Family System

AUTHORS: James L. Titchener, Jules Riskin, and Richard Emerson

PRECIS: A family case study presents the treatment of a young man's problem with colitis.

INTRODUCTION: The treatment approach set forth by the authors involves looking at all the family members to develop concepts of the family working as a whole system. In contrast to the view that a young person's symptoms result from a symbiotic relationship between mother and child, this study notes the mother's significant role but views it in the context of the whole family's psychodynamic patterns. The authors assert that since the ways in which mothers relate to their children develop within a family situation, their special relationships with ulcerative colitis patients are mainly determined by the dynamics of the family environment.

TREATMENT METHOD: The treatment method includes several procedures. All the family members are observed interacting with one another in one session and then each family member is interviewed separately a number of times. These individual interviews have a particular sequence whereby one member of the research team sees each person in the family. The series of interviews is repeated after the whole family has been seen. In the case presented, the series was repeated four times, except for a brother who was only seen once and two sisters who were unavailable. A family relations inventory is also completed. The interviews with each family member reveal some characteristic ways that members relate to one another. When a member tends to talk about specific incidents during the interview, he or she is encouraged to continue.

The Neal family's referring problem to the psychosomatic study service was the ulcerative colitis of the twenty-four-year-old son Bob. Bob had had this condition for a year and although he had received medical treatment experienced many physical setbacks. His weight had decreased from 170 to 115 pounds and he had difficulty talking with others because he found it emotionally difficult. The family consisted of Mr. and Mrs. Neal, twenty-nine-year-old Doris, twenty-seven-year-old Ken, twenty-four-year-old Bob, and twenty-two-year-old Dottie. An interesting and somewhat surprising interaction was noted between Bob and his mother after her first interview. Although Mrs. Neal appeared to be concerned about her son's illness, when she left the interview she went into Bob's room and said, "Your father is in an agony of stomach pain from worrying about you."

During Bob's sixteen-month hospital stay he received medical, surgical, and psychiatric treatment. The first month of psychotherapy was characterized by Bob's expressing his thoughts and feelings in a stereotyped way. As part of the process of establishng a working relationship with Bob, the therapist initiated role playing in which he was the "good doctor," on the patient's side, against the "bad doctors" who callously prescribed things to make him feel uncomfortable. Through this technique the therapist began to take control in the relationship, and Bob appeared to be more confident of his own feelings and less afraid of being abandoned. However, the therapeutic relationship could not be maintained at this balanced level because there were many painful issues to be explored. There was a constant push and pull in the relationship between Bob and his therapist. As therapy progressed, Bob often tested to see what would be required from him and what he could keep to himself without terminating the relationship. In one session Bob said, "You're just like my mother: You asked me if I wanted another appointment; I said, 'No,' and you came anyway." He also said that he did not know why the therapy had to involve such irritating matters as worry over finances (relationship with his father), dreams, and the notion that he was unable to let go of some feelings.

After this session, Bob became more overtly hostile toward the therapist. At this point, his bowel symptoms were replaced by headaches. The following stage of treatment found Bob viewing the therapist as a very reliable person who was his ally and who had taken or been given control of the relationship. It was seen as probable that this new relationship was repeating the early mother-child relationship.

Among the significant relationships within the Neal family were the following: Mr. Neal worked excessively long hours and allowed his wife to care for him only when he was troubled by his ulcer; he placed greater expectations on his son Bob than on the other children, which may have been due to his wife's overprotection of Bob. Mrs. Neal was undergoing the changes of menopause and had been given a great deal of responsibility for parenting over the years because of her husband's long work hours. Ken, the older brother, had a successful career in the air force but was casual and noncommittal in his relationships. During the one interview he attended, he stated, "I have one thing that bothers me. I can't express any emotion. I have a terrible time with it. I want to stay just as far away from emotion as I can. I hate to get emotionally involved, even with my family. It hurts me . . . it hurts them sometimes, I know." The two sisters were not available for interviews.

TREATMENT RESULTS: At the end of the treatment process for ulcerative colitis, which involved surgery, steroids, and psychotherapy over sixteen months, Bob was described as appearing full-faced. Regarding his psychological health, he was seen as displaying an air of complacent, assured stiffness. From an understanding of the family dynamics, the therapist suggested that the family would need to remain deeply committed to one another for as long as possible and to adhere to the family organization, which required that each member carry out his prescribed role.

COMMENTARY: The component of family therapy in the overall treatment of the young man's symptom of colitis was essential, as previous medical interventions alone had been unsuccessful. The authors propose that an understanding of the interlocking relationships in the family provides information about how a symptom develops and what course treatment should take.

SOURCE: Titchener, J. L., Riskin, J., and Emerson, R. "The Family in Psychosomatic Process." *Psychosomatic Medicine,* 1960, *22,* 127–142.

Techniques for Working with Families
of Failure-to-Thrive Infants

AUTHORS: Dennis Drotar and Charles Malone

PRECIS: Working with families of failure-to-thrive infants to improve relationships so that the infant can develop in a normal way.

INTRODUCTION: The authors state that an infant's failure-to-thrive conveys the message that there are problems in the mother-child relationship. In addition to the immediate problem of the infant not developing normally, there are also long-term effects, such as aggressive behavior in older children, severe feeding problems, and cognitive and learning deficits. Drotar and Malone report that intrafamilial relationships are directly connected with the development of failure-to-thrive. The treatment strategies employed by the authors view the problem within the family context. Many family relationships affect an infant's development: the husband-wife relationship has a profound effect on the parent-child relationship; the number of siblings and their ages influence the mother's ability to adequately care for the infant; extended family members, if available, can lend support to the parents; and the parents' relationships with their own parents also contribute. From their work with these families, the authors report that the way in which a traumatic or neglectful childhood experience influences the mother-infant relationship is significantly affected by the current transactional context of family life.

TREATMENT METHOD: Problems in family relationships may cause the infant's poor weight gain to go unnoticed. The authors state, "By the time the child's poor weight gain is significant enough to be recognized, many families have adapted to the infant's problem, and can be remarkably untroubled by it." If the situation reaches the crisis stage, the infant needs to be hospitalized. Although this step is necessary to treat the physical problem, it often focuses the family's emphasis on the poor weight gain rather than the intrafamilial relationships. Too, the infant's separation from the family may prompt the family to believe that they are not responsible for or participants in the treatment of the infant's condition. Thus the therapist must persistently reach out and inform parents and other family members that their participation is critical to the infant's development. After hospitalization, the initial step in the intervention process outlined by the authors, the treatment must be continued in the home environment. Three goals are pursued: altering patterns of family dysfunction that contribute to the infant's poor nurturing; facilitating more adaptive intrafamilial relationships and instituting better ways to control stress; and working toward improved family communication and problem solving in dealing with the infant's nurturing, which will secure a more prominent place in the family constellation for the infant.

The authors hypothesize that if one or more crucial relationships within the family improve, then the mother-child relationship might be strengthened.

CASE STUDY: Two-month-old Randy was referred after having been hospitalized once before for failure-to-thrive. His weight was far below the fifth percentile, and he was irritable, stiff, and inconsistent in his social responsiveness. Other members of the family were Randy's widowed mother and three siblings, ages two, four, and six. Extended family members included his great-grandparents, who lived next door, two uncles, and an aunt. Although having so many caretakers is sometimes beneficial to an infant, this was not so in Randy's case. As soon as problems arose, Randy was handed from his mother to her sister, and his siblings competed with him for their mother's attention. The first treatment goal was to position Randy's mother as the main caretaker by emphasizing the need for one person to be Randy's mother. Randy's mother had resisted assuming this role as she was fearful that he was physically sick. She was told that Randy was healthy but required her attention and nurturance. To aid in this process, the great-grandmother was asked to help out at mealtime by feeding his two-year-old sister. This intervention was aimed at strengthening the relationship between the mother and her grandmother.

The structuring of the mother and great-grandmother as a unit enabled the mother to spend more time with her son, rather than turning him over to her sister. By the time Randy was six months old, he and his mother had established a more consistent and satisfying relationship: "As Randy began to want his mother and no one else, she was helped to see this as a positive sign of his attachment to her and less as a sign of his being spoiled." Other family relationships were also addressed, including the slow process of fostering a more adaptive separation between Randy's mother and great-grandmother.

TREATMENT RESULTS: After two years Randy showed more normal weight and height, was appropriately attached to his mother, and had average cognitive development.

COMMENTARY: Drotar and Malone conclude by stating that the usefulness of their method of intervention would be evaluated in an ongoing study that included several variables: the child's overall psychological development, the child's physical growth, parental perceptions of family life, and parent-infant interventions as evaluated by monthly home observations.

Therapists working with families with failure-to-thrive infants are advised that maintaining a relationship with these families and keeping a focus on the goals is often extremely difficult. A comprehensive understanding of the lifestyles of these families is important in order to support their internal survival mechanisms while at the same time securing a safe place for the infant.

SOURCE: Drotar, D., and Malone, C. "Family-Oriented Intervention with the Failure-to-Thrive Infant." In M. H. Klaus and M. O. Robertson (Eds.), *Birth, Interaction, and Attachment: Pediatric Round Table*, vol. 6. Skillmon, N.J.: Johnson and Johnson, 1982.

A Family Treatment Approach to the Parents of Children with Nonorganic Failure-to-Thrive

AUTHOR: Judith B. Moore

PRECIS: The treatment of children with nonorganic failure-to-thrive employing supportive services to their families and emphasizing modeling techniques.

INTRODUCTION: Children who display the life-threatening symptoms of failure-to-thrive often do not respond to medical treatment alone. Although these children may gain weight in the hospital, they often experience recurring problems once they return home because the symptom is psychosocial in nature.

Project Thrive, a program in Tampa, Florida, was created to provide service to families of infants who had been hospitalized at least once for nonorganic failure-to-thrive. As Moore explains, "The project operates on the premise that failure-to-thrive is rarely the result of willful neglect, but is most frequently a symptom of family dysfunction, wherein the infant at risk becomes the receptacle of (usually unconscious) resentments, fears, conflicts, and stress points." Usually, the infant has difficulty eating as a result of the stress and fails to grow at a normal rate. The three measures of nonorganic failure-to-thrive noted in the article are: weight, height, and head circumference below the third percentile on normal growth charts; substantial weight gain during hospitalization; developmental retardation that decreases in the nurturing environment of the hospital.

TREATMENT METHOD: Project Thrive employed the services of social work students who were assigned cases of families whose children were hospitalized for failure-to-thrive. These students worked under close supervision by social workers. Before beginning work with the families the students were given an intensive course in the dynamics and treatment of the syndrome. The tasks assigned included: providing transportation if necessary to the parents so that they can visit and care for their child in the hospital; making appropriate referrals if other services are needed by the family; initiating and mobilizing support systems, for instance, relatives and friends; making home visits twice a week once the child returns home from the hospital, and providing role modeling, nurturing, and education to the parents; helping with medical appointments and watching the baby's progress.

The children in Project Thrive ranged from newborns to two year olds and had been hospitalized once for nonorganic failure-to-thrive. Two measurable objectives were stated: to prevent rehospitalization of the child and to continue weight gain at a rate appropriate to the child's age. Social work students were assigned cases while the child was still in the hospital. When the child was to be discharged, a referral was made to the public health nurse supervisor. The public health nurse and social work student coordinated the visiting schedule so that someone visited the family almost daily the first two weeks and thereafter twice a week for two months or longer if needed. At the termination of the program the student worker made a referral to an appropriate agency if follow-up was needed. Half of the project's cases were closed without outside referral.

CASE STUDY: Three-week-old Cindy had been hospitalized for failure-to-thrive when her weight had declined from seven pounds, ten ounces at birth to seven pounds. Cindy was the second child in the family; her sibling was a year and a half older. The parents were in their early twenties and had difficulty in their marital relationship as well as financial difficulties. During the two months following the baby's discharge from the hospital, the social work student visited the family twice a week. The mother was found to be distant from Cindy and appeared to be afraid to touch her even when feeding. Initially, the student cuddled and touched Cindy while feeding her and gradually encouraged the mother to do the same. As the mother became more comfortable caring for her baby, the student offered verbal reinforcement rather than physical involvement. The student also made positive comments about the mother's capabilities in running the household. At the end of two months Cindy weighed

eleven pounds, two ounces and was a more active and responsive baby.

TREATMENT RESULTS: Twenty-eight families were followed
over a year's time, and all the babies gained adequate amounts
of weight. The children spent between three and nine weeks in
the program. None of the children in the group had to be rehospitalized.

COMMENTARY: Although only a small number of children
and families were studied, some interesting results emerged in
that some common assumptions about the failure-to-thrive syndrome were negated. In the group studied, half the babies were
not first-borns; almost two thirds had two parents; and two of
the twenty-eight weighed less than five pounds at birth—all contrary to common belief.

The author attributes the program's success to the intensive support system provided by the social work students:
"Perhaps the secret to productive work with any troubled, isolated family is frequent contact, a supportive approach, and a
whole-hearted commitment to their well-being." Further, the
program was very cost-effective in that none of the children required rehospitalization and the students were not paid. The
success of this study suggests more extensive research of a similar kind.

SOURCE: Moore, J. B. "Project Thrive: A Supportive Treat-
    ment Approach to the Parents of Children with Nonorganic
    Failure-to-Thrive." *Child Welfare League of America*, 1982,
    61, 389–399.

Additional Readings

Bauknight, S. T. "Psychotherapeutic Treatment of a Gastrointestinal Disorder: Individual and Family Systems Perspectives." Paper presented at the annual convention of the Rocky Mountain Psychological Association, Denver, Colorado, April 1978.

This paper addresses the treatment of a seventeen-year-old boy who had suffered from chronic diarrhea for five years. Medical treatment had not been successful, and the problem resulted in erratic school attendance. It appeared that the patient was the focus of family conflicts that were generated by the mother's chronic schizophrenic condition. Specifically, the son's efforts at individuation were impeded by his mother's needs for constant care and support. The son's symptom was understood from two perspectives: intrapsychic and family systems. Within the family system, it served to keep him in the home, which seemed to be part of a family collusion demanding that someone stay home to watch the mother. Individual therapy was focused on facilitating ventilation of the patient's rage, and in family sessions a clarification of the nature and limits of the patient's responsibilities to his mother were addressed. Following several visits, the patient's diarrhea was in complete remission.

Blotcky, A. D. "Family Functioning and Physical Health: An Exploratory Study with Practical Implications." *Family Therapy*, 1981, *8*, 197–202.

This article concerns the relationship between family functioning and an individual's susceptibility to physical illness. Seventy-two undergraduate and graduate students participated in the study. The measures included the Physical Health Log and the Family Characteristics Inventory, both of which are questionnaires. Findings suggest that the level of family functioning is particularly related to the length or duration of physical health problems. The author advises that, through a family therapy approach, the therapist challenge the family's conflict-avoidance patterns so that family members can discuss conflicts, share their concerns and frustrations, and resolve problems.

Burks, H. L., and Serrano, A. C. "The Use of Family Therapy and Brief Hospitalization." *Disorders of the Nervous System,* 1965, *26,* 804–806.

Twenty-five children were treated through a short period of hospitalization in conjunction with intensive family-centered psychotherapy. The treatment was intended to maintain a continuity of the family unit during the physical separation caused by the hospitalization. While hospitalized, the children participated in the full hospital program and received intensive individual psychotherapy, usually every day. Most importantly, the child and family met together at planned intervals in team-family conferences in order to correlate the work of individual therapy sessions. Most of the patients were between twelve and sixteen years of age and 60 percent of them were girls. One case study concerns the treatment of a thirteen-year-old boy who had a peptic ulcer. Not until just prior to the boy's discharge from the hospital did the family begin meaningful interactions. This process continued and the first follow-up, four weeks later, found the boy back in school and free of pain. Continued healthy functioning was reported at a two-year follow-up.

Dietrich, K. N., Starr, R., and Weisfeld, G. E. "Infant Abuse, Neglect, and Failure-To-Thrive: Mother-Infant Interaction." Paper presented at the 90th annual convention of the American Psychological Association, Washington, D.C., Aug. 1982.

The basic issue investigated in this study is whether the degree of child maltreatment is related in some meaningful way to the interaction between the mother and infant and the infant's developmental status. A group of fifty-three mothers and infants were classified by five diagnostic groups (nonaccidental trauma combined with failure-to-thrive, nonaccidental trauma combined with iron deficiency anemia, nonaccidental trauma only, neglect only, and normal controls). All mothers and infants were observed during a feeding session. Results supported the hypothesized continuum of infants at risk, and dyads in which multiple forms of maltreatment occurred showed more severe interactional disturbances.

Fine, S. "Adolescent Somatic Symptoms: Masks for Individual and Family Psychopathology." *Comprehensive Psychiatry*, 1977, *18*, 135-140.

Three case studies are presented in which there was a family pattern of expressing emotions through somatic symptoms. The adolescents in the cases had recently been introduced to drugs or alcohol and feared they would cause irreparable harm, and the parents disagreed about how to handle their child. The author states that counseling these adolescents could be rewarding, but the therapist would have to expect many canceled appointments. A suggestion is to schedule several appointments in quick succession, for example, twice weekly, and then allow a break and resume the therapy. In family therapy, family members need to learn to express emotions and feelings in clear terms rather than as somatic complaints.

Friedman, P. H. "An Integrative Approach to the Creation and Alleviation of Dis-Ease Within the Family." *Family Therapy*, 1980, *1*(3), 179-195.

Among the several approaches to the alleviation of disease within the family described is the family systems approach. The attitudes, beliefs, and expectations of the family of origin in regard to illness, diet, exercise, and communicational patterns are explored in great detail, as are life stresses and crises experienced over time within the nuclear and extended families. One area of emphasis is the sources of secondary gain that both the patient and family members derive from the illness. Close collaboration with other professionals involved with the patient is necessary as is an understanding of the needs of families of different socioeconomic classes; a knowledge of patients of different ages and sexes enables the therapist to anticipate developmental stages of the patient's illness.

Grolnick, L. "A Family Perspective of Psychosomatic Factors in Illness: A Review of the Literature." *Family Process*, 1972, *2*, 457-486.

This comprehensive review of the literature on the relationship of the family to psychosomatic components of illness classifies the literature into intrapsychic, dyadic, and familial

categories. Among the findings are: that the family functions
as a system in relation to the physically ill member; that families with greater rigidity of structure usually show greater instances of psychosomatic illness and perhaps chronicity of illness; that these families tend to repress or suppress affects; that
within the family system, the mother usually plays a central
role in labeling illness, and other members, especially the father,
collude in this process.

Lask, B. "Emotional Considerations in Wheezy Children." *Journal of the Royal Society of Medicine,* 1979, *72,* 56–59.

The author notes that while wheezing is a primary organic disorder, a number of secondary factors can interact with
the condition. The illness can be triggered by such external factors as exercise, emotional stress, or frustration. Among asthmatic children identified as rapid remitters, the illness subsides
upon the removal of stress. Also, research shows that suggesti-
bility, attitudes toward illness, and internal factors may precipitate or aggravate an attack. Family therapy is briefly discussed
as a way to manage the illness. Some reactions of family members to the asthmatic child include denial, fear, guilt, anger, and
resentment.

Lask, B., and Duncan, M. "Childhood Asthma: A Controlled
Trial of Family Psychotherapy." *Archives of Disease in Childhood,* 1979, *54,* 116–119.

A sample of thirty-seven children (between ages four and
fourteen) who had moderate to severe asthma was evaluated to
study the effectiveness of family therapy as an adjunct to conventional treatment. The children were randomly assigned to a
control or an experimental group; the latter group received six
hours of family therapy over a four-month period. Results show
no significant difference between the groups on three param-
eters, but the experimental group showed improvement in day
wheeze scores and thoracic gas volume. The authors recommend further study with families with asthmatic children.

Libo, S. S., Palmer, C., and Archibald, D. "Family Group Therapy for Children with Self-Induced Seizures." *American Journal of Orthopsychiatry,* 1971, *41,* 506–509.

Two children who displayed self-induced seizures and their parents joined a family group led by a psychologist and a social worker. The purpose of the group was to investigate the children's motivation for producing seizures and to explore the possibilities of behavioral controls. Over a one-year period, sixteen biweekly sessions were held. The summer months were used as an observation period, followed by three sessions of review. The authors conclude that involving all family members, especially fathers, is essential to effect change in the family structure, and that behavioral control of self-induced seizures is possible if the dynamics are understood and the families are able to alter their responses to the seizures.

Liebman, R., Minuchin, S., Baker, L., and Rosman, B. L. "The Role of the Family in the Treatment of Chronic Asthma." In P. J. Guerin (Ed.), *Family Therapy: Theory and Practice.* New York: Gardner Press, 1976.

Patterns of family organization and functioning in children that contribute to psychosomatic illness are discussed, and a family-oriented treatment program that proved successful in the treatment of chronic severe asthma is presented. This approach is explained as an alternative to "parentectomy" (the removal of the sick family member from the family to a safe place) that enables the child with chronic asthma to stay at home with his family. Weekly outpatient family therapy sessions were organized into three phases. The first phase concerned the alleviation of the symptom of asthma; the second consisted of identifying and changing the patterns in the family environment that tended to exacerbate and perpetuate the severe symptoms; and the third focused on interventions to promote lasting disengagement of the patient in order to prevent a recurrence of the symptoms. Among the many positive results reported are an alleviation of acute attacks of asthma and improvements in the family members' interpersonal relationships.

9

Anorexia Nervosa

Anorexia nervosa produces a weight loss of at least 20 to 25 percent of the patient's original body weight, and this loss is not due to organic causes. The majority of cases are female adolescents, although cases have been reported for children as young as nine and adults thirty or older. An inaccurate body image is often common with this disorder. In most female cases, a cessation of menstruation occurs as a result of the illness but 10 to 30 percent of the female patients stop menstruating prior to the onset of the illness, while others continue to menstruate until they have lost a lot of weight. Early in the illness, some patients display marked behavioral hyperactivity, while others do not. Cycles of binge eating and vomiting are characteristic of some anorectics. Several recent studies delineate different groups of anorectics based on developmental, descriptive, and psychological components.

In treating this disorder, a variety of therapy approaches are used, including family systems therapy, structural family therapy, and combinations of insight, structural, and strategic approaches. A large number of anorectic patients need to be hospitalized during the acute stage of the disorder, and the seriousness of this disorder cannot be overemphasized: the mortality rate is over 20 percent.

The Reorganization of a Family
with an Anorectic Child Through
Structural Family Therapy

AUTHORS: Harry Aponte and Lynn Hoffman

PRECIS: A structural family therapy approach to assist the family in reorganizing itself.

INTRODUCTION: The authors present a transcript of an initial interview with a family whose presenting problem was the excessive weight loss of the fourteen-year-old daughter. Salvador Minuchin was brought in as a consultant for the initial interview, and Mariano Barragan was the therapist who was to continue treating the family. The authors' commentary on the interview explains how a structural family approach was used to shift the structure in the family so that the symptom would no longer be needed.

TREATMENT METHOD: The two therapists and family members were seated in a semicircle, with the symptomatic daughter between her two siblings, her brother on her right. Next came the mother, father, and Drs. Minuchin and Barragan. The session was opened by asking the family to state their problem, to which they responded: the older daughter's inability to eat and her sudden weight loss. Minuchin then began to elicit a family history. As a young child, the older daughter had been overweight, but other than that, she and her sister, who was two years younger, were treated alike. For a short while, at the age of six, the older daughter saw a psychologist for school problems. At that time, the psychologist felt that the daughter was caught in the middle, between parents pulling in different directions.

Minuchin asked how the family handled disagreements and was told they had none. The daughter was asked if there was anything she would like to see changed and she said it bothered her when her parents urged her to eat. Minuchin asked her to reenact a situation in which she refused her father's request to

eat. During the reenactment the father kept after the daughter
to eat. When the mother and daughter were asked to role play a
similar situation only one request to eat was made.

At this point in the session, Minuchin's secretary entered
the therapy room to take lunch orders. Each member made a
selection, and Minuchin ordered food and a soda similar to
those ordered by the mother and children respectively. The
topic of agreement within the family was pursued by Minuchin's asking the younger daughter how it was when she and her
father disagreed. Her description of an incident revealed that
she felt she could not openly differ with her father. This led to
a discussion of how the family gathered in the parents' bedroom in the evening. A good deal of physical contact (massag-
ing, combing hair) took place between the father and his children, although less with his older daughter. Often the mother
did chores outside the bedroom and did not have as great a need
for physical contact as the father. Minuchin asked the mother if
she ever wished she could be alone with her husband and she
said no. In fact, it was explained that the door of the parents'
bedroom was open at night, as were all the other bedroom
doors, except when someone was dressing.

The authors' commentary on this segment of the interview emphasizes the lack of a boundary between the father and
his children, and also the distance between the parents, as revealed by the mother's not wanting to spend time alone with
her husband.

Minuchin then explored the family members' habit of
keeping their bedroom doors open. Although both daughters
wanted to close their doors at times, the older daughter hesi-
tated to ask her father to knock for fear of hurting his feelings.
The son also indicated his desire to close his door at times. The
subsequent authors' commentary explains Minuchin's technique
for helping the daughter to challenge her father. Minuchin did
this in a gentle way by saying to the family, "We can talk about
boundaries in terms of flower hedges; it doesn't have to be
guns." By eliciting the response of the two siblings, Minuchin
began to create an alliance among the children emphasizing the
generation line.

During the following segment, the father responded with a "we" statement. Minuchin told him not to speak for his wife, and while saying this, rested his hand on the father's shoulder. The mother was then drawn in to oppose the father and form an alliance with the children. The mother's difficulty in acknowledging disagreements was noted. At this point the father said, "We seem to communicate," and Minuchin replied, "If there is communication, there is disagreement."

In the next sequence the mother talked about her husband's receiving phone calls during dinner, a behavior she found annoying. Minuchin had them tell each other what was troubling them rather than explaining the behavior to him. After the exchange, Minuchin told the mother that she was not convincing and added, "If it is important, you will need to tell Dave in ways that he will think it is important." Minuchin noted that the open-door policy extended to outside the home by the father's allowing phone calls at any time. As the parents talked to each other about their feelings toward "open doors," Minuchin stood up and changed the seating arrangement; the new order was the younger sister, brother, patient, Minuchin, mother, father, and Barragan.

The commentary observes that Minuchin was placing a physical boundary between the parents and the children, as well as supporting the mother by sitting next to her. The father continued to discuss family closeness in the evenings, and Minuchin again changed the seating by putting the father next to the children and sitting between the parents. Minuchin said to the mother, "And he (father) is selling you the idea that his relationship with the kids is extremely important and that it's more important than you want at this particular time in your relationship with him—that's why I sat here; because he is bundling there with the kids, having Laura (mixing the girls again) huh? (correcting himself) having Jill unknotting his calf and Laura combing his hair (touching Mr. R's hair), and Steve rubbing his back (placing his hand on Mr. R's shoulder), and you (to Mrs. R) are there, kind of unemployed." It was acknowledged after some discussion that the parents did not have time to be alone and talk. Minuchin exchanged seats with the father and told him he belonged with his wife and that some day the kids would grow up and leave and he would not know his wife. The authors note that having the parents experience disagreements allowed them to get closer to one another.

While Minuchin was questioning the older daughter about baby-sitting when her parents went out, he asked the younger daughter and son to change seats so the two girls could discuss baby-sitting. At that moment the secretary returned with the lunch and was asked to bring it in. As this was happening, Minuchin picked up on the issue of baby-sitting and pointed out that both parents treated their fourteen-year-old daughter as if she were the same as their twelve-year-old daughter. Minuchin then asked the older daughter if she gave her parents the message that she was twelve. An interruption was made to ask the mother to serve the food.

The subsequent commentary emphasizes that Minuchin decided to bring the lunch in at a point when he had gotten the parents together. In addition, he was more clearly defining the family boundaries by discussing how the two girls were treated alike. A review of the session thus far noted that Minuchin first separated the children from their father, then moved to differentiate the children, and finally handled the difference in ages of the siblings. At this point, he felt he could talk about the "unacknowledged disagreement" between the parents and older daughter about her right to grow up.

As the group began to eat lunch, Minuchin announced to Barragan that the seating arrangement had made a wall between the parents and children in that they were sitting across from each other at the table. Minuchin said to his colleague, "We are moving them out (pointing to the children) and moving them together (pointing to the parents) but I tell you something, I think we'll need to push a lot." He added that he didn't think there would be a problem getting the older daughter to eat and said, "She will eat." The older daughter was told directly by Minuchin that she would eat without any problems when she was fourteen years old. Minuchin continued talking to her as she was eating about the things she could make choices about, such as buying clothes. Barragan made the point that the father's saying that everything was fine in the family left little room for the children to be able to fight and grow up. At the end of the segment, Minuchin gave the father the assignment of listening carefully to his wife and children. He pointed out to the older daughter that her voice could be heard.

Here the commentary discusses Minuchin's timing: how he talked about the symptom of eating when the food was in front of the family and how his comments about eating to the older daughter were timed to her eating or not eating the lunch.

Before closing the session, Minuchin gave each member an assignment. A differentiation in the daughters' ages was made by telling the older daughter to close her door whenever she wanted for at least two hours a day. The younger daughter was told to keep her door as it had always been, and the son was told to keep his door open. From 9 to 10 P.M., the mother was told to be with her husband alone and to close their door. The father was told to respect the privacy of his daughters by knocking on their doors. Minuchin told the older daughter that her problem with food would be solved as soon as she wanted to grow up. He encouraged her to insist on being fourteen years old with her family.

TREATMENT RESULTS: The treatment continued with Barragan working with the parents on their relationship; as more conflict between them emerged, the involvement between father and older daughter lessened. The mother was supported in asserting herself with her husband. The father had to be hospitalized twice for anxiety attacks. He complained that he had too heavy a load to carry within the family and the mother became more active. An assignment was given to the parents to have their daughter gain ten pounds in three weeks. Nothing happened for two weeks, but the third week she gained eight pounds, and two weeks later had gained twenty-four pounds. A six-month follow-up indicated that the daughter was in good physical condition and had an active social life.

COMMENTARY: The presentation of the interview and the accompanying commentary vividly illustrates the structural family approach. In just one session, a very definite foundation was outlined for further treatment. The issues that resulted in the anorectic symptom were brought out, and the consulting therapist suggested clear strategies for changing the structure of the family. All family members were brought into the process and became actively involved. The life-threatening symptom of anorexia was eliminated, and the communication pattern within the family significantly changed.

SOURCE: Aponte, H., and Hoffman, L. "The Open Door: A Structural Approach to a Family with an Anorectic Child." *Family Process*, 1973, *12*, 1–44.

The Integration of Inpatient Hospitalization and a Family Systems Approach in Treating Anorexia Nervosa

AUTHORS: Steven Stern, Carl Whitaker, Nancy Hagemann, Richard Anderson, and Gerald Bargman

PRECIS: The role of the hospital team in the treatment of anorexia nervosa using a five-stage treatment plan.

INTRODUCTION: A majority of anorectic patients require hospitalization during the acute stage of the illness. The authors emphasize that the whole family needs to be included in the treatment process when an anorectic patient is hospitalized, and their method combines the inpatient program with the family therapy process.

TREATMENT METHOD: The five-stage treatment model described is analogous to the "developmental" stages Whitaker*

*A. Y. Napier and C. A. Whitaker, *The Family Crucible* (New York: Harper & Row, 1978).

differentiates in the family therapy process. Although the various stages are outlined as distinct, parts of each stage arise throughout the process. The stages are holding, battle for structure, battle for initiative, availability, and separation. The order of these stages is similar to the way treatment issues are usually confronted.

The team working with the anorectic patients and their families was composed of a pediatric endocrinologist, who administered the program, a clinical psychologist, a clinical nurse specialist, a small nursing staff, and a nurse specially trained to coordinate the outpatient program. After admission, the anorectic patient was placed on total restriction from activities and a specific program for caloric intake was prescribed by the pediatrician. At this point, the patient had little choice about the daily routine. As the patient gained weight and showed other signs of recovery, she earned more freedom and could make weekly requests to the team for more free time, longer passes, and the like. Responsibility for weight gain was gradually transferred from the treatment team to the patient so that she had total control of her diet by the end of the inpatient phase of hospitalization. The majority of patients stayed in the hospital from two to eight weeks, with four weeks the average length of stay.

Holding. Throughout the treatment program the hospital acted as a holding environment for the family. Before hospitalization, the pediatrician acted as a "holding" parent to the family by confronting the members with the life-threatening situation of the anorectic patient. Right after admission, the patient and family were presented with the concept of the therapeutic team: all important decisions were to be made by the team, not by an individual, so that both the physical and psychological aspects of the patient's program were always considered. The team explained to the family that they would not allow the patient to die or act self-destructively. Food was the medicine prescribed by the pediatrician and dietician. The family was told that they must be involved in the treatment program from its inception.

Battle for structure. The battle for structure refers to the family's testing of the therapy team's ability to establish and maintain effective control over the therapeutic process. During

the initial phase of treatment, the family had to become assured
of the team's ability to direct the therapeutic process so that
the family could feel safe in revealing their deeper conflicts. The
battle had to be won in a way that did not leave the family feeling impotent. The primary message to the family was, "You are
in charge of your family, but we are in charge of the treatment.
You may decide to participate in treatment or not, but we, as
experts on anorexia nervosa, will decide what the necessary
treatment procedures will be."

Battle for initiative. During the course of hospitalization,
crises often evolved, such as the patient becoming self-destructive or perhaps suicidal. Although a difficult period for all involved, it was often in the face of a life-and-death situation that
the family took some initiative. The staff had to take a definite
stand on what the patient needed without overprotecting the
family. They had to let the family members know that they had
the ability to solve their own problems.

Availability. In the majority of cases in this study, the patient required only one hospitalization. However, multiple hos-
pitalizations were needed when the condition persisted for a
period of time or in families whose pathology was quite pervasive. The therapy team then responded by being available for a
prolonged period of time. Continued availability was also provided by an outpatient program administered by a specially
trained nurse. During weekly visits, the patient was weighed,
had blood drawn to determine electrolyte imbalance (if she was
a vomiter), and talked to the nurse for ten or twenty minutes
about her present circumstances. Patients showing a weight loss
were asked to explain it; if the weight loss was significant, the
nurse informed the other team members and the parents. If a
patient's weight fell dangerously low, she was told that readmis-
sion to the hospital would be necessary if her weight went
below a defined limit. The patient and her family were presented with the clear choice of her returning to the holding environment of the hospital or her gaining weight.

Separation. The course of treatment for most anorectic
patients was one brief hospital admission (one or two months)
followed by a longer period of outpatient family or individual

therapy or both. While hospitalized, the patient became more aware of her psychological and physical situation. During the last few weeks, her opinions and preferences entered the treatment process, including the setting of a discharge date. The family therapy sessions allowed the other family members to express their concerns. Weekly outpatient sessions after discharge formed another step in the separation process. Patients and families who were more chronically disturbed sometimes developed a "malignant dependency" on the hospital. The team then had the task of determining whether anything more could be done for the patient and if not, to terminate treatment.

COMMENTARY: The unique contribution of this paper is the conceptual model the authors propose for the hospitalization phase of the anorectic patient. By delineating five stages that occur during the patient's stay, the authors present a clear picture of the treatment process. Many conflict issues generally surface during the patient's hospitalization, and the team approach with the family allows these issues to be confronted and addressed. Also, the team's approach to coordinating the inpatient and outpatient phases with the family makes for a smooth transition.

SOURCE: Stern, S., Whitaker, C., Hagemann, N., Anderson, R., and Bargman, G. "Anorexia Nervosa: The Hospital's Role in Family Treatment." *Family Process*, 1981, *20*, 395–408.

Treatment of Anorexia Nervosa Combining Family, Behavioral, and Analytic Techniques

AUTHORS: Tom Peake and Charles Borduin

PRECIS: Treating anorexia nervosa by the use of an eclectic approach employing family, behavioral, and analytic processes.

INTRODUCTION: In treating anorexia nervosa the authors describe a family systems approach to change the structure of communication in the family. The behavioral approach focuses on finding the reinforcers of the eating problem and interpersonal conflict and changing them. Reducing the severity of the superego in the anorectic patient is the goal of the analytic process.

CASE STUDIES: Miss D was a thirteen-year-old girl whose weight had dropped to below 80 pounds; she expressed great conflict with her mother and compulsively tried to please people. This girl was the youngest in the family, with one sister and two brothers. Both parents had advanced degrees, and the father was successful in his professional career.

The behavioral approach consisted of giving the patient a balanced diet of 1800 calories daily and making her responsible for eating. If the patient's weight fell below a certain level, she was fed nasogastrically until her weight stabilized. Required weekly family sessions focused on discovering the patterns and conflict areas among family members. The patient also participated in individual and group sessions in the hospital.

Four aspects of the therapeutic focus were to: increase the father's contact with his daughter so that he—as well as the mother—could deal with negative interactions; use modeling techniques that allowed the parents to express their resentments and thus change the system; help Miss D to separate herself from the role of arbitrator in the parents' conflict; and encourage both parents to move toward a mutual goal of the mother finding a sense of herself outside the home.

A second case concerned Miss L, a thirteen-year-old girl whose weight had dropped to below 75 pounds. Severe conflict with her mother, problems in peer relationships, and the compulsive pursuit of good grades were also symptoms. This girl was a middle child having two sisters and two brothers. Both parents had good educations, and the father was a very successful professional. It was recommended to the family that Miss L be hospitalized, but the family refused. The family was involved in outpatient treatment for fifteen weeks and frequently requested individual treatment for Miss L in lieu of family sessions.

The goals of the therapeutic process were: to reduce the mother's role as the main parent figure and actively involve the father; to examine the resentment between the parents concerning parenting tasks; and to remove Miss L from the parental conflicts.

TREATMENT RESULTS: Miss D benefited from the multifaceted approach; at the end of her hospitalization her weight was over 100 pounds and was gradually increasing. The relationship between Miss D and her mother improved with fewer conflicts reported. At the same time a greater range of feelings was expressed between Miss D and her father. In contrast, Miss L was treated solely by a family therapy approach. She weighed 85 pounds on leaving treatment, but her weight was not increasing. Her parents did not deal openly with their resentments. An increase in the father's involvement in parenting was reported, but this resulted from the father's strong insistence that his daughter not be hospitalized. The conflicts between Miss L and her mother were still evident, and the relationships within the family were unchanged.

COMMENTARY: The authors highlight the importance of giving immediate attention to the behavioral symptom in anorexia nervosa. In the case of Miss D the involvement of the entire family in the program, which was set up as a condition of hospitalization, was very successful. But while Miss L gained weight, thus reducing the life-threatening aspect of the symptom, her weight gain did not increase and a relapse was quite possible. Her family's qualified commitment to the process of family therapy was evidenced by the resistance expressed during family sessions and the frequent requests that the patient be seen individually instead. Maintaining a certain flexibility in the emphasis of each therapeutic approach in treating anorexia nervosa seems optimum.

SOURCE: Peake, T., and Borduin, C. "Combining Systems, Behavioral and Analytic Approaches to the Treatment of Anorexia Nervosa: A Case Study." *Family Therapy*, 1977, *4*, 49–56.

Combined Approaches of Family Therapy in Dealing with an Adolescent's Anorexia Nervosa

AUTHOR: Richard A. Oberfield

PRECIS: Distinct characteristics of three types of family therapy (insight-oriented, structural, and strategic) are used in treating an adolescent girl's weight loss.

INTRODUCTION: Through a case presentation, Oberfield illustrates the techniques of three approaches in family therapy. In insight-oriented therapy the goals are to guide the family to understand its difficulties and to improve members' communication of thoughts and feelings. Through a structural orientation the therapist attempts to change the dysfunctional configurations within the family system by using active directives and little insight. The strategic approach emphasizes the symptom and uses indirect, paradoxical techniques to change the family's homeostasis.

CASE PRESENTATION: After losing almost ten pounds in two weeks, Susan, age twelve and a half, was hospitalized. Up until three weeks before admission she had been eating normally, but she reported that suddenly food was getting stuck in her throat and she had some dizziness. Following this episode, Susan refused to eat solid foods.

The family included Susan's fourteen-year-old sister Carol and her parents. An ongoing conflict between the parents concerned the father's relationship with his younger, unmarried brother. The mother felt that her husband was more loyal to his brother than to her. It was acknowledged within the family that Susan was her father's favorite, which angered both her mother and sister. Her father constantly asked her to eat more. Carol was her mother's favorite but was starting to have problems with her parents, especially regarding her relationship with boys.

Treatment was approached by using insight, structural, and strategic approaches in sequence. The task of the insight-oriented therapy was to help the family deal with feelings such as the mother's resentment of her husband's relationship with his brother and each daughter's angry feelings about the parental favoritism the other experienced. The father often blamed his wife for Susan's refusal to eat. Topics explored during this phase of therapy included the mother's resentment of men following a poor relationship with her own father and the father's covert reasons for getting married. An important fact was that the father had received a message from his mother before she died to look after his younger brother. In individual sessions, the therapist explored with Susan her feelings about becoming a woman and her ambivalence about her father's overly close relationship to her and her mother's distance from her.

When the family became unwilling to move beyond superficial emotions, the insight-oriented treatment was replaced by a structural approach. In structural terms, this family was enmeshed in a dysfunctional cross-generational relationship between Susan and her father that excluded her mother. One intervention sought to separate the sibling subsystem from the parental one; specific techniques included not permitting the daughters to interrupt their parents and placing them on the opposite side of the room from their parents. Carol's problems were discussed to take the focus off Susan and she was encouraged to engage in appropriate adolescent social activities. In addition, the sisters were encouraged to do more things together, and the parents were prompted to go out together as a couple. The therapist addressed the issue of Susan's eating habits by telling her that they were under her control and by instructing her father to stop commenting on her habits. As these interventions illustrate, the structural approach places more emphasis on active tasks and less on exploring feelings. Although there was positive response to the structural approach, the father was not able to stop his comments about Susan's eating habits and the parents were resistant to doing anything social on their own. Thus at this point, the strategic-paradoxical approach was initiated.

The strategic approach requires the therapist to look for the "family game" that encourages the psychosomatic symptoms. In this case the therapist found that "with the impending move of the family away from uncle, Susan unconsciously anticipated a huge crisis and, again unconsciously, came up with an even larger one of her own involving her very survival to reunite her worried parents." Susan was given a paradoxical prescription: to sacrifice herself for the sake of her parents' marriage by not eating. She responded with a definite no. Following this, Susan gained weight, went back to school, and adjusted to adolescence. At a follow-up six months later, the family was doing well.

COMMENTARY: The intervention in a family in which the psychosomatic illness of an adolescent is the symptom requires considerable skill. As illustrated by Oberfield, a variety of family therapy approaches can be successfully employed. In general, it is useful to follow one approach at any given time; as therapy proceeds techniques can be changed if strong resistance is met.

SOURCE: Oberfield, R. A. "Family Therapy with Adolescents." *Journal of the American Academy of Child Psychiatry,* 1981, *20,* 822–833.

Additional Readings

Barcai, A. "Family Therapy in the Treatment of Anorexia Nervosa." *American Journal of Psychiatry,* 1971, *128*(3), 286–290.

Two case examples illustrate a crisis-induced family therapy for the treatment of anorexia nervosa. During the first week of treatment the patients gained two to three pounds, and they continued to gain until a normal weight was reached, usually within three to four months. The approach described encourages the family to change their customary ways of interacting with one another. The author outlines the advantages of the techniques and cautions therapists about problems inherent in the approach.

Bruch, H. "Family Background in Eating Disorders." *The Child in His Family,* 1970, pp. 285–309.

    The author asserts that treatment for anorexia nervosa must clarify the disturbed interactional patterns within the family in order to be successful. Such clarification allows the child to develop internal controls and see him- or herself as self-directed and as owning his or her body. The therapist is advised to evaluate the total situation in order to decide whether individual or conjoint family therapy is more appropriate. A detailed case history of a young boy's anorectic symptom treated with a family therapy approach is presented.

Conrad, D. E. "A Starving Family: An Interactional View of Anorexia Nervosa." *Bulletin of the Menninger Clinic,* 1977, *41,* 487–495.

    In the case described, an anorectic young girl was viewed as the spokesman for two generations of family deprivation. Therapy uncovered a rigid pattern within the family that permeated the entire system. Paradoxically, the young girl's starvation filled the parents' needs for nurturance. Relationships within the family needed to be changed very carefully, and including extended family members in the treatment was deemed beneficial, especially in resolving the marital conflict when it appeared during the treatment process. The author advises those working with families in which anorexia nervosa is the symptom to conceptualize the problem from an interactional standpoint as well as an intrapsychic one.

Liebman, R., Minuchin, S., and Baker, L. "The Role of the Family in the Treatment of Anorexia Nervosa." *Journal of the American Academy of Child Psychiatry,* 1974, *13,* 264–274.

    A comprehensive case description illustrates structural family therapy techniques for treating a fourteen-year-old girl's anorectic symptom. From their work with twenty cases of anorexia nervosa, the authors found family therapy to be the most useful approach. They conclude that direct participation of the patient's family in the early stage of treatment can stimulate a rapid significant weight gain, as well as helping the young person to return to the family after only a two- to three-week hospitalization. They also recommend that the family remain involved in the treatment process on an outpatient basis to diminish the possibility of recurrence of the symptom.

Minuchin, S. "Structural Family Therapy." *American Handbook of Psychiatry*, 1974, *2*, 445–473.

Minuchin addresses various specific therapeutic strategies within structural family therapy. Coupling tactics are intended to help two different systems adjust themselves in terms of direction to become one system. The three types of coupling interventions described are *maintenance* (supporting the family structures), *tracking* (adopting the content of family communications), and *mimesis* (focusing on the family's style and affect). Tactics to produce change include some type of challenge to the family's natural style. A case study involving a family with an anorectic girl illustrates change-producing interventions with a family.

Rosman, B. L., Minuchin, S., Liebman, R., and Baker, L. "Input and Outcome of Family Therapy in Anorexia Nervosa." *Adolescent Psychiatry*, 1977, pp. 313–322.

The authors cite some critical aspects of the structural family approach to treatment and outline general characteristics of the psychosomatic family. In cases of anorexia nervosa, the first step is to eliminate the symptom of not eating. Among several strategies to accomplish this goal is holding one session with the patient and family around the lunch table. In order to reinforce the changes in family organization that originate in the therapy sessions, the family members are given tasks to be completed at home. After the eating problems lessen and greater differentiation occurs among family members, the last phase of treatment focuses on the enduring underlying problems. If necessary, marital difficulties or particular problems with siblings are dealt with in separate sessions. The authors emphasize that these problems must be addressed to avoid a recurrence of the referring symptom.

Schneider, S. "Anorexia Nervosa: The 'Subtle' Condition." *Family Therapy*, 1981, *8*, 49–58.

The sequence of understanding the illness of anorexia nervosa, devising a treatment plan, and exploring possible treatment strategies is illustrated by a case history of a young woman whose parents came together to participate in the family treatment after having been divorced for twelve years. Treatment was set in a psychiatric residential treatment facility, where a combination of approaches including systems, behavioral, and analytic were used.

Selvini Palazzolli, M. "The Families of Patients with Anorexia Nervosa." *The Child in His Family*, 1970, pp. 319–332.

The author briefly reviews the history of the treatment of families of anorectics. In the 1950s and up until 1965, the treatment consisted of working with the patient and mother, as this relationship was viewed as the pathogenic one. But beginning in 1965 the family was seen as the system of pathological interaction, and all the family members were invited to the initial interview. The author reports that it is sometimes possible during the first session for the family members to uncover and understand certain ways in which they interact with one another. During the process of family therapy, the designated patient is sent a verbal or nonverbal message by the therapist that indicates that the therapist understands the extreme difficulty of the patient's position.

Wold, P. "Family Structure in Three Cases of Anorexia Nervosa: The Role of the Father." *American Journal of Psychiatry*, 1973, *130*(12), 1394–1397.

In the three cases illustrated in this paper, each parent placed the daughter in the position of his or her own mother. The significant factor was that neither parent could express hostility toward their own mother. By being the focal point of this conflict, the daughter was unable to express her feelings of aggression or sexuality. The findings suggested that the weight loss was closely connected with the daughter's relationship with her father.

10

School Phobia

Experts consider the etiology of school phobia to be a child's fear of separation from a significant person. Refusal to attend school generally occurs at the beginning of a school year or after a vacation. In some cases, the death or serious illness of a family member may trigger the behavior. The child's mother has traditionally been involved in the treatment process, and in the last two decades the crucial role of the father has come to be recognized. Therapists agree that effective treatment of school phobia is contingent upon the child's early return to school. In addition to involving the family in the therapy, the therapist must keep school personnel apprised of the child's status. Abatement of the symptom is usually seen within a short period of time, but family sessions should continue to deal with the underlying causes. A high success rate using family therapy is reported with preschool and elementary school children, but this rate drops dramatically for junior high or high school students. Some therapists postulate that if school phobia is not treated in the acute stage and becomes chronic, a reversal is improbable.

Conjoint Family Therapy for the Treatment
of School Phobia

AUTHOR: A. C. Robin Skynner

PRECIS: The use of family therapy in the treatment of school phobia acknowledging the crucial role of the father in the syndrome.

INTRODUCTION: In reviewing the literature on school phobia, the author cited that psychotherapy has generally been offered only to the mother and child, but that since 1965 the role of the father has been given more emphasis. Skynner reviews some clinical findings regarding the father's part in the origin of the syndrome: in general, the fathers studied lacked strong paternal roles. The literature also suggests that the parents' encouraging of a powerful, controlling self-image results in the child resisting the challenging forum of the classroom. Through case presentations, the author highlights methods for treatment.

TREATMENT INTERVENTIONS: Six principles of a group-analytic approach to conjoint family therapy are outlined: (1) the interview includes all members of the nuclear family and any other individuals who are significant to family functioning; (2) history is minimized and the emphasis in the interviews is on the present situation; (3) the major interventions involve non-verbal communication, which serves to open up any underlying system, rules, and attitudes—interpretations of intrapsychic dynamics are seen as unnecessary. (4) The therapist seeks to specify the developmental stage that the parents have been unable to help their child through. Subsequent therapy is intended to help the parents and child accomplish the developmental tasks. In school phobia, the failed developmental stage is often that of separation-individuation, usually due to the father's inability to intrude in the mother-child couple and support both through the pain of separation. (5) One or two widely spaced sessions are usually recommended, with the focus being on the family handling the problem themselves. The objective is to facilitate interaction between family members so that most of the work can be done in the home. (6) Ideally, the goal is to effect change by increasing insight through interpretation and in this way allowing the family to apply the necessary skills. If this is not deemed possible, the therapist can provide the parental functions that are lacking by example or by referring the family to an appropriate outside agency.

CASE ILLUSTRATIONS: Ten-year-old Jacqueline had not attended school for several weeks and had experienced nausea and occasional vomiting for three months prior to her leaving school. Following an initial family interview by the supervising psychiatric social worker, the therapist and a social work student joined with him to see the family. The team was unable to initiate any meaningful discussion. The therapist then changed the focus to nonverbal communication by noting the fond way the mother looked at her daughter. An interpretation was made that the mother viewed Jacqueline as the embodiment of all that was valuable in herself. The mother responded dramatically and emotionally, fighting to hold back her tears. The father commented on how important raising this child properly was to the mother who had experienced a miserable childhood herself. The therapist asked the mother, "Who are you married to?" Her response was to look at the child, confirming the therapist's suspicion. A subsequent discussion of sleeping arrangements revealed that the daughter still slept in her parents' bedroom. Further exploration revealed that the mother was frigid and the father angrily interrupted that he was very dissatisfied with the current situation. The mother explained that she felt emotionally deserted by her husband and experienced the burden of family decision making. At the end of the session, the therapist suggested to the husband that if he could fulfill some of his wife's needs that had not been met in her childhood then she might be able to let go of her strong identification with their child. Because the family lived a great distance from the hospital, they were referred to a local clinic. The mother and daughter were seen by a psychiatrist at that clinic four months later, and it was reported that Jacqueline had been attending school since the first interview and was handling normal school stresses. No further treatment was recommended. A follow-up two years later evidenced no other problems with school attendance.

The second case illustrates an approach to be used when the therapist needs to share the task of presenting the challenge with the parents. Eleven-year-old Susan had been out of school for a little more than a year when she was referred to the hospital for a second opinion. A psychiatrist at a local clinic had failed in an attempt to get Susan to return to school. During the initial family interview, it was noted that the mother was critical of her child but not firm. In contrast, the father appeared passive and related that he had experienced school phobia as a child. Although Susan was depicted by her parents as anxious and depressed, she presented herself in a stubborn manipulative way. The therapist pointed out this behavior and was met with a furious look and an increase in stubborn oppositional behavior. Susan's wish to control the situation was presented to the family, and the older brother said that he saw Susan as manipulative and added that she generally got her own way at home. The therapist, noting Susan's lack of physical illness, announced that medical excuses for not attending school would be withdrawn immediately. Furthermore, he told her that she would be able to return to school, prescribed medication to relieve anxiety, and offered to recommend a residential school should there be further difficulty. Toward the end of the interview, Susan's demeanor changed to a warm and friendly mood. Two weeks later her parents reported that Susan was much happier and had returned to school. However, before this change, Susan had been openly aggressive and had had a fight with her mother, who was able to constructively counter her onslaught.

Follow-up contacts with the family showed that Susan attended school consistently for a year but then did not attend for a week. Fifteen months later Susan was again referred for not attending school. The original therapist had moved, and his successor held several family interviews and finally recommended residential placement. This recommendation was not carried out. The psychiatrist at the local clinic again supplied certificates of her unfitness to attend school, though she refused to see him. The author comments that this case illustrates the problems encountered when the medical, social, and educational networks do not collaborate.

Therapeutic approaches to parents who are colluding fully with their child and truants referred as school phobics are also presented. In essence, the therapist is advised to confront the whole family with the threat or reality of the child's separation from them, while supporting them in their response of pain and rage that this threat arouses.

Skynner also emphasizes that the family therapist working with school phobic children and their families needs support from any colleagues who become involved with any of the members of the family. The psychiatric team must guard against a danger inherent in co-therapy situations: that family pathology may be reproduced in their own relationships. One indication of this phenomenon is conflicts between the team members over the timing of the child's return to school.

COMMENTARY: The framework described for working with families in which a child has school phobia is detailed and comprehensive, including different types of family interaction patterns and various approaches. The therapist is advised to carefully consider the context for the suggested techniques: "The fact that the techniques described here are usually both successful and psychologically beneficial, rests on the psychological meaning of the actions taken which is designed to assist the family to cope with a developmental challenge they have previously failed to transcend." The author also notes the essential and often overlooked role of the father in the dynamics of school phobia. Issues of authority and control are explained as quite important when the focus of treatment is to confront and dilute the ideas of omnipotence in the child and the family system.

Multifamily therapy is proposed as another promising technique, especially when combined with therapy groups for mothers and for children. Two distinct benefits of this form of therapy are that families can often be more objective about other families' problems and can provide mutual support.

SOURCE: Skynner, A. C. R. "School Phobia: A Reappraisal."
British Journal of Medical Psychology, 1974, *47,* 1-16.

Family Crisis Therapy in the Treatment of School Phobia

AUTHOR: Dorothy Bruhl Anderson

PRECIS: A family therapy approach to a crisis, which is defined as "dysfunction in a family network resulting from delayed, incompleted, or anticipated mourning of a significant loss."

INTRODUCTION: The rural families that the author worked with in New Hampshire generally had family gatherings as part of their normal social life. Consequently, whenever a crisis developed, the therapist's request that the family come together to the clinic was usually accepted. However, at times a breakdown in family cohesiveness occurred and the oldest brother, the designated head of the family, had to be contacted. Frequently, the firm message "We need everyone here to make decisions" brought the family together.

TREATMENT METHOD: At the beginning of the initial interview, the therapist explained that the therapy would be short term (five or six sessions with an option to renew the contract if necessary) and that all information would be kept confidential. The family was told that other members might be included at times. The first session emphasized having the family reach some agreement on what troubled them. Each person was asked what was wrong within the family and when the problem began. The therapist usually asked about recent losses, whether any member had died or been sick in the last year. After memories and feelings were shared, the therapist sometimes made a tentative diagnostic comment regarding the family experiencing incomplete mourning or anticipated grief reaction. The first session lasted one to two hours, and by the last half hour the list of problems was completed. Any problems that could be addressed immediately were attended to; for instance, if the family asked whether their son receive remedial help with schoolwork, a referral was made. The emphasis was on taking action, rather than on talking, and homework assignments were given to family members. The family was reminded that the clinic was staffed at all times in case of emergency, and an appointment was made for the second session within the week.

The second session was sometimes used for problem solving; if a grief process was incomplete, the second and third sessions focused on sharing memories and feelings. Everyone was encouraged to reconstruct the event so that distortions were revealed. By the third or fourth meeting, the list of problems was reevaluated. Any behavioral change was recognized with praise. If the main problems had been eliminated, the family was asked to check back with the therapist in a month's time. If new problems had come to the surface, a new contract was agreed upon.

CASE ILLUSTRATION: Fourteen-year-old Betsy had complained to her mother that she had stomachaches in the morning and refused to board the school bus. Betsy and her parents were asked to come to the clinic together. The onset of the school phobia had occurred six months ago, but Betsy had been fine during the summer. The therapist asked if anything specific had happened six months ago. The mother and daughter cried, and the father stated that his brother had been murdered, allegedly by a former girlfriend. The three family members then painfully recalled their feelings about the uncle's death. The father did not see how his brother's death affected his daughter. The therapist then asked how the ten-year-old son had been doing, in particular whether he had been eating and sleeping well. The father was astonished and asked, "How did you know?" The therapist explained that a significant loss in a family affects everyone. Before the first session ended, arrangements were made for Betsy to take guitar lessons, as she had expressed a wish for some fun in her life.

At the next session, the father was asked to share his thoughts about the previous session. He reiterated his belief that his daughter's school phobia and the murder of his brother were unrelated. The children were asked whether they were ever afraid that something might happen to their parents while they were in school. When the children said they were, the father began to understand the connection. The parents and children shared their feelings about the uncle's death and how it touched their lives.

TREATMENT RESULTS: All family members were doing well when the follow-up contact was made. Through the relationship Betsy developed with her guitar teacher and her satisfaction in learning to play a musical instrument, she developed increased self-esteem. Her new accomplishment also contributed to her making new friendships in school.

COMMENTARY: The use of a family therapy approach in response to crisis was appropriate to the pattern of social relationships for the population the author studied. The framework described is practical and thorough. Placing the emphasis on action, rather than introspection, accelerated the rate of change so that the goals were met within the short-term treatment period. The day-and-night availability of a therapist was also crucial to the crisis work.

SOURCE: Anderson, D. B. "An Operational Framework for Working with Rural Families in Crisis." *Journal of Marriage and Family Counseling,* 1976, *2,* 145-154.

Decreasing School Phobia by Helping
the Family to Reorganize Roles

AUTHORS: Roland G. Tharp and Gerald D. Otis

PRECIS: Restructuring the role functions within a family so that a symptom is eliminated.

INTRODUCTION: From an analysis of family roles authors identify five functional classes of family behavior. *Solidarity* includes intimacy, understanding, and companionship. *Sexuality* refers to the control of sexual activity in children as well as the expression of sexual feelings between spouses. *External relations* includes the family's relationship with others such as friends, school personnel, shopkeepers, and the like. *Internal instrumentality* denotes the responsibilities within the family such as cooking, cleaning, and so on. *Division of responsibility* refers to the arrangements within the other four functional classes.

According to the authors, a change in one element of family action results in other accommodating changes, and changes in behavior can effect changes in feeling states. They hypothesize that: "adjustment of a family interaction pattern may render a symptom dysfunctional and thus cause its disappearance."

TREATMENT METHOD: The focus of treatment is to negotiate role allocation so that each family member experiences role satisfaction. One technique for achieving this goal is family bargaining and compromise mediated by the therapist. Such bargaining in effect consists of one family member saying to another, "I'll change this if you change that." A second technique involves the attempt by family members to change another's behavior by applying negative sanctions. In order to effect change these sanctions are sometimes quite extreme, including threats to divorce, run away, or take a lover. During a session these threats may be made many times in a subtle way, with the therapist clarifying them and emphasizing the choice the individuals have to accept the requested change or the sanction. The last

step in the therapy process is the creation of a strategy acceptable to the family that enables them to negotiate the role revision once therapy has ended.

CASE STUDY: Thirteen-year-old Kay was referred for treatment of school phobia after unsuccessful treatment at a child
guidance center. The family constellation included Kay's mother, who was confined to a wheelchair, her maternal grandparents, and an older sister. Within the family, Kay assumed the
responsibility for internal instrumentality. A conflict existed between Kay and her mother in the area of external relations,
with Kay expecting her mother to perform her role in a way
similar to her friends' mothers. In addition, Kay was dissatisfied
with the division of responsibility within the family and desired
more free time for herself.

The whole family, except the grandfather, was seen for
one hour a week for five months. During the early sessions the
family members delineated their expectations. Next, the members were encouraged to bargain for changes in role functions
that would satisfy one another. The therapist emphasized the
consequences of the suggested role revisions. Finally, they drew
up some strategies to facilitate the continuance of the agreed-
upon role revision. These strategies included making a work
schedule and planning weekly menus. In addition, a family reconciliation agreement was drawn up that required each member to write down her particular responsibilities.

TREATMENT RESULTS: Following two months of therapy
Kay's phobia symptoms decreased dramatically. Her school ab-
sences had decreased by half at the conclusion of treatment. Before treatment Kay had been failing some subjects; afterwards
she achieved B's and C's. Also, she lost twenty-five pounds and
was more socially appropriate.

COMMENTARY: The therapy process described is specific and
short term. A unique feature of this therapy intervention is the
focus on planning strategies for the negotiation of role revision
once the formal therapy has ended, a technique that helps rein-

force and continue the new roles within the family. As noted by the authors, "For this treatment, different from all schools of psychotherapy, the significant healing relationship is not with the therapist, but for the family, it is with one another."

SOURCE: Tharp, R. G., and Otis, G. D. "Toward a Theory for Therapeutic Intervention in Families." *Journal of Consulting Psychology,* 1966, *30,* 426–434.

Family Therapy: A Method of Treatment for School Phobia

AUTHOR: Carl P. Malmquist

PRECIS: The use of family therapy for school phobia with four types of families showing a variety of disturbed functioning.

INTRODUCTION: Malmquist defines *family* to include "any relative or significant person interacting with the nuclear group at a particular time." His review of the literature shows three phases in the understanding of school phobia. Originally, it was seen as a problem solely with the child; then, as an expression of problems in the mother-child relationship. More recent approaches view school phobia as a reflection of difficulties involving the child and both parents, and possibly the entire family. The author then uses a classification of families devised by Voiland* and her associates to describe various cases and methods of treatment for school phobia.

DYNAMICS AND TREATMENT: In presenting the dynamics of families with children who have shown problems in attending

---

*A. J. Voiland and others, *Family Casework Diagnosis* (New York: Columbia University Press, 1962).

school, Malmquist uses a classification system developed by Voiland and her associates from a study of 888 families. The four categories, in order of increasing severity of disturbance, are: (1) the *perfectionistic family*, in which open conflict is avoided and expectations are unrealistic; (2) the *inadequate family*, in which family structures are resisted and members look to outside sources for validation and help in problem solving; (3) the *egocentric family*, characterized by the self-centered, opinionated stance of the parents, which intensifies any problems in child rearing; and (4) the *unsocial family*, whose members lack social skills and more than one of whom is seriously socially maladjusted.

The case example illustrating the perfectionistic family concerns a fourteen-year-old boy who was referred for treatment having had somatic complaints over several years and the recent problem of not attending school for several months. Family sessions with Glen, his parents, and twelve-year-old sister revealed that the father had not involved himself in disciplining the children. The mother often complained to the children about her dissatisfaction with being the dominant parent, but these complaints were never communicated to the father. Glen's anger increased as his father supported him in resisting the mother's authority. The younger sister was also placed in a similar bind and had come to disrespect both parents. Although initial resistance was put up, both parents continued family sessions, which had positive results for the whole family.

Specific case material is not presented for the inadequate family. These families have one or more members functioning at a subnormal mental level. The school phobia generally becomes an overt problem when academic and other expectations of the child alter the level of adjustment within the family.

The egocentric family is illustrated by the case of an eleven-year-old girl who had not attended school for six weeks. The dynamics of the family included physically assaultive behavior by Becky toward her mother; the two younger daughters would also sometimes assault their mother. The father's response to this behavior was a passive one. Becky was also self-destructive at times, hanging outside an eleventh-floor window in hopes that her father would rescue her. Further, Becky and her father often took naps together, and at these times Becky described experiencing "funny feelings." These feelings were approved of by the mother, who told Becky that she had experienced similar feelings when napping with her own father. Many of the important dynamics in this case were not revealed until the family was seen together. Previous sessions with the mother and daughter were unsuccessful, and not until Becky was hospitalized did movement occur through family sessions.

The unsocial family is represented by the case of eight-year-old Laurie, who had dropped out of school after attending the first week of third grade. She related that many times when she returned from school her mother was lying on the floor. In later sessions, Laurie spoke about the fears that her mother had told her about a neighbor planning to control her while Laurie was in school. During family sessions, the father said he would not hospitalize his wife and stated that he believed there was a plot by some relatives to kidnap his wife. The serious nature of the problem made it necessary to temporarily place the children outside the home and hospitalize the mother in order to get the children to return to school.

COMMENTARY: The case material presented shows the importance of including the father and other family members in the treatment of school phobia. According to the author, "In the most frequently cited pattern of the ambivalent mother-child relationship, there is always a father who is directly involved and aware of the situation." Therapists working in child guidance clinics are advised to include the father in the ongoing treatment, and individual sessions with the child or other family members is viewed as an integral part of the process.

SOURCE: Malmquist, C. P. "School Phobia: A Problem in Family Neurosis." *Journal of Child Psychiatry*, 1965, *4*, 293-319.

A Family Therapy Approach
to the Problem of School Phobia

AUTHOR: Alfred A. Messer

PRECIS: The treatment of all family members to eliminate the symptom of school phobia and restore the equilibrium in the family.

INTRODUCTION: Messer describes school phobia as "a symbolic public expression of breakdown in the equilibrium of the family." He hypothesizes that if the equilibrium is restored, the phobia should disappear. If all members of the family are seen together, the author proposes, the unconscious problems and motivations of the family members can be revealed and directly treated.

CASE STUDY: The members of the A family included the middle-aged parents and their children. The designated patient was the youngest child, B, an eight-year-old boy. B refused to attend school and resisted the attempts of his family and school personnel to get him to return. His brother, D, was twenty-one and his sister, C, was twenty-five.

The previous spring, the mother had suffered a heart attack while visiting her daughter in a faraway city. She was hospitalized twice, and the two sons stayed with relatives while she was away. During the summer, B experienced severe stomach cramps and hyperventilation at day camp. The mother was rehospitalized in August and remained in the hospital through the first two weeks of September. B attended school in the beginning of September, but when his mother came home he refused to go to school. During that month D went away to college. B described his feelings of increasing panic with accompanying stomach cramps on the way to school. The family placed a high value on education, and B had always been a good student.

The family was seen weekly for two years. Some of the family members were at times seen individually as well as in family sessions. The first four sessions were filmed as was a session a year and a half after therapy started.

During the initial session, B was quite active and made derogatory remarks about everyone in the room. A discussion of B's refusal to go to school was initiated by the family. The therapist changed the topic to the mother's illness and the family's concern about her. At first the family members denied their concern, but after numerous questions they admitted their true feelings. B described having fears that his mother would die. Both B and D talked about their lonely feelings being at home while their parents worked and the resulting resentment they felt. With the therapist's support the husband was able to express his upset and worry about his wife's illness. He expressed his dependence on his wife and commented, "I'll die first."

At the end of the session the therapist took a direct approach, saying to B that he most likely wanted to stay home with his mother so that she wouldn't become sick again. However, the therapist added that attending school was the law and that B must go to school. If necessary, a member of his family could take him. The school phobia was put into context by the therapist telling B that the family was experiencing a problem and would receive help. In analyzing the first session, the therapist noted that the mother handled her own death anxiety by clinging to her family. After the older son had left for college, B's role as mother's protector took on greater significance.

The second family session was attended by the daughter C, who confirmed the mother's dominant role in the family. A number of themes were explored during the third session, including sexuality in the family. The parents had not shared information about human sexuality with their children, and the wife rationed sex to her husband. The discussion also revealed that B was born three years after his mother was told she could not conceive. Family members talked about how relatives warned B not to upset his mother because she might die. At the time of the third session B was being brought to school by his father and was attending regularly.

A hopeful feeling was expressed by the family at the fourth session. B had continued to go to school, and the mother commented that things in general seemed better and she wondered how it had happened. The therapist suggested that perhaps her improved health had resulted in her being less dominant in her family. Several family sessions were devoted to changing the equilibrium in the family, as all had agreed that the previous arrangement was undesirable. A homemaker was hired to do the housework and to assume some mothering responsibilities. The family's belief that there was complete harmony in the home was confronted and dispelled.

TREATMENT RESULTS: The school phobia symptom was eliminated and a new equilibrium was established within the family. The father became more dominant and active while the mother reluctantly assumed a more passive role due to her chronic illness. D became more independent and self-assured, and B acted much more like a typical eight-year-old boy. A setback occurred the following summer when the hot weather affected the mother's heart condition and D returned to college. Both family and individual sessions were held with good results. B attended school and excelled in his academic work, and the family compensated well for the mother's chronic condition.

COMMENTARY: The family therapy approach was effective in changing the homeostasis within the family so that members functioned more independently. The author suggests that the dynamics within the family were clarified quickly by seeing members together. The manipulative behavior of the younger son and the resulting school phobia were uncovered and successfully handled by a family systems approach.

SOURCE: Messer, A. A. "Family Treatment of a School Phobia Child." *Archives of General Psychiatry*, 1964, *11*, 548–555.

Additional Readings

Baideme, S. M., and Kern, R. M. "The Use of Adlerian Family
    Therapy in a Case of School Phobia." *Journal of Individual
    Psychology,* 1979, *35,* 58–69.

    The case of a nine-year-old child who had school phobia
is used to describe the application of Adlerian family therapy.
Although the symptom was manifested in one member of the
family, it was proposed that the family system was instrumental
in encouraging and maintaining the problem behavior. Engaging
the whole family in the treatment process enabled the members
to learn new ways of relating to the symptomatic child. Enlisting
the cooperation of school personnel is emphasized. The contributions of such Adlerian processes as disclosure of purpose,
antisuggestion, paradoxical directives, logical consequences, encouragement, and educating parents are also noted.

Eisonberg, L. "School Phobia: A Study in the Communication
    of Anxiety." *American Journal of Psychiatry,* 1958, *114,*
    712–718.

    In the treatment of school phobia, the author emphasizes
the importance of insisting that the child return to school as
soon as possible. During the first interview, an attempt is made
to assess the degree of sickness in family members. The parents
are reassured that the prognosis is relatively good. A program
for rapid return to school is outlined, and the child is told that
school attendance is prescribed by law and that the issue is not
whether he will return to school, but how and when. On the
first day back at school, the child is required to be in the school
building, although he is permitted to spend the day in the principal's office or have his mother attend class with him. In rare
cases when other methods fail, a hearing in juvenile court may
be scheduled. After the child returns to school, therapy continues with the family in order to change underlying pathological attitudes. Results were positive with ten of eleven preschool
children, and all ten elementary school children returned to
school. However, with junior high school and high school students, the success rate was between 30 and 50 percent.

Fife, B. R. "The Resolution of School Phobia Through Family Therapy." *Journal of Psychiatric Nursing and Mental Health Services*, 1980, *18*, 13–16.

A family systems approach was used in the case of a fourteen-year-old girl who developed school phobia. During the assessment phase, it became apparent that there were more extensive family problems. A significant event had been the death of a maternal grandmother who had played a dominant role in maintaining cohesiveness within the family. There was distance within the marital dyad and feelings of parental inadequacy. The major goals of therapy involved opening communication, focusing on the family rather than the phobia, strengthening relationships and boundaries between the parents, enhancing mutual respect among family members, and implementing the daughter's reentry into the school. Follow-up sessions were scheduled to guard against a return to previous dysfunctional patterns.

Hess, T. "Paradoxical Interventions in Systemic Family Therapy." *Familiendynamik*, 1980, *5*, 57–72.

The author describes the family therapy of an eleven-year-old girl who refused to attend school. The girl, who was an only child, and her parents were treated by a structural approach, with three co-therapists behind a one-way mirror assisting and advising the therapist, who sat with the family. Paradoxical interventions played a major role in the therapy process.

Miller, T. P. "The Child Who Refuses to Attend School." *American Journal of Psychiatry*, 1961, *118*, 398–404.

A child's refusal to attend school must be acted upon promptly, and the child's early return to regular school attendance is seen as contingent on effective treatment. The therapist is advised to deal directly with the concerns of the parents, the child, and the school personnel. The method described entails informing the parents that the child's problem is not in school and reminding them that the methods they had used to remediate the problem had not worked. A date a few days later was scheduled as the date for the return to school. Sometimes the father is then involved in the mechanics of getting the child to school. Parents are told that they can call the therapist in the mornings if problems develop. During an individual session the child is told that his problem is not at school and that his return to school is not a matter of choice. He is informed of the plan to begin to attend school regularly and told that he will be seeing the doctor regularly to discuss his concerns. The principal is then contacted and told of the plan. The author reports that such methods are usually effective within two weeks; however, therapy should be continued with the parents and child.

Radin, S. S. "Psychotherapeutic Consideration in School Phobia." *Adolescence*, 1968, *3*, 181-194.

The author presents therapeutic principles that were found to apply in most cases of school phobia. Usually parental attitudes must be changed, which can be accomplished through direct involvement of the parents in the treatment of their young child. If the child is older, the therapist interprets to the child the effects of the parental influence. Prior to any dynamic insight therapy, emergency emotional states must be corrected. Insight therapy can then be instituted to resolve the conflicts that perpetuate the psychodynamic cycle associated with school phobia.

Radin, S. S. "Psychodynamic Aspects of School Phobia." *Comprehensive Psychiatry*, 1967, *8*, 119-128.

The author discusses the complex psychological mechanisms seen in school phobia. The child's feelings of omnipotence fostered in the home and a special kind of nurturance are not reinforced in the school setting. The child discovers instead that in school reward and punishment are based on realistic performance, and the illusion of omnipotence is dispelled sooner or later by either real or imagined school failure. These events elicit fear and rage reactions, which the phobic mechanism is called upon to contain and to restore homeostasis. The author concludes that although critical intrapsychic phenomena are involved, the larger picture involves the family dynamics, sometimes over successive generations.

Veltkamp, L. J. "School Phobia." *Journal of Family Counseling,* 1975, *3,* 47–51.

The author defines school phobia, explains its etiology, describes experiences with school-phobic children, and outlines a specific treatment approach. Three steps are considered as essential if the child is to return to school immediately. First, the child should have a physical exam to uncover any organic problems. Prior to the exam, the physician should be advised of the situation so that he does not reinforce the symptoms by assigning a home instruction teacher or prescribing medication. Second, the therapist should meet with the family and evaluate their feelings and interactions. After the family history is elicited, the family is told that there is nothing physically wrong with the child and that the symptoms will subside when he returns to school on a regular basis. Third, the therapist should talk to the school personnel, including the bus driver, to assure them that he will provide help if needed and will assume responsibility for whatever happens.

Over a seven-year period, the author and his colleagues report an 85 percent success rate with this method for returning the acute school-phobic child to school. However, the success rate was only 20 percent for chronic cases, a result that emphasizes the need for early identification of the school phobia.

Waldron, S., Shrier, D. K., Stone, B., and Tobin, F. "School Phobia and Other Childhood Neuroses: A Systematic Study of the Children and Their Families." *American Journal of Psychiatry,* 1975, *132,* 802–808.

The authors developed reliable, clinical rating scales and used them to compare thirty-five school-phobic children and their families with a matched sample of children having other neuroses and their families. The school-phobic children showed a mutually hostile-dependent relationship with their mothers; the mothers demonstrated that they felt their children to be excessively important to them; marked separation anxiety was noted in the children's functioning; and faulty development of autonomy and self-esteem produced an impaired capacity to function independently, which conflicted with the demands of a school program. Finally, the development of school phobia appeared to be dependent on defects in character development in the child.

11

Suicidal Behavior

Suicide is the second highest cause of death in the United States for adolescents and young adults between fifteen and twenty-four years of age. Once a rare occurrence, child suicide is becoming increasingly more frequent. This section reviews and discusses some of the major literature concerning suicide and depression in children, including the family dynamics that surround children's attempted suicide. Suicidal behavior is multi-determined and based on a diversity of precipitating factors, of which family conflicts and strains as well as disordered and maladaptive patterns of interaction are primary. The suicidogenic family, its salient features and characteristics, is the subject of several articles reviewed here. The approaches offered are pre-

239

ventive and concentrate on restructuring dysfunctional family patterns of interrelating, interacting, and communicating in order to reduce the risk of further suicide attempts by children within the family.

An Integration of Suicidology
and Family Therapy

AUTHOR: Joseph Richman

PRECIS: Suicide is a multidetermined act. Although tensions and faulty interaction patterns within the family are among the reasons for attempted suicide, family therapy has been an underutilized intervention method.

INTRODUCTION: Richman offers an extensive and thoughtful review of the literature on suicide. He then presents a logically convincing and humane argument for the integration of suicidology and family therapy. Empirical data and clinical experience are presented to illustrate that suicide attempts are intrinsically related to family dynamics, and practitioners working with suicidal patients are advised to obtain a thorough knowledge of suicide prevention as well as family dynamics, processes, and therapy, for successful treatment depends on an integration of these factors.

TREATMENT: Richman hypothesizes that "intense symbiotic ties combined with inordinate fears of separation and change are intrinsic parts of the suicidogenic family pattern. The maintenance of the bond among members is therefore a life-and-death matter, and unless the family is properly dealt with, both the patient and the relatives may sabotage treatment." Thus suicide is a psychosocial event, a self-destructive act that assures the maintenance of the family's homeostasis. Richman also offers substantial information on the motives for suicide, the assessment of suicidal potential within a family, and the salient features in the individual and family members that may indicate a high risk for suicide.

Among the treatment issues discussed are transference and countertransference, rapport in family treatment, the monitoring of the suicidal person and family members, symbiotic relationships within the family, communication, and aggression and hostility within suicidogenic families. Since the risk of suicide usually increases when the patient begins improving and family members complain that the patient no longer confides in them, the "special dangers" of therapeutic success are elaborated.

Richman recommends five requirements for any program intended to train family therapists to work with suicidal patients: self-awareness on the part of the therapist, an awareness of environmental and social-interpersonal stresses upon the therapist and patient, availability of a support network for the therapist, training in suicide prevention, and training in family therapy.

COMMENTARY: Richman's review of the literature on suicidology is thorough and thoughtful. He offers theoretical and empirical foundations for his assertions, and gives an excellent and convincing argument in favor of the integration of suicidology and family therapy. His approach is clearly detailed and tailored to suicidal patients and their families. Although his case histories concern adult subjects, his presentation has much to offer therapists working with children.

Richman's approach offers a broadly human and humanistic perspective on the problem of suicide. His effective suggestions and delineation of criteria for training family therapists to treat suicidal individuals make this approach practical and applicable. Because the procedure and integration are not as germane as the goal or cure—the saving of lives—the author presents the characteristics of patients who are at risk for suicide, special concerns of therapists treating suicidogenic families, and the dangers inherent in cure. The emphasis on prevention and life saving makes this article essential reading for all therapists working with families in conflict and with members who are at risk for suicide.

SOURCE: Richman, J. "The Family Therapy of Attempted Suicide." *Family Process,* 1979, pp. 131–142.

Childhood Depression and Attempted Suicide

AUTHORS: Alfred P. French and Margaret S. Steward

PRECIS: The concept of childhood depression and family dynamics are related to attempted suicide.

INTRODUCTION: Reference to depression in children appears only recently in the literature on childhood suicide. French and Steward present a review of the concept of childhood depression and clinical data that illustrate its application to suicides by children. They address the wide variability of the depression syndrome in children and the ways in which intrafamilial dynamics can compound this problem.

In the authors propose that helplessness and hopelessness, which are common to all depressions, result from an individual's being confronted with a nonsupportive environment and a disruption of the caretaking process. Therefore, depression in children can be viewed as a disturbance of object relationships.

CASE REPORT: Tommy, age seven, the second youngest of five children, had an extensive history of violent temper outbursts. For several years prior to therapy he was prescribed antiseizure medication. The acute episode that preceded treatment involved a suicide attempt in which Tommy tightly knotted a jumping rope around his neck. He manifested a wide range of symptomatic behaviors, including self-injurious and accident-prone behaviors, violent and uncontrollable temper outbursts, and bullying smaller children.

Tommy was seen in play therapy for five months. His parents were seen jointly by the same therapist. Tommy's father exhibited an obsessive-compulsive personality pattern. He perceived Tommy as a "bad boy" who was intrinsically different from other children. Tommy's mother demonstrated features of the hysterical personality. She believed her son was suffering from a form of epilepsy. In the course of therapy the parents gradually realized that the youngster was reacting to the rigid demands and the stresses within the family unit. Tommy perceived his parents as distant and threatening. He felt caught between a cold and hostile father and a warm but destructively infantilizing mother, and in effect perceived himself to be helpless in a hopeless situation.

COMMENTARY: The therapist readily understood Tommy's symptomatology in terms of the model of childhood depression, that is, Tommy's behaviors reflected the hidden stresses operative within his family. The authors point out that the current literature on suicide in children would not have identified Tommy as a high risk for suicide. Indeed, he manifested no depressive affect; rather he attempted to cope with the depression through impulsive and acting-out behaviors. In reviewing the literature and presenting a case report, the authors demonstrate the utility of the concept of childhood depression and show the clinical applicability of the theory.

French and Steward's presentation is an invaluable addition to the current literature on childhood suicide. The discussion of symptoms and behaviors that may be "depressive equivalents" is important because the greatest danger may well be the therapist's failure to recognize the patient's potential for suicide, thereby augmenting an existing risk. By demonstrating the link between family dynamics, childhood depression, and suicide, the authors make significant, perhaps life-saving, contributions toward a reduction of that risk.

SOURCE: French, A. P., and Steward, M. S. "Family Dynamics, Childhood Depression, and Attempted Suicide in a 7-Year-Old Boy: A Case Study." *Suicide*, 1975, *5*, 29–37.

Family Reconstruction with a Suicidal Youth

AUTHOR: Peter L. Sheras

PRECIS: Role playing is one of several reconstruction techniques in family therapy that emphasize the explication of family patterns.

INTRODCUTION: Sheras presents a descriptive approach to
several family reconstruction techniques used with families in
therapy. Case histories are supplied to help illustrate these various dynamic resources and valuable adjuncts to therapeutic intervention. Reconstruction techniques emphasize the explication of family patterns, thereby enabling clients to better understand and appreciate their own personhood. Each family member is given the opportunity to observe the family from a perspective other than his or her own.

The author briefly describes several family reconstruction techniques and the benefits that can result from their effective use. The reconstruction tools discussed are: family sculpting, family choreography, family fact chronology, family role
playing, family stress ballet, and family portraits. These various
techniques allow for "the 'translation' of forces into a different
representational system, one that is more concrete and one that
can more easily then be structurally and experientially changed."
These different perspectives on family intervention patterns require the active participation of all family members.

CASE HISTORY: The case of Jimmy, age nine, illustrates the
value of the family role-playing reconstructive technique. The
Smith family—father, mother, Bob, age thirteen, and Jimmy—
came to therapy following a suicide attempt by Jimmy and his
subsequent threat to kill himself. Jimmy was resistant to therapy and accused the therapist of prying into private family matters. To break through the resistance, the therapist suggested
role playing. He invited Jimmy to play the therapist while he
played Jimmy's mother. The therapist, playing the role of the
mother, expressed concern that her son might be suicidal. Jim-

my, as therapist, responded: " 'I wouldn't worry about Jimmy killing himself, he is probably just trying to get everyone's attention. Just pay a bit more attention to him and he will be fine.' "

This technique allowed Jimmy to experience himself and his family in a new perspective. It gave him an opportunity to observe his mother's concern, and it helped to clarify some of the clouded communications within the family. The discussion following the reconstructive technique emphasized the observation of how other members of the family perceive each other's roles. The technique allows each family member the opportunity to play another member's role, which facilitates a change of perspective, a shift in interaction patterns, a reappraisal of roles within the family constellation, and thus improves communication and understanding on the part of all.

COMMENTARY: Sheras offers an excellent introduction to some of the major family reconstruction techniques. His descriptions of the various techniques are clear and straightforward, free of jargon, and illustrated with case studies. The therapist using these techniques for the first time, however, would do well to refer to some of the original sources in order to gain a fuller grasp of these family therapy tools.

The author successfully condenses a wealth of family therapy resources, but the brevity of the presentation precludes detailed explanations of the rationale and method of each technique. Nonetheless, this excellent panoramic overview is particularly effective in outlining the benefits of family reconstruction techniques. In addition to allowing family members to observe how others view them in the family constellation, these techniques offer the opportunity to examine the experience of restructuring family patterns and forces. Furthermore, as the author states, these techniques effectively use the family in itself as a dynamic resource.

SOURCE: Sheras, P. L. "Using Family Reconstruction Techniques with Families in Therapy." Paper presented at the convention of the American Psychological Association, Toronto, 1978.

Additional Readings

Corder, B. F., Page, P. V., and Corder, R. F. "Parental History, Family Communication and Interaction Patterns in Adolescent Suicide." *Family Therapy,* 1974, *3,* 285-290.

The authors studied matched groups of suicidal and nonsuicidal adolescents referred to a county mental health clinic. They report significant differences between the two groups, differences that could prove invaluable in the early identification, screening, treatment, and prognosis of both the high-risk suicidal patient and the families who may tend to foster suicidal impulses in adolescents.

Significant differences in family organization, functioning, and interaction patterns between suicidal and nonsuicidal adolescents indicate the necessity for family intervention and counseling when the adolescent appears to be uniquely confined by parental conflicts and areas of family dysfunctioning.

Corder, B. F., Shorr, W., and Corder, R. F. "A Study of Social and Psychological Characteristics of Adolescent Suicide Attempters in an Urban, Disadvantaged Area." *Adolescence,* 1974, *9*(33), 1-6.

Eleven adolescent suicidal inpatients at a mental health center adolescent unit were equally matched with eleven patients who had a variety of diagnoses but no history of suicide attempts. The two groups shared some sense of social isolation and a low level of communication with their parents; neither group showed strong evidence of religious affiliations. The differences between the suicidal and nonsuicidal groups were marked: the suicidal group had a history of suicide within the family or with a close friend with whom the patient identified; a history of an absence of strong identification with a positive adult figure; lack of investment in the future and depression and hopelessness concerning the future; poor impulse control and hyperactivity; a lack of involvement in school; and open and active conflict with parents or guardians.

This study thus offers immense predictive value. Any combination of these "suicidal characteristics" may be present in an adolescent whose family is experiencing conflicts, but the presence of a majority of these characteristics dramatically increases the likelihood of suicide.

Kerfoot, M. "Parent-Child Role Reversal and Adolescent Suicidal Behaviour." *Journal of Adolescence,* 1979, *2,* 337–343.

The author uses the valuable insights of role theory to examine the etiological impact of role reversal in relation to disordered parent-child relationships. Dependency needs are at the core of role-reversal situations, and serious conflicts arise when the parents' unresolved dependency needs clash with the needs of the child. These dysfunctional dynamics are conducive to the formation of suicidal ideas and behavior in the child.

The author uses the case studies of Janet, age fifteen, and Tracy, age eleven, to illustrate the manner in which suicide attempts and threats may be an adolescent's ultimate responses to the stresses created by role reversals. Parent-child role reversals occur in various situations and for a variety of reasons. The mode of occurrence is contingent upon situational variables and personal characteristics within the family members who are involved in the tensions produced by the role reversals. Role reversals can have positive aspects—such as the learning of responsibility, reciprocity, and caring—however, usually the awesome burden outweighs the value of the role reversal as a positive learning experience conducive to continued growth and development.

Morrison, G. C., and Collier, J. G. "Family Treatment Approaches to Suicidal Children and Adolescents." *Journal of Child Psychiatry,* 1969, *8,* 140–153.

The authors propose that suicide attempts and threats by a child or adolescent are not merely an individual cry for help but also symptomatic of a major family disruption, conflict, or dysfunctional pattern of interrelating that has persisted for a prolonged period of time. In 76 percent of the families studied an important loss or separation (or the anniversary of that loss or separation) precipitated the child's suicide threat or attempt. Such precipitating events included the death, illness, divorce, hospitalization, or household move of a parent or parent surrogate.

The authors' family systems approach involved treatment of family patterns of interaction, communication limitations, and relatedness problems. Prognosis improved as interaction patterns became more positive and healthy. Techniques were selected in accordance with the family's and designated patient's abilities to work within the therapeutic problem-solving process.

Orbach, I., Gross, Y., and Glaubman, H. "Some Common Characteristics of Latency-Age Suicidal Children: A Tentative Model Based on Case Study Analyses." *Suicide and Life-Threatening Behavior,* 1981, *11*(3), 180–190.

The authors studied eleven latency-age boys and girls who had attempted or threatened suicide. Their investigations included intensive interviews, therapeutic meetings, direct observation in school, discussions with teachers, and a review of each child's school records. Among the factors common to these children were: a suicidal parent, usually the mother; an absence of satisfying relationships with adults; and the presence of responsibilities and demands that the children felt to be beyond their capabilities.

The study also presents a preliminary model for describing and predicting suicidal behavior. The theoretical base proposes that a person's attitude toward death and his patterns of life are related. Self-destructive behavior is a process composed of opposing forces that operate simultaneously. In children who have attempted or threatened suicide these forces can be classified into four dimensions, each composed of cognitive, emotional, and motivational aspects centering around attitudes toward life and death. The four aspects identified are: (1) the attractiveness of life, which is determined by the degree of need fulfillment, self-esteem, social relationships, and the like; (2) the repulsiveness of life, which involves mental and physical suffering such as rejection, identification with a suicidal parent, and poor peer relationships; (3) the attractiveness of death, which develops from various cultural and religious beliefs about death, and fantasies about death as an improved mode of life or a preferred state of peacefulness; and (4) the repulsiveness of death, that is, the degree to which death arouses fear and anxiety.

This is thus an important study of the core characteristics of the suicidal child or adolescent. An understanding of these typical features can promote preventive and life-saving interventions. Obviously, the earlier the intervention, the more readily is the risk of suicide reduced.

Stone, M. H. "The Parental Factor in Adolescent Suicide." *International Journal of Child Psychiatry*, 1973, *2*, 163–201.

The author presents the cases of six suicidal adolescents with functional psychoses to illustrate the predominant etiological role of parent-child interactions and to correlate these interactions with the prognosis and treatment. The parental attitudes toward the identified patient and the hospital staff ranged from intrusive but cooperative to uncooperative and destructive. The uncooperative and destructive attitude was correlated with the poorest prognosis for positive changes. Indeed, the parents' opposition and undermining of treatment may increase the risk of suicide; in such cases enforced separation of the child from the home environment may be essential.

Pfeffer, C. R. "The Family System of Suicidal Children." *American Journal of Psychotherapy*, 1981, *35*, 330–341.

Five cases are used to illustrate the range of family pathology, the system of family organization, and the effects of the family system on the child's suicidal tendencies and impulses. In sum, the families of suicidal children experience what E. H. Erikson terms "failure of generativity" (*Identity, Youth, and Crisis* [New York: Norton, 1978]) and M. Bowen describes as a lack of self-differentiation (*Therapy in Clinical Practice* [New York: Aronson, 1978]).

The family system of the psychiatrically hospitalized suicidal latency-age child is usually characterized by rigid patterns of interaction, poor identity as a family due to lack of differentiation of generational boundaries, functioning with low self-esteem and depression, repression to states of collective and primitive ego functioning, and intense ambivalence. The parents have a limited capacity for caring, and the suicidal child fulfills the special role of providing gratification to the parents and accepting the displaced parental hostility. In such families, the child's symbiotic relationship with the parent hampers his or her psychological individuation and personal autonomy. The family system produces pathological identifications in the child. The suicidal behavior of the child may be an acted-out last-resort mechanism employed by the child to remove from consciousness his or her negative self-perceptions.

Wetherill, P. S. "Predictability, Failure, and Guilt in Suicide: A Personal Account." *Family Process,* 1975, *14*(3), 339–370.

The author presents a sensitive and insightful examination of the predictability, failure, and guilt surrounding the suicide (or a suicidal motorcycle "accident") of a young man. The study is all the more poignant because it is a personal account involving the writer's son George, who died shortly before his twenty-second birthday as a result of his first suicide attempt. The study chronicles the failures, insensitivities, responsibility, and guilt of the family, school, church, several friends, and many psychiatrists. The author uses the individual case history, drawings, and personal data to support her contention that evidence for the possibility, if not the certainty, of suicide began to accumulate from the time George was four years of age.

The assignation of responsibility and guilt involves a series of philosophical questions: Is an individual completely responsible for his or her suicide? Or do other people within the individual's life system contribute to and influence his or her decisions, including the decision for suicide? Does suicide represent a failure for the individual, the family, and the professional community? As well as offering astute insights into the predictability of suicide, Wetherill poses a wide range of such provocative questions.

12

Schizophrenia

Schizophrenic disorder reactions are typically not seen in extremely young children; rather they arise between six and thirteen years of age. The onset may be gradual and insidious with a progressive movement from symptomatic behaviors to marked and primitive denial and projection and a looseness of association in the thought process. In the course of time the child's thinking regresses to an increasingly concrete level; his capacity for impulse control and frustration tolerance becomes limited, and oftentimes the child manifests marked social and interpersonal isolation. In other instances more acute and immediate eruptions surface.

Because the precise etiology of the schizophrenic syndrome remains an enigma, clinicians have proposed a wide and diverse range of treatment strategies. Intervention may involve one or a combination of the following approaches: genetic and biochemical, inter- and intrapsychic, psychosocial, cognitive, behavioral, and familial. Among the topics reviewed in this chapter are therapeutic perspectives that focus on dysfunctional family relations; patterns and styles of communication; and disordered and inappropriate roles, boundaries, and structures within the family constellation. As the studies presented illustrate, there is as yet no clear evidence for a predominance of any one specific set of familial or parental attitudes and characteristics.

Schizophrenogenic Communication

AUTHOR: Loren R. Mosher

PRECIS: This article focuses on the treatment of a family's "transactional thought disorder," a schizophrenogenic communication pattern that perpetuates irrationality and invalidates communication.

INTRODUCTION: Mosher posits a technique of conjoint family therapy used with the family of a seventeen-year-old diagnosed borderline schizophrenic. After reviewing research relating to disordered thinking and communications in families with schizophrenic offspring, the author proposes that the research findings concerning the communication theory of schizophrenia have not been systematically applied to the practice of family therapy.

Schizophrenogenic communication plays a pivotal role in the etiology and maintenance of the cognitive and communication disorder found in families with a schizophrenic offspring. Therapy is directed at minimizing the unclarified, vague, inconsistent, and distorted patterns of communication within the family. The pattern is pathognomic and serves to invalidate the meaning of a speaker. The therapist utilizing this procedure must be particularly attentive to statements that are inherently contradictory and unclear. Responses that invalidate the speaker's meaning must be questioned and restated. The therapist also remains alert to the disruption of the focus of attention, elicits a comparison of various family members' viewpoints, and must often ask directly for a metastatement.

TREATMENT: The following transcript illustrates the disordered pattern of communication within a family that was seen weekly in conjoint family therapy. The session included Bill, a seventeen-year-old diagnosed borderline schizophrenic, his mother, his father, and the therapist. Bill was discussing his doubts that anyone takes a genuine interest in the study of human relationships; specifically, he was questioning whether anyone, including the therapist, was interested in him. Then Bill's mother invalidated his statement (Mosher's comments about the material are bracketed, and nonverbal material is in parentheses):

Mother: (Laughs) Oh, dear—you're trying to say something else I'm sure—you couldn't really mean . . .

Bill: I don't think so, no. [I mean it as I've said it.]

Therapist: (To mother) What else would you think Bill is trying to say? [Asking directly for a metastatement.]

Bill: Not much . . .

Mother: Uhh (pause). No, I don't know—what . . . I don't feel what you're saying can be real. [Invalidates Bill by defining his feeling as unreal.] I can't see what reason you have for saying it. (To father) Can you? Just because you've perhaps been trying to put yourself across to your friends and they've not (inaudible) . . . or something like that . . . can't see any cause. Have you been trying to interest people in school in your various ideas and things?

Bill: I think . . .

Mother: Yes, and they haven't responded to that sort of (mumbles).

Bill: I think it's—I've been depressed. [Begins to back down from his original position.]

Mother: You mean you've just felt generally depressed— that nobody's interested?

Bill: No, even Dr. Mosher, no.

Mother: Well, that's what I thought. . . [Mother has gotten Bill to change his position to agree with her view.]

Bill: I don't like to say that. (Laughs)

Therapist: What don't you like to say?

Bill: Well, it must be mixed up but when I came in last (week) . . . felt that it wasn't going to do much good—feeling you (therapist) were just going to say to be superfluous, you know it—to (inaudible) . . . a waste of time. [Bill defines his feeling of hopelessness as "mixed up," i.e., as disagreeing with what his mother says he is feeling.]

Mother: What, for you?

Bill: For himself (referring to the therapist). I remember
               now.
Therapist: You were expecting me to not be interested?
Bill: Might be more correct to say I'm expecting not
               enough.
Father: What is this, I'm sorry, don't remember. [Father ac-
               tively disrupts the focus.] (Mother and Bill laugh.)
               [A frequent joint response to father's inattention.]
Bill: Well, the fact that I may be frustrated doesn't
               mean to say that I've a right to expect that frustra-
               tion be alleviated.
Therapist: You know, I would tie what you said with that—
               you said you don't expect enough in sense of . . .
               you hadn't really expected I'd be interested in
               you, *per se,* and in the family's way of being with
               one another. You had not experienced, as you said
               it, person or persons who are interested in relation-
               ships—which is how you based what you said.
Bill: Yes—yes. . .

This excerpt illustrates an instance of the mother's invalidation of Bill's statements, her vagueness, the father's inexplica-
ble disruption of the focus of attention, and Bill's "thought disorder." As Mosher notes, "schizophrenogenic communication
seems to be 'designed' to insure that human behavior is regarded
as unpredictable." Therapy, in contrast, is designed to establish
and maintain a clear and consistently focused pattern of communication within the family. This focus on clarity reduces the
risk of invalidation.

COMMENTARY: Mosher's procedure uses and illustrates the
"communications theory" model of schizophrenia. The establishment of reasonably clear transactions is posited as a necessary prerequisite to psychodynamic therapy with schizogenic
families, and family therapy can assist the family in achieving
this clarity. Furthermore, a clarification of the cognitive and
communication distortions can foster a "rational" and "demys-
tified" view of the patient.
        Clarity, consistency, and validation are initial prerequi-

sites for therapy, necessary but not sufficient. The author employs a communications theory model in order to make the process of communication and family transactions lucid, rational, and amenable to a psychodynamic approach. There is also recourse to a more traditional therapy, but Mosher insightfully points out the need to clarify the communication process prior to a more traditional psychodynamic intervention: "unstructured therapy would seem to subject the schizophrenic to an experience only quantitatively different from that he has experienced in his family; rather than being invalidated, he is not validated, and rather than unclear or inconsistent messages, there are few messages."

Still further, this procedure attempts to bridge the gap between the "communications theory" of schizophrenia that has emerged from current empirical research and the psychotherapeutic context of family therapy. The establishment and maintenance of clear and rational communications are essential to any method of therapy; as such, the author's procedure has unequivocal relevance for any therapeutic approach.

SOURCE: Mosher, L. R. "Schizophrenogenic Communication and Family Therapy." *Family Process*, 1969, *18*, 43–63.

Co-Therapy with Schizophrenic Families

AUTHORS: Peter S. Mueller and Monica McGoldrick Orfanidis

PRECIS: Male and female co-therapists adopt structural roles to observe and explore interactional patterns in families with a schizophrenic member. Therapy focuses on defining generational and sexual boundaries, and resolving separation and loss.

INTRODUCTION: The authors present a theoretical model that serves as a guide to the fragmented communication pattern and confusion inherent in schizophrenic families. The basis for this model proposes that schizophrenia is a disturbance that emanates from within a malfunctioning family system. The model employed rests on a three-generational triadic hypothesis in which schizophrenia is perceived as a lifelong mode of relating that renders one family member vulnerable to chronic and repeated psychotic episodes. The child is expected to meet the needs of the opposite-sexed parent by allowing this parent to take care of him or her. This child, then, remains in an unspoken collusion with the parent, whose needs derive from his or her own unresolved sense of loss from the opposite-sexed parent. The target-patient is used as a substitute or replacement for the lost grandparent.

The schizophrenic syndrome leaves the child confused, dependent, and unable to separate from the symbiotic fusion with the opposite-sexed parent. This dysfunctional alliance ensures that the enmeshed parent does not lose both a child and a parent. The other parent remains emotionally isolated from the child, thereby reinforcing and perpetuating the schizophrenic bond.

METHOD OF THERAPY: The methodological procedure advanced addresses the disturbed family relationship. The therapy included only intact families, wherein all members living in and outside the home were encouraged to participate. The use of male and female co-therapists is essential to this procedure since the structured roles foster a definition and strengthening of sexual boundaries. Co-therapists also limit the family's power to maintain rigid familial boundaries that serve to keep out nonmembers.

The authors discuss and outline four stages of therapy. In the first stage, the initiation of therapy, timing is crucial and the family is highly motivated. The repair of active pathology in the patient must be a pivotal concern. History taking also occurs at this stage. The second stage—the breaking of fusion—can prove to be the most explosive period. Mourned losses are linked to the differentiation process, and anxiety mounts as the patient begins to break infantile ties. Depression often results from the threatened loss of the fused relationship. In the third stage, the alienation between the patient and the parent of the same sex must be resolved. The fourth and longest stage concerns the solidifying of the marital alliance and generational boundaries. The therapists must encourage the extension of social relationships beyond the confines of the family, and marital conflicts must be resolved by the parents. Furthermore, during this phase, the therapists begin to pull back as the family's agents for change. The expansion of all meaningful relationships is encouraged for all the members of the family.

COMMENTARY: The authors propose an excellent treatment model of co-therapy for schizophrenic families. Their three-generational hypothesis is based on an extensive review of applicable literature and a detailed rationale. Their therapeutic model is not intended to be applied rigidly to all cases of schizophrenic families; rather, it is offered as a guide. Furthermore, the approach does not discount the role of heredity or biological predisposition in the etiology of schizophrenia.

The study offers decisive evidence for the use of co-therapists: the co-therapists' structured roles facilitate differentiation and strengthen the generational boundaries, and the co-therapists also provide mutual support and monitoring, thereby assuring that neither inadvertently gets drawn into the family's murky boundaries.

SOURCE: Mueller, P. S., and McGoldrick Orfanidis, M. "A Method of Co-Therapy for Schizophrenic Families." *Family Process*, 1976, *15*, 179-191.

Facilitating Intimacy Through
Cognitive Family Therapy

AUTHOR: E. M. Waring

PRECIS: A lack of intimacy in marriage is related to a vulnerability to some forms of psychopathology. Cognitive family therapy, based on self-disclosure, is proposed as a method of choice.

INTRODUCTION: Marriages of parents of schizophrenic offspring are often filled with conflict and disharmony and marked by an absence of affection, warmth, and intimacy. Waring hypothesizes that this negative affective potential, this lack of interpersonal intimacy in the marriage, "may be a necessary but not necessarily sufficient etiological variable in the development of schizophrenic illness."

Intimacy is operationally defined in this study as "the interpersonal dimension in marriage which most determines marital adjustment." The eight facets of this interpersonal dimension are: affection, cohesion, expressiveness, compatibility, conflict resolution, sexuality, autonomy, and identity. Cognitive family therapy, which is based on evidence that self-disclosure is the prime determinant of the married couple's level of intimacy, is suggested as the preferred method of treatment.

TREATMENT: Cognitive family therapy begins with an evaluation interview wherein all the family members focus on each member's "theory" of why the problems exist within the family unit. During this interview, only responses that answer the question "Why?" are elicited; affective expressions and behavioral interpretations are avoided. At the interview the therapist also explains the theory upon which cognitive family therapy is based, and the rules for the sessions are negotiated with the family. Following the initial interview, only the parents are involved in sessions; the schizophrenic child receives individual treatment from another therapist.

The lack of interpersonal intimacy and the absence of self-disclosure is usually revealed in the sessions. The cognitive process allows both partners the opportunity to uncover previously unrevealed assumptions that have created and serve to maintain the debilitating distance within the family structure. Furthermore, the context of the offspring's delusions often implies the parents' nondisclosed reasons for the lack of intimacy. As self-disclosure facilitates an increase in closeness, familial and marital tensions decrease, which results in less expressed concern about the schizophrenic target-patient.

COMMENTARY: Waring offers a number of stimulating and provocative clinical observations. As he notes, "these clinical observations are preliminary and may be a result of observer bias. However, they are presented in the context of our current lack of knowledge about the possible role of family dynamics in the predisposition, precipitation, or perpetuation of schizophrenia."

Waring also makes clear suggestions for further research; for example, the marriages of parents of schizophrenic children should be reliably evaluated for levels of intimacy compared to patient and normal controls. Since intimacy is operationally defined and subdivided into eight measurable categories, such an evaluation would be feasible. Another recommendation that has empirical and practical value concerns evaluating the effectiveness of cognitive family therapy in facilitating intimacy through cognitive self-disclosure at various developmental stages in the life cycle.

Waring also offers some excellent recommendations for treatment. He presents a technique that not only fosters self-disclosure but also bridges the isolation and distance within the parents' relationship. Waring's procedure could be incorporated into other theoretical and clinical approaches, and it has particular value in treating families who are experiencing difficulties with communication, openness, and the expression of intimacy. The technique can also help alert troubled families to the existence of conflict, for often schizophrenic families and families with a schizophrenic member view themselves as typically well-adjusted and are not cognizant of their severe lack of interpersonal intimacy. Cognitive family therapy serves to facilitate awareness and increase intimacy within the family.

SOURCE: Waring, E. M. "Cognitive Family Therapy in the
Treatment of Schizophrenia." *Psychiatric Journal of the University of Ottawa: An International Journal of Psychiatry*,
1981, *6*(4), 229-233.

Family Resistance to Change

AUTHORS: Norman L. Paul and George H. Grosser

PRECIS: Using both individual psychotherapy and the conjoint
patient-family therapy setting, the authors report on a series of
family units, each with a schizophrenic patient, to delineate the
fixity in family role relationships.

INTRODUCTION: Families tend to develop and establish specific interactional patterns that are rigidly resistant to change.
Role transactions are fixed, all the family members strive to preserve these relationships over time, and attempts to alter these
constellations meet with adamant opposition. The etiology and
maintenance of schizophrenia is related to, and an integral part
of, the designated patterns of interrelationships.
      The responses of the patient, his psychopathology, and
the responses of family members to him are all resistant to
change. Although the family comes to therapy seeking a cure,
members' behavior, responses, and interactional patterns betray
a staunch fixation and loyalty to the dysfunctional role structures and patterns within the family unit.

THEORY: Paul and Grosser present detailed and scholarly observations on the interactional characteristics of families with
a schizophrenic member. Their astute observations on the fixity
of role relationships are based on their experience in the early
phases of conjoint patient-family therapy. They highlight four
mechanisms most commonly employed by family members to
maintain the family's homeostasis, which thereby reinforces the

patient's pathology. The first mechanism is *denial*, which assumes a variety of forms: denial of the existence of patient's emotional disorder with or without attribution of dysfunction to nonpsychological causes; denial of the existence of the patient's problems or the legitimacy of his impulses and needs for gratification, which in turn provokes regressive or counterhostile behavior in the patient; attributing the patient's responses to defective character or deviance, which provokes the patient's perplexity or counterhostile behavior; denial of the possibility of improvement in the patient. The three other mechanisms are: the expectation of psychotic behavior and recurrence of symptoms; the denial of separate existence or possibility of separate existence for patient or other family member; and the provoking of anxiety in the patient by threatening abandonment. These mechanisms are illustrated by eight case studies.

The authors also discuss the role of projection and distortion as they are frequently observed in the course of therapy. The image of the patient as "an uncontrollable monster" or "freak of nature" is a recurrent projective theme. Such projections tend to allow the family members to deny and defend their own intrafamilial hostility. These projections also permit the parents to present themselves as long-suffering victims of the patient's idiosyncratic needs and demands. Of course, they also reinforce the patient's negative self-image and ensure the perpetuation of his role as the family's pathological and deviant member, which in turn solidifies and reaffirms the existing fixed and rigid structure: "Family members feel reinforced in their assumption that they need not change for the patient will never change."

To maintain their fixed interrelational pattern the family members may make incessant attempts to seduce the therapist into an alliance against the schizophrenic member. "Doctor, why can't you make him see this simple point?" is an example of one such maneuver. Consequently, the therapist must be family oriented. He or she must take a firm stance in empathically supporting and judiciously confronting family members.

COMMENTARY: The authors clearly illustrate the interactional characteristics observed in families with a schizophrenic member, focusing on the rigidly fixed role structure within the family, which they perceive to be at the core of the etiology and maintenance of schizophrenia. The authors explicitly discuss the function of this fixed structure; it perpetuates a static equilibrium within the family at the expense of the patient. Four mechanisms by which the family maintains its structure are explained and illustrated by case histories.

The authors assert that the features of family interaction discussed in this study are present to a greater or lesser degree in families whose members experience other forms of psychopathology as well as schizophrenia. Offering directions for further research, the authors pose a series of thought-provoking questions concerning the family's maneuvers for reinforcing the patient's pathology, and the possible existence of specific kinds of interactional patterns with the different types of schizophrenia.

SOURCE: Paul, N. L., and Grosser, G. H. "Family Resistance to Change in Schizophrenic Patients." *Family Process,* 1978, *17,* 377–401.

Therapy with an Enmeshed Schizophrenic Family

AUTHORS: Rachael T. Hare-Mustin and Carter Umbarger

PRECIS: A method for structuring therapy interviews that disengages the child from an enmeshed schizophrenic family.

TECHNIQUE: Families with a schizophrenic child are sometimes described as "enmeshed." The family members tend to be tightly interlocked, and this structure tends to be adamantly resistant to change. The family strives toward a continued balance within its system by undermining and destroying meaningful communication and rendering the therapist ineffective by drawing him or her into the dysfunctional system.

The authors offer a specific structural approach to treatment that enables the schizophrenic child to begin to differentiate himself or herself from the entangled disorder inherent within the schizophrenogenic family structure. The family is seen by two therapists, each of whom sees the family on alternate weeks. The therapist who is not with the family observes behind a one-way mirror, and he or she is not discussed during the session. This method thus focuses the family on problem-oriented, rather than therapist-oriented, issues. Further, the risk of "splitting the therapists" is reduced by focusing on different topics with each.

Each session is divided into two periods. In the first half, dubbed "family time," issues related to the target child are discussed. Following a mid-session break, therapist and child confer with the observing therapist. In the second part of the session the therapist returns to the couple to discuss essentially adult themes, that is, the marital relationship and their roles as husband and wife rather than as parents of a child with deviant behavior.

The structure of these therapy sessions thus mirrors the therapeutic intention: When issues of the child's and parents' individuation and independence are discussed, child and parents are physically separate. This structured approach makes explicit the generational boundaries between parents and child, the focus and content of the sessions, and the problem-oriented format, and it minimizes the possibility of the therapists inadvertently becoming inducted into the family structure.

CASE REPORT: The Decker family sought help because their twelve-year-old son had been diagnosed as schizophrenic. Although the boy was of normal intelligence and attended public school, he exhibited many bizarre mannerisms, incoherent speech, and numerous fears and somatic complaints. The boy was inappropriately enmeshed with his parents. The family persistently undermined previous attempts at therapeutic intervention.

The Deckers were seen for fifteen sessions over a five-month period. The family was seen by alternating therapists and in split sessions. The "family" sessions, wherein the son and parents were together, were devoted to issues of the boy's school life, outside activities, and enhancing his personal autonomy and break from the unhealthy collusion. The second half of the sessions, which separated parents and child, concentrated on marital conflicts and the hostility that existed between the husband and wife.

As a result of these structured sessions noticeable positive changes occurred. The son began to develop a sense of self-differentiation; his mannerisms and speech improved, somatic complaints diminished, and his affect became more subdued and less volatile. The parents also became less hostile, toward their son and each other and increasingly tolerant of their son's growing independence.

COMMENTARY: Hare-Mustin and Umbarger present a well-documented and richly illustrated argument for the effective use of a structural approach to therapy with schizophrenic families. Their perceptive recommendations for a therapeutic approach serve to increase meaningful communication and the possibility of breaking through rigid and destructive family boundaries. At the same time, these suggestions diminish the likelihood that the therapist will be drawn into the dysfunctional system. The rationale for the use of co-therapists is similar to that offered by Mueller and McGoldrick Orfanidis, reviewed earlier in this chapter; both articles present extensive empirical and clinical supports for the use of co-therapists.

The authors note that their method is not proposed as a cure for schizophrenia, but rather a means of reducing stresses and tensions in the family system in order to effect change. Theirs is a strategy that could be used in a wide variety of therapeutic approaches, and the authors so expertly delineate the goals of therapy, especially the sense of self-demarcation and differentiation, and the procedure for achieving these goals, that readers can readily apply the procedures in accordance with their needs. The applicability of this structural approach by other therapists is enhanced by the authors' detailed and clear statements of the procedural concerns and the logistics of the structural approach; for example, they outline the rationale for using split sessions and co-therapists and also explain the logistics for applying the structural strategy. This approach appears to be an effective method of choice when splitting, differentiation, and blurred and inappropriate roles and boundaries are at issue in working with schizophrenic patients and schizophrenogenic families.

SOURCE: Hare-Mustin, R. T., and Umbarger, C. "A Structural Approach to Therapy with Schizophrenic Families." Paper presented at the annual meeting of the American Psychological Association, Montreal, August 1973.

Characteristics and Treatment of Families with Schizophrenic Sons

AUTHOR: Richard H. Fulmer

PRECIS: Families of young schizophrenic males share certain characteristics, which are described and for which therapeutic strategies are suggested.

INTRODUCTION: Fulmer presents a clinical view of the symptoms and strategies for treatment of families with schizophrenic sons. The identified patient in these families is a male in early adulthood. He typically is depressed, dependent, and passive. He tends to be obese, has potential for explosive anger, and finds it difficult to establish meaningful sexual relationships with women. He often has homosexual confusion. His depressive tendencies are sometimes accompanied by suicidal ideation.

The families are perceived as struggling with a specific stage in the family life cycle, which Jay Haley and Milton Erickson call weaning parents from children (J. Haley, *Uncommon Therapy: The Psychiatric Techniques of Milton H. Erickson, M.D.* [New York: Norton, 1973]). Characteristically, the family does not establish clear boundaries. The mother and son are often fused and enmeshed, whereas the father tends to be isolated and disengaged. The father and son rarely have a way of resolving conflicts that arise between them, and the mother usually allays the problem. She sees herself as a mediator and feels she protects the father and son from doing violence to each other. Her position as "go-between" reduces the possibility of negotiation between father and son.

TREATMENT METHOD: Given that so much emotional pressure approaches the surface and little can be resolved because of the explosive nature of these stresses, the treatment method avoids the expression of affect. Concrete, specific, and common tasks are contracted that help accomplish the following therapeutic goals: loosening the relationship between mother and son, strengthening the relationship between father and son, increasing the son's independence and responsibility, and increasing the closeness between husband and wife.

Therapy also addresses the mother's and father's resistance maneuvers, the parents' marital conflicts, and the importance of follow-up to avoid backsliding. The training of practical living skills for the son is also emphasized; as the author explains, "An extremely important part of treating such a family is to be able to provide training in independent living skills for the son, and, eventually, a sheltered, supervised apartment into which he can move. This aspect of the treatment is often quite essential and in the cases about which this paper is written was accomplished by a large staff in a day hospital. It is perhaps thus counterindicated to attempt this treatment method with such a family privately without such a program being available for the son. The parents are usually *not* good trainers because they so habitually overindulge the son that he learns nothing."

COMMENTARY: Fulmer presents an excellent model of the typical characteristics of families with a schizophrenic son. He

also addresses the primary characteristics of the schizophrenogenic family pattern, particularly concentrating on the issues of
fusion (between mother and son) and exclusion (of the father).
His approach has important theoretical, empirical, and practical
implications. His practical emphasis upon behavioral living strategies makes for an applicable procedure. The general efficacy of
this approach appears to be contingent on this practical training
in day-to-day living skills and independence. As Fulmer states,
this program may not be effectively employed by private practitioners who do not have training resources available, since the
parents do not make good trainers.

The attempt to discourage explosive affective expression
and to focus on practical solutions is not dissimilar from many
other cognitive family therapy approaches. Contracts and negotiation strategies can be worked out with the parents and family
members to help the patient assimilate and apply practical living skills.

This stimulating and thought-provoking study describes a
style of treatment that appears tailored to work with a specific
"family type." Fulmer does not propose this strategy as a cure
for schizophrenia; rather the procedure allows a fuller understanding of the family dynamics and a means to reduce tensions
within the system in order to effect change. The approach expertly combines family, marital, and individual therapy in a specific sequence for the purposes of achieving constructive changes
in the interactional dynamics within the family and practical
solutions to existing conflicts.

SOURCE: Fulmer, R. H. "Families with Schizophrenic Sons: A
    Description of Family Characteristics and a Strategy for Fam-
    ily Therapy." *Family Therapy*, 1977, 4(2), 101–111.

Additional Readings

Beels, C. C. "Family and Social Management of Schizophrenia."
In P. Guerin (Ed.), *Family Therapy: Theory and Practice.*
New York: Gardner Press, 1976.

Beels's perceptive discussion of the management of
schizophrenic patients includes an extensive review of the literature and theories on the schizophrenic and his family. The series
of theoretical questions and answers posed could spawn vol-
umes of research. The author also details the social setting of
the schizophrenic and his family. Typically, the families of
schizophrenics lack a network of social connections and are isolated and alienated from the larger community. This isolation
fosters a myriad of problems, not the least of which is that the
family's closed system tends to reinforce its own dysfunctional
processes, which can lead to *folie à famille,* shared familial delusions, attitudes, ideas, and beliefs. The family's isolation allows
these delusions to become locked and perpetuated within the
family structure; they are not open to scrutiny and reality testing.

Beels also classifies various types of schizophrenia, detail-
ing the major differences among "first breaks," "periodic patients," and "chronic patients." The case studies presented are
rich with illustrations of the schizophrenic process that un-
folds within the disordered and dysfunctional family structure.

Bowen, M. "Family Psychotherapy." *American Journal of Orthopsychiatry,* 1961, *31*(1), 40–60.

The author, one of the pioneers in the field of family research in schizophrenia, discusses some of the essential principles, rules, goals, and techniques used in family therapy. Specific topics include the treatment of families with a psychotic
member, the avoidance mechanisms that involve the therapist
in the emotional problems of individual family members, and
the therapist's attitude about anxiety. To illustrate the degree
to which parents go along with their children's irrational behaviors, the case of a seventeen-year-old psychotic male is presented. This case also illustrates the change that occurs in family members when the passive father takes a positive stand, and

when the therapist refuses to label the patient as "sick." This article has immense historic value as well as theoretical and clinical implications.

Clower, C. G., Jr., and Brody, L. "Conjoint Family Therapy in Outpatient Practice." *American Journal of Psychotherapy,* 1964, *18,* 670–677.

    Clower and Brody present techniques, selection criteria, and treatment process and goals for outpatient conjoint family therapy with families who have a schizophrenic patient within their unit. In the initial session of the family therapy a contract is discussed with the entire family. The contract concerns such issues as the family as a unit needing treatment and treatment as seeking to modify maladaptive communication patterns and interpersonal relationships. Conjoint family therapy aims at clarifying the family communication process through focusing on nonverbal communications and behavior, as well as verbalized concerns, especially when they are contradictory, confusing, or debilitating to growth and authentic communication within the family system. Members are encouraged to ventilate hostile feelings within the therapy sessions. Therapy also seeks to resolve significant conflicts in the role relationships, particularly the parental roles.

    Conjoint family therapy is similar in many ways to traditional group therapy, although the processes and goals differ somewhat. For example, group therapy emphasizes the individual and his or her needs and improvement, while family therapy focuses on improving disturbed communication patterns and interpersonal relationships in order to foster and enhance the growth of the family unit.

Doane, J. A., Goldstein, M. J., and Rodnick, E. H. "Parental Patterns of Affective Style and the Development of Schizophrenia Spectrum Disorders." *Family Process,* 1981, *20,* 337–349.

    The authors analyzed measures of parental affective styles of communication from a sample of fifty-two families of disturbed but nonpsychotic adolescents. Data obtained from cross-situational measures of parental interactive behavior are

found to afford better prediction of offspring diagnosis than indices obtained from a single measurement source. Styles of
communication in dyadic and triadic discussions were also observed and analyzed. Adolescents with at least one parent who
consistently manifested a disordered affective style of communication in both dyadic and triadic discussions developed
schizophrenia-spectrum disorders as young adults. Adolescents
with at least one parent who was consistently benign in his or
her affective style of communication exhibited much healthier
behavior patterns in young adulthood. When both parents displayed pathological affective styles of communication and inconsistent styles in dyadic and triadic interactions, more serious
psychopathology was noted in early adulthood. The authors discuss the methodological implications for family research and
implications for clinical application.

Franklin, P. "Family Therapy of Psychotics." *American Journal
of Psychoanalysis,* 1969, *29,* 50–58.
     Franklin offers a case illustration to demonstrate the in-
terrelationship between the symptomatology of a schizophrenic
individual and the emotional life of his or her primary family:
the psychosis experienced by the identified patient is a symptom of the disturbed and maladaptive processes in the family
structure. Franklin further proposes that the family therapist
working with psychotics is never a neutral observer, but rather
an active participant in the family's life. The case of Susan,
a fifteen-and-a-half-year-old female, and her family illustrates
how the therapist may elicit the family's dormant healthy emotions by modeling and introjecting positive emotions and attitudes and by uncovering and resolving previously concealed and
displaced conflicts.

Gartner, R. B., Fulmer, R. H., Weinshel, M., and Goldklank, S.
"The Family Life Cycle: Developmental Crises and Their
Structural Impact on Families in a Community Mental Health
Center." *Family Process,* 1978, *17*(1), 47–58.
     The authors developed a typology for troubled families
based on the configuration of family members and the position
of the patient in the family unit. They then investigated the

proposed typology by surveying the demographic and clinical characteristics of 110 families of patients treated in a day hospital. The four family constellations defined are: families in which the identified patient is (1) currently a spouse; (2) the grown child of a couple in an ongoing marriage; (3) the grown child of a single parent, that is, one parent has left the family through death, divorce, desertion, or separation; and (4) a single adult living with relatives other than parents. Significant differences among the four constellations include: family income, the identified patient's sex, age of onset of the patient's conflict, age of presenting at the day hospital, and diagnosis. No significant differences were indicated for ethnic background, religious preference, identified patient's place of birth, occupation of the family's principal wage earner, or the identified patient's level of education.

As a whole, the constellations appear to constitute specific clinical entities in the population studied. Family stresses, especially those tensions and constrictions that occurred in the early and formative years of the identified patient's life, seem to account for the differences among the entities. For example, the second constellation contained the highest proportion of chronic schizophrenics, and these patients had experienced disruptive and debilitating familial conflicts at a very early age.

Haley, J. "The Family of the Schizophrenic: A Model System." *Journal of Nervous and Mental Disease,* 1959, *129,* 357–374.
In this classic article, a product of research conducted by Gregory Bateson, Haley attempts to show that schizophrenic behavior serves a function within a dysfunctional family organization. Focusing on the interactive behavior of the schizophrenic and his parents—rather than on the family's beliefs, attitudes, or psychodynamic concerns—he asserts that schizophrenic behavior originates within the family structure and its inherent patterns of communication, interrelationship, and interaction. The total family is pathological, rather than solely the identified patient within the family unit.

Referring frequently to classic studies and issues, Haley presents a wealth of case histories that illustrate maladaptive family structures and behaviors. He examines the manner in which patterns of interaction become constricted and rigidified, noting how over time the family members come to behave as though involved and bound in a *compulsory* relationship. He discloses the varied and complex ways in which family members form alliances and dysfunctional collusions within the family, observing also how family members qualify their own and others' statements, and use typical defensive maneuvers and strategies. In sum, the family seeks to maintain its homeostasis at all costs, no matter how painful. Thus schizophrenia can be described as both a product and parody of a dysfunctional family system.

Jackson, D. D., and Weakland, J. H. "Conjoint Family Therapy: Some Considerations on Theory, Technique, and Results." *Psychiatry,* 1961, *24,* 30–45.

The authors, pioneers of the Family Therapy in Schizophrenia Project of the Palo Alto Medical Research Foundation, address theoretical and technical considerations of conjoint family therapy, that is, therapy that treats the identified schizophrenic patient and other members of the family together as a functioning natural unit. They discuss the purpose of active intervention in, and management of, family interactions in the initial phases of therapy. They also consider the manner in which the therapist can help the family shift its patterns of meaning and intent. Still further, they elaborate various therapeutic techniques for altering self-reinforcing and mutually destructive networks of interaction within the family structure. Fragments of case studies are used throughout to clarify and illustrate essential points of theory and clinical practice.

Midlarsky, E. "Family Therapy: Two Case Studies." *Journal of Psychiatric Treatment and Evaluation,* 1981, *3,* 411–415.

The author presents two cases that illustrate a family systems approach to therapy. The psychopathology is perceived as rooted within the dysfunctional family unit. Although conjoint family therapy is usually the method of choice for intervening in disordered family systems, its effectiveness is limited in some cases. For example, in the first case study presented not all members of the family cooperated with the therapeutic sessions, process, and goals. In the second case, some family members were unable to participate because of their immaturity, youth, or psychological vulnerability. In some families members may be too rigid and inflexible to cooperate or participate productively in the therapy sessions. In instances of this sort, family therapy may not be the most effective intervention method.

13

Elective Mutism

Elective mutism is operationally defined as a condition in which an individual refuses or is unable to communicate verbally with certain people. The electively mute child has no particular speech or language deficit, has learned language and is capable of effective verbal expression, yet does not speak with anyone outside the immediate family. The condition is relatively rare and may represent a dysfunctional family system.

Electively mute children share many common features: they are particularly shy, sensitive, suspicious, and fearful; they can be strong-willed, oppositional, and particularly restrained in their aggression. Family therapy is suggested as an effective method of choice in working with these children. The specific strategic techniques depend on the age of the child, the degree of behavioral constriction, and the nature and structure of the family system. The two articles reviewed in this chapter present detailed case studies and invaluable suggestions for clinical intervention.

Behavioral and Family Therapies
for Elective Mutism

AUTHORS: John B. Rosenberg and Marion B. Lindblad

PRECIS: A combination of behavior therapy and family therapy is used to treat electively mute children.

INTRODUCTION: The authors discuss the need to employ a combined approach to the treatment of elective mutism, operationally defined as a child's refusal or inability to communicate with people outside the immediate family. Many electively mute children will speak only to their parents and siblings, often refusing to speak with grandparents or any other members of the extended family. Children diagnosed as being electively mute characteristically are behaviorally constricted in the presence of people other than the immediate family. They tend to be of average or better intelligence and are often verbally fluent with parents or siblings. The parents typically view these youngsters as controlling and determined to maintain their symptom. The problem particularly comes to the fore at about the age of four or five years, that is, the age at which children usually begin school and their social interactions extend beyond the boundaries of the family unit.

Rosenberg and Lindblad's approach combines family and behavioral therapies. A family approach enables all family members to understand the function of the target-patient's symptom within the family constellation, while the behavioral approach is intended to address the symptom. Because the symptom is particularly resistant to most forms of therapy, counter-conditioning, successive approximations, and reinforcement are useful. This combined approach thus seeks to both remove the symptom and examine the dysfunctional family unit.

CASE STUDY: The case of Tony, age six, is used to illustrate the combined approach. Tony manifested the typical characteristics of elective mutism: he appeared to be behaviorally constricted with strangers, had average intelligence, and refused to speak and participate in school. Treatment clarified the function of Tony's symptom and the structural aspect of the family system. Tony and his mother were enmeshed in an alliance that the mother used to retaliate against her husband, who was distant from the family. Therapy encouraged both parents to be more actively involved with each other. Once Tony was no longer triangulated by his parents he began speaking in school.

COMMENTARY: The authors' combined approach is clearly tailored to the treatment of elective mutism, allowing for the treatment of both the inhibiting symptom and the dysfunctioning family. The authors note that this method does not address the complex problems of speech disturbances exhibited by autistic or severely retarded children. According to them, the general efficacy of the approach demands that family therapy is always indicated in cases of elective mutism. Depending on the child's age and the severity of the behavioral constriction, it may also be necessary to formulate a reinforcement paradigm with the school, the family, and subsystems within the family.

    The case presented confirms the authors' conviction that an approach combining behavioral techniques in a family context ensures greater success than either approach alone. Through the integration of the empirical and practical contributions of behavior and family therapies, the symptom is ameliorated and the family system that produced the symptom is changed.

SOURCE: Rosenberg, J. B., and Lindblad, M. B. "Behavior Therapy in a Family Context: Treating Elective Mutism." *Family Process*, 1978, *17*, 77-82.

The Importance of Environmental Changes in the Treatment of Elective Mutism

AUTHOR: H. Wergeland

PRECIS: A follow-up study of eleven children with elective mutism shows that changes in environment such that the child no longer had to meet expectations of being "the one who does not speak" were the most crucial contribution to improvement.

INTRODUCTION: Wergeland briefly reviews the condition of elective mutism, the characteristics of the symptom, and its differences from similar syndromes. Children who experience elective mutism are particularly shy, stubborn, and suspicious of anything or anyone new; the family background of most of these children suggests that elective mutism is the result of a family neurosis.

METHOD: Wergeland studied eleven children who were admitted to the Children's Psychiatric Clinic of the University of Oslo between 1955 and 1970. All were diagnosed as having elective mutism. Initial examinations included case histories, somatic and neurological tests, and psychological evaluations. Among the ninety-five variables recorded were age, hereditary factors, family atmosphere, developmental patterns, and related issues. A similar list of approximately seventy variables was used for the follow-up study, including: development after discharge, school accomplishments, and work history. At the time of the follow-up the patients were between sixteen and twenty-six, with an average age of twenty-three years.

RESULTS: The results of the preliminary investigation indicated that in addition to elective mutism, repressed aggression was present in all eleven patients. Six of the children received treatment at the time of original admission (psychotherapy, milieu therapy, occupational therapy, and the like). Five did not receive treatment because their parents would not allow them to be taken from the home for an extended period of time. The backgrounds of both the treated and the untreated children were similar, with the exception of the father's age at the time of the child's birth.

The data confirm the author's hypothesis that family neurosis is often present. Typically, the father's advanced age and his absence from the home led the mother to establish close ties with the child and to become overprotective. A change of environment proved to be the most important factor in improvement. By implication, a change of school may be a prime consideration for children diagnosed as having elective mutism. Various methods of treatment appeared to be ineffective or to involve secondary traumata, namely, separation from the home and the immediate family. Consequently, preventive measures should be emphasized, and these should not stigmatize the child as mute.

COMMENTARY: Although this follow-up study involved only eleven subjects, the results yield feasible and effective suggestions. This sensitive and insightful investigation into elective mutism is commendable both for the emphasis on preventive measures and the reappraisal and confirmation of the characteristics of the families and children involved.

Wergeland notes the limitations of his study: for two of the five untreated children only the parents' evaluations were available, and, of course, further work must be done on larger populations. Nevertheless, the study serves as an excellent preliminary base for future research. Furthermore, the findings confirm most current empirical data and literature in showing that elective mutism is more often than not symptomatic of a dysfunctional family system; indeed, it may be a product of that dysfunction. Researchers should also pay attention to those factors that this follow-up study did not confirm, for instance, the contentions that the symptoms tend to disappear around puberty and that the patient is rarely inhibited by this symptom for more than two years.

This preliminary study should be read by all family practitioners working with children who experience elective mutism. It offers astute observations and superb clinical guidelines for understanding some of the family dynamics, family conflicts and characteristics, and features characteristically present in the child. Wergeland's suggestions and directives, especially his call for more preventive approaches, merit full and immediate attention and action.

SOURCE: Wergeland, H. "Elective Mutism." *Acktiv Psychiatry-Skandinaviska* [*Clinical Psychiatry: Scandinavia*], 1979, *59*, 218–228.

Additional Readings

Bradley, S., and Sloman, L. "Elective Mutism in Immigrant Families." *Journal of Child Psychiatry*, 1975, *14*, 510–514.

Bradley and Sloman present a comparative survey and four case studies of children with elective mutism. The preponderance of elective mutism among children whose parents recently immigrated to Canada led the authors to review the literature, study the cultural factors in the development of childhood disorders, and make clinical observations of the parent-child relationship and family interaction patterns. The authors propose that elective mutism, at least in the population studied, may exist on a continuum; the more resistant and pathological cases are referred to a clinic, whereas milder forms typically respond to treatment within the school setting.

Observation of the four clinic-referred children and their families suggests that the relationship between mother and child was hostile and dependent. This situation was exacerbated by the mother's depression, her loneliness in a foreign country, her sense of isolation, and her refusal to learn the language of her new country. These factors reinforced the dysfunctional bond between the mother and child, and hampered the development of the child's sense of autonomy and independence. In these cases, clearly parental reactions to immigration contributed to the etiology and dynamics of elective mutism in the child.

Goll, K. "Role Structure and Subculture in Families of Elective Mutists." *Family Process*, 1979, *18*, 55-68.

Goll presents an excellent and thorough overview of the literature on elective mutism. He poses two hypothetical conditions prerequisite to the development and maintenance of elective mutism: a society that produces outsiders and outsider groups, and a family that has little support from, and confidence in, the mainstream of society.

The study is richly illustrated with ten cases of families containing an elective mutist. The significant similarities in these families' role structures have crucial implications for therapy; for example, treatment must be based on alleviating the family's suspiciousness, hostility, and distrust of the "outside" world. Also, because the therapist is a member of the social realm external to the family structure, he or she must elicit the family's basic trust before attempting any therapeutic interventions addressed to the social training of the elective mutist.

14

Incontinence

Most children are toilet trained by eighteen to twenty-four months of age, although individual differences are large, even among children in the same family. Some children, however, for a variety of reasons, refuse or are unable to be toilet trained. In the absence of physical or urogenital disorders, these children are diagnosed as enuretic or encopretic. Nocturnal enuresis, defined as urinary incontinence during sleep in children three years of age or older, can be a significant symptom and may occur in as many as 20 percent of all children. For some unknown reason it is more prevalent in boys than in girls. Like enuresis, encopresis, the persistent fecal soiling in a child over the age of four, is more common in boys. Soiling usually occurs once to several times a day. The parents usually request therapeutic help

285

when their child begins school, as the encopresis then becomes particularly problematic. Both enuresis and encopresis can be categorized as primary or secondary. In the primary condition the child has never developed control over his bladder (enuresis) or bowels (encopresis). The secondary condition refers to those children who developed control and later regressed to bed-wetting or fecal soiling.

The articles reviewed in this chapter offer interesting and different approaches for intervention with families attempting to cope with an incontinent child.

Strategic Therapy for Childhood Incontinence

AUTHOR: Jay Haley

PRECIS: Three strategic approaches to the presenting problem of incontinence are discussed and illustrated by case studies.

INTRODUCTION: Typically, when a child is brought to a clinic the parents state that the problem resides in the youngster. The therapist may agree or may perceive the problem to be dyadic (within the mother-child or father-child unit) or triadic, wherein the parents use the child in a power struggle. The unit that the therapist addresses is determined, at least in part, by the presenting problem.

If the child's problem is conceptualized as an overintense, overinvolved dyad between an adult and child, the goal of therapy is a structural separation. Most often an overinvolved dyad exists between the mother and child, with the father seen as peripheral. The achievement of separation, however, is far more complicated than its definition. The stages of treatment are determined by the approach employed. To disengage an intense dyad, the therapist might enter the relationship between the mother and child, father and child, or mother and father.

Haley describes and discusses each of these three approaches for entering the family, emphasizing that the presenting problem is the determining factor in selecting an approach:

> The main purpose in having a clearly defined symptom, or problem, is that the entrance into the family structure is through the symptom. That is the issue the family is most concerned about. Another advantage is that a clearly defined problem allows the therapist and the family to judge the success of the treatment. However, the family need not offer a clearly defined symptom in the beginning, since a vague problem can be defined into a specific one when a competent therapist uses these approaches.
>
> Given a two-parent family, these approaches are most effective with a severely disturbed child and

family and are often most useful when previous individual child treatment has failed because of the severity of the symptom and the difficulty in obtaining
the cooperation of the family. It is the task of the
therapist to motivate disturbed parents to cooperate,
and approaching families in these ways leads to the
cooperation. Generally, family approaches of this
type can be used with the majority of cases that arrive in the average middle-class child treatment facility.

TREATMENT: In the first approach, the therapist enters the
family through the peripheral person, in the case presented, the
father. During the initial stage, father, son, and therapist become
engaged in a task, while the mother shifts to the peripheral position. Next, the parents and therapist become involved, while
the child drops out of the adult struggle and interacts with
peers. In the third stage, the therapist must drop out, leaving
the parents involved with each other and the boy involved with
peers.

If the therapist decides that he cannot enter the family
through the peripheral person, he may attempt to enter through
the overinvolved dyad. Foreseeing that the overinvolved parent
will resist the interpretation that he or she is overinvolved and
overprotective, the therapist can make an effective intervention
through the use of a task. The approach is to divert the parent
to activities that are more productive and appropriate than hov-
ering over the child.

A third approach is to initiate therapy by focusing on the
child's problems and then shifting to the marital struggle in
which the child is involved. In this approach it is not unusual
for coalitions with the therapist to form and change without the
clients' being aware of them.

CASE EXAMPLES: As an example of the therapist entering the
family through the overinvolved dyad through the effective use
of a task, Haley describes a case reported by Milton Erickson
(J. Haley, *Uncommon Therapy: The Psychiatric Techniques of
Milton H. Erickson, M.D.* [New York: Norton, 1973], chap. 6).

Johnny, a twelve-year-old boy, was wetting his bed every night. Johnny's father proved to be uncooperative, so the therapist focused on the mother-child dyad. Having detected Johnny's hostility toward his mother, the therapist suggested that Johnny engage in a task that he would dislike but that his mother would dislike even more. It was proposed to Johnny that his mother wake up at 4:00 A.M. to check his bed. If it was wet she would wake him; if it was dry she would let him sleep. If she had to wake him, he would have to copy pages from a book until 7 A.M., and his mother would watch him to ensure that he improved his poor handwriting. Both agreed to this unpleasant task. Soon Johnny stopped wetting every night, and in time, he wet his bed about once a month. At about that time he also formed his first friendship. Haley comments, "Now that was playing mother against son and son against mother. It's the simple approach of 'I've got a remedy for you, but you won't like it.' Then [the therapist] digresses to the fact that mother will hate it even more."

Another case concerns a five-year-old boy who had never been toilet trained; several times a day he had bowel movements in his pants. The therapist first aimed at restraining the family from improving, focusing concern on what would happen to the family if the child became normal. At the end of the initial interview the therapist asked the parents to state the consequences of their child's becoming toilet trained. Naturally, the parents expressed delight at this prospect. But the therapist responded that although he could help the family resolve the problem of the boy's soiling, he preferred to wait until he was sure of the consequences for the entire family.

In the second session the therapist pointed out some of the negative consequences of the child being successfully toilet trained. Within the mother-child dyad, for example, effective toilet-training indicates that the mother is successful in her role as a mother. Some women, he suggested, cannot tolerate this success: if a mother is not condemned as unsuccessful and instead is supported as successful, she is motivated to prove it. The therapist asked her if she could stand being more successful than her own mother. He also asked what she would do all day if no longer occupied with the boy's problem (changing and washing his clothes, and so forth). The therapist then shifted attention to the husband-wife dyad and asked about the consequence of their becoming a normal married couple without this problem child. For instance, they had never hired a baby-sitter or had an outing alone because of the boy's soiling problem. The couple became highly motivated to solve their problem to prove that they could tolerate being a normal married couple.

The family returned the following week and stated that the boy was now regularly using the toilet. The mother reported that she enjoyed her free time, and the husband and wife enjoyed going out together. The therapist began to disengage himself by registering surprise and delight that the problem had resolved itself. Credit was given to the family for the constructive changes. Haley closes his discussion of this case by noting, "This approach of restraining the family from changing is effective with sensitive, overconcerned middle-class parents, but is not as effective with working-class or poor families. The family must be keenly tuned to the therapist's opinion of them."

COMMENTARY: Haley presents a thought-provoking study of strategic interventions that illustrate different points for entering the family, and his case examples are intriguing. At least one of the techniques described might be best used by experienced therapists; the ploy to restrain the family from improving, like paradoxical intention, demands professional expertise and clinical acumen.

One of Haley's central points is that the approach, course of therapy, and therapeutic goals are determined by the presenting problem. Intervention must be problem- and symptom-oriented, and not determined by a rigid theoretical or clinical stance. Further, the progression from overinvolvement to disengagement occurs in stages, with the approach determining the stages and the presenting problem determining the approach.

Haley also offers certain rules that afford effectiveness in this approach to therapy. The therapist cannot confront or oppose the family's behaviors; rather he must "accept" them and attempt to make changes within that framework. The therapist must motivate the family toward constructive changes, rather than interpret the dysfunctional behavior or patterns of interrelating. And the therapist should focus on the present situation and family structure, and aim for a brief, intensive intervention.

Haley, a pioneer in the field of family therapy and the use of strategic interventions, offers a wealth of helpful suggestions and guidelines based on the literature, empirical data, and extensive clinical experience. In particular, the suggestions to focus on the presenting symptoms and to select an appropriate entry point and approach are invaluable, open to modification, and applicable to a diverse range of situations.

SOURCE: Haley, J. "Strategic Therapy When a Child Is Presented as the Problem." *Journal of Child Psychiatry,* 1973, *12,* 642–659.

Cognitive Family Therapy with an Encopretic Child

AUTHORS: Axel Russell, Lila Russell, and E. M. Waring

PRECIS: The use of cognitive skills in a structured treatment approach encourages family members to think of "explanations" and theorize about reasons for the family's dysfunction.

INTRODUCTION: Cognitive family therapy is an empirically based treatment approach that attempts to decrease criticism and hostility and increase intimacy in order to resolve some of the conflicts within the family constellation and reduce pathological elements. The authors outline some of the theoretical rationale for this intervention procedure, as well as the methodology and structure provided in therapy.

Cognitive family therapy begins with an assessment interview with all members of the family present. This interview focuses on each member's theory to explain the family's problem. Cognitive family therapy attempts to create a supportive and noncritical atmosphere that facilitates the statement of opinions and theories. Any discussion or expression of affect is discouraged, while questions that ask for explanations are encouraged, such as: Why was your father so strict? Why do you think your son rebels? By their very nature such questions foster theorizing, and to answer them family members must summon their cognitive skills. Also, family members are instructed to address the therapist only. This approach thus seeks to minimize hostility while encouraging parental intimacy. Furthermore, it offers many opportunities for the family members to learn how to listen.

CASE STUDY: To illustrate the cognitive family therapy approach, the authors present the case of the Smith family. The Smiths have four children, two older, fourteen and twelve years, and two younger, four and two years of age. The family presented with their four-year-old child who was encopretic. The initial sessions were devoted to a thorough review of the parents' families of origin that sought to determine the possible sources of some of the current conflicts.

Mr. Smith said that his father vented much of his rage at him; his father was physically abusive, while his mother failed to intervene. Mrs. Smith described her father as strict and punitive, yet loving. Both Mr. and Mrs. Smith were encouraged to formulate theories and explanations about their respective families of origin. This approach helped them to better understand their own parents' marital conflicts and the nature of the parenting they received. They began to suggest that they themselves did not know how to communicate intimacy and closeness because they lacked appropriate models in their original families.

Through the use of cognitive methods of intervention and contracts Mr. and Mrs. Smith made significant gains. They were able to support each other, negotiate disagreements, and communicate constructively. As their marital conflicts moved toward resolution, their son's encopresis completely cleared up.

COMMENTARY: Although the authors do not discuss the details of the therapy sessions, they offer an excellent and readable overview of the core features of cognitive family therapy, and the case history presented successfully illustrates the essential elements of this procedure. Because this cognitive therapy approach is intended to discourage parental criticism and increase parental intimacy, the case presentation emphasizes the parents' families of origin, their current marital conflicts, and their explanations for these difficulties; however, it would have been helpful and interesting had some details of the encopretic child's responses and explanations been elaborated. Nonetheless, the authors present a particularly strong discussion of the rationale for the cognitive method, emphasizing its empirical foundations and clinical advantages. By fostering "why" questions, discouraging affective expression in the therapy sessions, and modeling listening skills, the therapist is able to establish and maintain a neutral and objective position.

SOURCE: Russell, A., Russell, L., and Waring, E. M. "Cognitive Family Therapy: A Preliminary Report." *Canadian Journal of Psychiatry*, 1980, *25*, 64–67.

Short-Term Treatment of Nocturnal Enuresis

AUTHOR: Andrew Lee Selig

PRECIS: In this case study nocturnal enuresis was treated in one session of family therapy.

INTRODUCTION: This study illustrates the powerful effect of

brief family therapy. Despite failures of more traditional intervention methods, family therapy was effective in eliminating long-standing enuresis.

CASE STUDY: Brian, a six-and-a-half-year-old boy, was brought to a child development center because of nocturnal enuresis that persisted over a three-year period. Brian's parents had separated before his birth, and he then lived with his mother and nine-year-old sister. When Brian was about three-and-a-half-years old, his mother's boyfriend moved in with her and her children. Since that time Brian had become increasingly enuretic. Other attempts at therapy, including fluid restrictions prior to bedtime, medication, and hypnosis, all proved unsuccessful.

Brian, his mother, her boyfriend, and the sister all attended the family assessment interview. During the interview it was revealed that the mother had become increasingly uninvolved in her children's lives. She felt she was unable to control her children and relinquished discipline and behavior management to her boyfriend. Both the mother and boyfriend agreed that the mother was too lenient and that Brian tended to cling to her. Toward the end of the session the family was asked to cooperate on a task: the boyfriend was not to engage in any disciplinary activity when he and the mother were both present with the children. This task was to be carried out for the six days preceding the next family meeting, which was to take place in two weeks.

The author explains the rationale for treatment thus: "The treatment described here is based on four principles: (1) altering interactional patterns, (2) giving clients homework and directives, (3) brief, symptom-focused psychotherapy, and (4) accentuating the positive in individuals and their interactions." Selig notes that the enuresis began after the boyfriend moved in with Brian and his mother, and that Brian's behavior and statements indicated he was afraid of the boyfriend and wanted a closer relationship with his mother. Brian sought to achieve this closeness by bed-wetting and receiving negative attention from her.

RESULTS: In the second and final family session the family reported that Brian was dry the night following the first session and that he stayed dry for two weeks. The boyfriend reported that the relationship between him and Brian had improved, and the boyfriend felt relieved that he was no longer "always the heavy hand" in the family. The mother became more involved and again assumed the responsibilities of parenting. In all, she began to feel better about herself and both her self-esteem and her relationship with her children showed marked improvement.

COMMENTARY: Selig presents an approach to therapy that ameliorated the child's symptomatic behavior in a very short period of time. The behavior served a function within the family system—it was the child's attempt to get his uninvolved mother involved. The task assignment altered the interactional patterns, forcing the mother to become an involved parent and allowing the youngster to see his mother's boyfriend in a role other than the family disciplinarian. As his relationship with his mother and her boyfriend improved, the symptom no longer served a purpose and was dropped. The symptom-focused psychotherapy had halted the repetitive circular processes within the family unit.

Selig points out that family therapy is not always an effective or appropriate method of choice and that problems are not always resolved in so short a time. Approaching the child's difficulties as a dispensable part of the family interaction pattern also opens divergent and alternative methods of therapeutic intervention. Success in this case was achieved by focusing on the child's caretakers and his interrelational and interactional patterns with them. This appears to be a practical and focused approach applicable to similar problems. By altering interactional patterns within the family, therapy can alleviate symptomatic behavior within the family members.

SOURCE: Selig, A. L. "Treating Nocturnal Enuresis in One Session of Family Therapy—A Case Study." *Journal of Clinical Child Psychology*, in press.

Additional Readings

Andolfi, M. "A Structural Approach to a Family with an Encopretic Child." *Journal of Marriage and Family Counseling,*
1978, *4*(1), 25–29.

   The author presents a case in which brief therapy within
a structural framework was used to treat a preadolescent boy
whose encopretic behavior was seen as a symptom of a dysfunctioning family structure. The roles and behaviors of all family members were observed in relation to the interaction and
structure within the family unit.

Brandzel, E. "The Inclusion of a Three-Year-Old Child in Family Therapy." *Bulletin of the Family Mental Health Clinic of
Jewish Family Service,* 1970, *2*, 6–8.

   The author describes the case of Mr. and Mrs. L and their
three-year-old adopted son David. The family was disturbed by
David's refusal to use the toilet except for urinating and by his
soiling his pants while hiding behind a curtain or door. David's
symptom represented one aspect of the family system in which
control was used as a means of allaying anxiety. Controlling behaviors were also used by the family members as a substitute for
genuine understanding and affection.

   Mrs. L was depressed, infantile, and self-derogatory in her
comments, while Mr. L was a pleasant, but anxious and compulsive individual. Mrs. L displaced her hostility toward her husband and dead mother by overcontrolling David's eating habits;
meals became a competitive struggle between mother and child.
Mr. L felt he had no part in his son's conflicts; family therapy
helped him to become aware of the subtle manner in which he
encouraged his son to defy his wife. David's encopresis and
temper tantrums were seen as age-appropriate retaliations
against the family's dysfunctional system. Family therapy
helped the child to realize he had a place in the family and he
could work toward effecting a change within the family system.

Cecchin, G. F., Selvini Palazzolli, M., Boscolo, L., and Prata, G.
"The Treatment of Children Through Brief Therapy of Their
Parents." *Family Process,* 1974, *13*, 429–442.

The authors discuss a method of intervention involving brief therapy including two co-therapists who work, in most cases, with the entire family. A team of therapists observes from behind a one-way screen and discuss intervention strategies to be used by the co-therapists. The treatment model is grounded in the work of Gregory Bateson and later extensions of Bateson's work formulated by Jay Haley, which views the family as "an interacting error-controlled system."

The treatment of a nine-year-old boy exhibiting stool incontinence and his parents addressed the manner in which the boy became the scapegoat for the family. The boy was physically puny and cross-eyed, had surgery to correct strabismus and now wore awkward prescription glasses, and wore heavy orthopedic shoes to correct a knock-kneed condition. He was also being treated by an orthodontist because his permanent teeth were growing irregularly. In sum, he was fed up with all the specialists and treatment he was receiving. The therapists proposed a contract: the orthodontist's appointments would be canceled and the special glasses replaced by regular ones if the youngster agreed to stop soiling. The contract was formal and adultlike; every effort was made to underscore the seriousness of this commitment by the child and his parents. The boy delightedly accepted the terms of the contract and the encopresis stopped immediately.

Ringdahl, I. C. "Hospital Treatment of the Encopretic Child." *Psychosomatics,* 1980, *21*(1), 65, 69–71.

The author's discussion of the treatment and complications involved in treating encopresis in children focuses particularly on behavioral management. Encopresis is seen as a symptom of a dysfunctional family unit. The hostile power struggle that often exists within a family having an encopretic child requires that treatment of the target patient hinge on separating the child from the maladaptive family structure.

Following a review of case studies concerning the successful treatment of encopresis in a hospital setting, Ringdahl presents an in-depth case report and discussion of a six-year-old boy who was treated in a hospital setting. The study suggests that effective intervention demands a multitreatment approach, a combination of behavior modification strategies and individual, group, family, and occupational therapy within a hospital milieu.

Wright, L. "Counseling with Parents of Chronically Ill Children." *Postgraduate Medicine,* 1970, *47*(6), 173–177.

Wright discusses an approach to consultation with parents that involves fifteen to twenty sessions in which the parents are taught the basic principles of behavior modification through discussions in individual or group sessions. A consultant is also available to teach and provide information. The approach differs from Thomas Gordon's parent effectiveness training (PET) in that the parents actively participate and are taught in group and individual discussion sessions (T. Gordon, *Parent Effectiveness Training* [New York: Wyden, 1970]).

A case report of an eight-year-old encopretic boy and his family illustrates this approach. Physical examination revealed the boy had a somewhat distended bowel or megacolon. His parents were trained in behavioral modification techniques and encouraged to exert less control over the child, engage in more activities of the boy's choosing, and, in general, improve their supportive skills. Finally, the parents were counseled to refrain from punishing the boy for soiling "accidents," and to praise him for periods in which soiling did not occur. Within nine months the encopresis was completely eliminated.

15

Obsessive-Compulsive Behaviors

Retrospective research studies of obsessive-compulsive adults suggest that the onset of the repetitive and irrational actions usually occurs in childhood or adolescence. In 60 percent of these adults onset occurred before the age of twenty, and in 20 percent before the age of fifteen. The terms *obsessive* and *compulsive* define repetitive, fixed, and stereotyped functioning. An obsessive person repeats the same thoughts and is intensely pre-occupied with an irrational idea, belief, or feeling. Compulsive behavior, the repetition of actions, is related to the compelling and irresistible impulse to behave in a given manner; and the compulsive and ritualistic behaviors are used to control the impulses and to bind anxiety. In almost all instances the rituals assume a certain sequence; if the compulsive character pattern is disrupted the individual becomes extremely anxious, angry, and agitated. Obsessive thoughts and compulsive acts run the gamut from mildly annoying to overwhelmingly disordered, distressful, complicated, and burdensome.

The two studies reviewed in this chapter present the successful treatments of obsessive-compulsive children and their families. Case illustrations help to describe and clarify particular therapeutic techniques, such as the combined use of behavioral approaches and multiple-family therapy, and the prescription of an ordeal.

Multiple-Family Therapy and the
Extinguishing of Rituals

AUTHOR: Stuart Fine

PRECIS: Family therapy and a behavioral approach were employed to extinguish rituals in childhood obsessive-compulsive neurosis, and multiple-family therapy was used to offer the families mutual support.

INTRODUCTION: Although full-blown obsessive-compulsive neurosis is rare in children, retrospective studies of adults with obsessive-compulsive neurosis indicate that the onset of compulsive rituals usually occurs in childhood or adolescence. In general, children exhibiting obsessive-compulsive neurosis tend to have ambivalent feelings toward their parents, who tend to be isolated from the larger community. A strong emphasis on cleanliness and social protocol often exists within the family. As a whole, the family does not readily express feelings, particularly angry and hostile feelings.

Fine presents two cases of childhood obsessive-compulsive neuroses. The families of both boys were seen on an outpatient basis and at one point the two families were treated together in multiple-family therapy. Both boys experienced guilt feelings about their ritualistic behaviors, and these actions affected their social adjustments. The rituals were also perceived as symptomatic of family abnormalities.

CASE REPORTS: D, an eleven-and-a-half-year-old, good-looking, asthenic prepubertal boy was seen individually on a weekly basis for two months and then every two weeks for two months. His family was seen in therapy monthly. D had a compulsion to touch his peers on the buttocks, and he enacted a series of rituals at bedtime. He also attempted to get his parents to repeat statements, commands, and questions. The family was instructed to refuse to repeat statements, commands, and questions, and to interrupt his bedtime ritual of getting up to urinate if anyone spoke to him once he was in bed. D became very angry when these rituals were interrupted. Nevertheless, they were gradually extinguished, he became more verbally expressive, and his family began to function more as a unit.

E, a fair-haired and anxious nine-year-old boy, had bedroom and dressing rituals, and anxieties about school and a deceased adult friend. In brief, the rituals were interpreted as a means of E's preventing himself from changing, perhaps from dying. The family of E was seen on six occasions and E was seen twice individually. Following an angry outburst in school, E's school difficulties decreased. Marked improvement was also seen in E's parents, who had difficulty expressing warm or angry feelings to one another.

D's and E's families were eventually seen together in multiple-family therapy. This approach proved to be beneficial and supportive for both families.

COMMENTARY: Fine presents an excellent procedure for therapeutic intervention in childhood obsessive-compulsive neurosis. In the case histories presented the rituals were deemed symptomatic of family conflicts and abnormalities, particularly of the families' marked difficulty in verbally expressing anxiety or anger. Indeed, the major premise of this method is that children develop motor rituals and ruminative thoughts because they are unable to verbalize angry feelings; family therapy then aids the family members in becoming more adept at expressing these feelings.

As Fine states, more traditional therapy approaches are reluctant to recommend interrupting symptoms. But, he adds, most parents do not hesitate to interrupt undesirable behaviors, and in time, the children develop internal controls. One of the many insights of this approach is that it follows the developmental order of establishing internal controls.

The combination of family therapy, the behavioral approach, and multiple-family therapy appears to have been more effective for the two cases presented than any one of these strategies used in isolation. This procedure could be adapted to other behavioral methods, and multiple-family therapy could similarly be used effectively with a wide variety of theoretical and therapeutic orientations, particularly in the treatment of families who are isolated from the larger community. For the multiple-family approach by its very nature penetrates the debilitating isolation while also offering the families mutual support and encouragement, the awareness that they are not alone in their dilemmas, and a format for reality testing and an exchange of problem-solving strategies.

SOURCE: Fine, S. "Family Therapy and a Behavioral Approach to Childhood Obsessive-Compulsive Neurosis." *Archives of General Psychiatry*, 1973, *28*, 695–697.

The Prescription of an Ordeal

AUTHOR: Henry T. Harbin

PRECIS: After multiple therapeutic interventions failed with an adolescent girl who had a severe obsessive-compulsive neurosis, a behavioral intervention using the prescription of an ordeal succeeded.

INTRODUCTION: Sue, a sixteen-year-old girl, was the presenting patient. She was attractive, neat, serious, and articulate. She was also hypersensitive and angry; irritability surfaced with the slightest provocation. Sue was diagnosed as an obsessive-compulsive neurotic with evidence of obsessive-compulsive personality traits. She had been unsuccessfully treated for almost thirty months in insight-oriented individual therapies. Sue presented with several obsessive worries about failing in school and worries that she may have cheated in school even though she knew that was not the case. She developed a compulsion to reread and rewrite her assignments, sometimes working four or five hours each night.

THERAPEUTIC PROCEDURE: The course of therapy focused on the family as a unit, the mother, and a prescribed ordeal for

Sue. The family was encouraged to communicate more openly, and the parents were encouraged to set firm limits with their children. Also, attention was given to the mother's depressive status. After about five months of therapy, Sue stopped her self-destructive behaviors and decreased her temper tantrums, but her obsessive ruminations and her ritualistic behavior continued. Despite some constructive changes within the family, resistance was still evident. In response to this, the therapist prescribed an ordeal.

To encourage Sue's interest in the task the therapist appealed to her sense of independence and resistance. He suggested that the prescribed ordeal remain a confidential matter and within her personal control. On any night that Sue considered herself to have acted obsessively or compulsively in doing her homework, she was to do half an hour of exercises in her bedroom at midnight. She was also to keep a chart to follow her progress. This prescription led to a significant reduction in the frequency of Sue's obsessive ruminations and compulsive behaviors. Therapy was terminated, and a follow-up indicated that progress continued.

COMMENTARY: Harbin proposes that behavioral-cognitive changes emerge from the interaction of a variety of additions to and changes in the family system. This approach clearly fits into a learning paradigm wherein self-imposed aversive behavior is used to effect a reduction in self-imposed anxiety-imposing behavior. The therapist insightfully appealed to the patient's need for adolescent oppositional expression and independence by suggesting that the ordeal be self-imposed and totally within the patient's control. Still further, by having the ordeal a confidential matter between Sue and himself, he met her resistances directly and afforded her an occasion to express her emerging sense of independence from her family. As the author states, "The real effectiveness of this ordeal prescription may not lie solely in its self-conditioning aspect or its intrapsychic use, but may be more related to the relationship between Sue and the therapist."

In this particular instance it appears that Sue's potential for change was contingent on the dynamics operative within her family. The symptom, obsessive-compulsive behaviors, was intricately enmeshed within the family's dysfunctional system and pattern of interaction. Treatment, then, included the family as well as, and prior to, a behavioral intervention, namely, the prescription of the ordeal.

SOURCE: Harbin, H. T. "Cure by Ordeal: Treatment of an Obsessive-Compulsive Neurotic." *International Journal of Family Therapy*, 1979, pp. 324–332.

Additional Readings

Friedmann, C. T., and Silvers, F. M. "A Multimodality Approach to Inpatient Treatment of Obsessive-Compulsive Disorder." *American Journal of Psychotherapy*, 1977, *31*, 456–465.

The authors present the case of James M, an eighteen-year-old male who was treated for a severely incapacitating obsessive-compulsive neurosis in an inpatient setting for thirteen weeks. The patient reported obsessional thoughts, experienced a failure to complete sentences and maintain eye contact, and devoted an extremely large amount of time to ritualistic dressing, washing, and walking from place to place. On admission the patient was observed to be almost noncommunicative and depressed; he threatened suicide if his symptoms did not quickly disappear. Because of the severity of his symptoms a multimodal intervention approach was employed. For thirteen weeks he was treated with a combination of insight-oriented, group, family, and behavioral therapies. Since James was in a highly structured therapeutic environment, it was felt that diverse techniques could be applied in a consistent, coherent, and meaningful manner. Still further, the patient's behaviors could be monitored by the hospital staff. Consequently, stable changes were effected in a relatively short period of time.

The authors discuss the synergistic effects of the various intervention modalities and the therapeutic community. A follow-up study thirty months after hospital discharge confirmed that the positive changes were still in effect; there was no recurrence of the symptomatic behaviors.

Safer, D. "Conjoint Play Therapy for the Young Child and His Parent." *Archives of General Psychiatry*, 1965, *13*, 320–326.

Conjoint play therapy is a variation of family treatment that seeks to limit mutually unrewarding conflictive patterns of interaction between the child and his parent. In the playroom setting the child, his parent, and the therapist participate in various forms of play selected by the child. Typically interactive behavior reactions become evident. The child's play is representative of, and mirrors, the dysfunctional parent-child relationship.

The author discusses the general format of conjoint play therapy, the parental involvement in therapy, variations in conjoint play therapy, the therapist's role, and specific difficulties (for example, the therapist risks being maneuvered by the parent-child "team"). The case of a four-and-a-half-year-old boy seen for ten sessions illustrates the techniques of conjoint play therapy. S, the identified patient, was living with both parents and his ten-month-old sister. The parents complained that he had temper outbursts, no apparent interest in peers, spoke in an infantile manner, frequently made up his own words, and was fearful of riding unfamiliar routes in the car. Since the age of seven months he insisted on separate bowls for each of his foods. He banged his head hard enough and often enough to raise calluses. At the age of three he used his cat's name to refer to himself.

In therapy S was compulsively clean in his sand play and became extremely angry when the therapist interfered with his pattern of drawing and play. Therapy concentrated on facilitating S's direct expression of hostility and anger and helping him accept individual responsibility. The mother joined in many of the sessions; the father joined when he was able. The author details the events of each of the ten sessions—the agreed limit for the conjoint play therapy approach in this case—indicating the steady progress S made in achieving some of the delineated goals. The role of the therapist was both active and relatively directive. Treatment results were successful and maintained five months later at the time of a follow-up study.

Part Three

Children
at Risk

Traditional intervention in the problems and concerns of the child tends to focus diagnostically and therapeutically on intrapsychic conflicts. The child is perceived as the primary, if not the only, patient. However, family-oriented approaches to therapy work with the concerns of the parents and the total family unit as more than merely adjunctive to the major child-centered tasks. Indeed, the family structure, patterns of relationship and interaction, styles of communication, and the family system's functioning all become the focus of the therapeutic process. The child's problems and symptomatic behaviors may be the initial issues of concern; nevertheless, these are only one manifestation of discord and tension in a dysfunctional family system. Therapeutic intervention is not directed solely at the

307

child's disordered behaviors. The entire family system and the interplay of forces within that structure become critical features of clinical observation and intervention.

The disharmony, tensions, and stresses inherent in a dysfunctional family constellation place the child at risk for emotional disorders, psychopathological behaviors, and somatic problems, and, in general, delay the developmental process. The degree and urgency of the risk depends upon a variety of contingencies, including the intensity and duration of the stress-provoking situation; the child's age and the developmental tasks appropriate to that age and stage of growth; the resources available to the child and his family; and the nature and level of disequilibrium that the problems have wrought upon the family structure.

The process of divorce instigates dramatic and often traumatic changes in the family system. The security of a two-parent family is threatened. Parents and children are all involved in the divorce, and all must develop new relationship patterns and new mechanisms of adaptation and defense. The demands of divorce, the marital and family struggles that precipitated the divorce, single-parenthood, and remarriage often overwhelm family members and deplete the psychological and emotional resources at their disposal. Therapy with the entire family, often including the original family as well as the reconstituted family, may be a primary means of facilitating continuation of the family's growth and the development of individuals within the family, of ameliorating the identified patient's maladaptive symptoms, and of restructuring the family system in a way that is conducive to effective functioning.

The transitions related to divorce call for a major reorganization of family roles and structures. Deaths within a family and any loss of significant members similarly demand a reappraisal and reorganization of the family. The process of reorganization in itself creates risks. The family's homeostasis is temporarily lost, and family members experience a period characterized by blurred definition of boundaries, roles, and expectations. Intricate family patterns dissolve and new ones begin to form. Family members must resolve former alliances and establish new relationships. A diversity of family-oriented therapeutic strategies and intervention techniques can help the family through the arduous task of formulating a viable new family structure. Children of families that are in the process of restructuring are in a particularly delicate position as they attempt to cope with the demands of development simultaneously with the strains of family reorganization.

The multiproblem family is a particularly vulnerable unit. A complex of interrelated problems mesh and place the family members at high risk for disorders. Single-parent families, racial-minority families, and socioeconomically impoverished families exhibit features that are somewhat different from those of white, middle-class, intact families. They have special needs that require a treatment approach which is flexible and expansive enough to address their needs in an effective manner. Nontraditional therapeutic approaches, innovative strategies, the resources of the community and social support networks, and collaborative intervention programs are all used in an attempt to minimize the risk factors present within the multiproblem family system.

The abused child is a child at risk for disorders and pathological conditions. Empirical research clearly indicates that the abused child typically feels depressed, has a low sense of self-worth and self-esteem, has a fragile sense of self-identity, and is subject to more behavioral disorders, psychological conflicts, and somatic complaints than nonabused children. Likewise, abusive parents manifest a specific set of characteristics, including a sense of hopelessness, worthlessness, and social isolation, together with a pervasive sense of guilt and shame linked to the stigma of being a child-abuser. However, although all child-abusers share certain characteristics, the phenomenon is not limited by class, race, socioeconomic status, or educational background. Similarly, child abuse is not restricted to a particular behavior; children can be abused physically, sexually, emotionally, and psychologically. Child abuse can be a direct act or the omission of an act, such as neglect or the withholding of nurturance and affection. Child abuse is symptomatic of a severely disordered and dysfunctional family. Because it can be used to maintain the family's balance, alliances, and structures, the entire family constellation needs treatment. Therapeutic intervention into the child-abusing family is particularly difficult because of the legal and criminal ramifications of child abuse, as well as the emotional and psychological implications. The prevalence of child abuse, and the specific difficulties that therapists working with child-abusing families encounter, make it imperative that clinicians have guidelines and successful therapeutic models to assist them in the formation and implementation of treatment goals.

The list of handicaps that can beset a child is endless. Of course, since the child is part of a family structure, the handicaps also affect the family as a unified system. Mental retardation, memory and attention problems, brain dysfunction, psychoses, and physical illnesses and limitations are but a few of the conditions that can place a child at risk for current and future problems, halt the appropriate course of development, and negatively affect family functioning. Special therapeutic techniques are needed to deal with the families of handicapped children and to help them cope with the child's special needs and the demands the handicap places on the family unit.

Just as the families of handicapped children demonstrate unique needs, so, too, families in crisis are in a position of special vulnerability. The crisis situation compounds the usual stresses of family life and exacerbates the tensions provoked by the child's developmental stage. Therapists engaged in family-oriented crisis intervention must consider the family's weaknesses in relation to its strengths. They must be prepared to help the family regroup during and after a crisis. They may even be called upon to prepare the family for an impending crisis. Common crisis situations include a death, suicide, chronic disease, or terminal illness in the family, to name but a few. In each case, the therapist must help the family to express their doubts and fears, open channels of communication, become aware of their own resources and those of the community, and develop adaptive strategies that facilitate family cohesiveness and growth, not only despite the crisis but also as a result of it.

There are times when the child does not manifest any

personal psychopathologies, handicaps, or disorders but is part of a disordered family structure. Membership in a psychotic and dysfunctional family places the child at a definite disadvantage. The child's reservoir of defenses and coping mechanisms is tested to the limit on a daily basis. Oftentimes, the child must contend with shared delusional systems. The persecutory nature of such delusions makes it difficult for an outsider to break through. Therefore, the family therapist must employ every available therapeutic strategy just to gain entry into the family. Effective therapy depends on the intensity and duration of the delusional system, the degree of the family's isolation from the community at large, the ages of the children involved, and the therapist's expertise and patience in chipping away at the barrier to reality.

In short, the practitioner utilizing a family therapy approach is called upon to be flexible, innovative, and willing to use collaborative programs and expand his or her definition of what is included in therapy. The family therapist must be alert to the complex patterns that exist within a family structure. He or she must be aware of the family's resources and limitations as well as those of the community and social service agencies. In some instances networking may be in order, while in other cases attention may be focused exclusively on the family unit in order to facilitate cohesiveness. The clinician must be knowledgeable about relevant research, the implications of empirical and experiential data, and a diverse range of clinical intervention strategies. This section attempts to help the practitioner achieve these aims as they relate to families having children at risk.

16

Children
of Divorce

In our society, divorce is taking place at a rate of one out of every three first marriages, and is rapidly approaching one out of two. The process of mourning the loss of the original family unit and adjusting to the new family roles and structure creates disequilibrium, psychological and emotional conflicts, and myriad other strains on all family members. Children react differently to divorce depending on their ages, the intensity and duration of family conflicts prior to the separation, their own individual ego strengths and resources, and the support they receive from significant adults and peers. Many children feel responsible for the breakup. They experience tremendous ambivalence, anxiety, and anger. Their loyalties are torn and they dread having to make a choice between the mother and the fa-

313

ther. Too often, parents, in an attempt to vent their hostility to each other, compound the children's confusion by fighting over economic issues of ownership, alimony, child support, and custody, and over visitation rights and privileges.

Many parents are so drained by the tumultuous experience of the divorce that they cannot provide adequate emotional suport to their children. Oftentimes, the oldest siblings become so-called parental children, who are burdened with responsibilities inappropriate to their age. Yet all the children, including the oldest, are in dire need of support and reassurance. Empirical findings indicate that the first two years after a divorce is the most conflict-ridden period for children. It is not unusual for children to become troubled and symptomatic at this time. They may lose interest in school, become depressed and withdrawn, act out in a hostile and aggressive manner, or develop irritability, loss of appetite, and insomnia. Individual and family therapy are often indicated. It is essential that the children be assured that they are not at fault for the divorce. Therapy may be a means of helping to resolve the mourning process as it relates to the family of origin. It helps the parents to focus on the emotional needs of the children, and offers all members an occasion and model for communication, particularly the expression of fears, doubts, expectations, and hopes. Therapy also helps the children to affirm and accept the divorce, and it fosters an effective adjustment to living in a single-parent family or a reconstituted family structure.

Structural Family Therapy Techniques
for Children of Divorce

AUTHOR: Stuart L. Kaplan

PRECIS: Structural family therapy strategies for treating post-divorce families in which a child is symptomatic are described. Case illustrations of six family configurations are included.

INTRODUCTION: The process of divorce involves a number of disruptions in the family. These disruptions begin with the conflicts that precipitate the divorce itself and progress to the separation and divorce. Following these phases, each spouse attempts to go through the process of individuation. Remarriage often follows. Each of the phases is disruptive of the child's development. Symptoms may reflect the dysfunctional family structure. Structural family therapy techniques, based on the theories and strategies of Salvador Minuchin, can help repair some of these disruptive interactional patterns.

THEORY AND CASE ILLUSTRATIONS: To illustrate the structural family therapy approach, Kaplan presents six family configurations, together with cases that illustrate each pattern.

Mother, Child, and Maternal Grandparents. Following a divorce, the mother and her children often return to live with the maternal grandparents or turn to them for support.

A, an exceptionally bright six-year-old boy, was presented for fecal soiling of lifelong duration. Both grandparents and mother refused to allow A any independence with regard to toilet habits. They held his penis when he urinated because they feared he would fail to urinate in the toilet bowl. They also complained that he might flood the bathroom so he was not allowed to use the sink or wash his hands. The mother, a twenty-six-year-old college-educated woman, presented herself as helpless and incompetent. She was unemployed. The family as a whole did not delineate generational boundaries. Co-therapists were introduced to facilitate the development of these boundaries. An elderly woman co-therapist was part of the therapeutic process. She formed an alliance with the grandparents, while the primary therapist allied himself with the mother and child.

In the course of therapy, the mother gradually assumed more adult and parental responsibility. She became more competent. The growth of the mother facilitated the separation of mother and child from the grandparents and from each other. The grandparents were made aware of the mother's newly acquired adeptness. The entire family constellation became less dysfunctional as generational boundaries and individual lines of demarcation began to take form.

Overprotective Mother and Child. After a divorce the overprotected child may cling more tenaciously to the mother. In such instances, the divorced father plays a pivotal role.

B, a nine-year-old girl, was inattentive in class, sucked her thumb, and refused to interact with her classmates. The relationship between B and her mother was overly close. At the initial interview, she separated from her mother but behaved bizarrely. In the next twenty sessions she was seen together with her mother. She ignored the therapist and related only to her mother. It was proposed that B's aversion to the therapist was due to the fact that he reminded her of the painful loss and separation from her father. After four months of therapy, the therapist met with B and her father. B's behavior with her father and the therapist was markedly different from the way she behaved with the mother and the therapist. Her behavior, comments, and complaints were much more age-appropriate. Improvements began to be evident. B's ability to be alone with the therapist paralleled her growth in maturity at home and at school.

Helpless and Mildly Neglectful Mother. Mothers who are generally neglectful of their children prior to the divorce tend to be even more neglectful afterward. They find the child intolerable, and therapy focuses on giving the mother and child occasions for mutually pleasurable interaction.

Mrs. Z came to therapy with her six-year-old son, C, complaining that he was too demanding of her time, stole from her, had temper tantrums, and lied. Confusion centered on the financial aspects of the divorce and Mr. Z's visitation schedule. The therapist saw Mr. and Mrs. Z together and attempted to establish some order in C's chaotic life. The mother started to realize that the father's visitation time gave her some time for herself away from C. The therapist also explored some activities that were mutually enjoyable to mother and son. Therapy also concentrated on improving Mrs. Z's child management and discipline skills. The educational focus of therapy resulted in improved relations among all family members and a definite symptomatic relief for C.

The Father. Maintaining contact with each other appears to have important psychological advantages for both the children and the father. A parent who continually complains about the other parent splits the children's loyalties. Too often, the children are used as go-betweens for the separated couple. The therapist attempts to provide alternate means of communication between the separated parents other than the children.

New Family Formation. The formation of a new family is always stressful. Children from the previous marriage must either be abandoned or integrated into it. Either decision precipitates tension and conflict.

The case of Y, a seven-year-old boy, illustrates how difficult it is to integrate children into a new family. Despite the fact that Y was a bright youngster, he was having problems in school. His attention wandered and he was unable to learn; moreover, he was chronically sad and had frequent temper outbursts. Following her divorce, the mother took Y and two younger siblings to live with another man. In the interview, the children related only to their mother; they made no contact—verbal, visual, or tactile—with their stepfather-to-be. The stepfather made no efforts to relate to the children, and the mother remained aloof from her children for fear of alienating the stepfather. The therapist encouraged increased involvement on the part of both parents. As a result, Y's symptoms cleared rapidly.

Couples Who Remarry. Oftentimes divorced parents marry again and the child from the first marriage becomes the focus of disagreements. In this case, a joint meeting with both couples can be helpful.

E, a bright ten-year-old boy, was performing poorly in school. Both his parents had remarried and there were frequent arguments about the financial obligations toward the boy. The therapist hypothesized that E's mother attempted to provoke changes in the financial rules regarding E in order to establish communication with E's father. A meeting was held with E's mother and father and their new spouses. E was not included in this meeting in order to protect him from interfamilial conflict. At the meeting, ground rules were established for each parent's financial responsibilities to E. These rules reduced the stress that their quarreling was creating for E.

COMMENTARY: Kaplan's study points out the manner in which a child's symptomatic behavior may reflect disruptive patterns of interaction stemming from the child's family of origin. It offers a glimpse into some of the problems that follow a divorce, such as the conflicts that relate to the formation of the reconstituted family.

The study goes beyond the family conflicts that precipitated the divorce. It also goes beyond the difficulties that the separation or divorce may provoke in the child. It includes the problems of the current experiential situation (remarriage or single-parenthood) that act upon the initial tensions or create new ones. We are reminded that the child's symptoms can represent pain and loss following the parents' separation (and remarriages), or unresolved mourning related to the original family, or a dysfunctional parent-child relationship during any of the phases of divorce, separation, and remarriage.

Structural family therapy is a method of choice for intervening in a family's disruptive patterns. Only by focusing on family configurations can therapy correct disruptive structures. The child's symptoms reflect the family's dysfunctional patterns of interacting and interrelating. An effective alleviation of these symptoms demand that family configurations be observed, evaluated, and restructured. The six cases studied elaborate on primary family patterns and the manner in which each can create problems and perpetuate a disruptive and debilitating family system.

SOURCE: Kaplan, S. L. "Structural Family Therapy for Children of Divorce: Case Reports." *Family Process,* 1977, *16* (1), 75–83.

<hr>

Counseling Families in the Midst of Divorce

AUTHORS: Judith S. Wallerstein and Joan B. Kelly

PRECIS: A clinical intervention program offering services to children and parents in families going through divorce.

INTRODUCTION: The authors present an experimental, child-centered, preventive intervention program for divorcing families. The program evolved as part of a research project observing the experience of divorce among normal children and adolescents. The project focused on tracing the effects of divorce on psychological and social development, particularly in regard to vicissitudes in the parent-child dyad at three points: the time of separation, one year following the divorce, and four years later. The program drew heavily upon crisis theory and the literature on loss and mourning. It was designed mainly as a preventive measure that would establish psychological, social, and educational strategies to alleviate the dysfunctional effects of divorce on children.

Some of the study's findings, which are central to the development of clinical programs, are as follows: (1) Divorce is a disorganizing and reorganizing process that extends over time. Years of disruption and disequilibrium within the family result. (2) The entire postseparation period is a central determinant of the child's well-being. The manner in which the parents function and relate following the divorce affects the child as significantly as the behaviors and interactions that preceded the divorce. (3) The child's capacity to maintain his or her developmental stride is related to the custodial parent's needs. The more the parent leans on the child for emotional and social support, the more negatively it will affect the child's course of development. There appears to be an optimal distance between the older child and the custodial parent. The older child needs space in which to develop in an autonomous manner. (4) The period immediately following the separation is crucial; as crisis theory emphasizes, opportunities for effective change are greatly enhanced in a fluid system. Following divorce, parents are usually involved in long-term, important decisions concerning the child. (5) Loss is a common denominator in divorce and death. Divorce, like death, provokes a process of mourning and loss. Unlike death, however, divorce still affords the child contact with the separated parent. (6) Even though many of the parents were in therapy at various times in their lives, the therapy rarely focused on the parental relationship with the children at the time of the divorce. Thus, divorce counseling with parents and children seems relatively unaffected by the parents' participation in any other ongoing form of psychotherapy.

The authors conceptualize the intervention strategies as primarily child-centered, relationship-centered, or adult-centered. These can occur in any combination, to various degrees, and at different times in the course of therapy.

Child-Centered Intervention. The child-centered intervention strategy concentrates on the children. Parents apparently have great difficulty in explaining their decision to divorce to the children. Children, particularly younger children, often display symptomatic behavior due, at least in part, to the absence of any explanations and assurances of parental support.

Child-centered intervention can train the parents to relieve symptomatic behavior by offering explanations. An example is the case of four-year-old Mary, who refused to lie down at bedtime because her parents used to argue at night. The mother was advised to explain to Mary that she could now sleep uninterrupted because the fights that had occurred between the parents in the past would not happen anymore. The purpose of the divorce was to terminate the fights.

Relationship-Centered Intervention. Relationship-centered intervention is the strategy of choice when parents are unable to respond effectively. Many parents feel immobilized by the pressures of the divorce. The case of Mrs. V and her ten-year-old daughter, Alice, illustrates an instance in which relationship-intervention is appropriate. Mrs. V complained that she was victimized by her daughter's controlling temper and screaming outbursts. She wanted to be firmer but was unable. Alice was pressing for a reconciliation between her parents. Mrs. V was advised to make it clear to Alice that she would not return to the marriage under any circumstances. Alice reacted with an outburst but then calmed down and stated, "Mom, I'm so unhappy." Alice confided that she thought she was the only one who loved her father and could not choose between her parents. Mrs. V and Alice began to talk regularly; the temper tantrums gradually lessened.

Parent-Centered Intervention. In the parent-centered intervention strategy, emphasis is placed on the parent and his or her needs. Divorce counseling is geared toward facilitating the transition to the single-parent role. Parents are helped to deal with their own anxieties, doubts, and insecurities.

COMMENTARY: The authors present an excellent illustration of the use of crisis theory. Their approach offers temporary support and direction that could lead to continued services and resources. As such, it is a clinical intervention program that offers services to both parents and children who are attempting to cope with the ambivalence and conflict that is in evidence during and after a divorce.

One of the primary advantages of this approach is its immense flexibility. It focuses on the individual or family unit that is in the greatest need. The approach can meet the needs of the child, the relationship, or the parent in an equally effective manner. Further, it offers a complex array of services, and places the therapist in a variety of roles. In any and all instances, however, the overriding goal is to recommend or develop psychological, social, and educational strategies that will alleviate tension and diminish the likelihood of dysfunctional outcomes. Because of the flexibility of this approach, it is widely applicable and can serve the needs of a large and diverse population.

SOURCE: Wallerstein, J. S., and Kelly, J. B. "Divorce Counseling: A Community Service for Families in the Midst of Divorce." *American Journal of Orthopsychiatry*, 1977, *47*(1), 4–22.

Dysfunctional Elements in Civilized Divorces

AUTHOR: Edward H. Futterman

PRECIS: Civilized divorces may undermine the psychological processes necessary for completion of the divorce work.

INTRODUCTION: A great deal has been written in the literature of divorce about the traumas, conflicts, and dilemmas that occur because of the animosity and continuing squabbles that often accompany divorce. However, little has been said about the effects of a civilized or friendly divorce. Futterman addresses this very issue.

Mutually cooperative and agreed-upon divorce settlements apparently take place in the absence of antagonism and struggles over custody, support, and visitation rights. Yet despite the absence of acrimony, the children of these benign marriage dissolutions may develop symptoms. For example, aggressive acting out, poor school performance and a decline in academic achievement, night terrors, psychosomatic complaints, and constrained social and interpersonal relationships with peers and adults may all be manifestations of unresolved issues linked to the parents' divorce. "While such 'civilized,' 'friendly' divorces may prevent the tumultuous consequences of continued battles between bitter ex-spouses, the constraint and consideration that typify such 'civilized' divorces may deny parents and their children the opportunity to work through important issues and consequently may undermine the psychological processes necessary for completion of the divorce work."

In this study, Futterman draws from both clinical and private practice to illustrate the psychological, social, and behavioral consequences of such unresolved feelings. The process of working through divorce is essential. The fragments of cases presented in this study demonstrate the debilitating power of unresolved issues, for conflicts can surface years after the divorce.

TREATMENT ISSUES: The procedure outlined in this paper proposes that the entire original family reconvene. Therapy focuses on a review of the marriage as well as the divorce. All parties are encouraged to express their feelings, fears, doubts, questions, and hostilities. This type of therapy, of course, reopens old wounds and can be very difficult for all involved. Nevertheless, it is essential to the course of therapy that past and painful issues surface. Unresolved and concealed feelings are uncovered. Bitterness and wishes for retaliation often come to the fore. It is crucial that the children be given permission to discuss their feelings of rejection and isolation as well as their anger toward both parents. Children often harbor shame and guilt over the divorce. It is not unusual for the children of divorce to feel that something they did precipitated the separation. These feelings, along with depression and separation anxiety, must be expressed and dealt with in a therapeutic manner.

The parents also have unresolved issues that demand attention. The pseudomutuality that colored the divorce often masks feelings of distrust and anger. The partners need an occasion to disengage from each other, to express their anxieties and insecurities, and, in general, to work through the divorce process.

Civilized divorces often allow the children to harbor reconciliation fantasies. The children may be led to believe that since the parents parted company so amiably, no real problems existed between them; consequently, there are no insurmountable barriers to reunion. They may believe it is just a matter of time until their parents come to their senses. Since they have not completely accepted the finality of the divorce, a remarriage may be particularly difficult for these children. They feel a loyalty to the original parents and family unit and do not easily become part of the second family. Indeed, the symptomatic behavior and resistance to the parents' remarriage may be a function of that loyalty.

COMMENTARY: This article presents a timely and perceptive look at the civilized divorce. Timely because today so many middle-class divorces are theoretically friendly; perceptive because the effects of such divorces can be long range and subtly disguised.

By reconvening the original family in a therapeutic setting, the therapist gives all members the opportunity to resolve problems that may have been glossed over in the pseudocooperative divorce processs. A myriad of intense feelings may have been denied; they can only be resolved if first brought to the surface and then worked through in the process of therapy.

This article has serious implications for childhood pathology, prevention, and treatment approaches. Practitioners should be particularly suspicious when a child begins to manifest pathological behaviors and symptoms and his parents are going through (or have gone through) a divorce that is (was) just too friendly, conflict-free, and cooperative.

SOURCE: Futterman, E. H. "After the 'Civilized' Divorce." *Journal of Child Psychiatry*, 1980, *19*, 525–530.

Stalemating the Divorce Process

AUTHOR: Marla Beth Isaacs

PRECIS: The use of a systems approach and behavioral techniques to alleviate the problems of a child who became symptomatic as a result of her parents' separation.

INTRODUCTION: A developed systems approach is necessary

to help ameliorate children's symptomatic responses to their parents' dysfunctional behavior. The family unit functions as a system; when that system is disrupted, children often manifest symptoms that represent the disorder in the family. Divorce is a major disruption to the family system. Therapy is often a necessary intervention to correct the conflicts that divorce creates.

The author proposes four essential features that characterize the divorcing process: "1. Individuals begin the divorcing process when the wish to leave the marriage becomes sufficiently crystalized on the part of at least one partner such that a separation is precipitated. 2. Divorce is a process through which parents and children leave one family organization and enter a new one. 3. Family members enter the process with their own agendas from which they devise 'strategies,' often unconscious, for navigating the divorcing process. . . . 4. The meshing of people's own agendas creates a temporary 'divorcing process system' that may produce behavioral sequences that prevent family members from fully navigating the divorcing process."

CASE EXAMPLE: The case of Kimberly D illustrates the creation of a stalemate in the divorcing process. Kimberly, aged nine, an only child, was brought by her mother to the Families of Divorce Project. Kimberly's mother complained that her daughter had an uncontrollable temper and screaming outbursts and did not like sleeping alone. Furthermore, peers teased her and she did not have any friends.

Kimberly was almost six years old when her parents separated, about three years prior to her presentation at the clinic. About a year before the divorce, Mrs. D grew increasingly depressed and isolated. Mr. D told his wife that he was seeing other women. After the separation, Mr. and Mrs. D argued less and their relationship became "comfortable and friendly." Mrs. D only saw her ex-husband when he visited Kimberly, although they occasionally talked on the phone about their daughter and issues that concerned her. Clearly, Kimberly became the medium and occasion for their reunion or speaking.

Following the separation, Mrs. D became more and more isolated and withdrawn from adult social life. She became enmeshed in a symbiotic relationship with her daughter. When in the house together, Kimberly and her mother spent all their time with each other instead of engaging in separate activities. The mother and daughter even slept in the same bed together and retired at the same time. Apparently, this helped to alleviate Mrs. D's loneliness and ensured that mother and daughter did not become differentiated. Generational boundaries were not established. The two lived more like sisters than like mother and daughter.

The mother presented herself as helpless. She was helpless in controlling Kimberly's temper outbursts and disruptive behavior. She called upon her mother and husband for assistance, thereby confirming her incompetence, inducing the grandmother's criticism of her parenting role, and using Kimberly's behavior as a way of pulling her husband back into a relationship. The mother's helplessness also kept Kimberly close to her and served to keep the daughter regressed.

For his part, the father simply wanted to disengage himself and become less involved with the family. He colluded in sustaining his ex-wife's incompetence, so that he could relieve his guilt by periodically "saving" Kimberly from a helpless mother.

The grandmother used her daughter's helplessness as an excuse for becoming more involved with her daughter and granddaughter. This gave her a chance to compensate for the time during the marriage when she had felt pushed out.

Kimberly's behaviors helped her mother to fail. At some level, she seemed to sense her mother's need to be in contact with the father. She gave her mother every excuse for calling the father, thereby reaffirming the mother's incompetence and failure.

In sum, mother, father, grandmother, and daughter all produced a dysfunctional system in which each one had certain needs met. The mother's incompetence was a means of pulling the husband back into a relationship, keeping her daughter close to her, and remaining infantilized in relation to her own mother. The father was given a chance to relieve his guilt for deserting his daughter. The grandmother had a chance to become more involved in her daughter's and granddaughter's lives. Kimberly cooperated with the entire venture.

THERAPEUTIC INTERVENTION: Therapy aimed at the management of specific symptoms. The mother was advised to leave the room when Kimberly threw a temper tantrum, to establish boundaries around sleeping arrangements, to allow her daughter to sleep alone, and, in general, to differentiate herself from her daughter. In the process, the mother became more assertive and aware of her needs with respect to both her mother and her husband. She also became aware of her isolation and loneliness and her need for adult companions.

The therapist made attempts to return self-control to Kimberly. She was given a diary with a key, which symbolized her right to and need for privacy and autonomy, and was advised to record incidents of screaming and what occasioned them. Kimberly began to feel that she was solving her own problems. She began to feel a sense of pride in her own identity and independence, as well as in her self-control.

COMMENTARY: This article presents a clear illustration of the manner in which a divorce process can be stalemated. The strategies employed by the various family members—mother, father, daughter, and grandmother—meshed to create a dysfunctional sequence in which all family members became stuck. The family became a dysfunctional unit and the daughter's symptomatic behavior reflected that disorder. It is interesting to note the subtle and unconscious collusion of all the members to stalemate the divorcing process. Kimberly's pathological behavior was merely a dramatic manifestation of that stalemate.

Isaacs's case study exemplifies the manner in which a systems approach to family therapy can help break the stalemate and allow family members to proceed with appropriate developmental tasks. The therapist's insightful use of behavioral techniques directly addressed the specific symptomatic behaviors. When the mother left the room, Kimberly was no longer reinforced for her infantile temper tantrums. Furthermore, allowing Kimberly to record her own incidents in the diary not only served as a behavioral check but also gave her a much-needed sense of self-control. Behavioral research indicates that the very process of self-monitoring one's behavior is therapeutic. It forces one into an awareness of the frequency and intensity of one's behavior, which helps to ameliorate undesired behavior. By keeping a diary of temper outbursts, Kimberly was involved in the process of monitoring her own behavior.

This study outlines an approach directed toward the awareness, understanding, and reduction of unproductive strategies that serve to maintain a dysfunctional interrelational system. It also poses practical, specific techniques for breaking the stalemate and eliminating symptomatic and disordered behavior patterns. Family members are then free to progress and develop in the areas of individuation, independence and autonomy, and self-control and self-assertion. Each member is facilitated in achieving full functioning, and the dysfunctional patterns within the family are corrected.

SOURCE: Isaacs, M. B. "Helping Mom Fail: A Case of a Stalemated Divorcing Process." *Family Process,* 1982, *21,* 225-234.

Family Therapy in a Residential Treatment Setting

AUTHORS: David Weisfeld and Martin S. Laser

PRECIS: A family therapy treatment procedure that reconvenes the divorced parents of children in a residential program.

INTRODUCTION: This article elaborates on a family therapy treatment program that takes place at The Alpha House Boys Program, a residential treatment program for emotionally disturbed boys aged eight through fifteen. Family involvement is required in two ways: the children return home on weekends for visits, and family therapy sessions occur on a continual basis. Many of the children come from broken homes; in these situations, the divorced parents are required to participate together in the family therapy sessions. The approach emphasizes

to the in-parent (the parent with custody of the child) that continued contact between the out-parent and the child means that
a relationship continues to exist between the divorced parents.
They still have a common interest in the well-being of the child
and their parenting function. Divorced parents often approach
the initial sessions of therapy with marked caution, and new
mates may or may not be included in treatment, depending on
whether their participation would help or hinder the process of
therapy. However, all family members having a psychosocial
relationship with the child should participate in the family
treatment program.

CASE STUDIES: Fragments of sessions are presented that illustrate the types of resistances and sabotaging maneuvers that
often occur in the process of therapy.

Family A had twenty sessions of family therapy. The son
apparently got into trouble during his weekend visits. Both parents agreed that they had failed in giving the youngster too
much independence. An instance is cited from the fourth therapy session, when the father came to visit his son and the boy's
uncle accompanied him. The father made it clear that he, the
uncle, and other family members were opposed to having both
parents attend the sessions together. A discussion of the rationale
for the attendance of both parents helped the father and uncle to
accept the idea of family therapy with both parents participating.
They in turn convinced other family members of the value of the
approach. Consequently, the possibility of therapy being sabo-
taged by extended family members was eliminated.

Family B had eighteen sessions together. In this case, the
son's love for his parents was being manifested through his attempts to control and manipulate them in order to protect
them, especially the mother. The authors present an instance of
the fifth therapy session to illustrate the resistance and sabotage
that takes place. At this session, the boy's paternal grandparents
come to visit him. They exhibited great concern for their grand-
son, yet they felt that therapy with both parents was a waste of
time and doomed to failure. They also used the occasion to attack the boy's mother. It was obvious that the grandparents

could form a collusion to hinder therapeutic progress. The purpose of the family therapy approach was explained to the grandparents. They left with a more open, wait-and-see attitude.

Attempts are made to motivate parents and to recognize and redirect efforts at sabotage. Sabotage may include the parents using the sessions as an occasion to attack rather than to help the treatment process. Subtle sabotages include the parents cancelling sessions, arriving late, or being unable to implement the weekend visits of the therapeutic program. Each of these resistance strategies must be confronted and directly addressed or therapy may be stalemated.

COMMENTARY: This study illustrates an effective technique for family therapy in residential treatment settings. It is particularly instructive in that it points out characteristic kinds of resistance and sabotage that may occur. These can take place overtly or on a more hidden level. Such maneuvers may be made by either one of the parents, by the child, or by extended family members. The therapist must be prepared to deal with these resistance strategies whenever they occur and regardless of who originates them. Opposition typically focuses on the participation of both parents in the family therapy sessions, regardless of the legal status of the divorce or separation. Bringing both parents together leads to the reemergence of family conflicts that have been dormant since the divorce. Nevertheless, mutual participation is crucial since both parents are invested in the child and both function in a parental role. Again, the therapist must be ready to deal with these oppositions; unless they are confronted, the course of therapy will be hampered.

SOURCE: Weisfeld, D., and Laser, M. S. "Divorced Parents in Family Therapy in a Residential Treatment Setting." *Family Process,* 1977, 22, 229-236.

Additional Readings

American Institutes for Research. "Mourning the Divorce: A Project in Marin County, California." *International Journal of Family Therapy,* 1982, *4*(3), 164–176.

This study presents a brief counseling program developed for divorcing parents and their offspring living in Marin County, California, where the divorce rate is perhaps the highest in the United States. The program described is a short-term approach that seeks to meet specific goals. Some of its major objectives are: (1) to provide skilled, clinical intervention to all members of a divorcing family; (2) to make interventions short-term (six sessions with the parents, three or four with children and parents); (3) to meet the needs of a nonpathological population; (4) to gear the services toward prevention; (5) to help parents adjust to divorce in a competent and fully functioning manner; (6) to help the children resolve cognitive confusion surrounding the divorce of their parents; and (6) to build awareness in the community concerning the normative nature of divorce-related problems.

Beal, E. W. "Children of Divorce: A Family Systems Perspective." *Journal of Social Issues,* 1979, *35*(4), 140–154.

The author reports on a study of marriage and divorce as processes through which emotional attachments are established and resolved. The concepts of family systems theory and therapy are used to describe the manner in which emotional attachments in general, and attachments to children in particular, operate in families undergoing the process of separation and divorce.

The author gives a general description of family systems theory. This includes an examination of the family's patterns of managing emotional attachments, the relationship of these patterns to the child's experience of the parents' separation and divorce, and the arrangements made for custody of the child.

A comparative description is offered of the management of emotional attachments in families with a mild or severe degree of child orientation. The objectives, processes, and specific intervention strategies of family therapy are considered in relation to these issues.

Hancock, E. "The Dimensions of Meaning and Belonging in the Process of Divorce." *American Journal of Orthopsychiatry,* 1980, *50*(1), 18-27.

The meaning of marital disruption and divorce is derived from the meanings and functions of marriage and the family. There are direct connections between the structure of family relationships and their meaning. For children in particular, disruption of the family matrix constitutes a crisis of meaning and belonging. This crisis may be central to the impact of divorce.

Men and women experience divorce differently and society assigns different responsibilities according to gender. Herein lies the central impact of the divorce on the couple. Divorce results in the loss of social definition by members of the separating family. Each must redefine his or her identity. The dimensions of meaning and belonging lie at the core of the experience of separation and divorce, just as they are central to the social bonds we all require. Divorce is accompanied by intense emotional reactions created by a shift in bond formations, and these shifts have implications for the individual's social connectedness. Divorce is a period of delicate readjustment and redefinition. The individual's sense of integrity must be reclaimed. Oftentimes family members need temporary buttressing while formulating and establishing new patterns of definition, meaning, belonging, and relatedness.

Jenkins, S. "Children of Divorce." *Children Today,* March-April 1978, pp. 16-20.

Three current trends tend to underscore the need to direct attention to children of divorce. The first is the continuing high divorce rate in the United States. The second is the high rate of remarriage. The third is the increasing percentage of divorces involving young children.

The author aims toward an evaluation of the specific needs of children in a divorcing family, based on four considerations: economic problems and child support; custody issues and court involvement; essential problems and therapeutic intervention, including peer group support; and kinship patterns in step relationships and the reconstituted family. Suggestions are given for child advocacy, age-appropriate intervention strategies, and areas of specific concern.

Kelly, J. B., and Wallerstein, J. "Brief Interventions with Children in Divorcing Families." *American Journal of Orthopsychiatry*, 1977, 47(1), 23–39.

The authors present a detailed description of preventive clinical intervention strategies developed for children of various ages in divorcing families. They also present their views regarding the assessment and treatment of children at the time of divorce, with reference to the strategies and limitations of brief interventions.

The assessment process, within the framework of a short-term intervention with a specific focus such as divorce, has special characteristics that differentiate it from the standard psychodiagnostic evaluation. As a divorce-specific process, it evolved in the course of clinical research. It includes an overall assessment of the developmental levels and achievements of each child in the family. The assessment also focuses on each child's reactions and unique set of responses to the parents' separation and divorce. Finally, it concentrates on an evaluation of the social support network surrounding, and available to, each child.

The authors have developed two models of intervention with children. Both models use the divorce-specific assessment process. The first intervention model is designed for those children who are too young to allow the therapist significant access to their feelings or conflicts. This model is also used with children who, for a variety of reasons besides age, are unable or unwilling to express and openly discuss affect-laden issues. The second model, an extended, focused crisis intervention, is more often appropriate for older children. Both models seek to reduce suffering and conflict; limit cognitive confusion about the divorce; increase psychological distance between the divorce and the child, where the child has been directly involved in the parental conflicts; and effectively resolve various idiosyncratic issues, such as having to choose between parents.

Regardless of the child's age, divorce is stressful. The in-

terventions discussed in this study have as their goal the amelioration of the short-term effects of divorce and the prevention
of their consolidation into long-range effects.

17

Reconstituted
Families

During periods of separation, divorce, single parenthood, and re-marriage, family structures undergo a radical process of change and restructuring. These phases of transition force a reappraisal of family roles, tasks, values, norms, and expectations. Reevaluation, expansion, and rearrangement are necessary within the family constellation. The change in the family structure in and of itself affects the operations of the family. Although the changes are not necessarily always negative, family members nonetheless need time in which to adjust to the demands of the new structural system. Parents and children must develop and establish new perspectives and new adaptive mechanisms. The parent, for example, must adapt to the new role of a single parent. If a remarriage occurs, all members involved must adjust to the new spouse as well as to the new roles of stepparent and stepchild. Even though the spouses dissolve the original marital unit, they still remain parents. Consequently, issues of visitation and financial responsibility to the children need consideration and demand some level of contact between the ex-husband and ex-wife. The family members must redefine their relationships within the original family.

The phases of separation, divorce, single parenthood, and remarriage each manifest a specific set of characteristics. In each case, new attachments, alliances, and boundaries are formed while old ones are disintegrating or, at least, changing. The articles by Schulman, Whiteside, and Auerbach discuss these complex family arrangements as well as the multiplicity of problems that can occur at each stage and in all parts of the system. They offer the clinician suggestions for effective intervention into the family structure at each stage of the transition, and therapeutic techniques that facilitate growth for all members, both as individuals and as part of an integrated family system.

Transitions in Family Structure

AUTHOR: Gerda L. Schulman

PRECIS: Family therapy can be an effective resource during times of transition in the family structure. It aids during the divorce as well as during the later stages of single parenthood and the reconstituted family.

INTRODUCTION: No rituals have yet been developed to guide the family and society through the process of divorce. The roles of husband or wife in a second marriage, or of stepparents or stepchildren, are not clearly defined. This article considers some of these roles. It deals with the consequences that a family must face when the family structure changes because of the partial loss of a parental figure through divorce. It also presents the similarities and differences between the crisis of divorce and the crisis of a parent's death.

A change in the family constellation has an impact on all members of the family. The author states: "It is my contention that the change in the structure in and of itself affects the operation of the family and creates certain phenomena regardless of the personality development of the members. To live successfully through the crisis, the family has to master certain tasks which eventually lead to the establishment of a new family unit. To the extent that the family accomplishes these tasks the unit will be able to grow and develop into a viable system. If for whatever reason this does not take place, dysfunctioning patterns will develop and the family will experience considerable stress." Clearly, family structure changes during the divorce as well as in the following phases of single parenthood and remarriage.

DIVORCE: The period preceding and following the actual separation and divorce is one of acute instability. Divorce constitutes a time-limited crisis in the life of a family, and during this time essential tasks must be accomplished. Some of the tasks belong to the marital partners while others need to be dealt with by the entire family as a unit. For example, one of the primary tasks for the couple is to decide whether or not to separate and divorce. The therapist must help the couple differentiate threats from action. The couple must also be helped toward a realistic appraisal of the consequences of divorce. Following the decision to separate, the first task to be accomplished is the dissolution of the marital relationship. The next task involves a recognition on the part of the couple that parenthood is not divorceable. It is essential that children feel they can rely on the support and guidance of both parents.

After the Separation: The Single Parent. The structure of the family changes in this stage. Where there were two adults before, there is now only one. This change forces the family into a new adaptation. One adaptive strategy that often occurs involves placing the oldest child in the role of a parent. The tasks and responsibilities of the missing parent are given to this child. In view of the age-inappropriate stresses and demands of this role, the parental child may react in a disordered and symptomatic manner. Oftentimes the single parent is totally unaware of the source of this child's problems. In working with this situation, the therapist must appreciate the implications of the structural changes for the family unit and for the oldest child.

Disequilibrium may also arise following a remarriage. Adding a second adult changes the structure of the family again. From the perspective of the parental child, the remarriage is seen as both a threat and a relief. The parental child resents the loss of status, but at the same time welcomes relief from the burdens of adult responsibility.

The Stepfamily. The reconstituted family has to deal simultaneously with several tasks. In the normal course of events, two adults who marry have a period of time in which they can adjust to each other and the new role of husband or wife. Later, a child is born, and this birth creates new roles for the adults. They are no longer merely a married couple; they are now parents. The birth also brings about a restructuring of the family unit. The reconstituted family does not have the luxury of time to adjust to these roles. They accept the roles of married individuals and parents at one and the same time. The family enters into new living arrangements, yet old struggles, conflicts, loyalties, and jealousies often linger. Family therapy may be a method of choice for helping the family members deal with the dilemmas that beset them.

The Family with Two Sets of Children. A complex situation is created when two individuals marry and both have children from a previous marriage. The family now consists of three subunits whose task is to unite sufficiently for the family to function. The simultaneous adaptation of the three units to each other is often accompanied by a great deal of competition. The natural parents tend to act as champions of their biological children. While there is some debate concerning status (for example, who is smarter or more helpful), the conflict appears to center around who had to give up the most in order to resolve past loss and become part of the new family. Therapists working with this family structure must emphasize similarities rather than differences. It may also be necessary to point out that the stepparent or the stepsibling is not responsible for the remarriage. The task confronting the new family is multiple. The family's members must give up the original family structure while also setting the boundaries of the new structure; expansion and rearrangement are necessary.

COMMENTARY: The core of this article is that structure influences operations. The author presents a structural position and offers excellent and timely examples of the manner in which structural changes affect the entire family. Crises may arise at various stages before and after the divorce and separation. This study presents a discussion with illustrations of some of the conflicts and dilemmas that typically come to the fore. Each of the major stages is discussed: the divorce itself, the conflicts following the separation, the problems that exist in the formation of a family after remarriage, and the issues that arise during the establishment of a family involving children from both spouses.

The author offers clear and informative examples of conflicts that may arise at any and all of the stages of transition. The cases presented are grounded in research as well as clinical experience. In each case, the structural changes have implications for the entire family unit and family environment. Changes in roles, alliances, parenting arrangements, household responsibilities, rules and norms, expectations and demands, and other aspects of family structure are all discussed in an effective and illuminating manner. The author discusses and offers suggestions for therapeutic intervention in the many problems that can occur at each of the stages of divorce and its aftermath.

SOURCE: Schulman, G. L. "Divorce, Single Parenthood and Stepfamilies: Structural Implications of These Transitions." *International Journal of Family Therapy*, Summer 1981, pp. 87–112.

Structural Challenges Within the Reconstituted Family

AUTHORS: Mary F. Whiteside and Lynn S. Auerbach

PRECIS: Data from family therapy interviews are used to delineate common structural problems that occur in remarriages.

INTRODUCTION: This article discusses the problems involved in the reconstituted or blended family. This is a family in which one or both parents has been previously married and brings children to the second marriage. A functioning family structure must be developed out of this network of relationships. Members of the blended family have mixed loyalties, as they are emotionally torn between the original family and the new family. Feelings are complex and ambivalent. Part of the task of the reconstituted family is to develop an arrangement that maintains the valuable intimacy of the nuclear family structure, yet preserves connections with important extended-family members such as parents and grandparents. The children need contact with both parents that does not provoke old conflicts. They also need to develop new family ties.

Symptomatic behavior in the reconstituted family often indicates that the family is having difficulties adjusting to the challenges of integration. Family interviews can help ascertain the relation between the symptoms and the family dynamics. Significant problems usually come to the surface. For example, the child's role during the marital conflicts, age at the time of the divorce, and problems during the period of the one-parent family all may precipitate dysfunctional behavior or contribute to existing problems.

The primary clinical data for this study come from four families. Each of the families was seen by a co-therapist team in a family therapy setting, and each came to the clinic at various stages in the development of the new family structure. The stage of family development at the start of treatment has significant implications for the diagnostic picture. It affects the course of intervention, the tenacity with which family members hold on to past roles, and the prognosis for effective change.

The initial adjustment period, occurring in the early stages of the development of the new family, can be a highly stressful time. The new couple is particularly vulnerable. Familiar experiences in the marital relationship are associated with guilt, hurt feelings, and expectations formed in the original marriage. A sense of chaos often marks this early transitional state. Pathological structures may form through premature and rigid crystallization of roles. For instance, the stepparent may adamantly withdraw from any discipline issues concerning the stepchildren.

CONFLICTS BETWEEN SPOUSES: The case of a twelve-year-old girl is used to illustrate the problems that occur when two family subgroups attempt to merge. The mother complained that since her remarriage the daughter had had destructive temper outbursts and had become withdrawn, and that her grades in school suddenly dropped. There was also a suspicion of sexual involvement with a stepbrother. The family interview disclosed that the father feared setting firm limits on the son for fear he would return to his mother. Further complications existed, as the son was attracted to the stepmother. Sexual issues were blocked and there was no established incest barrier. The marital relationship was still in the formative stage and the couple had difficulty in dealing with their vulnerability to one another. The children's problems allowed the parents a first line of defense. An essential task for such a couple is the development of a close relationship that allows conflicts to be resolved without using the children as go-betweens.

CONFLICTS IN THE STEPCHILD ROLE: The stepchild role in the family has some advantages. For example, there is a close relationship with the natural parent. However, this is a relationship with only half of the family. The stepchild must develop appropriate ties with three parents. If there is a stepchild from only one marriage, the role is a particularly isolated one.

MOURNING ISSUES: The reconstituted family must rework the investment in the original family. Anxiety over separation and loss must be resolved. New roles and new relationships must be clarified with the same people.

The case of the H family illustrates how problems can be precipitated by the extended family. The H family was in constant turmoil resulting from the interference of Mr. H's ex-wife. This interference masked many of the difficulties that existed in the reconstituted family. Mr. H felt he had to protect his ex-wife. He perceived her as fragile and vulnerable. Furthermore, she would often threaten suicide. Mrs. H protected the ex-wife's image in spite of strong wishes to the contrary. True feelings were blocked and conflictual issues were not discussed. Problems in the remarriage were hidden below the surface. The symptomatic behaviors were alleviated only when channels of communication were opened and feelings concerning the ex-wife could be honestly expressed.

COMMENTARY: The authors present an informative and empathic portrayal of the major issues that confront the members of a reconstituted family. The approach employed is practical and flexible. It remains open to modifications depending on a variety of considerations, such as the nature of the circumstances that lead a family to experience the remarriage as a crisis, the developmental stage of the reconstituted family, the presence of stepchildren, the roles the stepchildren play in the new and original families, and the problems of unresolved mourning related to the loss of the original family.

Although the authors discuss major problem areas within the reconstituted family, they are quick to point out that this article may present an overly problematic view. Many such families do not request outside help. Indeed, in some cases the remarriage brings renewed strength and optimism. After the initial adjustment period, many new marriages culminate in interactional patterns, styles of communication, and a family structure that are healthier than, and far superior to, those which existed in the original family system. The second marriage may better facilitate growth and functioning for all involved.

The authors have presented an objective, flexible, and feasible approach to coping with the challenges of the reconstituted family. The case histories offer clear illustrations of some of the typical problems that such families may experience. In discussing the major types of conflicts that characteristically occur in blended families, the authors have offered suggestions and guidelines from their own therapy experiences with these families. This is an article that could help any practitioner working with reconstituted families. It illustrates the manner in which symptomatic behavior represents both the presence of dysfunctional relationships and the reconstituted family's inability to adequately cope with the challenges inherent in the new family. In addition, the authors have presented illustrations of the major role dysfunctions that may occur in the remarriage. The examples and suggestions offered regarding the relationship between stepparents and stepchildren are particularly valuable. The study has implications for further research on the structures and challenges of the reconstituted family.

SOURCE: Whiteside, M. F., and Auerbach, L. S. "Can the Daughter of My Father's New Wife Be My Sister? Families of Remarriage in Family Therapy." *Journal of Divorce,* 1978, *1* (3), 271–283.

Additional Readings

Johnson, H. C. "Working with Stepfamilies: Principles of Practice." *Social Work,* 1980, *25,* 304–308.

Families that include stepparents and stepchildren are becoming prevalent. There are some common features that tend to characterize these families. They manifest a high degree of complexity. The greater the number of newly acquired family members, the greater the complexity of the relationships with which family members must cope. When people who are already parents marry, a new form of extended family comes into being. The combination of different life-styles and values, along with the number of different relationships with which the family must cope, contribute to the high degree of intensity that is present in reconstituted family units.

Characteristics of the reconstituted family are given. The most common of these include a high degree of complexity and variability, unexpressed role expectations, and competition for resources of time, money, and affection. The author also discusses some of the benefits of blended families.

Messer, A. A. "The 'Phaedra Complex.' " *Archives of General Psychiatry,* 1969, *21,* 213–218.

The Phaedra complex deals with the nonpathological stepparent-stepchild attraction. The Phaedra complex is to that relationship what the Oedipus complex is to the natural parent-child relationship. In view of the increasing number of remarriages, it is not surprising that the Phaedra complex should currently engage our attention.

The author proposes that the typical case illustrating the Phaedra complex is the couple who divorce after several years of marriage. They may have several young children; these usually stay in the mother's custody. Seven or eight years later the woman remarries. At this time, the daughter is entering adolescence and beginning to notice adults of the opposite sex. Oftentimes the stepfather is the focus of this interest. To illustrate this scenario, the case of Mr. and Mrs. R and Susan, the seventeen-year-old daughter, is presented. Susan was Mrs. R's daughter from a previous marriage. Mrs. R's marriage to Mr. R was a second marriage. In this marriage the husband and wife were growing apart. The conflicts between husband and wife pushed Mr. R closer to his stepdaughter, which caused him considerable anxiety. The author discusses these issues in the light of preventive measures.

Messinger, L. "Remarriage Between Divorced People with Children from Previous Marriages: A Proposal for Preparation for Remarriage." *Journal of Marriage and Family Counseling,* April 1976, pp. 193–200.

On the basis of the clinical experiences of the author and interviews with seventy couples, this study suggests remarriage preparation courses. Remarriage after divorce is an increasingly common phenomenon. It is an experience replete with tension and stress, especially when children from previous marriages are involved. Indeed, the remarriage family is identified as a high-risk group for which society has not yet established stable norms.

In this article, the author discusses the complexities and problems that are specific to separation and divorce and remarriage between divorced people. Role stress is discussed in detail. It involves the intricacies of relationships past and present, and the ambiguity of role functions and expectations, especially with respect to the roles of stepparent, stepsibling, and half sibling. The issues of custody and visitation rights and financial support and responsibility also present conflicts in the remarriage of divorced people with children.

With regard to formulating an educational program in preparation for remarriage, the author suggests some specific topics that might serve as the content of such a venture. The proposed content includes: (1) feelings related to the first marriage and divorce; (2) adjustment to remarriage; (3) division of labor in the present household; (4) perception of role relations; (5) responsibilities of the new partner; (6) exchange of views between the present spouses on child-rearing; (7) perceptions of what constitutes a happy family life; (8) feelings about financial arrangements; (9) feelings about continued relations with a former spouse and his or her kin, and between children and absent parents and kin; (10) feelings about having stepchildren who live with the ex-spouse visit regularly in the present household; and (11) discussion allowing for recognition of a range of difficulties, such as privacy for the couple, acquiring a ready-made family, and the like.

Ransom, J. W., Schlesinger, S., and Derdeyn, A. P. "A Stepfamily in Formation." *American Journal of Orthopsychiatry,* 1979, *49*(1), 36–43.

The increasing number of divorces and remarriages indicates a need for mental health clinicians to develop skills that facilitate the growth of viable new family systems. Clinicians must come to understand the reconstituted family as a legitimate form in its own right. In an attempt to meet this need, the authors have conceptualized three developmental phases of the reconstituting family: (1) recovering from loss and entering the new relationship; (2) conceptualizing and planning the new marriage; and (3) reconstituting the family.

In the first phase, feelings of anger, guilt, sadness, grief, anxiety, and loss relating to the predivorce family must be expressed and worked through. The presence of children can complicate issues. In the second phase, the partners in the planned marriage must come to terms with their doubts and insecurities concerning their ability to sustain an intimate relationship. Time and effort is required to enable family members to become emotionally invested in the new family as a primary source of emotional gratification. For some parents, the children may represent a reincarnation of the former spouse. This can complicate and delay the resolution of the loss. These children often become the target of misdirected anger and ambivalence. In the third phase, the reconstitution of the family focuses on a restructuring of family roles. Because children are involved, a delineation of the relationship with the divorced biological parent must be established.

The authors present the case of a thirteen-year-old girl to illustrate the manner in which a child's symptomatic behavior may represent the family's conflicts in progressing through the various phases of development. The role of the symptomatic child is a complex and crucial one, as it embodies the ambivalence and fears surrounding the new family unit.

The authors present an excellent and readable approach that can enhance any clinician's understanding of the process involved in coming to terms with the predivorce family, the issues related to that family, and the conflicts involved in the formation of the reconstituted family.

Rosenberg, E. B. "Therapy with Siblings in Reorganizing Families." *International Journal of Family Therapy,* 1980, *2* (3), 139-150.

The loss of parenting figures through divorce, death, and other forms of separation often leaves children without consistent parental support and with increased fears of abandonment. Siblings are in a position to offer each other a significant support system. Since they usually maintain an almost lifelong relationship with each other, they can form a stable and consistent support system throughout the various phases of development. Work with sibling groups can help children resolve the destructive forces that are often present in families and can facilitate the establishment of adaptive mechanisms.

The author presents three case illustrations that clearly demonstrate the powerful impact a sibling group can have within a family. These cases illustrate the manner in which a mutually supportive sibling group can be a resource for physical and emotional survival. Focusing on sibling groups is particularly advised as a method of choice when the parents are unavailable or unable to provide the support the family needs and when the children, by virtue of age and circumstance, can function as a support system for each other.

Visher, E. B., and Visher, J. S. "Common Problems of Stepparents and Their Spouses." *American Journal of Orthopsychiatry,* 1978, *48*(2), 252-262.

In this article, the authors discuss some of the common myths that circulate concerning stepparents. Vignettes of cases are offered to demonstrate how the myth operates and how it works contrary to the truth of the situation. The following are some of the common myths: Stepfamilies are nuclear families. The death of a spouse makes stepparenting easier. Stepchildren are easier to deal with when not living in the home. Love happens instantly. Each of these myths serves to confuse and complicate an already vulnerable relationship, that between the stepparent and the stepchildren.

The article also outlines some of the characteristic conflicts that occur in second marriages when children from the original marriage are involved. These conflicts focus on discipline issues, money, guilt concerning mixed feelings and loyalties to the original family, sexual issues that may arise when there is no natural incest taboo, and the issue of renaming the stepchildren. This is a valuable article that should be read by all clinicians working with reconstituted marriages in which stepchildren-stepparent relationships are involved. It offers a clarification of myths, suggestions for dealing with common problem areas, and perceptive insights into the dynamics of the stepparent-stepchild relationship.

18

Multiproblem
Families

The following three articles discuss and illustrate some of the similarities and differences between impoverished black families and white middle-class families. Each of the authors in this section proposes that the multiproblem family manifests special and unique styles of communication, role playing, cognition, and ways of experiencing affect. Because of the uniqueness of these styles, the usual techniques of therapeutic intervention are often ineffectual. Clinicians who work with multiproblem families soon learn that the differences are critical and must be taken into account if therapy is to be effective. Therapists must therefore be flexible, willing to expand the traditional therapeutic stance, and willing to modify their perceptions of the family and its individual and experiential mode of functioning.

349

Adaptation of Family Therapy Techniques: Working with Disorganized Low Socioeconomic Families

AUTHORS: Salvador Minuchin and Braulio Montalvo

PRECIS: Adaptation of family therapy techniques is often in order when dealing with the specific needs, characteristics, and demands of disorganized families from low socioeconomic backgrounds.

INTRODUCTION: In order to work with disorganized families from a low socioeconomic background, traditional family therapy techniques must be modified. The specific characteristics of these families must be taken into account. Characteristic styles of communication, cognition, and ways of experiencing affect must all be addressed. Therapy attends to the natural subgroups within the family. This may involve manipulating the subgroups in relation to the entire family unit.

SPECIFIC ISSUES: Disorganized families from a low socioeconomic population risk the loss of their boundaries. Members tend to mesh into an undifferentiated whole. Dysfunctional behaviors among individual family members are provoked by different subgroupings. Consistency in the composition of the family group is essential if structural conflicts are to be uncovered and openly expressed within a therapeutic setting. However, such consistency is often absent in the disorganized family unit; consequently, the therapist must change family subgroupings and shift observational sets if therapy is to prove effective. "The active manipulation of family subgroups in their relation to the whole group seems to us an effective therapeutic strategy to sharpen affective experience. The traditional therapeutic emphasis is predicated on the reclaiming of 'repressed' feelings, on the patient's own ability to define affect and to dislodge it from the totality of experience. This emphasis was developed for a patient population with a more differentiated psychological inner organization; but for the families discussed here, therapy must attempt to dislodge affect from amorphous experience and to modulate and expand the range of emotional events. Active alterations in the composition of groupings are such vivid and unescapable events that they facilitate sharper experiencing; the reorganization of contexts fosters the emergence and dislodgment of affect."

CHANGING GROUP COMPOSITION: To illustrate the adaptation of family therapy techniques to natural subgroups within the family structure, the authors present the case of the Parrington family.

This family was composed of the mother, her boyfriend, and eight children. The children tended to cluster into two primary groupings, each of which experienced different dynamics. One group involved the three older daughters. The dynamics of this group focused on their need for autonomy. The second group, composed of the five smaller children (between two and eight years of age), manifested the need for guidance and nurturance. The mother found it easier to cope with the younger group of children; they did not challenge her with needs for independence and autonomy.

Therapy was conducted along the lines of the family's natural subgroupings. Alternate sessions were conducted with the mother and the three older daughters, aged thirteen to seventeen, and with the mother and the five younger children. Sessions of couple therapy were also interspersed to include the youngest child's father and the mother. Later on in the course of treatment, the entire family was seen as a whole.

In working with the mother and the three adolescent daughters, it became clear that they were involved in a power struggle. The mother became authoritarian toward them. The rigidity of this interactional pattern demanded that the therapists completely reorganize the situation. One therapist conducted sibling therapy with the three girls, while the other therapist joined the mother behind a one-way mirror for co-observational therapy. In therapy with the daughters, it became evident that the feelings that each family member felt for the others were covered over with aggression. At one point in the therapy, one girl expressed a protective feeling for another. This gave the therapist a chance to focus on unexpressed or poorly expressed affect, particularly the issue of concern. The word *concern* was incorporated into the family's communication system, and was established as a frame of reference for distinguishing "tenderness" from "being a sucker."

The compositional move brought about the emergence of a new affective cluster among the siblings. In the traditional setting, the adolescent girls would probably have remained deadlocked by transactions of a controlling nature passed down from mother to daughters. Therapy with this natural sibling subgroup generated an awareness of concern and facilitated the development of concern-oriented patterns of interaction. This technique actively uses compositional ploys in order to dislodge affect. It stresses observation more than introspection.

This form of therapy appears to correspond to the family's capacities for experience. Small subgroupings allow the expression of interpersonal feelings within a narrower and more manageable range. The smaller groups also serve to buffer the impulsive nature of the responses of individuals. The individual members are less hesitant to express their feelings in a small-group setting. Compositional changes also foster the expression of more distinct affective reactions. This allows the therapist a chance to focus in on specific examples of affect, such as the issue of concern in the example cited. The use of small subgroups also forces the family members to consider alternative responses to the members present. For example, with the mother absent the girls could no longer rely on her for cues in relating to each other.

The study also discusses therapeutic styles. "The well-timed exaggeration or diminution of the therapist's own affective components is essential for promoting 'cognitive-affective' reorganization and expansion, for dislodging affects, and for allowing the initial articulation of new interaffective patterns."

COMMENTARY: The authors present an insightful and provocative approach to working with disorganized low socioeconomic families. The active use of compositional ploys is apparently an effective way of dislodging affect and forcing family members into a reappraisal of each others' roles and interactional patterns. It is a means of breaking the family unit down into more manageable and workable units. It is noteworthy that these units are not arbitrarily or artificially established. They are natural subgroups existing within the family structure. Therapeutic intervention with small subgroupings affords a concentrated focus of attention on specific affective interactions and fosters a reappraisal of roles and role expectations.

This is an excellent article by pioneers within the field of family therapy. They present techniques that afford a novel use of traditional intervention approaches. The techniques offered not only change the composition of the family subgroups but also shift observational sets and facilitate the differentiation of global responses within the family unit. By encouraging family members to observe their behaviors and patterns of interaction, this technique of therapeutic intervention fosters productive changes within the family. This article should be read by all practitioners working with disorganized low socioeconomic families, as well as by clinicians who would like to develop a modification of traditional therapeutic approaches.

SOURCE: Minuchin, S., and Montalvo, B. "Techniques for Working with Disorganized Low Socioeconomic Families." *American Journal of Orthopsychiatry*, 1967, *37*, 880-887.

Therapy with Impoverished Disorganized Families

AUTHOR: Gerald Fleischer

PRECIS: Families that are impoverished and disorganized tend to lack stability and consistency; consequently, traditional intervention techniques may be ineffective with such families. Therapy must often be supplemented by the mobilization of community resources.

INTRODUCTION: Impoverished and disorganized families lack stability and consistency. Roles are not firmly established or solidified; channels of communication remain closed. Consistent limits and controls are not set. Because of these limitations, impoverished disorganized families do not readily respond to the format and expectations of traditional family therapy.

In working with impoverished families, the therapist may find it necessary to function in a variety of roles. Oftentimes, the problems do not lie solely within the confines of the family structure. Environmental forces impinge on the family in a dramatic fashion and render its members dysfunctional. The therapist, not unlike an anthropologist, must study the family *in vivo*. Contrary to traditional therapeutic techniques of neutrality, in working with impoverished and disorganized families the therapist may have to gain acceptance in order to observe how the family copes with everyday problems in the environment. Thus, the therapist may have to function as a community specialist as well as a traditional family therapist. The mobilization of community resources, as well as of family resources and strengths, becomes essential in assuring the effectiveness of treatment.

The author presents the case of the Steele family in order to illustrate the specific needs of the impoverished disorganized family and the manner in which the therapist must change his or her perceptions of the family in order to effect therapeutic changes within it.

CASE REPORT: The Steeles, a black family, consisted of a mother, her husband of two years, and her six children (five by previous fathers), who were all living at home. The children ranged in age from sixteen to one and one-half years old; the youngest, a boy, was the child of the present union. The court referred the two oldest boys, Charles, aged sixteen, and Calvin, aged fifteen, for physically assaulting their stepfather.

The therapist initially hypothesized that the boys attacked the stepfather because his marriage to their mother threatened their own status within the family. While this "oedipal rivalry" explanation provided a theoretical framework for the therapist, it did not provide him a means of intervening in the family system. In actuality, there was a reversal of generational roles. The stepfather appeared to be passive. He did not provoke, nor was he able to control, the aggression against him. The mother did not seem too sympathetic to the stepfather. Indeed, it was possible that she covertly encouraged the boys in their attacks on the stepfather.

By the second session, progress had been made in the family relationships, but not in the relationship between the boys and their stepfather. The two boys did not appear for the third session. At this session, however, the mother reported the existence of another child, Ruth, aged nineteen, who was not living in the home. Ruth had left her boyfriend and for the past six months had spent much of her time with the Steeles. Ruth actually instigated the latest assault against the stepfather.

A home visit impressed upon the therapist how extremely impoverished the family actually was. It also gave him a chance to meet Ruth. However, once again, the two boys were not present. A debilitating sense of apathy and helplessness pervaded the family. Their problems were complex and multiple. The stepfather was financially dependent upon the family. Prior to his marriage to the mother, he contributed some money to the family. Furthermore, one of the boys involved in the assault, Charles, had an active case of tuberculosis but would not go to the hospital for assessment or treatment. A four-year-old child had a hernia that required surgery but was neglected. Ruth was unemployed. Her appearance was marred by the absence of all her front teeth (knocked out by her boyfriend), which made employment for her unlikely. This had important psychological, economic, and cosmetic implications.

The therapist managed to establish a relationship with Ruth. She proved an ally in the therapeutic process. Ruth was helped in the following ways: She received dental care, vocational training, and help in obtaining employment. Although this was a long and difficult process, Ruth became more motivated and hopeful. She no longer encouraged attacks on the stepfather, and she disengaged herself from the two older boys. She also promised to work with the parents in getting Charles into the hospital to have his tuberculosis treated. The attitude of apathy had been temporarily conquered, and the family was acting as an integrated unit, even though the two boys were still absent from the therapy sessions.

A follow-up revealed that for over eighteen months there had been no attacks upon the stepfather. Charles's condition was inactive and did not require hospitalization. Ruth was going to a dentist. The parents reported that the situation had improved. However, the parents' drinking had increased, placing the younger children at risk, particularly in a neighborhood that was deteriorated and crime-ridden.

COMMENTARY: Fleischer presents a thought-provoking case illustrating the complex problems that besiege an impoverished and disorganized family. The traditional approaches to therapy fall short of resolving many of these problems. The difficulties the family faces are not only individual and interpersonal; they are imposed in part by the family's impoverished condition. They include environmental stresses as well as psychological, familial, interpersonal, health-related, and economic problems. It is apparent that the resources of such a family must quickly become strained. In view of these problems, the therapist must operate at a variety of levels, as a community resource person as much as a family practitioner.

Fleischer offers a sensitive, compassionate, and highly involved glimpse of the Steele family. He clarifies the manner in which therapy is contingent upon the resolution of external and environmental dilemmas. The problems provoked by unemployment, health concerns, economic limitations, impoverished living conditions, and the like must all be addressed if traditional psychotherapeutic intervention is to be effective.

SOURCE: Fleischer, G. "Producing Effective Change in Impoverished, Disorganized Families: Is Family Therapy Enough?" *Family Therapy*, 1975, *11*(3), 277-289.

Family Therapy with Disadvantaged Black Families

AUTHOR: Vincent D. Foley

PRECIS: Disadvantaged families are evaluated on the basis of fifteen years of experience. Suggestions are made for effective intervention, highlighting certain features of a black, disadvantaged family system.

INTRODUCTION: Foley discusses the relationship of roles and communication in a systems concept of family therapy, and in relation to disadvantaged black families. Therapy with white families from similar economic backgrounds yields different results, or if similar, less extensive results. Cultural dimensions and differences are real and attention to these differences is essential if therapy is to be successful. It must be kept in mind that a black family system operates according to certain rules and norms just as a white one does. However, these rules are not necessarily the same.

FAMILY ROLES: Therapeutically, the concept of roles involves two levels. First, it involves the delineation of roles within the family structure. Secondly, it involves the therapist's goal of getting family members to perceive each others' roles in a different light. There is an attempt to move away from rigidly fixed role expectations.

Disharmony over role fulfillment leads to a consideration of four issues specific to black families: (1) Black families have often had multiple unpleasant and unfulfilling experiences with social and helping services. Therefore, they tend to be defensive and untrusting of these services. Oftentimes, these families are not self-referred but are sent by the court or school. In view of these factors, success in therapy must be immediate. (2) There is a strong need for self-observation. For this purpose, videotape equipment or a co-therapist is often employed. (3) The assignment of family tasks allows various members to gain awareness of their interaction patterns. (4) It is not unusual for the oldest daughter to be treated as a surrogate parent rather than as a sibling. Conflicts often arise because too much responsibility is placed on her.

COMMUNICATION: The concepts of role and communication are interrelated. Communication in black families tends to be in generalizations. For example, the therapist may hear responses like "He's jiving me." An expression like this is open to a variety of possible interpretations. There is also a frequent neglect of metacommunication; it is difficult to understand what is actually being said. Factors critical to family interaction are often neglected or overlooked.

It is not unusual for black families to label behaviors in a negative way. Family interactions need to be relabeled. Members need help in seeing the positive as well as the negative side of specific behaviors. In a similar fashion, affective exchanges in these families tend to have an all-or-nothing quality. Extremes of involvement or total lack of interest are frequently seen. Complete shifts or changes in affect are often in order.

TECHNIQUES: Suggestions are offered for ways of intervening in and changing roles and communications within disadvantaged black families. Audio and video tapes are particularly helpful, as is the use of a co-therapist. A multiple-family approach is a valuable method of choice in working with this population. When two or more families are seen together, they can mirror each others' behaviors and roles. Models are offered. Furthermore, the use of multiple families introduces multiple perspectives and this directly addresses issues such as the all-or-nothing tendency in affective exchanges and the necessity for relabeling.

COMMENTARY: This study offers a wealth of experiential data, case vignettes to illustrate the issues discussed, and practical suggestions for intervention techniques in working with disadvantaged black families. What emerges are invaluable therapeutic insights and strategies that address specific factors from a cultural and socioeconomic perspective. The realities of social class are considered in relation to therapy.

In attempting to discern whether these findings are consistent with the objective realities of disadvantaged black families, the author concludes his study with the following statement: "Some readers conversant with other ethnic groups may say that family therapy with black, disadvantaged [families] is not basically different than therapy with lower-class Italian, Polish, or Irish families, arguing that economics is the key factor in determining family structure and that the roles and communication outlined here are found also in white families. On the other hand, the sociologist Robert Staples ["Toward a Sociology of the Black Family: A Theoretical and Methodological Assessment," *Journal of Marriage and the Family*, 1971, *33*, 38], after observing the lack of research variables, concludes his study by saying that '. . . the black family had evolved a unique structure and style to cope with the circumstances that it has confronted.' He seems to be suggesting that despite similarities, black families have 'a unique structure.' "

This informative and thought-provoking article should be read by any clinician working with disadvantaged black families. The reader may or may not agree with Foley's contention that such families have a unique family structure and that this structure is intimately linked to cultural realities. Nevertheless, his arguments are documented by significant literature, research data, and his own clinical experiences. The suggestions for intervention techniques, particularly the use of co-therapists and audio and video equipment, are practical; moreover, they are based on the characteristics of the family interactions of the involved population. The suggested use of multiple families in therapy is certainly valuable and is grounded in a relatively large body of research findings confirming the efficacy of this approach when applied to specific populations.

SOURCE: Foley, V. D. "Family Therapy with Black, Disadvantaged Families: Some Observations on Roles, Communication, and Technique." *Journal of Marriage and Family Counseling*, 1975, *1*(1), 29–38.

Additional Readings

Combrinck-Graham, L., Gursky, E. J., and Brendler, J. "Hospitalization of Single-Parent Families of Disturbed Children." *Family Process,* 1982, *21,* 141-152.

The authors describe six years of experience using well-planned, short-term family hospitalization. Issues to be considered in selecting families for hospital treatment are discussed. The authors present case studies of six families treated in this manner. Each of the families discussed had at least one severely symptomatic member other than the identified patient. The single-parent families presented also had problems involving isolation from other adults and peers, which led the parents to overinvest in their children. The parents, though sensitive to changes in their children's behavior, tended to perpetuate the symptomatic behavior as a way of maintaining involvement with the child. The approach to treatment is systematic and structural. For intervention to be effective, the changes that begin in therapy need to be generalized to the totality of the family's life. The treatment in most cases sought to disengage an overinvolved family system and develop individuation and a sense of competence in each of the family members.

Goldensohn, S. S. "Psychotherapy for the Economically Disadvantaged: Contributions from the Social Sciences." *Journal of the American Academy of Psychoanalysis,* 1981, *9*(2), 291-302.

Private practitioners have become increasingly involved in providing health care for the economically disadvantaged. This study presents clinical strategies that utilize sociological and psychiatric insights to treat the socioeconomically disadvantaged. The author suggests five issues that demand attention: (1) Therapeutic emphasis must be focused on functional competence rather than self-actualization. (2) Clinicians must adhere to a perception of etiology as multidetermined. (3) Value orientations are determinants of behavior. (4) Intervention should take place *in vivo,* within the actual family and community setting. (5) Primary therapeutic reliance should be placed on the natural helpers, such as parents, spouses, extended family members, and friends.

Family therapy is presented as the method of choice to meet the complex needs of multiproblem families. Two therapeutic techniques are particularly recommended within the framework of a family therapy approach: role-playing and advocacy-mediation.

Heinicke, C. M. "Aiding 'At Risk' Children Through Psychoanalytic Social Work with Parents." *American Journal of Orthopsychiatry,* 1976, *46*(1), 89–103.

The author presents psychoanalytic social work as an approach to family interventions. Research and clinical data are offered regarding its impact on parents and their children. The study contrasts two methods of psychoanalytic social work, the open-ended and the problem-oriented. The results stress the importance of including family intervention in early childhood intervention programs. The problem-oriented approach still requires further testing. Follow-up studies suggested that the open-ended approach, which allows access to certain unresolved problems in the parents, appears to facilitate conditions that sustain the child's development.

McKinney, G. E. "Adapting Family Therapy to Multideficit Families." *Social Casework,* 1979, *15,* 327–339.

This study demonstrates that family-group casework concepts, such as outreach, advocacy, attention to initial engagement, limited and specific goals, and emphasis on growth potential and flexibility, can be more effective with multiproblem families when the family is viewed as a structural unit. Attempts must be made to alter the transactions, family interactions, and styles of communication in a positive manner. One of the primary aims of therapy is to facilitate the family members' adoption of appropriate social roles and tasks. Parents and children who have been emotionally deprived learn to grow and develop in intervention approaches that emphasize communication and interdependence within the family.

Mostwin, D. "Multidimensional Model of Working with the Family." *Social Casework,* 1974, *55,* 209–215.

The multidimensional model for working with a family is presented as a valuable and practical method of choice for working with multiproblem families. This approach involves the concentrated efforts of a group of professionals directed toward a family as a system of interacting individuals. It aims at restructuring the family system so that problems can be addressed and indirectly resolved.

The case of the P family, a lower-middle-class black family experiencing a multitude of interrelated problems, is used to illustrate the multidimensional model. A team of professionals, working within definite time limits, concentrated on specific task-oriented goals in order to modify the family structure and restore productive family processes.

Orcutt, B. A. "Family Treatment of Poverty Level Families." *Social Casework*, 1977, *58*, 92–100.

This article describes the socioeconomically impoverished family with multiple difficulties. Case studies richly illustrate some of the primary problems these families confront on a daily basis. Changes for family functioning are complex and often demand a combination of intervention strategies. Attention is given to parental life patterns that are self-defeating.

19

Child-Abusing
Families

One of the more appalling manifestations of the disordered and dysfunctional family is child abuse. Child abuse takes a variety of forms and results in a wide array of tragic and traumatic consequences. The abuse can be physical, sexual, psychological, or linked to neglect. It can also be a combination of any and all of these.

The characteristics of the battered child syndrome are too frequently seen by physicians, psychiatrists, psychologists, social workers, and helping agency personnel who work with families. The abused child and the abusive parent both experience a complex array of problems including depression, low self-esteem, low frustration tolerance, guilt, and a marked isolation from peers and the community at large.

The understanding of incest and other forms of sexual

abuse involving children is clouded by confusion, contradiction, misinformation, and myth. These distortions are compounded and perpetuated by the fact that the family's shame and guilt over the sexual abuse of children leads to insistence on keeping any incidents secret.

Research into the sexual abuse of children indicates that it occurs in all social, economic, and educational brackets and that in 80 to 90 percent of the cases the offender is a male. Furthermore, about 80 percent of the time he is a relative or friend of the abused child's family. This accounts for only one of the reasons why physical and sexual child abuse is underreported. Since he is known to the family or is a member of the family, family members often collude to protect the offender. The abuse is underplayed, forgotten, or merely ignored.

The articles discussed in this section examine the problem of child abuse within the context of the family structure. Child abuse represents one possible manifestation of the family's dysfunctional status. Therefore, family therapy addresses the problem within the structure of the family unit. It examines the interplay among all family members. The family intervention approach studies the personality characteristics of the parents that appear to contribute to their abusive behaviors, the characteristics of the child that may increase his or her likelihood of being abused, and the immediate and chronic family stresses that maximize the possibility of child abuse within the family.

The digests in this section discuss family systems approaches, psychodynamic strategies, group therapies, cognitive and behavioral interventions, techniques that develop listening skills and social and interpersonal abilities, conjoint and multiple-family approaches, and collaborative programs involving a combination of therapeutic ploys. Informed and experienced clinicians offer treatment suggestions for intervening in the dysfunctional family, changing family patterns of interaction, and enhancing constructive development in the abused child and the abusing parent. In each case the therapist is a child advocate. The immediate goal is always to protect the child and break the child-abusing pattern within the family. The long-range goal involves reeducation and restructuring of the family in a manner that reduces the risk of continued child abuse.

A Family Systems Approach to Child Abuse

AUTHOR: Brian Grodner

PRECIS: An intervention approach with abused children that focuses on the entire family or parent-child interaction as a system.

INTRODUCTION: Prior to presenting the family systems perspective on child abuse, Grodner reviews two traditional theories regarding the etiology of child abuse and techniques for intervention; namely, the psychopathological model and the sociological-environmental model. In the psychopathological model, child abusers are perceived as having a general character defect, emotional problems, inadequate self-esteem, and childhood experiences that result in abusive behaviors. The sociological-environmental model generally attributes the etiology of child abuse to external stresses such as multiple socioeconomic, cultural, and environmental handicaps.

A family systems approach to child abuse can be used alone or with more traditional approaches. It is grounded in the general systems theory which states that "organized systems are the product of the dynamic interaction among their parts." The family systems approach focuses on the entire family. It is sensitive to reciprocal transactions between parent and child and other family members. It investigates patterns and relationships within the family; consequently, the family is viewed as a dynamic unit. As is the case in most general family therapy and interactive play, the family systems mode of intervention may focus on more than one member of a family simultaneously. It can also focus on both parent and child separately while studying the reciprocity or mutual effect of a given behavior on either party. The value of this approach is that the focus of treatment is on the parent and child as a unit.

In working with both parent and child as a unit, consideration must be given to logistic issues. There has to be a time and place in which the parent-child unit can be observed. The Peanut Butter and Jelly Therapeutic Pre-School, Infant and Family Center in Albuquerque, New Mexico, of which the author is the

director, was established in 1972 to meet this very need. The
program serves preschool children and infants who are labeled
abused, neglected, emotionally disturbed, autistic, or developmentally delayed. In general, the parents are experiencing severe
stress and have significant emotional conflicts and limited parenting skills. The families run the gamut from broken and disorganized to intact.

TREATMENT PROCEDURE: During the intake procedure,
parent and child are seen together and the interactions, reciprocity of behaviors, and parental expectations are monitored.
The emphasis is on listening to parental goals, expectations, and
problems. Observations are made concerning family configurations, strengths, and motivations; the influences of friends and
extended family members; the nature of the family's stress; and
the degree of danger present for the child. Topics that may
prove too stressful for the child to hear are discussed privately
with the parents while the child is observed interacting with
staff and materials in a classroom situation. Decisions about
classes for the child, the frequency of parents' visits to the classroom to interact with their child, and counseling goals are based
on the aforementioned observations. The treatment plans for
child abusers vary and allowances are made for individual differences.

The therapeutic center affords parents a chance not only
to interact with their child but also to observe the interactions
between teachers and staff and their child. Parents, therefore,
have ample opportunity for direct training, modeling, and feedback experimentation. A range of techniques from behavior
modification to parent effectiveness training are employed.
These techniques, combined with continuous support and a
mood of friendliness, are used to foster positive changes in the
parent-child interactions. Parents are not treated as villains.
Such positive treatment has a direct therapeutic effect on the
abuser's self-concept and has the added advantage of resolving
parental antagonism toward social service agencies. Changes in
both the parents' and child's behavior can have an advantageous
effect on mutual interactions. Improvement in the interactions
of the parent-child unit can, in turn, help resolve the child abuse.

COMMENTARY: This article describes an innovative and promising approach to child abuse. In view of the current literature of social-developmental theory concerning reciprocal interactions between parents and children, the family systems approach to the parent-child unit is timely and essential. Initiates embarking on a family systems approach must be flexible and willing to depart from more traditional methods, which often, for the child's safety, separate parent and child. Observation of, and intervention in, the family unit is the salient feature of this approach.

This perspective has the added advantage of viewing the parent in a positive light. This affords the parent a chance to enhance self-esteem and also assures a greater likelihood of cooperation between the parent and social agencies. Furthermore, as described by Grodner, the family systems approach has the advantage of allowing for a diversity of techniques. Direct modeling of positive parenting skills and attitudes, the application of behavior modification, techniques of learning and generalization, and the beneficial effects of group therapy are but a few of the approaches discussed in the article. As a clinical intervention, the family systems approach can be used alone or in conjunction with the psychopathological model and the sociological-environmental stress model.

SOURCE: Grodner, B. "A Family Systems Approach to Child Abuse: Etiology and Intervention." *Journal of Clinical Child Psychology*, 1977, 6(1), 32-35.

Distorted Patterns of Interaction
in Child-Abusing Families

AUTHOR: Arthur H. Green

PRECIS: A psychodynamic approach to the treatment of child-abusing parents that seeks to modify the major components of the child abuse syndrome.

INTRODUCTION: Green proposes that the problem of child abuse is a severe dysfunction of parenting. He presents a brief outline of observations by various researchers who have described abusing parents as impulsive, rigid, dependent, narcissistic, and overidentified with a bad childhood self-image. The author concludes that "a specific 'abusive' personality does not exist; rather individuals with a certain psychological makeup operating in combination with the burden of a painfully perceived childhood and immediate environmental stress, might be likely to abuse the offspring who most readily elicits the unhappy childhood imagery of the past."

Using this frame of reference, Green conducted a study of mothers of abused children at the Downstate Medical Center in Brooklyn, New York. His study also utilized nonabusing controls; sixty mothers of abused children were compared with thirty neglecting mothers and thirty normal controls. The neglecting families were socioeconomically comparable to the abusing families. The normal mothers also resided in inner-city regions. Each mother was interviewed for an average of one and one-half hours. Although a large variety of family interaction patterns was associated with child abuse, the following three primary features characterized most abusing families: environmental stress, abuse-prone personality characteristics of the parents, and behavior of the child that increases his or her susceptibility to abuse. Case histories are presented to elucidate each of these factors.

CASE HISTORIES: The case of Calvin, aged ten, illustrates the environmental stress that occurs when the equilibrium between the limited capacity for parenting and the pressures of child-rearing is disrupted. Mr. A, Calvin's alcoholic father, left his job following his wife's stroke in order to care for Calvin and two younger children. The pressures of full-time child care resulted in an increase in Mr. A's drinking and a progressive loss of impulse control.

The case of Sonia, aged six, is used to illustrate the personality characteristics of the abuse-prone parent. Sonia's mother, Mrs. G, demonstrated impaired impulse control as a result of early childhood exposure to punishment and identification with her adult aggressors. In a manner characteristic of most abusive parents, Mrs. G suffers from feelings of worthlessness, a poor self-concept, and unstable identifications as a consequence of the rejection and hostility she received from her own parents. As a result, although she identifies with Sonia, she displaces her rage toward her ex-husband and her abusive godparents onto her daughter and abuses her in the same manner in which she had been abused as a child by her godparents.

The contributions of a child's behavior to his being scapegoated are illustrated by the case of eight-year-old Ira. At the age of four, Ira was hospitalized for multiple bruises following beatings administered by his father. Ira was born prematurely and his parents perceived him to be disruptive. Ira's speech was incoherent. His full scale IQ on the WISC was 54 and the neurological examination indicated signs of cerebral dysfunction. Ira's case suggests that physically or psychologically deviant children are especially vulnerable to child abuse.

In the remainder of the article, Green discusses psychodynamic considerations. He proposes that the "key psychodynamic elements in child abuse are role reversal, excessive use of denial and projection as defenses, rapidly shifting identifications and displacement of aggression from extraneous sources onto the child."

The author also discusses the treatment of abusing parents, emphasizing a multidisciplinary approach that would provide parents and children with a variety of comprehensive services, such as daycare facilities for infants and outpatient psychiatric treatment for school-age children. He stresses the importance of involving the parents in a corrective emotional experience with an accepting and uncritical adult. This is particularly crucial since abusive parents typically are mistrusting of authority, have fragile self-esteem, feel threatened by changes in their relationship with the abused child, and often have had humiliating interactions with their own parents and spouses. If not handled with sensitivity and caution, these characteristics can become formidable obstacles to treatment.

COMMENTARY: Green regards child abuse as a dysfunction of parenting. His treatment approach combines a psychodynamic orientation with a multidisciplinary approach. The aim is to modify the major components of the child abuse syndrome, all of which foster and maintain dysfunctions of parenting. His observations on abusing parents, as well as his study of abusing, neglecting, and normal control parents, utilize psychodynamic insights while incorporating community and agency services to reduce environmental stress. He has presented a historically grounded and impeccably researched treatment approach for child-abusing parents. This approach seems to be highly effective in modifying long-standing negative patterns of parent-child interaction.

In the last paragraph of his article, Green states that traditional psychiatric treatment must be greatly modified if it is to successfully hurdle the obstacles posed by the characteristics of abuse-prone parents. He suggests that the therapist must be supportive, active, and adaptable. The flexibility of his approach shows that he puts his own advice into practice. He addresses the negative and rigid responses that might exist in the community and service agencies as well as in the therapist (in the guise of countertransference). Similarly, the distrust and rigidity that may be present within the abusive family is discussed. While remaining loyal to the tenets of psychodynamic theory and application, he expands his approach to include the complexities of a multidisciplinary intervention strategy.

SOURCE: Green, A. H. "A Psychodynamic Approach to the

Study and Treatment of Child-Abusing Parents." *Journal of Child Psychiatry*, 1974, *69*, 414–428.

Multiple-Family Therapy for Child Abuse

AUTHOR: L. R. McKamy

PRECIS: Child abuse is conceptualized as a family system's malfunction.

INTRODUCTION: In this article, the author presents some preliminary considerations. First and foremost, since families operate as a system, family therapy must address itself to the client in the family and to the interplay among various family members. The system is a wholistic force that is more powerful than the individuals who comprise it. It is a force that seeks to maintain homeostasis even at the expense of the individual. The author discusses family therapy, the goal of which is to influence the operation of the family system. Although this goal is achieved through different techniques, the majority of family therapists agree on the following principles: Families should be treated as a unit and all members should be present at therapy sessions; emphasis should be placed on the interrelationship of members; and treatment should be directed toward changing the family rather than the individual.

Individual family therapy has proven to be an effective mode of treatment with child-abusing families. However, due to the stigma of child abuse, families in which it occurs usually remain socially isolated. Consequently, multiple-family therapy as developed by H. Peter Laquer can be an invaluable adjunct. Multiple-family therapy is a therapeutic system consisting of three or more co-therapists and four to six family units who meet weekly. The individual family units are comprised of everyone who lives in the home, plus significant extended-family members such as grandparents. An entire therapeutic network is established, having the properties of a living system. Because of this, the focus in therapy may be diffuse, which makes the issues less intolerable and reduces resistance. Furthermore, the families can offer information, advice, and support to each other. Indeed, families in the same predicament can more readily understand and bolster each other.

CASE STUDY: The Hill family entered a time-limited multiple-family therapy group in order to treat child abuse. Mr. Hill was hospitalized for the treatment of alcoholism. Mrs. Hill appeared to be an angry individual, particularly with regard to her husband's drinking and his abuse of their three children, though she too admitted to being abusive toward the middle child, Suzy, aged nine, who had been admitted to the emergency ward at the local hospital twice within the previous two years. Upon beginning treatment, Mrs. Hill did not feel that she had a problem; she wanted to focus on her husband's drinking. While in the multiple-family treatment group, several of the other parents related experiences similar to those of the Hill family, namely, situations in which they turned their anger over stresses in their lives onto their children. The message of understanding, support, and empathy was emphatically clear.

The group composition of multiple-family treatment also allows occasions for role playing. For example, rather than confront her husband at too early a stage in the therapy, Mrs. Hill was given the opportunity to verbalize her anger toward him using a surrogate Mr. Hill. Mr. Hill not only witnessed this event but later was asked to step in and negotiate an acceptable contract with his wife concerning some specific needs she had expressed. The victim also benefits from this form of group encounter. By receiving support from the group and responding verbally to situations in other families, the abused child, Suzy, was able to interact with her family in a more constructive manner. Her school performance and socialization skills also improved.

COMMENTARY: The approach espoused by McKamy offers a myriad of benefits. The structure of the multiple-family therapy group, in which a number of families and co-therapists work toward a common therapeutic goal, offers infinite possibilities. Families not only learn from other families with similar problems but also profit from families whose concerns are different from their own. In a similar fashion, the co-therapists benefit both the families involved and each other. By interacting in a clinical setting with other and varied professionals (psychiatrists, psychologists, social workers, and so on), they acquire new clinical skills.

Research indicates that abusive families are typically socially isolated. If they do participate in their community, it is only at a superficial level. Involvement in multiple-family therapy places them in a social framework and so reduces their former isolation. It also puts them in contact with a socially, interpersonally, and therapeutically supportive group of individuals. It serves to enhance their awareness of community services and social agencies. Certainly not least in importance, social involvement and awareness of social support serve to establish and maintain a sense of self-esteem and dignity. For many families, this is the first opportunity to verbalize frustrations and needs in a nonthreatening and therapeutically-oriented atmosphere. This very expression and acceptance helps to curtail the abusive behavior patterns.

SOURCE: McKamy, L. R. "Multiple Family Therapy: A Treatment Modality for Child Abuse Cases." *Child Abuse and Neglect,* 1977, *1,* 339–345.

A Cognitive Behavioral Intervention for Child Abuse

AUTHORS: Mary L. Otto and David G. Smith

PRECIS: The restructuring of parenting styles of child abusers via a six-step cognitive behavioral intervention model.

INTRODUCTION: Otto and Smith describe a child abuse intervention paradigm that allows the immediate alleviation of abuse even if only one adult family member is in contact with the assisting agency. This method focuses on changing parental behaviors and cognitive structures. It seeks to put an immediate halt to the abusive behavior and presents a strategy for allowing parents to learn new information and acquire new behaviors that will initiate and maintain a nonabusive pattern of behavior.

INTERVENTION PROCESS: The child abuse intervention paradigm is composed of six service-oriented steps. The crisis intervention step focuses on stopping the current abuse sequence. Parents can receive relief of anxiety by talking to a nonjudgmental and supportive individual either on the phone or in person; at this point in the intervention, emphasis is on deescalation of feelings.

The second step, cognitive restructuring, seeks to eliminate the myth that most parents enjoy parenting and find it easy, natural, and rewarding. The abusive parents learn that they are not alone with this particular problem. Specific thoughts and beliefs that may be fostering the abusive cycle are clarified and examined.

The third step seeks to reeducate the parents concerning specific normative information regarding child development. The therapist aids the parents in uncovering and exploring their unrealistic expectations of their children.

The fourth step is to link the child and/or parent with therapeutic structures. Within a group setting, the other members provide information, modeling, support, and assistance. Similarly, marital and family therapists can prove invaluable at this stage.

At the fifth stage, an alternative and more constructive culture is established. The development of new personal identities and norms that can serve as a basis of self-esteem is emphasized.

In the final stage, the focus on cognitive behavior changes may be replaced by more traditional psychotherapy if required.

COMMENTARY: Because of the usefulness this approach has for family therapists, this article merits inclusion here. The authors have described a step-by-step cognitive behavior intervention process that has the advantage of immediately interrupting the abusive cycle. It also teaches new, nonabusive behaviors. By examining the links between the parents' behaviors and the child's responses, this process emphasizes the cognitive restructuring that must take place in both the abusive parents and the child. Like many of the other techniques discussed in this book, this method is applicable within a wide variety of therapeutic frameworks to augment an existing theoretical and clinical orientation. This article presents a positive, flexible, and supportive group model that gives the parents assistance while in a crisis state, provides immediate relief from abusive behavior, and offers a systematic plan for instigating and maintaining constructive behavioral and cognitive changes.

SOURCE: Otto, M. L., and Smith, D. G. "Child Abuse: A Cognitive Behavioral Intervention Model." *Journal of Marital and Family Therapy*, 1980, 6(4), 425–430.

The Use of Behavioral Parent Training to Reduce Child Abuse

AUTHORS: David A. Wolfe and Jack Sandler

PRECIS: The use of behavioral training methods with abusive parents can substantially reduce the risk of recurring child abuse by equipping parents with appropriate and effective child management techniques.

INTRODUCTION: An abusive act by a parent toward a child represents the parent's inability to effectively manage the child's behavior or appropriately respond to the child's developmental needs and changes. By providing the parents with appropriate child management skills, the risk of further child abuse can be significantly lowered. The study by Wolfe and Sandler analyzes the specific contributions of parent training and contingency contracting in substantially reducing the probability of future child abuse.

BEHAVIORAL TRAINING METHOD: This study involves three abusive mothers and their families. Each mother and family constellation was studied independently. Prior to intervention, family interactions were observed and analyzed in the context of the family interaction coding system. During home visits, the experimenter observed the interactions of all members of the family. All members were present at the same time and all interactions were confined to two adjoining rooms. Each family member was the focus of attention for five minutes at a time, and the observer coded the individual's behavior at six-second intervals, as well as the behavior of any other family member with whom the observed subject interacted. The experimenter used these five-minute interaction blocks for each family member in each observation session, for a total of one hundred entries.

Two specific measures were analyzed: command compliance, reflecting the percentage of parental commands followed by child compliance, and total aversive behavior for each target child and each adult. Total aversive behavior includes destructiveness, negativism, humiliation, disapproval, and the like. This measure was selected as an analogue to abuse due to its high correlation with physical and verbal aggression.

Undergraduate students who learned the coding system but were not involved in treatment nor aware of the status of the families were used to check agreement among experimenters.

Two treatment modes were employed: parent training

and contingency contracting. Parent training involved reviewing chapters in the book, *Parents Are Teachers* by W. C. Becker (Champaign, Illinois: Research Press, 1971), studying selective typical problems and solutions, and role playing and rehearsing appropriate techniques for solving the problems. Contingency contracting involved rewarding the parent with a previously selected reinforcer contingent on the parent's use of a given appropriate child management skill for one week. Contracts specifically outlined what the parents intended to do and how it was to be done. If the contract was not fulfilled, rewards were withheld and a new contract was negotiated. Follow-up observations took place at one, two, and three months for each family. Constructive changes occurred and were maintained. The risk of recurring abuse was substantially reduced and the parents reported satisfaction with the program.

In addition to demonstrating changes in parent-child interactions, different patterns of family interaction were uncovered. The primary determinant for child abuse may be an abusive parent, who uses excessive and inappropriate discipline, an abuse-prone child, who contributes to the probability of abuse, and an abusive partnership, consisting of mutually hostile and competitive behavior between parent and child.

COMMENTARY: Wolfe and Sandler have provided significant research to support the growing body of empirical data that affirms the efficacy of behavioral training methods with abusive parents. Their approach is straightforward, descriptive, and systematic. Behavioral assessment and intervention methods to train child abusers in child management skills successfully reduce the risk of further child abuse. It follows logically that if an abusive act represents the parents' inability to deal effectively with a child's behavior, then training methods can decrease abuse by increasing the parents' child management skills.

This article is helpful in that it illustrates two concrete and specific techniques of training: parent training in everyday child-management skills, and contingency contracting. While some programs recommend contingency contracts with children, the authors inject a novel and insightful twist in that they negotiate contracts with the parents.

As Wolfe and Sandler note, conclusions regarding the efficacy of this intervention strategy still await investigation with other families. Their study does not presume to be conclusive based on three family units. Nevertheless, the strong theoretical and empirical base for their method and the substantial reduction in the risk of continued child abuse make this an invaluable pilot study. Their findings are further validated by empirical confirmation of the distinct patterns of family interaction in the three abusive homes.

SOURCE: Wolfe, D. A., and Sandler, J. "Training Abusive Parents in Effective Child Management." *Behavior Modification,* 1981, *5*(3), 320-335.

A Comprehensive Treatment Program for Abusive Parents

AUTHOR: John S. Wodarski

PRECIS: The implementation and evaluation of an approach to child abuse that addresses multiple causation.

INTRODUCTION: Following an extensive review of current treatment methods for child abuse, Wodarski outlines a comprehensive treatment program. Research data indicate that parents who are abusive with their children suffer under multiple social and psychological burdens. Indeed, most agencies working with the problem of child abuse fail to meet the multiplicity of parental needs. They tend to focus on only one aspect of the problem and therefore have not produced significant treatment results. Since empirical evidence clearly indicates that the problem is multidetermined, it follows that services should be similarly structured. Thus, the demand for a comprehensive treatment program.

THE COMPREHENSIVE TREATMENT PROGRAM: Research data indicate that a comprehensive treatment program would involve provision of services in four areas:

Child Management. Substantial evidence reveals that abusive parents lack consistency and effectiveness in the handling of their children. They tend to have unrealistic expectations of what constitutes appropriate behavior at each developmental level.

Marital Enrichment. Substantial research evidence indicates that abusive parents experience a high degree of interpersonal strain and marital discord.

Vocational Skills Enrichment. Recent data show that many parents who abuse their children are dissatisfied with their vocational occupations. Limited skills and occupational choices often compound this dissatisfaction.

Interpersonal Enrichment. Findings suggest that abusive parents tend to be dissatisfied with their interpersonal relationships. They tend to have poor self-concepts and feelings of worthlessness.

PROGRAM IMPLEMENTATION AND EVALUATION: Parents are referred by a network of agencies. They are administered a battery of self-inventory tests assessing parental attitudes toward children, and marital, vocational, and social satisfaction. A strong empirical base exists for each of the programs to develop the requisite skills in child management, and marital, vocational, and interpersonal enrichment.

Treatment consists primarily of programs spanning eight weeks for each area delineated, that is, eight weeks for child management, eight weeks for marital enrichment, and eight weeks for a combined vocational and social enrichment program. It is noteworthy that measurements occur during baseline, at the conclusion of each eight-week program, and at the conclusion of the first (eight weeks after conclusion), second (six months later), and third (one year later) follow-up periods. The results suggest that there is not only a reduction in the recurrence of child abuse but also a modification in service programs.

COMMENTARY: Wodarski's article elucidates the relationship between conceptual knowledge, research evaluation, and the possible subsequent alteration of services provided. Empirical research serves as the primary foundation of the treatment program, which itself focuses on the multidetermined causes of child abuse. The complexities of social and psychological conflict are given comprehensive attention. No single aspect is accentuated at the expense of the overall picture.

Only a program this extensive, solidly grounded on empirical findings, and attentive to issues of assessment and follow-up evaluation can assure satisfactory results. It appears to offer concrete assistance to mental health and social service workers as well as to parents and children.

SOURCE: Wodarski, J. S. "Comprehensive Treatment of Parents Who Abuse Their Children." *Adolescence,* 1981, *16*(64), 959–972.

Family Therapy in Crisis Situations

AUTHOR: Anthony John Siracusa

PRECIS: Crisis treatment for child abuse is conceptualized as a three-phase process that alters maladaptive patterns of behavior within the family.

INTRODUCTION: Family units are transactional systems that maintain their own homeostasis. For this reason, emphasis in therapy should be placed on relationships between members of the family as opposed to individual behavior. As a homeostatic system, the family strives to maintain its current functioning even in the face of a crisis such as child abuse. In order to restore healthy and appropriate functioning to family members, the system must be influenced as a whole. The approach employed by Siracusa combines crisis intervention techniques with family therapy as a means of intervening in the family structure to reduce or halt incidents of abuse.

CRISIS INTERVENTION: The primary goal of intervention is to minimize or prevent child abuse within the family unit as well as ameliorate the effects of crisis. Crisis intervention is conceptualized as a three-phase process including the emergency intake phase, the assessment phase, and the therapeutic intervention phase.

Phase One. During the emergency intake or initial contact phase, the clinician's role is to meet with the family within twenty-four hours of the reported abuse. Intervention occurs at an extremely sensitive time. Guilt and shame foster resistance on the part of the parents, and the parent's identity, therefore, should not revolve solely around being a child abuser.

Phase Two. In the assessment phase, the clinician focuses on many levels—ties between family members, family boundaries, and the psychosocial climate within the home. The following questions are frequently asked: "What is the crisis, whom does it affect, why is it disorganizing, what were the family's resources and plans for coping with it prior to intervention, . . . what are the specific tasks to be carried out to help resolve or reduce the crisis?"

Phase Three. During the therapeutic intervention phase, the clinician works with the family to stabilize their current functioning while presenting the family with meaningful alternatives. An understanding of the crisis and an appropriate expression of feelings such as guilt, anxiety, and anger are encouraged. Previously used coping strategies and alternatives to them are examined. Community resources such as day care facilities, crisis nurseries, parent support groups, and parenting skills courses are discussed with the parents as viable options.

COMMENTARY: Siracusa's approach makes provision for twenty-four-hour emergency service to families. Child abuse is recognized as a symptom of a dysfunctional family system. While every consideration is made for the immediate protection of the child, the crisis intervention technique does not necessarily advocate removal of the child from the home and punishment of the parents. This method is sensitive to the research which indicates that placement of children in foster care is traumatic, and which suggests that the longer children are separated from their primary caregivers, the less likely they will be to rejoin the family unit.

Success in this crisis intervention technique is contingent upon cooperation in the service network. Furthermore, the services must function so that the response to crisis situations is immediate. A lack of mutual cooperation and immediate response from these agencies could make the procedure less effective.

The intervention method detailed by the author of this article recognizes and seeks to reduce the parents' resistance to any intervention or treatment plan. Siracusa's procedure also addresses the parents' distrust of social service agencies. By dealing with this resistance, Siracusa's three-phase approach not only reduces distrust of community services but also increases the likelihood that the parents will continue with the treatment plans and that any gains from the initial intervention and treatment will be maintained.

SOURCE: Siracusa, A. J. "Brief Interventions for Families Facing the Crisis of Child Abuse." Paper presented at the 3rd International Congress on Child Abuse and Neglect, Amsterdam, Holland, April 21–25, 1981.

Child Abuse in the Single-Parent Family

AUTHORS: Alvin E. Winder, Ann C. Greif, and Evelyn P. Kelso

PRECIS. A treatment focus on interventions that work toward appropriate role restructuring within the single-parent family.

INTRODUCTION: Winder, Greif, and Kelso employ a family

systems theoretical base and a perspective that is consistent with Boszormenyi-Nagy's concept of parentification. In instances of parentification, the child assumes the role of the parent. An excessive burden of responsibility is placed on the child and other family members fail to balance or alleviate this burden. Restructuring the family helps to assure that the mother assumes parental responsibilities and the children are allowed to develop in an age-appropriate manner.

The authors describe a family therapy experience with a single-parent family, one of whose members is a battered child. They address the following questions: What familial roles are assigned to each of the children? How does the parent unconsciously carry out an assignment related to her family of origin? How does the parent relive her own parental experience through her children? Which therapeutic maneuver would work most effectively in changing the inappropriate configuration of a given family?

"Pathologic family systems are characterized by the use of children as objects upon whom both conscious and unconscious feelings and attitudes are projected by their parents." Consequently, children can be assigned a variety of inappropriate roles and they can be easily exploited in these roles. A complex pattern of interrelationships within various familial subsystems is established, and the manner in which each member affects the other members must be carefully examined.

CASE PRESENTATION: The La Belle family, which consisted of Carol, aged twenty-six, and her two children, Sally, seven, and Tommy, six, were presented as a family in search of a good parent. The mother had recently secured a divorce and complained that both children had been abused by their father. She had custody of both children and became enraged when the father and his girlfriend visited them. He brought the children toys and Carol felt he was trying to take their love from her. The father's visits usually resulted in Tommy having bouts of enuresis and school misbehavior. Carol often physically punished Tommy for his looks, which she felt were silly, and for a way in which Tommy laughed at her. They reminded her of her ex-husband.

Carol appeared to carry out unconsciously an assignment related to her family of origin. She felt needy and unloved. Her mother gave love conditionally, that is, if Carol kept her distance from the father. Carol chose a husband who proved men were ineffectual and worthless as parents. As well as being subject to many external stresses, Carol also suffered from colitis and gynecological problems (the result of being beaten by her ex-husband). She perceived both her children as obstacles to her obtaining nurturance. She rejected her role as mother and was continually frustrated because her children were incapable of fulfilling her needs.

The role of the parent was split between Sally and Tommy. Sally overidentified with the underdeveloped parent in Carol. She was maternal toward Tommy and Carol. Tommy was identified with the child. He was repeatedly told that he was like his father, unworthy of love and destructive, and that he ultimately deserved punishment instead of love. Tommy acted out in a destructive fashion at home and at school. His neediness demanded that Carol assume her parental role, and this in turn provoked her abusive behavior.

FAMILY THERAPY INTERVENTION: The therapist intervened to fill the role of the needed parent for mother and children and to restructure the family so that in time Carol would be able to assume her appropriate parental role within the family system. By taking on the responsibility for disciplining the children during the sessions, the therapist also afforded Carol a model of the good parent. Through the therapeutic use of modeling, Carol was guided toward becoming a more secure and effective parent, and was able to accept and cope with her role as a parent.

COMMENTARY: This case presentation is characteristic of the type of family currently being referred to family agencies. The multiproblem single-parent family with a battered child is an all too frequent state of affairs. Winder, Greif, and Kelso have not only presented a thoroughly researched article on parentification and inappropriate role assignment but have also documented a current societal malady. The case they selected was excellent in its lucid delineation of the family's fragmented quality and disordered role assignments.

The therapist's intervention appears to be directly on target in creating a receptive climate in which restructuring can become the primary means of achieving therapeutic goals. The technique whereby the therapist initially meets the patient's needs by relieving her of discipline responsibilities, parenting her and the children, and modeling for them, and then, in keeping with the patient's readiness and abilities, gradually shifts the focus of parenting responsibilities back onto the parent, is one that could supplement diverse intervention methods. The concept of restructuring is apropos. In any disordered family constellation, children may be called upon to fill a variety of inappropriate assignments. Since one partner is absent in the single-parent family, this situation is more conducive to parentification, and the need for restructuring may therefore prove more immediate and vital.

SOURCE: Winder, A. E., Greif, A. C., and Kelso, E. P. "Family Therapy: The Single Parent Family and the Battered Child." *Family Therapy*, 1976, *3*(2), 97-107.

A Psychodynamic Approach to Incest

AUTHORS: Thomas G. Gutheil and Nicholas C. Avery

PRECIS: Overt incest can function as a multidetermined familial defense against separation and loss.

INTRODUCTION: Gutheil and Avery, adopting the psychodynamic view that incest expresses the collective psychopathology within the family system, present a case study in which all members of the family were relevant to the etiology of the problem. This includes the nonparticipant member, in this case, the mother in father-daughter incest. Beyond the manifestation of the familial pathology, the incestuous relationship serves to ward off the dissolution of the family. It functions as a defense against separation anxiety and loss.

THE JONES FAMILY: The family described in this article consisted of Mr. Jones, aged forty-one, Mrs. Jones, thirty-eight, and seven daughters, ranging in age from nine to nineteen years. Overt father-daughter incest occurred with five out of the seven daughters. The authors highlight four aspects of the Jones family's world view that underscore the central importance of separation and loss; these are separation as a family preoccupation, the nature of family bonds, the interface between the family, and outsiders, and extrafamilial pleasures.

A signal that separation was a family preoccupation was the parents' strictness and the children's wish to elude it. Yet despite this preoccupation, the issue of separation anxiety was rarely confronted directly.

The nature of the family ties was unusual in that the emotional component was deemed irrelevant. Allegiance and obedience to parental authority replaced the affective element.

A definite line of demarcation was drawn between inside and outside the family unit. The outside represented freedom and pleasure, and as such was tempting and dangerous. Imagined pleasures also differentiated the outside from the inside. The parents perceived such extrafamilial pleasures as a tremendous threat. This view of the outside as dangerous occasionally took on a paranoid cast.

TREATMENT ISSUES: The Jones's marriage was burdened by chronic sexual difficulties as well as significant separations of several kinds. Mr. Jones had been absent from home at the time the older children were born. In addition, both Mr. and Mrs. Jones had experienced traumatic and impulsive separations from their own parents, and they had just separated from each other when the overt incest began. The mother was ostensibly unaware of the incestuous behaviors until treatment began.

The authors suggest that "the incest thus appeared to forestall separation: (a) by allowing mother a vicarious acting-out of her own unresolved Oedipal wishes and thus serving to 'discharge' these disruptive tensions; (b) by relieving the sexual pressure on Mrs. Jones, thus allowing her actually to tolerate staying; (c) by improving the marital relationship (according to the daughters), since father's guilty secret would 'force' him to be tender to mother."

Thus, incest may have been used as an alliance whereby mother was excluded and the daughters bound to the father by a shared secret and a shared guilt. The authors further note that although the incest in the Jones family represents a total family involvement, the mother's role is pivotal. "This is so to the degree that mother either grossly denies evidence of the incest or takes no consequent action if she does acknowledge it."

COMMENTARY: Gutheil and Avery have presented a classical psychodynamic interpretation of incest. In the context of family therapy, they have shown the manner in which incest expresses the collective psychopathology of all the family members. In this case, incest served as a bond and as an alliance that protected the family unit from the shared dread of separation.

The case report illustrates an instance of father-daughter incest that is fairly consistent with the family configuration outlined in psychoanalytic literature, wherein the mother feels unloved and shuns the maternal role, seeking instead to be mothered by her daughter. The daughter, on the other hand, feels rejected by the mother. When his marriage reaches an impasse, the father turns to the daughter as a relief from fear of abandonment. In the case presented, the father turns to several daughters; consequently, we are concerned with multiple incest.

The authors present a clear case of incest utilized as a homeostatic family defense against disintegration. It is noteworthy that Gutheil and Avery emphasize the complex and subtle manner in which all family members are involved in the incestuous relationship, including nonparticipant members. This unconscious collusion serves as an incestuous alternative to the conjugal bond and as a secret alliance for assuring the family's intactness.

SOURCE: Gutheil, T. G., and Avery, N. C. "Multiple Overt Incest as Family Defense Against Loss." *Family Process*, 1977, *16*, 105-116.

The Contribution of Nonparticipating Members in the Incestuous Family

AUTHORS: Pavel Machotka, Frank S. Pittman III, and Kalman Flomenhaft

PRECIS: The denial of an incestuous relationship by participating and nonparticipating members avoids responsibility and creates a secret collusion within the family.

INTRODUCTION: The authors, members of the family treatment unit of the University of Colorado Medical Center, provide crisis-oriented family therapy as an alternative to hospitalization. They propose that incest is determined by an interpersonal triangle, and they are particularly sensitive to the contribution of the nonparticipating member. Therapy is directed toward helping each member to see his or her involvement in the problem. Furthermore, the therapists strive to encourage each member to achieve healthier family relationships and role assignments.

Following a brief review of the psychiatric literature on incest—suggesting, in essence, that an incestuous liaison is made possible and maintained by the collusion of several family members—the authors present three case studies. The following is one such study of a protracted incest relationship.

CASE STUDY: The most detailed of the three cases presented involved the Carlson family. All three members of the triangular relationship—mother, father, and daughter—had been hospitalized at one time or another for psychiatric problems. Mrs. Carlson is described as a frigid, dependent woman, the mother of three children. Mr. Carlson appears to be an ineffectual and unsuccessful man who is unhappy in his marriage and work. He had been admitted several times to the hospital for alcoholism. Mary, the victim, is the oldest of three children; while Mrs. Carlson worked, Mary cared for the home and younger children.

Following an argument with her father at the age of sixteen, Mary was hospitalized and given electroshock therapy (EST). She was accused of becoming "wildly hysterical." Mary insisted that during a three-year period she had been raped by her father. She further stated that the argument ensued because she refused her father sexually. The father denied these claims. The issue of incest was not raised again until two years later. At this time, Mr. Carlson opposed Mary's engagement, an argument erupted, and again Mary became "hysterical" and was hospitalized and given EST. At the age of seventeen, Mary had an illegitimate child which she put up for adoption. It was not mentioned who the father of the infant was. Following her release from the hospital, Mary went to live with her grandmother. All this time, Mr. Carlson continued to oppose the marriage and made efforts to exert greater control over his daughter. Due to these pressures from her father, Mary repeated the incest story and was again hospitalized. This time she came under the care of the family treatment unit.

Mr. and Mrs. Carlson both denied the possibility of incest. At times they even denied that the issue had ever been mentioned. Privately, Mr. Carlson admitted that it might have happened once or twice while he was drunk. In actuality, both parents appeared to believe that incest had occurred but denied their belief. This secret gave Mary the power to upset her parents by reiterating the incest incidents, a power that she fully utilized when she felt her freedom was in jeopardy. Further power was given to Mary in her role as a buffer between her parents. Moreover, because she performed the necessary household duties, her mother sought to keep her at home. Mr. Carlson felt deserted by both women; he felt powerless and afraid of both. He isolated himself from the family and drank.

The authors present a transcript of an interview between Mrs. Carlson and Mary in which Mrs. Carlson asserts her disbelief of the incestuous relationship, and, despite adamant protests to the contrary from Mary, insists she never heard any mention of the incidents. The authors use the transcript to illustrate that the women see the incest as a problem between them. Mary's use of the incest story is taunting, aggressive, and complex. Mrs. Carlson's staunch denial continues to give the story power. Therapy focused on the denial of the incest, on the disordered relations within the family, and on the collusion of the nonparticipant member, Mrs. Carlson.

COMMENTARY: This article describes an interesting and complex secret collusion within a disordered family. The denial of the incestuous relationship served a function for each member of the triangular system. The needs served continued to give the secret a power the victim learned to manipulate. Appropriately, therapy concentrated on the denial, not only of the incestuous activity but also of the disordered relations and the collusion of the nonparticipant. By concentrating on this collusion, the therapist could effect the desired change within the family and assure appropriate role assignments. It is clearly desirable to break through the denial and have each member of the family face their responsibility for family conflicts. This includes the nonparticipating member. Because of this emphasis, the article warrants careful reading. The authors persuasively argue that concentrating on the issues of denial and collusion within the abusive family, and on a restructuring of disordered relations and inappropriate role assignments, should be a primary concern for all family therapists.

SOURCE: Machotka, P., Pittman, F. S., III, and Flomenhaft, K. "Incest as a Family Affair." *Family Process,* 1967, *6,* 98–116.

Additional Readings

Brant, R. S. T., and Tisza, V. B. "The Sexually Misused Child."
American Journal of Orthopsychiatry, 1977, *47*(1), 80–90.

This study is based on pediatric emergency room records
and clinical experience. The data suggest that the sexual abuse
of children often goes undetected. For example, long-term cases
of incest do not come to hospitals too often. Occasionally, the
family homeostasis will be disrupted and angry and upset parents will present the child at the emergency room. It is not unusual for the child to be brought in because of guilt or anger
toward the abusive spouse rather than because of concern for
the health and well-being of the child. Because of the element
of secretiveness surrounding this problem, the diagnosis of sexual abuse should be considered for all children seen for genital
injury, irritation, or infection. Sexual abuse is often a symptom
of family dysfunction. The authors present eleven case studies
illustrating these issues. They also discuss the guidelines for
management of acute cases.

Finkelhor, D. "Sexual Abuse: A Sociological Perspective."
Child Abuse and Neglect, 1982, *6,* 95–102.

Sexual abuse is rapidly emerging as one of the major
forms of child abuse. The problem has reached epidemic and international proportions. It has recently entered the public lime-
light not primarily because it has been steadily on the increase,
but because it has been championed by a coalition of groups,
particularly the women's movement and the children's protection movement. These two movements tend to perceive sexual
abuse from different perspectives. The child protectors have
tended to group sexual abuse with other forms of child abuse
and neglect, whereas feminists have identified sexual abuse with
the phenomenon of rape.

The two factors primarily associated with the sexual abuse
of children are social isolation and male domination. Sexually
abusive families have been noted for being patriarchal. The social isolation of the family serves to keep neighbors and social
agencies unaware of the abusive behaviors within the family. In
addition, the rising divorce rate, erosion of sexual norms, and

changes in the expectations of social roles all place children at greater risk.

The article asserts that the sexual abuse of children needs to be seen as a problem distinct from the physical abuse of children. Sexual abuse incriminates a particular sex, namely, men; it may therefore be described as a problem of masculine socialization. In attempting to solve the problem, emphasis should be placed on male sexual socialization rather than on dysfunctional and inadequate parenting. This is not to say that the dysfunctional elements in the family unit should be ignored, only that the emphasis should be placed elsewhere.

This study presents an interesting variation on the usual approach to child abuse and child-abusing families. The focus is on cultural factors, such as issues surrounding socialization, rather than on dysfunctional behaviors and relationships in the family.

Geismar, L. L. "Family Disorganization: A Sociological Perspective." *Social Casework*, November 1978, pp. 545–550.

Research data suggest that family disorganization is not necessarily a universal phenomenon; rather, its prevalence is affected by the economic and cultural factors that shape family life. While this does not discount the possibility that biologically determined factors may also contribute to family malfunctioning, it appears that culturally determined factors are primary. Consequently, intervention must go beyond individual and family treatment. Forces must be mobilized at the community, state, and national levels. The dominance of cultural factors highlights the need for intervention at the sociocultural level.

Green, A. H., Gaines, R. W., and Sandgrund, A. "Child Abuse: Pathological Syndrome of Family Interaction." *American Journal of Psychiatry*, 1974, *131*(8), 152–160.

A typical psychodynamic pattern operates in the abusive mother (or maternal caretaker) during interaction with the scapegoated child. The child's increased demand for nurturance intensifies the mother's own unsatisfied dependency needs, and the mother often turns to the child for the satisfaction of these needs. The child, of course, is not psychologically able to meet the mother's needs. At this point, the mother unconsciously equates the child with her own critical and rejecting mother, and unconsciously enacts with the abused child her own original rejection. This provokes low self-esteem, guilt, and a sense of worthlessness in the mother, who then displaces her bad self-image onto the abused child. With this shift, the mother assumes identification with the aggressive mother. This allows her a chance to master the rejecting situation. In addition to representing the bad mother and bad childhood self, the abused child may become linked to other individuals who have come to be associated with ambivalence or rejection.

Child abuse may be regarded as a dysfunction of parenting in which the parent displaces past feelings onto the child. The etiology of child abuse is based on an interaction among three factors: the personality traits of the parents that contribute to abuse, the characteristics of the child that tend to foster the scapegoating process, and increased environmental demands for child care. Any viable intervention technique must respond to these crucial variables. Strategies for intervention must also be able to acknowledge the influence of past events, situations, and relationships on the parents' current relationship and interactions with the abused child.

Halperin, S. L. "Abused and Non-Abused Children's Perceptions of Their Mothers, Fathers and Siblings: Implications for a Comprehensive Family Treatment Plan." *Family Relations,* January 1981, pp. 89-96.

Different patterns arise when children from abusive families are compared with those from nonabusive families. Both abused and nonabused children from abusive families have more negative perceptions of their parents and siblings than do children from nonabusive families. Children from abusive families also manifest more ambivalence toward their parents than children from nonabusive families.

The author proposes a comprehensive treatment model for intervention with abusive families. Since abuse affects the entire family system, all family members individually, and the family as a unit, must be assessed and treated. A three-phase intervention model is proposed, involving not only individual, marital, and sibling dynamics, but also family dynamics. A combination of treatment approaches completes the comprehensive intervention program.

Holmes, S. A., Barnhart, C., Cantoni, L., and Reymer, E. "Working with the Parent in Child-Abuse Cases." *Social Casework,* 1975, *56,* 3–12.

Child abuse is often one of the problems of the multiproblem family. In this article, the authors present a definition of child abuse and discuss the resistance to treatment manifested by abusive parents. For example, abusive parents are usually socially isolated from other families and from the larger community. These parents also suffer from severe deficiencies in interactional skills. Because of these resistances, it is very difficult to develop a treatment relationship. Suggestions for doing so are offered. The authors argue that child abuse may bear no relation to the child's behavior but may relate instead to the abusive parent's limitations, low self-esteem, and negative feelings about himself or his situation. These issues must be addressed if therapy is to be considered as a method of intervention and if it is to be successful.

Kroth, J. A. "Family Therapy Impact on Intrafamilial Child Sexual Abuse." *Child Abuse and Neglect,* 1979, *3*(1), 297–302.

The author proposes a family therapy treatment program to deal with intrafamilial sexual abuse of children. The program was evaluated using a cross-sectional longitudinal design. Three groups of clients at different phases in therapy were measured on forty-four indices of behavioral and attitudinal change. The study results are analyzed in terms of the psychosomatic symptomatology, social isolation, emotional disorders, aberrant behavior, and marital relationships of the parents. The study emphasizes the need for further empirical research on the causes and treatment of incest.

Paulson, M. J., and Blake, P. R. "The Physically Abused Child: A Focus on Prevention." *Child Welfare,* 1969, *48*(2), 86–95.

Following a brief review of the literature on child abuse, the authors compare the results of a study in one area of Los Angeles County with results of other studies reported in the literature. Although caution should be exercised in making generalizations from such a sample, the data reveal the primary characteristics of abusive parents, their home life, and their family structure.

The study elaborates on some of the following issues: the responsibility of the physician once child abuse is suspected; the similarities and differences between abuse and neglect; the goals of future research into maltreatment of children; and strategies for the early identification of possible offenders.

20

Families with Handicapped Children

The usual day-to-day demands of family life can tax the resources and coping mechanisms of all family members. Many families, however, face a composite of stresses that are exacerbated by the unique physical, emotional, and caretaking needs of handicapped children. Families with a child who is handicapped are more likely to experience stress, all things being equal, than families with normal children. The articles in this section use case studies to illustrate the myriad problems that confront families of handicapped children and to demonstrate the ways in which various family therapy techniques can facilitate the development of the family's coping mechanisms.

The papers by Wikler, Turner, and Loeb discuss some of the developmental disabilities, transitions, and crises that plague

397

mentally retarded children. They each offer suggestions of therapeutic strategies that deal with both the immediate and the long-term needs of families with mentally retarded children. Weltner discusses the single-parent family structure. He elaborates on the risks that are inherent to this type of family and offers a structural approach to therapy that seeks to minimize these risks. Serrano and Wilson present a multidisciplinary approach to the diagnosis and treatment of the brain-damaged child with associated behavioral disorders. The article by Todd and Satz details some of the disruptive effects of traumatic and long-term memory deficits on a young man and his family.

Stresses Confronting Families of
Mentally Retarded Children

AUTHOR: Lynn Wikler

PRECIS: The stresses that confront the families of mentally retarded children are chronic; they recur over time. Discrepancies
between parental expectations and the performance of the mentally handicapped child exacerbate these stresses.

INTRODUCTION: Wikler presents an overview of the stresses
that occur in families of mentally retarded children, and offers a
preventive approach to them. If clinicians were alerted to those
times when the family most needs extra help and support, coping mechanisms could be strengthened, and problems and risks
reduced.

Types of chronic stress that are unique to families of
mentally retarded children include the prolonged burden of care
the child demands, stigmatized social interactions, lack of specific child management information, and the parents' emotional
response to the diagnosis of retardation in their child. These are
stresses that the parents and family do not cope with on a one-
time basis only; rather, they recur over time.

It is hypothesized that ten critical periods are potentially
stressful for families of mentally retarded children. Five of these
crises are developmental and occur as the child successively
starts to walk, learns to talk, begins school, goes through puberty,
and reaches early adulthood, when the parents may expect that
independence is possible.

The second series of five crises involves transitions away
from the traditional carrying out of parental responsibilities,
that is, recourse to professional services in making key decisions. These stresses center on the diagnosis of mental retardation, on younger siblings who are intellectually superior to the
retarded child, on discussion of possible placement of the retarded child, on behavior and health problems specific to the
retarded child, and on discussion of the guardianship and care
of the mentally retarded older child or adult.

COMMENTARY: This study not only discusses some of the major issues confronting families with a mentally retarded child but also considers implications for further research and clinical interventions. For example, since the majority of retarded children have traditionally been institutionalized, professionals are not fully alert as to what stresses may occur when the child is reared at home. An awareness of these stresses is invaluable from a preventive perspective. Knowing which times and stages produce the greatest stress can reduce the risk factor.

The author perceptively indicates that coping is not merely a linear process. The coping strategies developed within the family are complex. Like the crises they attempt to meet, these adaptive mechanisms undergo various changes as they recur.

The thorough discussion of the five developmental crises and the five crises centering on transitions in familial responsibility should be read by any practitioners who may be working with families of retarded children for the first time. The article also offers a wealth of information for researchers interested in studying families of retarded children, particularly their coping mechanisms and the issue of living at home versus institutional placement for the child.

SOURCE: Wikler, L. "Chronic Stresses of Families of Mentally Retarded Children." *Family Relations,* 1981, *30,* 281–288.

Therapy with the Families of Mentally Retarded Children

AUTHOR: Andrew L. Turner

PRECIS. Therapy with families having a mentally retarded child involves a two-pronged approach. It must serve as immediate crisis intervention as well as long-term counseling.

INTRODUCTION: Family therapy provides a means of dealing with the continuous tensions facing families that include a mentally retarded child. The presence of the handicapped child places the family at a higher risk for marital conflicts, sibling rivalry, and ongoing stress and frustration. Therefore, therapy with these families should be designed to meet immediate as well as long-term needs.

Turner elucidates the major goals of therapy with families of mentally retarded children. Therapy aims at helping the family members cope effectively with some of the following problems: acceptance of the child's diagnosis; the implications that the diagnosis will have for the family; assignment of appropriate family roles; appropriate expressions of affect regarding the child and the situation; and the like. All these issues should be considered in the light of long-range planning for the family, rather than only as a means of immediate crisis intervention.

Turner also points out that the definition of crisis is contingent on the family members' reactions to the mentally retarded child and the constraints his or her condition may place upon the family. The event itself does not constitute a crisis; rather, the *response* to that event may precipitate a crisis. Certainly the birth of the mentally retarded child disrupts the family's homeostasis, demands some role restructuring, and puts a strain on the family's coping mechanisms. However, the manner in which the family individually and as a unit reacts to the child may predispose the family to a crisis situation.

An invaluable and essential part of Turner's article deals with the techniques of family therapy as it is directed to families with a mentally retarded child. His list of guidelines for therapeutic intervention includes three crucial goals: to provide the family with a rapid and accurate assessment of family functioning, to encourage an open expression of feelings, and to focus attention on the family unit and its strategies for coping with problems and crises. This list is particularly recommended as a set of guidelines for practitioners who have not had much prior experience doing therapy with families of mentally retarded children.

COMMENTARY: Turner has offered a perceptive and practical article on therapy with families of mentally retarded children. His lists of significant goals and therapeutic guidelines are particularly valuable as a resource for therapists working with these families. An appraisal of these goals and guidelines makes it clear that this approach is sensitive to the needs of both child and family. This study advocates a therapeutic intervention procedure that deals realistically with everyday problems and their implications, yet offers hope.

It is noteworthy that the author focuses on the family unit rather than the target child. Since all members of the family are affected by the presence of the retarded child, this orientation is extremely practical. It is only by concentrating on the family constellation that stresses affecting all the members can realistically be addressed. Such an approach serves both the immediate and long-term needs of the family.

SOURCE: Turner, A. L. "Therapy with Families of a Mentally Retarded Child." *Journal of Marital and Family Therapy,* 1980, *6,* 167–171.

Peer Therapy for Parents of Mentally Retarded Children

AUTHOR: Roger C. Loeb

PRECIS: An eclectic group therapy approach for helping parents of mentally retarded children deal with day-to-day stress.

INTRODUCTION: For a variety of reasons, fewer mentally retarded children are being institutionalized every year; instead, they remain at home as an integral part of the family structure. This places the parents of mentally retarded children under many special and chronic stresses. On a daily basis, these parents experience and attempt to cope with the child's limitations; the intrusive questions and advice of well-meaning, but ill-informed, friends and strangers; their own resentment and guilt; and the common stresses that confront any family. Clearly, these parents need and deserve an opportunity to explore their own concerns in a therapeutic setting.

Loeb offers a technique of group therapy that provides parents of mentally retarded children with a means of meeting their special needs. The essence of the method is group therapy with several parents of retarded children. These parents have learned how to confront avoidance reactions, overcompensating tolerance, concern about genetic inferiority, and the like. By forming small groups with other parents of mentally retarded children, they can share their knowledge and resources. The peer group sessions fulfill several needs. The parents have an occasion to ventilate their feelings, hopes, and fears. They are given a chance to share common problems and possible solutions. They are able to provide each other with understanding and empathy. As a result, all the parents involved are able to reduce their sense of isolation and feelings of guilt and are able to increase their self-confidence.

THERAPEUTIC TECHNIQUE: The groups in Loeb's study consisted of parents having Down's Syndrome or brain-damaged children between the ages of two and four living at home. Parents were only admitted as couples, thereby assuring the involvement of the father as well as the mother. Co-therapists, one male and one female, offered sex-role perspectives and models for both parents. An eclectic approach combining Freudian interpretation, Gestalt techniques, Ellis's reality therapy, Rogerian reflection, and behavior modification was employed.

The groups characteristically focused on the children's behavior problems and allowed the parents a chance to let down the facade that everything was going smoothly. This offered the parents a chance to recognize and accept their true feelings. Furthermore, the parents were able to share practical solutions to commonly experienced problems. For example, the author discusses a shared solution to the issue of the children's head-banging behavior. One parent shared his technique with the group. He permitted head banging only in certain places, such as the back of a well-padded couch. The child was reinforced for engaging in head banging only when it took place in this safe and acceptable environment. Instead of punishing head banging, behavioral management and reinforcement techniques were used to modify the behavior in a safe and controlled manner. The parents in this group were particularly effective in dealing with everyday problems.

COMMENTARY: This paper investigates an interesting and effective technique for using parents as active and supportive participants within group therapy. Since the parents share these problems in common, they become the most logical and valuable agents of therapy. They are also in a position to offer each other appropriate and practical suggestions, support, empathy, optimism, and confidence. Support is also offered by the co-therapists, who share leadership and therapy responsibilities.

This procedure also encompasses the best of a variety of theoretical and clinical perspectives. The eclectic orientation allows incorporation of a variety of approaches. Furthermore, this approach demands that the parents take an active participant role. Hope and confidence replace passive defeatism. As active agents of change, the parents have as much to teach the helping services as they do each other. Techniques for the behavioral management of mentally retarded children and solutions for commonly experienced family problems are no longer merely passed down in a linear fashion.

The structure of the therapy sessions demands that both parents be present. Although this is the ideal, it is certainly possible when the family is intact. It would be interesting and valuable to develop a variation of this approach that could be applied to the single-parent family or to families that are not intact.

SOURCE: Loeb, R. C. "Group Therapy for Parents of Mentally Retarded Children." *Journal of Marriage and Family Counseling*, 1977, 3(2), 77-83.

Structural Theory and the Single-Parent Family

AUTHOR: John S. Weltner

PRECIS: The single-parent family is a family at risk plagued by multiple problems. The structural approach seeks to resolve some of these conflicts by creating new organizational patterns.

INTRODUCTION: The structural approach focuses on subsystems, generational boundaries, and organizational patterns. There are inherent problems with the structure of any family in which there is only one parent. Single parenthood imposes stresses on the individual parent and on the family as a unit. Weltner discusses some of the major problems that the single parent faces. For example, because single parents do not have spouses to support or validate them, confirmation and validation become major issues. Moreover, generational boundaries tend to become blurred in the single-parent family. As a consequence of the failure of generational boundaries, symbiosis becomes a serious problem.

THERAPEUTIC PRIORITIES: In view of the problems faced by the single-parent family, certain therapeutic priorities must be established. The author outlines three primary priorities.

Support of Executive System Function. Most of the problems discussed result from an undermining of the competency of the single parent. The therapist, then, must ensure that all executive functions can be performed by the parent. This involves a thorough examination of the roles of the parental child, the extended family, family friends and allied groups, home health resources, and even the therapist since he or she must be careful not to assume, and thereby undermine, the parent's executive position and functions.

Establishment of Generational Boundaries. Various strategies can be employed to establish and maintain appropriate generational boundaries. For example, certain topics can be labeled as specifically adult issues for discussion. Power relationships are discussed, as are issues that naturally separate the two generations; for instance, the assignment of chores, supervisory tasks, and the like.

Dealing with Individual or Family System Issues. Once these crucial therapeutic priorities are addressed, then the therapist can concentrate on individual problems, symptoms, and system issues in the family.

COMMENTARY: The structural system has the distinct advantage of focusing on issues that relate to subsystems, boundaries, and organizational patterns. The family unit is affected by the inner workings of its particular interactional constellation. Because the problems are a product of the family's structural organization, they cannot be resolved unless this pattern is clarified, confronted, and, if necessary, corrected.

This study presents a sequential approach to treatment issues within the single-parent family. The author is sensitive to the constraints suffered by the single parent. For instance, he makes it clear that the course of therapy cannot progress until basic core issues are dealt with. First and foremost, the executive role of the single parent is clarified. Too often, children in a single-parent family assume, by choice or by default, a parental role. In this situation, roles and responsibilities become confused for all involved. By clarifying the parent's executive function, the therapist initiates appropriate organizational structures and role definitions in the family, thus laying the foundation for therapy. In addition, the author alerts the practitioner to the danger of the therapist unwittingly assuming the parent's executive function. All involved must be aware that the single parent —not an outside authority figure—is in charge of the family unit.

The structural approach to therapy also addresses sensitive and crucial family issues, such as generational boundaries, role definition, symbiosis between parents and children, and the role of support groups such as the extended family. It is noteworthy that the needs of the single parent as an individual are also addressed. The single parent, as the author points out, is particularly in need of confirmation and validation. The single parent experiences a degree of alienation and isolation that does not occur in the typical intact family. Parental responsibilities are not shared, and individual needs for support are not met. Extended family members, friends, community and agency services, and neighbors are particularly important to the well-being of the single parent. It is, therefore, essential that the single parent be aided in gaining awareness of, and access to, community, religious, neighborhood, and social groups, services, and agencies. The single parent risks isolation from friends and community, and this danger must be reduced.

Weltner has offered a sensitive, perceptive, and knowledgeable approach to therapeutic intervention in the single-parent family. This is an approach grounded in the concrete day-to-day concerns of the single-parent family. It is a method that can be incorporated into a variety of theoretical and clinical orientations. It appears to be a particularly valuable method of choice when dealing with the single-parent family.

SOURCE: Weltner, J. S. "A Structural Approach to the Single-Parent Family." *Family Process,* 1982, *21,* 203–210.

Use of Multiple Impact Therapy in Treating the Brain-Damaged Child

AUTHORS: Alberto C. Serrano and Norman J. Wilson

PRECIS: A multidisciplinary approach to the diagnosis and treatment of the brain-damaged child.

INTRODUCTION: Serrano and Wilson present an overview of the characteristics of the brain-damaged behavior syndrome as discussed in the literature. These include hyperactivity, low frustration tolerance, distractibility and limited attention span, impulsivity, and antisocial behavior. Following this introduction, they propose a family-centered approach to diagnosis and treatment of the brain-damaged child utilizing a brief, intensive psychotherapy procedure called Multiple Impact Therapy: "Starting with a team-family conference, it proceeds through a series of different combinations of the people involved. It includes multiple therapist situations, individual interviews, and group therapy interspersed with brief staff conferences."

Treatment, then, employs a multidisciplinary team involving psychiatrists, clinical psychologists, and psychiatric social workers. Along with traditional studies of the physical and psychological problems facing the family, an evaluation is made of the total family configuration. Treatment is tailored to the specific data obtained in each case, and drug therapy frequently proves useful. The child's disturbance appears to be a combination of at least three primary factors: soma, psyche, and family.

CASE STUDY: The authors offer the case history of A, aged nine, who was referred for hyperactivity, soiling, impulsivity, and an inability to relate to his peers. The family was interviewed as a group and all members including siblings were given the chance to openly express their feelings, doubts, and fears. A battery of psychological tests was administered as were the usual physical examinations and EEG studies. The treatment program included 300 milligrams of Deanol daily. Furthermore, it was recommended that A attend special education classes.

The family was advised to establish firm and consistent rules. They were also encouraged to allow the patient to assume more personal responsibility for his bowel functions and the related troubles. Although as a result of his hyperactivity and impulsivity, A still experienced behavior problems, treatment helped to reduce incidents of encopresis. His coordination and speech improved, and he experienced pride in his achievements.

COMMENTARY: This article presents a viable multidimensional evaluation and treatment approach to the problems faced by the brain-damaged child and his or her family. Since the problems are perceived as multidetermined, the approach is multidisciplinary and flexible. The authors propose that all essential aspects of the problem—soma, psyche, and family—be addressed.

The team approach affords the family greater resources to call upon, as well as greater access to community and agency services. Furthermore, the team members can offer each other support, suggestions, and increased potential to utilize their skills to the fullest. Multiple Impact Therapy appears to be a method of choice, especially for a problem like brain damage which is so very complex and has physical aspects as well as psychological.

SOURCE: Serrano, A. C., and Wilson, N. J. "Family Therapy in the Treatment of the Brain Damaged Child." *Diseases of the Nervous System,* 1963, *24*(12), 686–691.

The Disruptive Effects
of Long-Term Memory Disorders

AUTHORS: John Todd and Paul Satz

PRECIS: Traumatic and long-term memory deficits can have a serious disruptive impact on an adolescent and his family.

INTRODUCTION: Traumatic head injuries resulting in long-term memory deficits affect an adolescent's vocational, social, and emotional functioning. Furthermore, such a memory disorder puts stress on the family and on the adolescent's relationships within the family. These stresses place the family at risk for continued dysfunctioning and conflicts. Consequently, guidance may be in order from professionals who know the condition, prognosis, and limitations of the adolescent's memory deficits. Todd and Satz propose a collaborative effort between neuropsychologists and family therapists.

CASE STUDY: Mr. A is a twenty-year-old male who was involved in a motorcycle accident when he was seventeen. He suf-

fered bilateral brain damage due to trauma. Following hospitalization, Mr. A was sent home to a caring and supportive family.
He had severe difficulties dealing with his environment and was
hindered by feelings of depression, vulnerability, and inadequacy. Some of these problems gradually resolved themselves
over the course of time; however, the long-term memory deficits remained unchanged.

Family therapy was the method of choice for helping Mr.
A and his family cope with his conflicts and the havoc they
wreaked upon the entire family unit. A realistic appraisal of Mr.
A's competencies and limitations became a focal point for family-oriented therapy. Therapy proved useful in relieving some of
the tensions by helping family members realize that they must
become more active in their own lives and less protective of Mr.
A. With support and encouragement, all members of the family
gradually returned to normal life activities. Mr. A enrolled at a
local community college and in time regained a sense of self-
confidence.

COMMENTARY: Todd and Satz present an excellent appraisal
of the competencies and limitations of long-term memory deficits. They not only outline the dramatic impact that this disorder has on the family but also offer a persuasive argument
favoring the use of both the neuropsychologist and the family
therapist. This collaborative approach has marked advantages,
especially since physiological factors are involved. The competencies of both specialists combine to offer the family a realistic
appraisal and prognosis of the condition.

The authors advocate an approach emphasizing empathic
support for the family and the target patient while also encouraging the patient to reassert his or her autonomy. The therapists
direct the family unit toward more effective functioning by
helping all family members to become aware of their limitations
and responsibilities, and by suggesting that they redirect attention to their own individual lives.

It appears that the main benefit of this approach is that it
fosters a multidisciplinary assessment of the disorder. This ensures that both assessment and prognosis will be realistic, there-

by affording the family an understanding of the patient's strengths and limitations. Unrealistic expectations are not placed on the patient, nor are unrealistic responsibilities asked of family members.

SOURCE: Todd, J., and Satz, P. "The Effects of Long-Term Verbal Memory Deficits: A Case Study of an Adolescent and His Family." *Journal of Marital and Family Therapy,* 1980, *6*(4), 431–438.

Additional Readings

Berdie, J., and Selig, A. L. "Family Functioning in Families with Children Who Have Handicapping Conditions." *Family Therapy,* 1981, *8,* 187–195.

Understanding family functioning is a key to assessing and influencing a disabled child's potential for achievement. This study presents six concepts that help to understand family dynamics in families of children with handicapping conditions. The concepts are based on family systems theory and therapy, and on the special experiences and problems of families with handicapped children.

The six concepts which the authors detail are:

1. The reverberation effect. As a system, a family's members are connected to one another in such a way that changes in one member affect the entire system.

2. Homeostasis. The family operates and interacts in such a way that homeostasis is maintained.

3. Change as stressor. Change alters homeostasis; as such, it creates stress. Whether positive or negative, change produces tensions. That is not to say that families resist change; rather, they attempt to cope with change.

4. Maintenance mechanisms and patterns of interaction. Families develop mechanisms to maintain order, balance, and

continuity. Patterns of interaction are important to understanding family functioning.

5. Familiar coping strategies. Family coping strategies are employed in order to maintain homeostasis. The coping mechanisms influence a host of other variables including family flexibility and problem-solving skills.

6. The effects of stress and crisis. Some of the stresses experienced by the families discussed are special to families with disabled children. Stress is the precursor of crisis. The manner in which stress is perceived and handled determines whether or not crisis ensues.

Understanding these dynamics is essential whether the clinician is working with the child, the partners, or the family as a whole.

Hall, J., and Taylor, K. "The Emergence of Eric: Co-Therapy in the Treatment of a Family with a Disabled Child." *Family Process,* 1971, *10,* 85–96.

Handicapped children are often highly dependent on their families. Consequently, disabled children are strongly influenced by parental attitudes. By the same token, the family is the most powerful force for the integration of the disabled child into society. Yet the family is too often overlooked as a resource. By treating the family as a unit, the practitioner is able to observe and understand what processes are enhancing or impeding the child's adjustment.

This study focuses on the problem of the socialization of the disabled child within the family structure. Socialization of the handicapped child is a particular challenge. It does no good to train the child in techniques of mobilization if the family does not allow the child a chance to be independent. Family therapy is an effective method of choice for intervening in these very problems. A case study is included to illustrate the usefulness of family interviewing and therapy with a congenitally blind thirteen-year-old boy, his mother, father, and two sighted brothers.

Mahon, E., and Egan, J. "The Use of Family Interviews in Child Psychotherapy." *International Journal of Child Psychotherapy,* 1973, *2,* 365–382.

The family interview has important diagnostic and therapeutic uses in child psychotherapy and at any stage in the treatment of the child and his or her family. The data gleaned from family interviews can provide a wealth of information that is often not available in individual interviews. In working with children, it is usually inappropriate to separate the identified patient from the family. Family interviews provide an opportunity to see the patient interact with the family. Patterns of interaction, styles of communication, and the structure of roles and interrelationships can be quickly disclosed. The authors present five richly illustrated and detailed examples of family interviews in child psychotherapy. Each case demonstrates the clinical usefulness and value of the family interview technique.

Robinson, L. D., and Weathers, O. D. "Family Therapy of Deaf Parents and Hearing Children: A New Dimension in Psychotherapeutic Intervention." *American Annals of the Deaf,* 1974, *119*(3), 325–330.
　　This article discusses the problems encountered in a family of deaf parents and hearing children. The identified patient, a ten-year-old boy, was experiencing weight loss, social and academic problems, and psychological conflicts. The problematic areas demanded crisis intervention by a psychiatrist-social worker team. Six months of conjoint family psychotherapy led to a positive outcome.

Seitz, S., and Riedell, G. "Parent-Child Interactions as the Therapy Target." *Journal of Communication Disorders,* 1974, 7, 295–304.
　　The subjects of this study were a severely retarded four-year-old girl and her mother and father. The study focused on the immediate and long-term results of an experimental language therapy program. Attempts were made to increase the verbal communication skills of the child in an indirect manner, through changing the language environment of the child, especially in the parent-child interactions. Some aspects of the parent-child interaction changed temporarily, while others were modified for a more extended period of time. Immediate improvement was seen in the child's nonverbal behavior. She be-

gan to respond positively to her parents and engage in independent play.

Steady improvements in the child's verbal behavior were reported in follow-up assessments at three months and again at one year. Within a year from the time the program terminated, educational assessment of the child's retardation had moved from severe to trainable, with prediction of functioning at the educable level. The authors propose that the parent-child interaction constitutes the child's language environment. It is the quality of this relationship that most affects the verbal behavior of the child.

Selig, A. L., and Berdie, J. "Assessing Families with a Developmentally Delayed/Handicapped Child." *Developmental and Behavioral Pediatrics,* 1981, 2(4), 151–154.

The nature of the behaviors and interactions within a family has a major influence upon the disabled child's development. Indeed, the influences of the family structure may have more impact on a child with a handicapping condition than the handicap itself. An assessment of family functioning can help the pediatrician understand the contribution of family dynamics to the etiology of dysfunctional symptoms. Family members usually register surprise that the entire family is being assessed; they expected the sole focus to be on the handicapped child. Consequently, families must be prepared for assessment.

The authors present insightful suggestions for conducting the family assessment. In particular, they offer twenty questions that should be included in the family assessment. These questions cover a wide range of issues affecting the family system. They serve as an excellent guide to the therapist and help determine therapeutic goals and intervention strategies.

The appendix of the article lists the following questions for the family assessment:

1. What do parents (and perhaps the identified child and other children) expect from an evaluation, and how do they currently explain the child's problems?

2. What are family members' concerns about the child starting a new program or school?

3. How does each parent see the identified child?

4. How do parents interact with the identified child and siblings?

5. What are parents' experiences in their families of origin (e.g., significant events, individuation, and current relationships)?

6. What is each parent's current satisfaction in work and social roles?

7. What roles does each parent have in relation to the identified child?

8. To what degree does parenthood dominate the marital relationship, and do parents use triangulation (focusing on a third person to relieve stress in a dyadic relationship)?

9. To what extent do family members have roles outside the family?

10. What are the support networks within and outside the extended family?

11. To what degree does each member have real input into various decisions? What amount of control can be exerted by various behaviors (e.g., what function does the child's handicapping condition have in the family)?

12. How are conflict, stress, and crises handled?

13. What are the family rules, especially in relation to (a) expectations of responsibility from each member and (b) topics that can and cannot be discussed? Who enforces the rules and how is it done? What are the consequences of breaking rules?

14. What are the boundaries between family members and between the family and the outside world?

15. What does each family member see as the family's strengths?

16. What would improve family functioning?

17. How do family members view each other's similarities and differences?

18. What do family members identify as stressors

and as annoying or pleasing behaviors in others? How
do they react to these behaviors?

19. How do family members perceive the developmental stage of the identified child, and how does the child differ from that perception?

20. How does each member deal with the issues of having a disabled child?

21

Families
in Crisis

Certain life events create hazards for individual and family growth. Events such as role transitions, separations, chronic or terminal illnesses, suicides, and deaths all place family members, and the family as a unit, in a vulnerable position. In order to mitigate the debilitating force of these crisis-producing situations, the family must call upon its collective functioning capability and recuperative power. The nature and degree of the family's resources determine how effectively the family will weather the crisis. Unless a family has developed a sense of integration, cohesiveness, adaptability, and organization, and has established open channels of communication, it may disintegrate in the face of tragedy. Not only is the family unit at risk, but individuals within the system are more vulnerable to emotional and psychological disorders.

417

In this chapter we discuss some of the critical events that strain a family's resources. In each instance, a complex set of factors determines how a crisis will affect the family. An adept clinician realizes that it is not only the crisis event that must be examined; attention must also be directed to the family's resources, the availability of outside support, and the family's perception of the crisis and the meaning they attribute to it. It is interesting to note that some of the authors of the articles suggest that the crisis can also *give* the family meaning. A crisis can be viewed as a period of transition that can reorient the family system in a positive as well as a negative way. A crisis can become the occasion for a family's reintegration, a chance for members to re-ally themselves with each other and to offer mutual compassion and support.

The digests in this section provide invaluable techniques of family-oriented crisis intervention. Strategies and therapeutic tools are offered that facilitate immediate and short-term crisis intervention as well as long-term crisis counseling. The family therapy techniques discussed cover a wide range of treatment programs, including psychodynamic, behavioral, cognitive, and conjoint and multiple-family approaches; the use of family network intervention; and therapeutic ploys that reestablish the family's communication process.

Vulnerability and Family Functioning

AUTHOR: Thomas C. Walsh

PRECIS: Any effective treatment program for families in crisis demands an understanding of the strengths and weaknesses of the family structure.

INTRODUCTION: This article offers a review of the family crisis literature in order to clarify the way assessment of a family's coping strategies relates to intervention approaches. Following Reuben Hill, the author presents the structure of the family crisis in the form of an equation: "A (the event) interacts with B (the family's crisis-meeting resources) interacts with C (the definition the family makes of the event), which produces X (the crisis). The importance of this framework lies in the identification of A, B, and C, which are all independent variables affecting the existence of X. The event alone does not determine the severity of a crisis. It must be measured against the family's ability to handle crisis, which in turn is at least partly correlated with whether or not they view A as being a serious threat to their equilibrium."

The "B" factor, the family's crisis-meeting resources, includes the degree of family integration, of adaptability, of organization, and of expressiveness. How a family copes depends on the sense of cohesiveness and belonging among its members. The family's integration depends on the development of boundaries that are permeable enough to allow the family to interact with society, but strong enough to keep the family a separate and differentiated unit.

The adaptability of the family is one of the major factors determining its vulnerability to crisis. The greater the family's rigidity, the more likely it is to be thrown off balance by a crisis. Adaptive coping demands flexibility, an openness to alternative problem-solving approaches.

Furthermore, a family that is crisis-prone is likely to be less well organized than a family that is more resistant to crisis. A clear delineation of family rules, roles, responsibilities, and structure affords the family an edge in maintaining its balance even in a crisis situation.

A family that allows little opportunity for the expression of thoughts and feelings is vulnerable to crisis. A family that is freely expressive has learned to cope with crisis-producing situations through open processing of disagreements, opinions, and diverse points of view. As a result, it is better able to resolve a crisis in a quick, responsive, and open manner.

In order to clarify the nature of the "B" factor, the author presents definitions of the healthy, "crisis-proof family," utilizing the theories of Hill, Satir, Minuchin, Beavers, Bowen, Haley, and other family theorists and clinicians. It is essential that the therapist working with families in crisis have a framework by which to assess the family's "B" factor. Understanding of the family's coping skills is necessary in order to make treatment decisions. The nature and goals of therapeutic intervention must be determined in light of the family's resources. This can only be achieved within the conceptual framework of an adequate theory of family functioning.

COMMENTARY: Walsh presents an excellent review of some of the major theoretical perspectives on family crisis and intervention in times of crisis. He suggests that any effective intervention demands a frame of reference. Without a theoretical framework for assessing and understanding the family's "B" factor, intervention strategies become hit and miss and are certainly less effective. A theoretical framework is necessary so the therapist can plan the course of therapy, make goals and major decisions within the therapeutic process, and remain sensitive to the family's strengths and weaknesses.

It is noteworthy that the author is open to a variety of theoretical perspectives. The article does not push in the direction of any given theory, nor does it present a stance that is theoretically rigid or closed. It does, however, stress the importance of having some theory as a foundation for major decisions and intervention plans. Naturally, the therapeutic plan of action should be congruent with the theoretical position. Only thus can the therapist appraise the family's skills and coping mechanisms.

Furthermore, an awareness of the family's strengths and vulnerabilities that is in line with a theoretical framework not only helps to determine the nature and course of therapy but also serves a preventative function. Knowing the family's "B" factor alerts the therapist to the kinds of situations that would place the family at risk. Working within the frame of an effective theory of crisis intervention and family functioning affords the therapist an awareness of and sensitivity to the family's limitations and areas of strain.

SOURCE: Walsh, T. C. "Families in Crisis: Relating Vulnerability and Family Functioning to Treatment." *Family Therapy*, 1981, *8*(2), 105–112.

Crisis and Enhanced Family Functioning

AUTHOR: Andrew L. Selig

PRECIS: A crisis may be the event that triggers a major breakthrough in family therapy and family growth.

INTRODUCTION: The author presents a brief outline of crisis theory, followed by a brief discussion of the principles of practice and rationale for its use. "Crisis Theory postulates that certain life events, such as role transitions and deaths or separations of significant others, create hazards for meeting basic needs and, therefore, increase the probability of either interpersonal disturbances, or new adaptions and increased functional capacity."

Resolutions of life crises usually lead either to deterioration or enhancement of functioning; only rarely do they leave the status quo unchanged. Crisis periods may be seen as transitional states, and growth can often be an outcome. In this study, Selig uses crisis theory to explain a breakthrough with a family which led to more productive and higher levels of functioning.

CASE HISTORY: The author reports the case of a four-member family. The R family included the mother, aged forty-eight; the father, aged fifty; the son, nineteen; and the daughter, sixteen. The identified patient was the mother, who was the major spokesperson for the family. She was hospitalized for drinking and symptoms of depression and anxiety. The author of the article was a co-therapist who met with the family for twelve sessions prior to the crisis. Until the crisis, the mother did all the talking for the family. She and her daughter argued frequently. The father and son were quiet and withdrawn. The family members were isolated from each other and rarely did anything socially; consequently, they were also alienated from the larger community.

Little progress was made with the R family and major conflict issues remained unresolved. At the eleventh session, the mother informed the group that the father's uncle had died. The father became more responsive and stated that he was very fond of the uncle. At the next session the mother, son, and daughter all stated that they wanted to be helpful to the father. He expressed surprise at their empathic remarks and positive feelings were engendered. The uncle's death turned out to be a crisis that brought the family closer together. It made them more aware of each other's needs and sensitivities, and more open and responsive to each other. Naturally, this resulted in enhanced functioning for the family as a unit. Sixteen months after the critical incident, the family still reported progress.

COMMENTARY: In this particular instance, the use of crisis theory proved to be a helpful method of intervention. The crisis event served as a precipitating factor that led to warm, and open expressions and acceptance within the family unit. It served to break through the father's barrier of passivity. It also afforded family members an opportunity to become allies. It bridged the distance from and indifference toward one another they formerly felt. The case presented offered a clear application of crisis theory, illustrating the manner in which a crisis can be used for the purpose of enhancing family functioning.

The author suggests that family therapists should seize every opportunity to intervene during crisis periods. Indeed, these periods could be viewed as transitional states. As such, they can be occasions to break a stalemate and mobilize the family. They can offer family members an opportunity to see each other in a different light and become a support system to each other.

SOURCE: Selig, A. L. "Crisis Theory and Family Growth." *The Family Coordinator,* July 1976, pp. 291–295.

Family Network Intervention

AUTHOR: Uri Rueveni

PRECIS: The development and implementation of crisis intervention strategies that help families to reconnect with sources of support and strength.

INTRODUCTION: Families in a state of crisis resulting from suicide, separation and loss, psychotic episodes, and the like, could oftentimes benefit from network intervention. Network intervention aims at mobilizing friends, neighbors, and extended family members who might serve as sources of support while the family attempts to cope during and after crisis situations. The network, then, is a support system that collaborates with the family to resolve a crisis.

NETWORK PHASES AND INTERVENTION GOALS: A small team of interventionists, usually two or three clinicians skilled in family and group psychodynamics, works with the network, which may include forty or more members. The network usually meets for two four-hour sessions spaced a week apart. Each network typically involves six distinct phases and any one network session may involve all of these phases or only some of them.

Retribalization is the first phase of the network process. It is the initial building and restructuring of connections between network members. Activities at this phase include milling around, singing, and similar forms of rapid verbal encounters.

Polarization, the second phase, is characterized by a diversity of opinions, disagreement, and increased tension as the therapists attempt to involve all members and their various perspectives on the problem issues. Family and network members begin to take sides. The team leader will encourage side-taking, for example, by fostering a discussion of controversial issues and splitting members into various camps depending on the sides they take.

The third phase, mobilization, is characterized by collaborative exploration. Communication is facilitated and network leaders become identified and more thoroughly involved. The mobilization phase is temporary and meets resistance to change.

During the depression phase little progress is made. Members experience a temporary setback; they feel helpless and frustrated. At this point, it is particularly important for the professional team to suggest various strategies that might facilitate further progress. For example, role playing may be used, or a sculpturing experience, or a psychodrama in which one or more family members are considered dead and others in the network are called upon to eulogize them.

The breakthrough period is marked by the formulation of solutions and problem-solving strategies. Small support groups begin to form around each family member. Hope is raised as specific options for each family member are discussed.

Feelings of satisfaction and accomplishment are typical during the exhaustion-elation phase. Network members usually remain with their support groups for additional time at the end of the meeting and plan the agenda of the next meeting. Support groups meet between network sessions. Any efforts toward effective resolution of conflicts can be diminished if the formation of these support groups does not take place.

Network goals differ depending on family members, their specific needs, and the problems involved. These goals are usually determined in the interview and prenetwork sessions. In general, the goals correspond to the various phases of the crisis. The first goal is to facilitate rapid connections and foster familiarity and high levels of energy and involvement. The second goal is to facilitate the family's readiness to share their problems. The therapists should foster increased involvement and the exchange of various opinions among network members and facilitate communication between the family and network members. A further goal is to underscore the significance of network leaders. Particularly during periods of impasse, the team needs to offer direct intervention and foster a deeper exploration into the problem areas. The team must encourage the development of temporary support groups. They must function as resource consultants.

CASE STUDY: The author presents four cases illustrating the effectiveness of the family network. The fourth case presentation involved Mrs. Q, a divorced mother living with five children ranging in age from nine to seventeen years. The family was experiencing hopelessness and desperation. Betty, the fourteen-year-old daughter, would attack her mother, refuse to eat or bathe, and lock herself in the garage for extended periods of time. After a few sessions using family therapy, the family was referred for network intervention. The network included Mrs. Q's former husband and his current wife, along with friends and family members. Betty adamantly refused to attend the network sessions; at first she stayed in the garage, later she listened from the basement.

The goal determined by the network was to help find a place where Betty could stop her psychotic behavior. The technique of family network intervention proved effective in mobilizing assistance and support for the family. Betty was sent to live with her aunt in another state.

Mrs. Q regained her self-confidence, made social contacts, and found a new job. A one-year follow-up indicated that all members of the family were functioning better. Betty was reported to be making definite progress.

COMMENTARY: Family network intervention seems to be a viable method of choice. The effectiveness of this approach appears to be contingent upon a myriad of factors. For instance, a relatively large body of people must be mobilized. The logistics of organizing so many individuals at one time, in one place, for one purpose could prove staggering. Furthermore, as Rueveni indicates, the approach provides crisis resolution, and is meant to be a temporary support. If the underlying conflict issues are not resolved, similar crisis situations may appear once the temporary support system is disbanded.

The intervention strategy, however, does rapidly mobilize a network system and activists who take the lead in helping the family members find solutions for the immediate crisis. Furthermore, the approach offers a temporary support system; in some cases, that may prove enough of a boost to the family to initiate productive changes. The support system can also help the family to realize a variety of options, such as securing employment, making career moves, changing residence, restructuring family roles and responsibilities, and related alternatives. Brainstorming with a large body of people certainly increases the likelihood of uncovering a variety of possible solutions because everyone involved focuses intently on the same issue, the crisis facing the target family. Networking appears to be a realistic method of solving day-to-day problems. Furthermore, network intervention of the scope described by this study appears to be an impressive strategy for resolving immediate crises.

SOURCE: Rueveni, U. "Family Network Intervention: Mobilizing Support for Families in Crisis." *The International Journal of Family Counseling*, 1977, *5*(2), 77–83.

Brief Dynamic Psychotherapies
Using the Focal Treatment Unit

AUTHORS: George MacLean, Bette-Ann MacIntosh, Eithne Taylor, and Marilen Gerber

PRECIS: The use of the focal treatment unit, an approach providing a brief assessment, a focal hypothesis, and a plan of treatment that can be applied to the family, to the individual, or to a combination of individuals.

INTRODUCTION: The authors review the position of brief psychotherapies in child psychiatry. An approach developed by an outpatient child psychiatry team is presented. Following a brief assessment of problem areas affecting the identified patient and his or her family, a focal hypothesis and plan of treatment are outlined:

> [The focal hypothesis] was defined as a dynamic statement accounting for the most important, manifest psychopathology presented by the family in the assessment interview. On occasion, this hypothesis was modified during the course of treatment; however, this happened rarely. . . .
>
> After forming this focal hypothesis, it was then necessary for the team member to make a treatment plan. By definition this plan was firmly based on the crucial focal hypothesis and was termed the Focal Plan. . . .
>
> Finally, in order to achieve the focal plan and to address the focal hypothesis expressing the manifest psychopathology, the individual team member then chose who should be treated according to who needed to be the focus of treatment, or, looked at another way, whom it was the most strategic to treat. We coined the phrase 'Focal Treatment Unit' to express this concept and, thus, had to choose for treatment either (i) the family as a group; (ii) the individual child; (iii) the parents, conjointly; or (iv) a parent, individually. . . .

A maximum of eight weekly sessions of psychotherapy was then offered to the focal treatment unit.

FOCAL TREATMENT UNIT—THE FAMILY GROUP: Heather,
aged six, was referred to an outpatient child psychiatric center
because she stole money from her teacher to buy candy for her
friends. In addition, her school performance had deteriorated
and she was bed-wetting. It was hypothesized that Heather's
symptomatic behaviors were expressions of the family's marked
depression and unresolved grief over the father's death. When
Heather was four and one-half years old, her father was killed in
an automobile accident. The family discussed his death in a
controlled and matter-of-fact manner.

The focal treatment unit involved the family group—the
mother, Heather, and Ida, Heather's thirteen-year-old sister with
whom the mother related in a peer-like fashion. The family was
seen as a unit for a series of six weekly sessions. The mother and
Ida had never resolved the father's death beyond a stage of denial. Heather, on the other hand, dealt with the father's death
through anger. Her anger persisted. She called the father by his
first name and she refused to recall any good times with him.
She recalled that he was mean because he "wouldn't let her eat
candy." The therapist interpreted Heather's symptomatic behaviors as a way of letting the family know how sad she was.
The treatment involved working through the unresolved grief.
The mother and Ida appeared to agree with the interpretation
and responded by crying. In a short time, Heather began to refer to her father as Daddy and was able to recall some happy
times with him. The last sessions of family therapy dealt with
the unresolved grief and mourning process related to the father's
death. A six-month follow-up indicated that Heather's school
performance had dramatically improved and she was free of
debilitating symptoms.

FOCAL TREATMENT UNIT—BOTH PARENTS: The follow-
ing is an illustration of a case involving brief conjoint psychotherapy with the parents. Joshua, an eight-year-old boy, his
parents, and his ten-year-old brother were referred for treat-

ment. The parents and school complained that Joshua broke
rules. It appeared as though he would go out of his way to
break a rule once he discovered its existence. The parents had a
constant battle with Joshua to get him to dress, eat, catch the
school bus, go to bed, and so on. The family's home life was a
continuous chaos. The parents blamed the school for Joshua's
problems; the school, in turn, criticized the parents. The parents
also blamed each other for failing as parents.

J oshua was assessed as educably mentally retarded and
oppositional. A focal hypothesis was formulated proposing
that the parents had never fully accepted their retarded son.
The parents' anger at each other and at the son was a displacement of their anger at their son's defect. They had never resolved their grief over the loss of the wished-for perfect son.

Therapy involved working with the parents in order to
facilitate their awareness of their grief, anger, and lack of acceptance of their handicapped son. The parents were seen in six
biweekly conjoint therapy sessions. They eventually saw how
they interplayed together to express their anger and grief. With
gains in the parents' awareness and acceptance of their unresolved grief, improvements were seen in Joshua's behavior.

COMMENTARY: The authors have presented an approach
which has the advantage of brevity and which addresses specific
symptomatic behaviors through the medium of the "focal treatment unit," that is, the person or group most in need of therapeutic intervention. The focused assessment, formation of a
working hypothesis, and development of a plan of therapeutic
action together assure that the course of therapy will be directed toward specific goals, namely, changes in individual actions and group relationships. This directed approach facilitates
brevity and a positive course of therapy. As such, it has great
functional value.

As the authors state in the discussion section of their
study, "The concept of cure in this context is not viewed as
being important. Although in terms of our brief work with families we have hoped that a little may be enough, we accept that
the families may need to return about the same problem or

other issues." They acknowledge that in some instances long-term psychotherapy may be indicated. Alternatively, the family and/or the identified patient may need to return to therapy at some point in the future. One of the major advantages of brief dynamic intervention, however, is the primacy given to child advocacy. No matter what focal treatment unit is seen, the child is always the focus of concern.

This appears to be an effective therapeutic method whenever time and a concentrated focus are essential in dealing with a troubled child. The intervention strategy is flexible enough that it could be applied within a variety of theoretical and clinical orientations. It offers an efficient and concentrated method that is applicable to diverse problems of family dysfunction.

SOURCE: MacLean, G., MacIntosh, B., Taylor, E., and Gerber, M. "A Clinical Approach to Brief Dynamic Psychotherapies in Child Psychiatry." *Canadian Journal of Psychiatry,* 1982, *27,* 113–118.

A Combination of Crisis Theory and Behavioral Techniques

AUTHORS: Richard M. Eisler and Michel Hersen

PRECIS: A discussion of behavioral techniques to be used with short-term crisis-oriented treatment.

INTRODUCTION: Eisler and Hersen discuss the value of combining crisis theory and behavior modification techniques. This appears to be a logical and feasible collaborative effort since both approaches emphasize the importance of environmental influences in the development and maintenance of maladaptive behaviors. The behavioral approaches to crisis intervention focus on the immediate social and environmental triggers of maladaptive family interaction patterns.

The authors stress three major goals of this combined approach. The first goal is to develop new problem-solving strategies and coping behaviors within the family. The second goal is to establish effective communication patterns, particularly with regard to the expression of positive and negative feelings concerning the precipitating problem. The third goal is to help the family generalize the newly acquired coping strategies to other problem areas.

A discussion follows of four specific behavioral techniques: feedback, modeling and role playing, behavioral rehearsal, and use of instructions and behavioral contracts to achieve reciprocal reinforcement in families.

Case presentations illustrate the use of various behavioral techniques in crisis-oriented family intervention approaches. One such case illustration is presented here.

CASE STUDY: Problems developed when Tom, a sixteen-year-old boy, went to live with his father and new stepmother following the death of Tom's natural mother. Shortly after Tom's arrival, his stepmother developed symptoms of depression and nervousness, and had outbursts of temper. Tom's failure to come home on time and to telephone precipitated her outbursts and conflicts. In therapy, the family was given videotape feedback of their interactions and communication patterns. They were directed to focus on aversive attacks that took place within the family unit. Such attacks were prevalent and continual. Role playing and modeling were also used to correct the aversive interaction patterns within the family. Progress was made in the course of treatment thanks to the use of these behavioral techniques.

COMMENTARY: The authors have presented a perceptive combination of therapeutic techniques. The combination of behavioral intervention techniques with crisis-oriented therapy appears to have distinct advantages, and is a viable method of choice for intervening in family crisis situations. The approach has the advantage of being immediate and short-term. It is also an extremely practical response to a wide range of problems. The family is also able to generalize the techniques learned in therapy to other conflict-ridden areas.

This combined approach appears to emphasize learning skills. The specific techniques are based on social learning theory and, as such, have immense value as a method of choice. The approach contrasts with psychodynamic approaches in that emphasis is on specific behaviors and interaction patterns. The development of learning skills is emphasized over self-awareness and insight. It appears to be an extremely effective approach for dealing with specific symptoms and crisis situations.

SOURCE: Eisler, R. M., and Hersen, M. "Behavioral Techniques in Family-Oriented Crisis Intervention." *Archives of General Psychiatry*, 1973, *28*, 111–116.

===

Adolescent Acting Out When a Parent Has Cancer

AUTHOR: David K. Wellisch

PRECIS: This article investigates the phenomenon of acting out in the cases of six adolescents whose mothers had cancer.

INTRODUCTION: This study focuses on adolescence in regard to the influence cancer in a parent may exert during this stormy time in life. Both situationally and developmentally, these stresses can be uniquely intense. The burdens upon the adolescent may be manifested in an overt manner; for example, the youngster may be called upon to assume the responsibilities of child care and household management. In a more covert manner, subtle role shifts between the child and both parents may occur. The adolescent, then, is bombarded with the usual pressures of this developmental phase plus the additional strains created by the disease.

In view of these tensions, it is not surprising that in some cases the adolescent may respond to the parent's illness by acting out. Wellisch proposes that the acting out and decompensation on the part of the adolescent take place as a reaction to role shifts. The adolescent may be prematurely and inappropriately placed in a parenting role. The adolescent may also experience shifts in oedipal relationships, and may be called on to take on the role of a pseudo-wife to the father. He or she may also become the father's confidant. Cancer in a parent instigates a rapid and traumatic restructuring of family roles, places unusual and demanding expectations on the adolescent, and can impair the developmental processes of adolescence, particularly the young person's attempts to establish sexual identity.

CASE REPORTS—TERMINAL ILLNESS: G, aged thirteen, experienced severe conflicts when role shifts began to occur after her mother was diagnosed as having acute myelogenous leukemia. G started to run away from home, became sexually promiscuous, and in a sullen and passive manner refused to become involved with her mother. In brief, she began to look, dress, and act more like an eighteen-year-old than a thirteen-year-old. It was felt that G was acting out in response to role shifts; she was put into the roles of pseudo-wife and confidante to her stepfather, and foster mother to her three-year-old half sister.

F, a seventeen-year-old male whose stepmother's abdominal cancer was diagnosed as metastatic and unresectable, reacted to role shifts by refusing to help around the house, driving recklessly, and using drugs. His behavior was perceived as a maladaptive attempt to gain his father's attention and thus deflect his consciousness away from the insoluble dilemma of the stepmother's cancer.

CASE REPORTS—LONG-TERM ILLNESS: In the first two cases presented death was imminent. However, the two cases that follow focus on families with adolescents where the cancerous parent was not in the terminal stages of the illness.

The third case illustrates what occurs during the deparentifying of the adolescent. L, an eighteen-year-old male, reacted to his mother's cancer with anxiety, agitation, and fear of separation. He experienced immense difficulty in making a decision to leave home and go to college. He said that he felt "like a rat leaving a sinking ship." With firm support from his father, L was able to separate from the family successfully and remain at college.

In the fourth case presented, A, a thirteen-year-old male, felt that his mother had been psychologically buried before her time. He was upset by the intrafamilial delineation of his mother as dead, and his acting out behavior was seen as an attempt to force his mother back to life.

CASE REPORTS—MASTECTOMIES: The case of S, a seventeen-year-old girl, illustrates how an adolescent's dysfunctionality can serve a functional purpose. S's drinking, associating with the wrong crowd, and failure to do schoolwork all served to bind the family's anxiety. The family's concentration on the daughter's problems distracted attention and energy from far more distressing issues, such as the mother's cancer, postmastectomy concerns, and marital and economic difficulties.

In this case, R, a seventeen-year-old female, was not seen in therapy with her parents nor did she necessarily require individual therapy. R was involved in an unconscious collusion with her mother wherein she acted out her mother's sexual concerns following the mother's mastectomy.

COMMENTARY: Wellisch has presented an interesting and thought-provoking article that attempts to explain the rationale for acting out, and the dynamics underlying it, when an adolescent's mother has cancer. His six case histories offer readable and clear illustrations of his conclusions. The cases demonstrate the overt and covert disruptive impact that the parent's illness has upon the adolescent member of the family. Undoubtedly, the entire family is under stress, and a dramatic restructuring of roles affects all members; the adolescent, however, is at a particularly sensitive and conflict-ridden developmental stage. The situational problem represented by the parent's cancer compounds and magnifies the adolescent's developmental stresses.

Wellisch's discussion makes it evident that the adolescent family member is anything but uninvolved in the mother's cancer. He or she is particularly reactive and sensitive to the tensions this illness creates and the traumatic role shifts it often demands. The adolescent experiences tremendous anger over the situation at the same time as he or she is facing strong and unmet dependency needs and fears of separation and loss. This article is highly recommended for any clinician working with a family, one of whose members is experiencing a serious illness. It is particularly recommended when there is an adolescent or young adult member in such a family and the family members are forced to confront a restructuring of roles. The article helps in deciphering the adolescent's acting out in such instances.

SOURCE: Wellisch, D. K. "Adolescent Acting Out When a Parent Has Cancer." *International Journal of Family Therapy,* 1979, *1*(3), 230-241.

A Crisis-Focused Treatment for Families of Bone Marrow Recipients and Donors

AUTHORS: Marie Cohen, Irene Goldenberg, and Herbert Goldenberg

PRECIS: The development and implementation of a crisis-focused family therapy approach that helps family members develop adaptive coping strategies and learn to deal realistically with bone marrow transplant treatments.

INTRODUCTION: Leukemia and aplastic anemia are now being treated by a technique involving replacement of the patient's bone marrow with matching marrow from a donor, typically a close relative. The technique is dangerous and understandably produces tensions and stresses within the family. The authors propose a physician-therapist team approach to these disorders, including psychological interventions on an oncology ward.

Families of bone marrow recipients and donors must interrupt employment and home routines often for several weeks to relocate to an unfamiliar city where treatment is available. For purposes of immunity, the patient must spend six to eight weeks or more in isolation. This requires the patient to be kept in a private room with limited outside contacts. No intimate physical contact is possible. This, of course, has severe intra-psychic and interpersonal repercussions for all involved.

A family therapy approach is used to help alleviate the high level of stress experienced by all family members. This procedure must be tailored to reflect the family's attitudes and expectations. The therapists involved typically can discern three phases in the coping process. At first, the family attempts to cope with the reality of impending death through the use of denial and avoidance. During the second phase, the patient and family accept the reality of cancer while denying its probable terminal prognosis. During the third phase, the patient and family, as well as the involved staff, come to an acceptance of the medical reality. If death occurs, all involved must work through the process of separation and loss.

It is crucial to note that the therapists and medical staff must also go through these sequential phases. They too must arrive at a realistic, yet hopeful, appraisal of the situation. They must exert caution not to ease their own distress by giving the family and patient false hopes and unrealistic expectations.

CASE REPORTS: The case of eighteen-year-old Tom and his family was used to illustrate shifts in roles within the family, and to discuss the areas that merited attention during the course of crisis-focused family therapy. Tom needed bone marrow transplants. His sister Dee, aged sixteen, was not only the chosen donor but was also put into the role of family caretaker because of the father's physical disability and limited status within the family. Dee, who appeared to be capable of handling her responsible role, was encouraged and given support in the therapy sessions.

The case of Carol, aged sixteen, was used to illustrate the flaws in a warm and supportive family veneer that was not strong enough to hold up under the strain of Carol's bone marrow transplants. Carol saw herself as the sole cause of her family's problems and as an emotional and financial burden. The therapists sought to break through the scapegoating and denial that are common strategies for avoiding painful confrontation during a family crisis. The crisis-focused family therapy approach helped all family members to accept Carol's leukemia as a family crisis requiring a collective effort to give support and develop effective coping strategies.

COMMENTARY: This reality-oriented, crisis-focused approach meets very serious needs. The stresses that impinge upon the families of bone marrow recipients and donors are not only intense but are also multidetermined. Physical realities, psychological concerns, interpersonal conflicts, communication difficulties, and environmental and financial stresses all combine to burden a family already depleted by the demands of serious illness. It is, therefore, crucial that the approach emphasizes both optimistic and realistic attitudes and expectations.

The authors make it clear that the therapists involved must remain in a position to be part of the family yet separate from it; obviously, this is an extremely difficult problem with respect to oncology patients. The therapist must be able to be sensitive to the needs of the patient, who is usually being scapegoated and rejected. On the other hand, he or she must avoid being drawn into the family's mythification of death and their processes of denial and avoidance. In addition, the therapist is called upon to maintain the delicate balance between hope and realistic expectations.

The authors have presented a readable discussion of a practical approach to crisis-focused family therapy. Their clear-cut delineation of coping strategies and phases is valuable to clinicians. They have taken great pains to illustrate the family therapist's role and conflicts, and the hopes, fears, and expectations of the patient and family members. In addition to an academically and experientially grounded approach, they have offered a balanced presentation, arguing for both hope and a reality-oriented therapeutic procedure. The approach is timely, sensible, and humane.

SOURCE: Cohen, M., Goldenberg, I., and Goldenberg, H. "Treating Families of Bone Marrow Recipients and Donors." *Journal of Marriage and Family Counseling,* 1977, *3,* 45–51.

Conflicts Linked to Unresolved Mourning

AUTHORS: Gordon D. Jensen and John G. Wallace

PRECIS: Mourning is not restricted to a given individual within a family, but, as is typical of all family crises, is reacted to by all family members and affects the patterns of family interaction.

INTRODUCTION: The authors present two studies of bereavement reactions in families. The cases illustrate applications of psychodynamics within a crisis theory framework. Flexible plans of therapy are indicated. In one case, the family was treated with individual and family psychotherapy. This case represents an example of the treatment of coexisting individual and interpersonal emotional disorders. The second case illustrates the development of dysfunctional family dynamics as a consequence of unresolved mourning. Therapeutic attempts were made to restore the families to healthy levels of interpersonal relating.

FIRST CASE STUDY: Sandra, aged fourteen, was brought to a child psychiatry outpatient clinic. Sandra complained of leg and joint pain. These symptoms appeared about four months after her brother's death. The brother had had Marfan's Syndrome, which terminated in his sudden death. He had suffered similar leg pains.

During the final two years of the boy's illness, the family focused all their time and attention on him. Sandra was openly jealous of her parents' preferential treatment of her brother. The parents felt that Sandra's symptoms were linked to unresolved grief concerning her brother's death. However, they were not aware of their contribution to her problems. They felt Sandra experienced guilt over her brother's death. She often stated that she wished she were present at the time of the brother's death. During temper outbursts, she said she wished she too were dead.

Sandra was an attractive, well-developed, and tense adolescent girl. Her mannerisms were shy and somewhat childish. She stated that she was very close to her brother and when she spoke of him she was on the verge of tears. She felt her father pushed her too hard in her schoolwork. The therapist hypothesized that she responded with passive-aggressive behavior (laziness). The relationship between mother and daughter was severely disordered. In family therapy, the parents were helped to see that Sandra's conflicts involved their view of her limited capacity for independent thought and action. They also felt she was becoming too sexually active. Therapy focused on their pathological relationships, and aimed at facilitating Sandra's independence and the parents' acceptance of her independence and self-assertion. The parents' attitude changed as they began to give Sandra individual responsibilities and trust her more.

The final session occurred two weeks after the anniversary of the brother's death. No debilitating grief reaction was in evidence. Both Sandra and her mother appeared cheerful, and Sandra did not complain of leg pains. A follow-up four months later confirmed steady gains and improvements in the family's interactional patterns.

It was suggested that Sandra's somatic symptoms, sexual acting out, school problems, and maladaptive behaviors were related to unresolved mourning. Still further, Sandra and her parents were unable to provide mutually satisfying relationships. In order to move toward resolution of these problems, individual psychotherapy was employed for Sandra's grief reaction and family therapy addressed the dysfunctional family interactions. It is important to note that the resolution of the mother's grief reaction was of primary importance in effecting positive alterations in family interactional patterns.

SECOND CASE STUDY: Brian, a six-year-old boy, entered therapy twenty-two months after his father's death from cancer. Both Brian and his mother gave evidence of unresolved grief. Brian apparently experienced no behavioral clashes with anyone except his mother. The boy threw temper tantrums whenever the mother left him. He would act out by throwing toys; he also threw rocks at his babysitter. The mother appeared to be unable to set limits; issues of discipline had ordinarily been left to the father. At a deeper level, it seemed that the mother wanted Brian to be stronger so that she could lean on him for support; she was angry that he did not take care of her. The mother related that she had no problems with her ten-year-old daughter, only with Brian.

In the course of therapy, it was disclosed that the intensified mother-son conflict was primarily related to the mother's unresolved mourning reaction. Brian's testing of limits was part of that unresolved grief in that the mother refused to accept the father's role of effective disciplinarian. Improvements in their relationship occurred during the course of therapy.

COMMENTARY: Jensen and Wallace have presented a study that underscores the importance of working through grief reactions. Grief is a family response to loss. Therefore, it is not only individuals who react to the death of a family member, rather, the family as a unit experiences the loss. Symptomatic behavior may represent the inability of the family as a unit to work through the mourning process.

The authors suggest an open and flexible therapy plan to accommodate the needs of the individuals and families involved. In some cases, both individual and family therapies may be in order. Therapeutic intervention aims at addressing both individual and interpersonal emotional disorders. The cases presented illustrate the flexible use of combined therapies and the manner in which these combined approaches are tailored to work with specific needs. This procedure appears to be applicable to the unresolved mourning reactions that may result from various situations such as death, separation, divorce, and the like. It is an excellent example of the combined application of psychodynamic approaches within a crisis theory framework.

SOURCE: Jensen, G. D., and Wallace, J. G. "Family Mourning Process." *Family Process*, 1967, *6*, 56–66.

Therapy Following a Child's Suicide

AUTHOR: Peter R. Whitis

PRECIS: Therapy is a means of confronting some of the conflicts that are precipitated by the suicide of a child.

INTRODUCTION: Whitis presents the case of Martin, aged thirteen, whose suicide had severe dysfunctional effects upon the remaining members of the family. The bereaved family was demoralized and their relationships were negatively affected. In addition, symptomatic behaviors were manifested in the ten-year-old son.

CASE REPORT: Kelly, aged ten, was referred by his parents to a child outpatient service. He appeared angry, depressed, frightened, and withdrawn, had unpredictable temper outbursts, and threatened suicide. Kelly's symptoms flared up on his dead brother's birthday. Martin was thirteen when he committed suicide. His death was so traumatic and shocking to the family that they never really worked through the grieving process.

The nuclear family included the parents, a sixteen-year-old sister, Nancy, Kelly, and the paternal grandmother, who had lived with the family for fourteen years but moved out a year before Martin's suicide. Each member was involved in the dysfunctional pattern that arose following Martin's death.

It appeared that each member of the family was still trying to work through their sense of separation and loss. For example, Kelly felt he could not cry because it would further upset his family. The parents were unable to support and comfort each other. The sixteen-year-old sister, Nancy, turned to a girlfriend for comfort; this adolescent friend moved into the house with her. There was no leadership in the family system. Everyone involved was caught up in, and debilitated by, hostility, recriminations, depression, guilt, and psychosomatic disorders. Family members seemed unaware of the fact that the family communication system had almost entirely disintegrated.

Each family member individually had a specific set of responses to Martin's suicide. The father attempted to deny it. He insisted that the cause of death was something other than suicide. He suspected foul play, and felt someday the truth would be uncovered. The mother became active after the suicide and adopted other children into the family. These were usually friends of her own children, often from broken homes. In part they were used as an attempt to replace the missing child. Nancy was the family member who most worked through her grief. Consistent with her stage of development, she became involved with her peers. Kelly developed hostile-dependent feelings toward his mother and manifested these feelings through angry episodes. He tried to manipulate the family and relieve his guilt by threatening suicide.

THERAPEUTIC INTERVENTION: A combined individual and family therapy approach was employed with this family. The family displayed marked emotional constriction and fear of expressing feelings. Each attempted to deal with Martin's suicide in unique and separate fashion. Therefore, the therapist initiated the mourning process and helped the family focus on Martin's death and examine their reactions to it. The family appeared to fixate on the how and why of Martin's suicide. Progress had to be facilitated. The stalemate had to be broken and new and positive family interaction patterns inaugurated.

COMMENTARY: Whitis presents a perceptive and sensitive first-hand account of working with a family who was trying to live with the painful legacy of a child's suicide. If each individual attempts to cope (or fails to cope) with the suicide in a separate and individual manner, such that it is never handled at the level of the family as a unit, grieving issues will never be resolved. The suicide of any family member affects each person within that family not only as an individual but also as an integral part of the family structure. The death of any family member, particularly a death by suicide, alters relationships within the family. Patterns of relating, interacting, and communicating are negatively affected. Kelly's symptomatic behavior was representative of the dysfunctional relationship within the family, which appeared to be linked to the unresolved process of grieving. Martin's suicide had a pathogenic impact on the marital, sibling, and parent-child relationships. Therapy was necessary as a means of intervening in these dysfunctional relationship patterns so that the channels of communication could be opened and the issues surrounding Martin's death could be examined. When grief is denied, it is likely to be acted out in the symptomatic manner evidenced in Kelly's behavior.

This is an insightful study that offers guidelines and a frame of reference for any therapist working with a family who have suffered the loss of one of their members through suicide. Suicide always has traumatic effects on surviving family members; guilt, depression, anger, and blame are common. However, when the suicide involves a young child, the painful consequences are magnified. This article should be read by any clinician working with families who are attempting to adjust after such a catastrophic loss.

SOURCE: Whitis, P. R. "The Legacy of a Child's Suicide." *Family Process*, 1968, 7, 159-169.

Unresolved Grief Following a Suicide

AUTHOR: Fady Hajal

PRECIS: Unresolved grief may play a destructive role in a family following the death by suicide of its principal male figure.

INTRODUCTION: After tracing a brief outline of mourning and unresolved grief reactions, Hajal presents the case of a family who suffered the loss by suicide of the father. Unresolved grief in survivors of suicide places the family at risk. The ultimate goal of therapy with these surviving family members is preventative. If the powerful affective experience of suicide remains repressed and arrested, the family members run the risk of actively or passively repeating the experience in an attempt to master or undo it.

CASE REPORT: The case used to illustrate the vicissitudes of the grief process in survivors was that of Jane, a ten-year-old girl. Jane's development had been normal prior to her father's suicide. After the suicide, Jane's mother complained of her daughter's constant complaining and testing behavior. She refused to communicate, repressed her feelings, and withdrew into her room. These conflicts occurred only at home. Jane's adjustment at school and in the community was described as excellent.

The father was described as frequently having somatic complaints, and as being quiet, and particularly uncommunicative when troubled. His behavior was erratic, and following the birth of his third daughter he avoided his wife and abstained from sexual contact for months. His suicide was totally unexpected and shattered the family.

Jane's obstinence, irritability, and desire for privacy were all traced to her identification with her lost father and her attempt to work through unresolved grief concerning his death. "In summary, Jane's behavior and verbal communications were thought to be expressing her identification with her father, one way of holding on to him and keeping him alive. What seemed to be difficulties in the mother/child relationship were in fact residual effects of the cataclysm that occurred in the family in the form of the father's suicide."

Therapy sought to enhance and promote the grief work. Time-limited therapy was considered the method of choice and seemed particularly suited to the needs of this family. Initially, the therapy focused on the undoing of the family's denial-repression system. The issue of identification with and idealization of the lost object, the father, was then addressed. In this identification process, Jane directed her hostility toward her mother, whom she saw as the rejecting parent, the rival who took the father away from her. At the same time, Jane clung tenaciously to an idealized image of her father.

Along with these issues, the family had to confront the guilt and rage that were associated with the suicide. Following this confrontation, the loss had to be worked through, which served to reinstate a more realistic image of the father.

Termination of therapy evoked fears of separation, abandonment, and rejection that were similar to those that occurred at the time of the suicide. These feelings warranted discussion. The grief work was conceptualized as an ongoing process demanding redefinition and serious reconsideration at each developmental stage for each member of the family.

COMMENTARY: Hajal presents a therapeutic approach for working through issues of grief and loss that holds immense value for families working through the process of mourning. This study has particular relevance since the majority of previous studies consider the effects of grief and loss on adults. Children's reactions to loss seemed an unapproachable enigma. Clearly, a study of postsuicide grief work involving children is long overdue.

This study is also valuable because, as the author notes, "The ultimate goal of such therapy is preventative." This article helps the reader to recognize acting out behavior in children following the death or loss (for example, through divorce) of a parent for what it really is, namely, unresolved grief reactions.

This approach is specifically tailored to work with families experiencing unresolved grief. Some of the major issues that must be dealt with, such as guilt, rage, identification, idealization, and denial, are considered. Furthermore, Hajal gives suggestions to aid the therapist from the initial phases of therapy through termination.

SOURCE: Hajal, F. "Post-Suicide Grief Work in Family Therapy." *Journal of Marriage and Family Counseling,* 1977, *4,* 35–42.

Additional Readings

Baider, L. "The Silent Message: Communication in a Family with a Dying Patient." *Journal of Marriage and Family Counseling,* 1977, *3,* 23–28.

This article discusses the functioning of the linguistic code in family communication processes in a crisis situation when the family is in need of concealing its dilemma. Two case studies are used to illustrate the basic concepts of verbal interaction and to demonstrate the difficulties involved in any open exchange of messages in a family with a dying member. The author discusses the nonverbal communication that takes place in family interactions as well as the verbalized communication. Intervention methods that are consistent with, and tailored to, the specific ways in which the family habitually interacts and communicates are suggested.

Brown, A. H. "A Use of Social Exchange Theory in Family Crisis Intervention." *Journal of Marriage and Family Counseling,* July 1975, pp. 259–267.

The author explores the practical application of social exchange theory to developing working hypotheses for family crisis intervention. Social exchange theory offers a way of relating the content of personal interactions to the level of satisfaction experienced in such interactions. It specifies the potential the outcome has for change or perpetuation of the interaction. The author investigates family interactions in relation to social exchange theory. The therapist does not resolve the family's existing crisis, but rather expands the range of exchange content. Specific behavioral exchange equivalents are offered to family members based upon need-response patterns. (A behavioral exchange equivalent is an alternative communication interchange that satisfies the needs of all involved without producing negative results or outcomes. It is an alternative to conflict-producing exchanges. For example, an open discussion of family roles and expectations is a behavioral exchange equivalent of arguing about who is "boss.") Such behavioral exchange equivalents facilitate a resolution of the crisis situation.

Cohen, P., Dizenhuz, I. M., and Winget, C. "Family Adaptation to Terminal Illness and Death of a Parent." *Social Casework*, 1977, *58*, 223–228.

This article highlights the importance of open communication among family members in coping with a crisis, especially with regard to post-death stabilization. The study indicates that when the terminal patient is the mother, who is often the family communicator, both she and the other family members are less likely to be informed about the terminal nature of the illness than when another member of the family is ill. It is important that in all cases caretakers establish strategies to inform patients and their families of the patient's terminal condition and to help family members develop alternative paths of communication when necessary.

Characteristically, the families reported the terminal illness and the death as the most stressful period they had experienced and the time during which most changes took place. It is essential that caretakers and support groups be alerted to the nature of these crucial periods, so that intervention can be appropriate and effective. Being prepared for the death (which requires being informed of the terminal nature of the illness) and being able to communicate fears and pain of loss with all family members helps reduce some of the stress and thus serves as a coping mechanism.

Grando, R. "An Approach to Family Crisis Intervention." *Family Therapy,* 1975, *2*(3), 201-214.

    The author describes an approach to crisis intervention that involves the active participation of all family members. The personal experience of crisis is determined by three factors: the crisis itself, the resources at the family's disposal to meet the crisis, and the meaning attached to the crisis. In effect, there are usually several interrelated crises existing simultaneously rather than a single crisis; this is because family members experience different crises. The process of crisis management involves an assessment of the problem areas, and the selection and implementation of intervention strategies. Three case examples are presented to illustrate the complex interrelationship among the three factors that determine the crisis.

Kaffman, M., and Elizur, E. "Children's Bereavement Reactions Following Death of a Father." *International Journal of Family Therapy,* 1979, *1*(3), 203-229.

    This study yielded no psychological syndrome that might be considered typical of bereavement reactions in normal children. Bereavement reactions are diverse and individual. The specific combination of symptoms and reactions, their intensity, and their duration differ from child to child. The developmental age of the child at the time of the death also affects the nature of the bereavement reaction.

    The study employed twenty-four normal kibbutz children who had suffered the loss of their fathers. The behaviors and changes reported by the mothers and teachers of these children over a period of one to six months after bereavement are reported. There is no doubt that the death of the father brought about a stressful situation and an abrupt disequilibrium in the child. However, reactions depended upon coping mechanisms of each child.

    The children reacted by attempting to restore their stability by increasing their dependence upon the mother and by searching for a father substitute. Some of the children denied the death. Some experienced depression, mourning, separation anxiety, and grief. Some children talked about the father; they recalled specific memories and longed for his return. Some identified with the dead father. Somatic symptoms were also in evidence in some of the children: these included anorexia, overindulgence in eating, sleep problems, and related conditions.

Despite the range of bereavement reactions, the study indicates that at least half of the children involved experienced acute emotional strain, and all of the children were considered at risk.

Kopel, K., and Mock, L. A. "The Use of Group Sessions for the Emotional Support of Families of Terminal Patients." *Death Education*, 1978, *1*, 409–422.

This article describes a group conducted within a medical setting. The group was formulated in order to meet the emotional needs of family members of terminal patients. It served as an emotional support and provided a formal point of contact for families undergoing similar experiences in having a terminally ill family member. Weekly group sessions were established on a cancer ward. Although very different in structure and process from traditional psychiatric group therapy, the group filled several needs for this particular population. It afforded members a chance to air emotional issues and attitudes, express feelings of anger and powerlessness, and manage the mourning process. It also gave patients and their family members a chance to verbalize complaints and questions concerning hospital treatment and care. It afforded occasions for communication and interaction between staff and patients. In addition, the attachments formed and losses suffered by the group leaders have made the group as growth enhancing for them as it was for the families of the terminally ill patients.

Krell, R., and Rabkin, L. "The Effects of Sibling Death on the Surviving Child: A Family Perspective." *Family Process*, 1979, *18*, 471–477.

The death of a child invariably affects the entire family unit. It leaves a legacy that influences all future transactions among the surviving members. It compounds the experience of grief and mourning with the problem of survivorhood. Adaptive mechanisms are usually employed that serve to establish a new family equilibrium following such a loss. Surviving siblings often become the focus of maneuvers unconsciously designed to alleviate guilt. Communication about the lost child is often shrouded and evasive. Parents and children often share a powerful bond, usually unspoken, that if they had acted differently the death could somehow have been avoided. Parents often remind the surviving children of their good fortune in having survived. Surviving children often come to view themselves as precious, lucky, and omnipotent. Often, the surviving child is used as a replacement for the deceased child. Substitution and replacement provide major themes for these surviving children. They often feel haunted or bound by the role of substitute for the deceased sibling. A definite relationship exists between the family's defensive strategies and the specific consequences these have for the surviving children.

Paul, N. L., and Grosser, G. H. "Operational Mourning and Its Role in Conjoint Family Therapy." *Community Mental Health Journal,* 1965, *1,* 339–345.

     The authors present a case that illustrates the technique of operational mourning within a family following the loss of one of its members. The example highlights the manner in which operational mourning in conjoint family therapy sessions can activate an empathic potential. The conjoint therapy sessions offer occasions for the family members to reactivate the experience of loss. They have a chance to work through their anger, ambivalence, and experience of separation and loss. In essence, operational mourning offers a corrective mourning experience to a family who previously may have denied the mourning process or, for a variety of reasons, had the experience aborted. It consists of mourning responses induced by direct inquiry about the reactions to various losses experienced by the family members. These inquiries raise unresolved issues and afford an opportunity to work through the grieving process.

22

Psychotic
Families

The two articles reviewed in this chapter describe an unusual disorder termed *folie à famille*. The literal meaning of the French term is "psychotic family." Children raised in this type of family are at risk for psychological disorders and problems. They are constantly exposed during critical developmental phases to a family structure that perpetuates persecutory, grandiose, and wish-fulfilling delusions. Because of the family's shared delusional system, the children are subjected to a bizarre, confusing, and chaotic home environment and life-style.

The papers by Wikler and Waltzer discuss and document the fascinating history of this unique disorder. Both authors describe the syndrome as it appears in literature and in individual case studies. They emphasize the functional aspect of *folie à famille*, namely, its role in warding off disintegration of the family as a unified entity.

451

Folie à Famille: *Shared Familial Delusions*

AUTHOR: Lynn Wikler

PRECIS: Shared familial delusions are viewed as a dramatic attempt to maintain family cohesiveness in the face of an environment perceived as hostile.

INTRODUCTION: Although an extremely infrequent phenomenon, *folie à famille* does occur and is apparently underreported. The syndrome is characterized as a commonly shared delusion permeating the family. Wikler traces the rather extensive history of this syndrome. In a century of psychiatric literature, the disorder is never mentioned in the *family* literature. The syndrome was first defined by Lasèque and Falret (1877) in a case involving two partners: "*Folie à deux* is the transmission of delusional ideas from a psychotic to closely associated individuals, who have experienced his/her domineering influence for a prolonged space of time. This condition may be transferred to three and/ or more individuals." Elsewhere, *folie à deux* is described as a shared paranoid disorder.

It is worth noting that the syndrome does not apply to a family in which the different members are experiencing various forms of mental illness, but rather describes an identical psychotic delusion shared by several family members. *Folie à famille* occurs when the outside world, which is perceived as a hostile intruder, threatens to break into the symbiotic relationship of the family. The shared beliefs are an attempt to maintain the family's homeostatic balance and the satisfaction that the family unit provides. The family sharing this delusional system is typically socially isolated. However, the cause-effect relationship is unclear; that is, it is uncertain whether the family is isolated because of their strange shared beliefs or whether an already isolated family is more prone to develop delusions. Certainly, isolation makes the delusions inaccessible to outsiders and contributes to maintaining them.

The family member who induces the delusional beliefs is usually perceived by the family as its most powerful member and is the one who believes that the family unit must be preserved in the face of threat. The inducer must be sufficiently powerful to mobilize the imagination of other family members. The induced, on the other hand, are usually passive, highly suggestible, and dependent. The delusional content commonly centers on themes of persecution, such as paranoia, grandeur, and/or wish-fulfillment.

CASE REPORT: Mary, a six-year-old child, was presented by her family because she "refused to act normally in public." Despite the fact that experts diagnosed Mary as severely retarded, her parents refused to accept this diagnosis. The parents' rejection of this evaluation constituted the major problem. To compound the situation, Mary was mildly cerebral palsied, suffered from petit-mal seizures, and had the language development of a nine-month-old infant. Mary was admitted to a children's ward that specialized in multidisciplinary evaluation and treatment.

Prior to her admission, Mary had never been separated from her family. Following her admission, several catastrophes occurred in the family in rapid succession, all within two weeks of each other. Her father suffered a major heart attack, her half sister experienced a severe industrial accident, and her brother suffered an outbreak of hives, serious blackout spells, and loss of memory. Family therapy was attempted but aborted. Contrary to advice, Mary's mother removed her from the ward. The family was diagnosed as delusional.

DISCUSSION OF THE CASE: When Mary was eighteen months old, her twelve-year-old brother drowned. Following his death, the mother experienced severe depressive episodes. At this same time, the father experienced professional failure. The author proposes that the precipitating events of the family's delusional belief system were probably the son's death, the father's professional failure and the resulting financial strain, and Mary's developmental delay. These multiple stresses placed the family at risk. The family remained isolated and turned inward for support. Further, they developed a fantasy world, a delusional belief system that served the individual and family needs for cohesiveness. In the place of a delusion of paranoia, the family developed a belief system about the retarded girl, Mary, who could neither defend herself nor correct the fallacy of the delusional system. The strain of Mary's separation from the family proved incapacitating; it became increasingly difficult to maintain the delusion in her absence.

COMMENTARY: Wikler has presented a fascinating article that is not only historically documented, expertly researched, and rich in case histories but also presents a problem which, the author believes, is underreported in family literature. In her concluding paragraph, Wikler remarks: "It seems essential for family therapists to acknowledge the existence of varying forms of shared familial beliefs, including *folie à famille*. As long as the therapist remains an outsider in the family's eyes, he or she will have little access to the family 'realities.' Assuming their presence and understanding their function enable the therapist to measure the extent to which he or she has been allowed to permeate the family boundaries and will be able to contribute to the family's improved functioning."

Wikler also spells out the importance of *folie à famille* to family therapists. It facilitates appropriate diagnosis of shared delusions. It serves as a metaphor for vulnerable and enmeshed families. Furthermore, although this disorder is not referred to in family literature, the functional-dysfunctional continuum is a familiar one. A delusion such as *folie à famille* is only one point on a hypothetical continuum of family beliefs. Such delusions keep the family inaccessible to outsiders and assure family cohesiveness. Yet the delusional system is functional in that it wards off the disintegration of the family.

SOURCE: Wikler, L. *"Folie à Famille*: A Family Therapist's Perspective." *Family Process,* 1980, *19,* 257–267.

Psychosis of Association: A Case Study

AUTHOR: Herbert Waltzer

PRECIS: A case report illustrating *folie à deux* (in this case, *folie à douze*) is discussed. The importance of environmental stimuli as an etiological factor is stressed, as is the delineation of the three phases involved in the process of developing and sustaining the psychosis of association.

INTRODUCTION: Waltzer presents a historical overview of *folie à deux*. He discusses etiological factors and the combined characteristics that mark this psychosis of association, namely, the association of the involved partners, similarity in the content of the shared delusion, and the mutual acceptance and support of the delusional ideas. The term *folie à douze* is used in this particular study because it concerns a family with twelve members.

The author also elaborates on the marked similarities between what occurs in the development of *folie à deux* and the phenomena of brainwashing, hypnosis, and psychotherapy. These similarities involve the phases through which the process develops. The first phase focuses on the breakdown of defenses. It is viewed as the "disorganizing or regressive phase." The second phase involves an identification with the dominant figure. The third phase is one of reindoctrination; during this period, family members adopt the delusional ideas.

CASE REPORT: The case of a twelve-member family with a shared delusional system is cited. The family consists of the parents and ten children, ranging in age from four to fifteen years. The parents and their thirteen-year-old son were remanded for observation. The mother, aged thirty-seven, of Jewish origin, was diagnosed schizophrenic reaction, paranoid type. However, although the mother was the more disturbed of the parents, the father was the primary agent in instigating the delusional system.

The father, aged seventy-two, was of Chinese descent.

Like the mother, he was diagnosed schizophrenic reaction, paranoid type. He reported experiencing auditory and visual hallucinations. His delusions focused on what he insisted was a plot to take his life. The children rotated guard to ensure that would-be assailants did not enter the home. He felt that the Jews, bookies and gangsters, Negroes, Puerto Ricans, poor whites, and the police were all involved in this plot. He wrote the following letter to his children: "I am sorry that the Jew bookies and gangsters had us framed up and forced into this crazy ward. I enclose you two four-cent stamps if you want to write Mama and me. Yesterday Mama was taken away to another crazy hospital. Remember these Jew gangsters did it to us and the Chinese race."

The children adopted the father's paranoid delusions. Of all the children, the thirteen-year-old son was the most seriously disturbed. He was guarded and evasive, and experienced auditory hallucinations in the form of gangsters' voices threatening to kill him. He also had visual hallucinations. Furthermore, he insisted that the teachers were against him because he was Chinese and was adamant in his belief that the principal wanted to have sexual relations with his sister. The boy was diagnosed schizophrenic reaction, paranoid type.

To a greater or lesser degree, each of the children shared the father's delusional system. Five of the ten children manifested a paranoid schizophrenic psychosis, while the remaining five were diagnosed as having a paranoid reaction. In discussing these diagnoses, the author does not discount genetic factors; however, he proposes that the disturbed environment and the presence of inflammatory agents (the parents) precipitated the *folie à douze.*

COMMENTARY: This study provides an impressive scholarly review and documentation of the phenomenon of *folie à deux.* Waltzer adds an interesting twist by presenting a case study in which the psychosis of association applies to twelve members of a family. In addition to delineating the major characteristics of the *folie à deux,* the author also elaborates on the similarities between this shared delusion and brainwashing, hypnosis, and psychotherapy.

Since the psychosis of association is not limited to family members but can also be observed in societies and cultures at large, and can be communicated from generation to generation, this article has far-reaching implications and merits a thorough study. The author points out that the occurrence of *folie à deux* may be more frequent and widespread than has been previously imagined. This, of course, has research implications for social and cultural psychology as well as clinical psychology and therapeutic practice.

SOURCE: Waltzer, H. "A Psychotic Family—*Folie à Douze.*" *Journal of Nervous and Mental Disease,* 1963, *137,* 67–75.

Author Index

459

Subject Index

A

Abdominal pain, psychosomatic, 180-182

Accommodation, in structural therapy, 4

Acting out, in families in crisis, 432-435

Aggression, repressed, and elective mutism, 281. *See also* Impulsive-aggressive behaviors

Alpha House Boys Program, 328

American Institutes for Research, 331

Anorexia nervosa: abstracts on, 199-215; background on, 168, 197-198; behavioral therapy for, 207-209, 215; boundaries in, 200, 201; case studies of, 199-203, 208-209, 210-212; crisis therapy for, 212-213; family systems therapy for, 204-209, 213, 215; hospitalization for, 204-207; insight therapy for, 207-212, 215; integrative therapy for, 204-212; mortality rate of, 198; paradoxical prescription for, 212; and sibling subsystem, 211; strategic therapy for, 210-212; structural therapy for, 199-204, 210-212, 213-214

Asthma, psychosomatic, 175-177, 195, 196

Autonomy: in families with handi-

465